Gender and Occupational Outcomes

Gender and Occupational Outcomes

LONGITUDINAL ASSESSMENTS
OF INDIVIDUAL, SOCIAL, AND
CULTURAL INFLUENCES

Edited by
Helen M. G. Watt and Jacquelynne S. Eccles

American Psychological Association
Washington, DC

Published by
American Psychological Association
750 First Street, NE
Washington, DC 20002
www.apa.org

To order
APA Order Department
P.O. Box 92984
Washington, DC 20090-2984
Tel: (800) 374-2721; Direct: (202) 336-5510
Fax: (202) 336-5502; TDD/TTY: (202) 336-6123
Online: www.apa.org/books/
E-mail: order@apa.org

In the U.K., Europe, Africa, and the Middle East, copies may be ordered from
American Psychological Association
3 Henrietta Street
Covent Garden, London
WC2E 8LU England

Typeset in Goudy by Circle Graphics, Columbia, MD

Printer: Maple-Vail Book Manufacturing Group, York, PA
Cover Designer: Naylor Design, Washington, DC
Technical/Production Editor: Harriet Kaplan

The opinions and statements published are the responsibility of the authors, and such opinions and statements do not necessarily represent the policies of the American Psychological Association.

Library of Congress Cataloging-in-Publication Data

Gender and occupational outcomes : longitudinal assessment of individual, social, and cultural influences / edited by Helen M. G. Watt and Jacquelynne S. Eccles. — 1st ed.
    p. cm.
  Includes bibliographical references and index.
  ISBN-13: 978-1-4338-0310-9
  ISBN-10: 1-4338-0310-0
  1. Sexual division of labor—Longitudinal studies. 2. Sex differences in education—Longitudinal studies. 3. Women—Education—Longitudinal studies. 4. Science—Study and teaching—Sex differences—Longitudinal studies. 5. Technical education—Sex differences— Longitudinal studies. 6. Women in technology. 7. Technical education. 8. Women in science. I. Watt, Helen M. G. II. Eccles, Jacquelynne S.

  HD6060.6.G448 2008
  331.4—dc22
                          2007027308

British Library Cataloguing-in-Publication Data
A CIP record is available from the British Library.

Printed in the United States of America
First Edition

CONTENTS

Contributors .... *ix*

List of Tables and Figures .... *xvii*

Gender and Occupational Outcomes: An Introduction 3
Helen M. G. Watt

I. Mathematics as the Critical Filter? **25**

Chapter 1.   Gender, Mathematics Achievement, and the
              Educational and Occupational Aspirations of
              Canadian Youth 27
              Jennifer D. Shapka, José F. Domene, and
              Daniel P. Keating

Chapter 2.   Mathematics as the Critical Filter:
              Curricular Effects on Gendered Career Choices 55
              Xin Ma and Willis Johnson

II. **Psychological Processes and Gendered Participation in Math, Science, and Technology-Based Careers** 85

Chapter 3.   What Motivates Females and Males to Pursue
             Sex-Stereotyped Careers? 87
             Helen M. G. Watt

Chapter 4.   Gendered High School Course Selection as a
             Precursor of Gendered Careers:
             The Mediating Role of Self-Concept and
             Intrinsic Value 115
             Gabriel Nagy, Jessica Garrett, Ulrich Trautwein,
             Kai S. Cortina, Jürgen Baumert,
             and Jacquelynne S. Eccles

Chapter 5.   Testing for Time-Invariant and Time-Varying
             Predictors of Self-Perceived Ability in Math,
             Language Arts, and Science: A Look at the
             Gender Factor 145
             Barbara M. Byrne

Chapter 6.   A Sociomotivational Analysis of Gender Effects on
             Persistence in Science and Technology: A 5-Year
             Longitudinal Study 171
             Simon Larose, Catherine F. Ratelle, Frédéric Guay,
             Caroline Senécal, Marylou Harvey, and Evelyne Drouin

III. **The Importance of Family Considerations, Family,
     and Biology in Gendered Career Choices** 193

Chapter 7.   Is the Desire for a Family-Flexible Job Keeping
             Young Women Out of Male-Dominated
             Occupations? 195
             Pamela M. Frome, Corinne J. Alfeld,
             Jacquelynne S. Eccles, and Bonnie L. Barber

Chapter 8.   Gender-Typed Occupational Choices:
             The Long-Term Impact of Parents' Beliefs
             and Expectations 215
             Christina S. Chhin, Martha M. Bleeker, and
             Janis E. Jacobs

Chapter 9.   Biological Contributors to Gendered Occupational
              Outcome: Prenatal Androgen Effects on Predictors
              of Outcome 235
              Sheri A. Berenbaum and Kristina L. Korman Bryk

**IV. Social and Institutional Constraints on Women's
     Career Development** **265**

Chapter 10.   Gendered Occupational Outcomes From
              Multilevel Perspectives: The Case of Professional
              Training and Work in Turkey 267
              Ahu Tatlı, Mustafa F. Özbilgin, and Fatma Küskü

Chapter 11.   Advancing Women Faculty in Science and
              Engineering: An Effort in Institutional
              Transformation 299
              Abigail Stewart and Danielle LaVaque-Manty

Chapter 12.   The Continuing Technological Revolution:
              A Comparison of Three Regions' Strategies for
              Creating Women-Inclusive Workplaces 323
              Christina M. Vogt

Author Index 353

Subject Index 365

About the Editors 383

CONTRIBUTORS

Corinne J. Alfeld, PhD, is the research director of the Duke University Talent Identification Program, Durham, North Carolina. She received her PhD in education and psychology from the University of Michigan, Ann Arbor, in 1999 and completed a postdoctoral research fellowship at the Max Planck Institute for Human Development in Berlin, Germany. Her research focuses on educational opportunities for adolescents and young adults from the perspectives of developmental psychology, social structure, and educational policy.

Bonnie L. Barber, PhD, is a professor of psychology at Murdoch University, Perth, Western Australia, and an adjunct professor of family studies and human development at the University of Arizona, Tucson. She completed her PhD in developmental psychology at the University of Michigan, Ann Arbor, in 1990. Her research interests include adolescent and young adult relationships, long-term benefits of organized activity participation, and positive development in divorced families.

Jürgen Baumert, PhD, is a professor of education and director of the Center for Educational Research at the Berlin Max Planck Institute for Human Development in Berlin, Germany. He is the author of numerous books, book chapters, and journal articles. His major research interests include teaching and learning, effects of social background on educational outcomes, large-scale assessment, and educational institutions as developmental environments.

Sheri A. Berenbaum, PhD, studies genetic and neuroendocrine influences on cognitive and social development. She earned her PhD in psychology from the University of California, Berkeley, and completed a postdoctoral fellowship at the University of Minnesota, Minneapolis. She was previously on the faculty at the University of Health Sciences/Chicago Medical School, North Chicago, Illinois, and Southern Illinois University School of Medicine, Carbondale. She has been at The Pennsylvania State University, University Park, since 2001, where she is professor of psychology and pediatrics and a member of the neuroscience program.

Martha M. Bleeker, PhD, is a survey researcher at Mathematica Policy Research in Princeton, New Jersey. She conducts national research on education policy issues, with a focus on the domains of math, science, and technology. She also studies the influence of gender and parental factors on achievement and career goals during adolescence.

Kristina L. Korman Bryk, MSW, earned her bachelor's degree in psychology from Lake Forest College, Lake Forest, Illinois, and her master's degree from Loyola University, Chicago. She has been involved in the longitudinal study of individuals with congenital adrenal hyperplasia since 1993 and has also worked as a school social worker. She has been a researcher at The Pennsylvania State University, University Park, since 2001.

Barbara M. Byrne, PhD, is professor emeritus in the School of Psychology at the University of Ottawa, Ottawa, Canada. She is the author of a resource book devoted to self-concept measurement as well as five books that focus on applications of structural equation modeling (SEM). Other publications include 11 book chapters and 68 papers in scholarly journals, most of which have addressed SEM application issues.

Christina S. Chhin, PhD, is an associate research scientist at the Institute of Education Sciences, U.S. Department of Education, Washington, DC. Her research interest is focused on the role of gender, ethnicity, and activity involvement on achievement and career goals during adolescence.

Kai S. Cortina, PhD, is an assistant professor of educational psychology at the University of Michigan, Ann Arbor. He received his doctoral degree in 1996 from the Free University, Berlin, Germany. As a tenured scientific investigator at the Max Planck Institute for Human Development in Berlin until 2000, he worked on a large-scale longitudinal study on adolescents' cognitive and psychosocial development. Current projects include a study on learning motivation and learning styles in foreign language classrooms and an evaluation project on improving reading skills in elementary schools.

José F. Domene, PhD, is an assistant professor of counseling psychology at Trinity Western University, Langley, British Columbia, Canada. His research interests include the roles of interpersonal relationships, gender, and spirituality in career development; adolescent development within the family; and methods of qualitative data collection and analysis.

Evelyne Drouin, MEd, is a research professional at Laval University, Québec City, Québec, Canada, where she also obtained her master's degree in education. Her research interests are mainly related to the factors influencing young adults' participation and persistence in science and technology studies and careers.

Jacquelynne S. Eccles, PhD, serves as the McKeachie Collegiate Professor of Psychology, University of Michigan, Ann Arbor. She received her PhD from the University of California, Los Angeles, in 1974 and has served on the faculties at Smith College, Northville, Massachusetts; the University of Colorado, Boulder; and the University of Michigan, Ann Arbor. She chaired the MacArthur Foundation Network on Successful Pathways Through Middle Childhood and was a member of the MacArthur Research Network on Successful Pathways Through Adolescence. She was Society for Research on Adolescence (SRA) program chair in 1996, has served on the SRA Council, and is now past president of SRA. She served as program chair and president for the American Psychological Association (APA) Division 35 (Society for the Psychology of Women) and chair of the National Academy of Sciences Committee on After School Programs for Youth. She has received numerous awards from professional and research organizations in the field of psychology. She is a fellow of the APA, the American Psychological Society, the Society for the Psychological Study of Social Issues, and the National Academy of Education. She has conducted research on topics ranging from gender-role socialization and classroom influences on motivation to social development in the family, school, peer, and wider cultural contexts.

Pamela M. Frome, PhD, is a research investigator at the Frank Porter Graham Child Development Institute, University of North Carolina, Chapel Hill. She completed her PhD in social psychology at the University of Michigan, Ann Arbor, in 1998. She is currently the project director for the Promoting Academic Success of Boys of Color initiative. Her research interests include gender issues, student achievement, academic self-concept, early literacy, and program evaluation.

Jessica Garrett, MEd, is a graduate student in the combined program in education and psychology at the University of Michigan, Ann Arbor. She received her bachelor's and master's degrees from Ohio State University, Columbus. Her main research interests include effects of multiple contexts on the many transitions to adulthood.

Frédéric Guay, PhD, finished his PhD studies in 1997 in social psychology at the University of Québec, Montreal, Canada. He is now a professor of guidance counseling in the faculty of education at Laval University, Québec City, Québec, Canada. Since 2003, he has been the chairholder of the Canada Research Chair on Motivation and Academic Success. In this capacity, his goals are to describe the incidence and patterns of development of student motivation and to ascertain whether those development patterns serve as predictors of academic adjustment.

Marylou Harvey, MEd, is a research professional at Laval University, Québec City, Québec, Canada, where she also obtained her master's degree in education. Her research and teaching interests are related to the factors influencing adolescents' persistence and motivation in science and technology studies and careers.

Janis E. Jacobs, PhD, was a professor of human development and family studies, professor of psychology, and vice president and dean of undergraduate education at Pennsylvania State University, University Park. Her research focused on the development of social cognitive processes during childhood and adolescence, gender differences in achievement motivation, and parents' influences on achievement.

Willis Johnson, PhD, is a professor of mathematics education at the University of Kentucky, Lexington, and the editor of *Kentucky Journal for Teachers of Mathematics*. He spent 20 years at Murray State University,

Murray, Kentucky, where he took many opportunities to serve teachers throughout the country. He is interested in technology applications that enhance teaching.

Daniel P. Keating, PhD, is director and research professor of the Center for Human Growth and Development at the University of Michigan, Ann Arbor, as well as a professor of psychology, psychiatry, and pediatrics at the university. He is also a fellow of the Canadian Institute for Advanced Research, Toronto, Ontario. His current research focus is integrating knowledge about biodevelopmental processes, population patterns in developmental health, and social factors affecting individual and population development.

Fatma Küskü, PhD, is an associate professor of management in the Faculty of Management at Istanbul Technical University, Turkey, where she also earned her PhD. Her research interests involve aspects of human resource management such as organizational trust, satisfaction of employees, employment interview processes, career choice, social responsibility, corporate citizenship, and corporate environmental citizenship.

Simon Larose, PhD, is a professor of educational psychology at Laval University, Québec City, Québec, Canada, where he also obtained his PhD in developmental psychology in 1994. His main fields of research and teaching are adolescent and young adult development, attachment and family relationships, mentoring, school transitions, and academic adjustment. Since 1999, he has been the principal investigator of longitudinal and experimental studies on the role of sociomotivational factors involved in young adults' participation in science and technology studies and careers.

Danielle LaVaque-Manty, PhD, holds a doctorate in political science and an MFA in creative writing. She worked on the National Science Foundation ADVANCE Project at the University of Michigan (UM), Ann Arbor, for several years and teaches composition at UM's Sweetland Writing Center, Ann Arbor.

Xin Ma, PhD, is a professor of mathematics education at the University of Kentucky, Lexington, and a fellow of the U.S. National Academy of Education. He received the Early Career Contribution Award from the American Educational Research Association. His research interests include mathematics education, school effectiveness, policy analysis, and quantitative methods.

Gabriel Nagy, PhD, is a research scientist at the Center for Educational Research at the Max Planck Institute for Human Development, Berlin, Germany. He recently completed his PhD thesis. His major research interests focus on determinants and consequences of self-selection into educational and occupational environments and cognitive and motivational development in adolescence and young adulthood.

Mustafa F. Özbilgin, PhD, performs research on comparative aspects of equality, diversity, and inclusion at work. He is a professor of human resource management at the University of East Anglia, Norwich, England. He previously worked at the University of London, England; the University of Surrey, Surrey, England; and the University of Hertfordshire, Hertford, England. He has authored, coauthored, and edited a number of books and has published papers in prominent human resource journals.

Catherine F. Ratelle, PhD, completed a doctorate in social psychology at the University of Québec, Montreal, Canada, and is now a professor of educational psychology at Laval University, Québec City, Québec, Canada. Her main area of work is school motivation and family relationships. More specifically, she studies relational dynamics within families and their role in predicting students' motivational processes as well as academic persistence and adjustment.

Caroline Senécal, PhD, received her doctoral degree in psychology in 1994 from the University of Québec, Montreal, Canada, and then had a postdoctoral fellowship at McGill University, Montreal, Québec, Canada. She is a professor of social psychology at Laval University, Québec City, Québec, Canada. Her research and writing span a range of topics in human motivation, including adherence to diabetes treatment, obesity, teacher burnout, and school persistence among women who study science and engineering.

Jennifer D. Shapka, PhD, is an associate professor in the Department of Educational and Counselling Psychology and Special Education at the University of British Columbia, Vancouver, Canada. Her research focuses on adolescent and youth development and particularly on understanding contextual influences on developmental well-being, such as the role of information technology.

Abigail Stewart, PhD, is Sandra Schwartz Tangri Professor of Psychology and Women's Studies at the University of Michigan, Ann Arbor, and director of the University of Michigan ADVANCE program. Her current research examines educated women's lives and personalities; race, gender, and generation among graduates of a Midwest high school; and gender, science, and technology among middle-school-age girls, undergraduate students, and faculty.

Ahu Tatlı, MA, is currently pursuing her doctoral study on a multilevel investigation of diversity managers' agency in the Centre for Business Management, at Queen Mary, University of London. She holds a bachelor of science degree in sociology from the Middle East Technical University, Ankara, Turkey, and has a master's degree in political science from Bilkent University, Ankara, Turkey, with a thesis titled "Islamist Women in the Post-1980's Turkey: Ambivalent Resistance." Prior to her doctoral study, she worked as a project coordinator in a women's nongovernmental organization in Ankara.

Ulrich Trautwein, PhD, is a research scientist at the Center for Educational Research at the Max Planck Institute for Human Development, Berlin, Germany. He received his PhD from the Free University of Berlin, Germany, in 2002. His main research interests include effects of learning environments on academic achievement, self-concept, and personality.

Christina M. Vogt, PhD, serves as a National Academy of Engineering Senior Scholar-in-Residence to implement a program designed to increase the number of young women in preengineering and engineering education programs. Previously, she was at the Rossier School of Education, University of Southern California, Los Angeles, where she worked in various teaching and research positions before relocating to the National Academies in Washington, DC. She is currently the cochair for the National Council of Women's Organizations Global Women's Task Force and a member of the ad hoc Committee for Global Feminist Strategies at the National Organization for Women, Washington, DC.

Helen M. G. Watt, PhD, is a faculty member at Monash University, Melbourne, Australia, and has previously served on the faculties of the University of Michigan, Ann Arbor; University of Western Sydney, Sydney, Australia; University of Sydney, Sydney, Australia; and Macquarie University, Sydney, Australia. She has received national and international early career awards since obtaining her PhD in educational psychology and measurement at the University of Sydney in 2002. Her interests include motivation, mathematics education, gendered educational and occupational choices, motivations for teaching, and teacher self-efficacy.

LIST OF TABLES
AND FIGURES

TABLES

Table 1.1.   Average Levels of Occupational Prestige for
Time Across all Participants 36

Table 1.2.   Descriptive Statistics for Grouping Variables and
Covariates 37

Table 1.3.   Variance Components Analysis for Null,
Unconditional, and Conditional Growth Models
for Occupational Prestige 39

Table 1.4.   Parameter Estimates for the Unconditional
Growth Curve Model for Occupational Prestige
and Educational Aspirations 39

Table 1.5.   Parameter Estimates for the Main Effects
Growth Curve Model for Occupational Prestige 40

Table 1.6.   Variance Components Analysis for Null,
Unconditional, and Conditional Growth Models
for Educational Aspirations 42

Table 1.7.   Parameter Estimates for the Main Effects
Growth Curve Model for Educational Aspirations 43

Table 2.1.   Effects of Mathematics Coursework in Grade 7
                on Career Choice in Grade 8 61
Table 2.2.   Effects of Mathematics Coursework in Grade 8
                on Career Choice in Grade 9 61
Table 2.3.   Effects of Mathematics Coursework in Grade 9
                on Career Choice in Grade 10 62
Table 2.4.   Effects of Mathematics Coursework in Grade 10
                on Career Choice in Grade 11 62
Table 2.5.   Effects of Mathematics Coursework in Grade 11
                on Career Choice in Grade 12 63
Table 2.6.   Effects of Mathematics Coursework in Grade 12
                on Likelihood of Majoring in Science 63
Table 2.7.   Proportions of Males and Females Undertaking
                Selected Mathematics Courses, Grades 7 to 12 64
Table 2.8.   Descriptive Statistics for Career Choice Prestige,
                Grades 7 to 12, by Gender 65
Table 2.9.   Proportions of Males and Females for College
                Major Choices Made in Grade 12 65
Table 2.10.   Effects of Mathematics Coursework in Grade 12
                on Likelihood of Majoring in Engineering 69
Table 2.11.   Effects of Mathematics Coursework in Grade 12
                on Likelihood of Majoring in Economics 70
Table 2.12.   Effects of Mathematics Coursework in Grade 12
                on Likelihood of Majoring in Law 70
Table 2.13.   Effects of Mathematics Coursework in Grade 12
                on Likelihood of Majoring in Medicine 71
Table 2.14.   Effects of Mathematics Coursework in Grade 12
                on Likelihood of Majoring in Liberal Arts 71
Table 2.15.   Effects of Mathematics Coursework in Grade 12
                on Likelihood of Majoring in Education 72
Table 3.1.   Participation at Each Grade for Math and English 95
Table 3.2.   Sample Construct Items to Measure Student
                Perceptions... 96
Table 3.3.   Pearson Correlations Among Prior Achievement,
                Perceived Difficulty, Intrinsic Value, Utility Value,
                and Self-Perceptions for Math and English 96
Table 3.4.   Gender Differences in Academic Choices as
                Measured by the d Statistic for Senior High Courses
                and Career Choices Related to Math and English 99
Table 3.5.   Summary of Regression Analyses Predicting
                Math-Related Educational and Occupational
                Participation 103

Table 3.6.   Summary of Regression Analyses Predicting
              English-Related Educational and Occupational
              Participation 105
Table 4.1.   Psychometric Properties of the Scales Analyzed 126
Table 4.2.   Gender Differences: Standard Deviations and
              Odds Ratios (Course Level) 128
Table 4.3.   Logistic Regression Models Predicting Course
              Enrollment in Math and English: Odds Ratios
              for the BIJU Sample 132
Table 4.4.   Multinomial Regression Models Predicting Course
              Enrollment in Math and English: Odds Ratios
              for the Michigan Study of Adolescent Life
              Transitions Sample 134
Table 5.1.   Parameter Estimates for Multiple Domain Model
              (Model 1a) 158
Table 5.2.   Parameter Estimates for Time-Invariant Predictor
              Model (Model 2) 161
Table 5.3.   Parameter Estimates for Time-Varying Predictor
              Model (Model 3): Males... 164
Table 5.4.   Parameter Estimates for Time-Varying Predictor
              Model (Model 3): Females.. 165
Table 6.1.   Overview of the Québec Scientific Career
              Project Design and of the Constructs Examined
              in This Chapter 178
Table 6.2.   Percentages of Men and Women Who Have
              Persevered in Science and Technology 181
Table 6.3.   Psychometric Measures Used to Conceptualize
              Motivational, Family, and Teacher Factors Specified
              in the Sociomotivational Model of Persistence 182
Table 6.4.   Descriptive Statistics of the Sociomotivational
              Measures by Gender 183
Table 6.5.   Summary of a Logistic Regression Analysis for
              Predicting Persistence in Science and Technology 185
Table 7.1.   Numbers of Young Women Who Aspired to
              Male-Typed Occupations 201
Table 7.2.   Numbers of Young Women Who Changed to
              Neutral Occupational Aspirations by Age 25 202
Table 7.3.   Numbers of Young Women Who Changed to
              Female-Typed Occupational Aspirations by
              Age 25 202
Table 7.4.   Correlations of Outcome and Predictor
              Variables 205

Table 7.5.   Statistics for the Final Logistic Regression Model—
               Includes Self-Concept of Ability 206
Table 7.6.   Statistics for the Final Logistic Regression Model—
               Includes Intrinsic Value 206
Table 8.1.   Parents' Occupational Prestige Expectations
               and Children's Occupational Choices 225
Table 8.2.   Relation Between Parents' and Children's
               Gender-Typed Career Expectations 226
Table 8.3.   Young Adults' Gender-Typed Career Choices
               at Age 28 227
Table 8.4.   Relation Between Parents' Earlier Career
               Expectations and the Child's Actual Career
               at Age 28 228
Table 9.1.   "Quasi-Longitudinal" Study of Individuals
               With Congenital Adrenal Hyperplasia
               and their Relatives: Behavioral Domains Assessed
               at Each Phase 242
Table 9.2.   "Quasi-Longitudinal" Study of Individuals
               With Congenital Adrenal Hyperplasia
               and Their Relatives: Number of Participants
               at Each Phase 242
Table 10.1.   Beliefs About Key Influences on Engineering Choice
               and Gender 275
Table 10.2.   Factor Descriptions 278
Table 10.3.   Pearson Correlations Between Factors 279
Table 10.4.   General Characteristics of the Students' Parents 280
Table 11.1.   Men and Women Hired in Natural Science
               and Engineering Departments in Three University
               of Michigan Colleges 310
Table 12.1.   Women's Share of Positions in Related Fields
               to Gender Equality 327
Table 12.2.   HDI, GEM, GDI, WEF, and CEDAW Ratification 334
Table 12.3.   Women's Empowerment in Several Spheres 336
Table 12.4.   Estimated Longitudinal Wages of Professionals
               From 1994 to 2003 340
Table 12.5.   Overall Employment Statistics 343

FIGURES

Figure 1.1.   Level of Occupational Prestige Through High School
               and Postsecondary as a Function of Grade 9 Math
               Achievement 41

Figure 1.2.   Level of Educational Aspirations Through
                High School and Postsecondary as a
                Function of Gender 44
Figure 1.3.   Level of Educational Aspirations Through
                High School and Postsecondary as a
                Function of Grade 9 Math Achievement 45
Figure 3.1.   Gendered Participation in Senior High Math
                and Senior High English by Course Level
                in New South Wales, Australia, 1991–1999 91
Figure 3.2.   Gendered Senior High Planned and Actual
                Math Course Selections and Gendered
                Math-Related Career Plans 98
Figure 3.3.   Gendered Senior High Planned and Actual
                English Course Selections and Gendered
                English-Related Career Plans 100
Figure 3.4.   Gendered Motivations Related to Math and
                English 101
Figure 3.5.   Conceptual Model to Predict Participation
                Choices 102
Figure 3.6.   Math-Relatedness of Boys' and Girls' Career Plans
                by Level of Math Utility Value 104
Figure 4.1.   Path Model Predicted by the Internal/External
                Frame of Reference Model 117
Figure 4.2.   Research Model Combining the Internal/External
                Frame of Reference Model and the Expectancy-Value
                Theory 120
Figure 4.3.   Path Diagram of the Structural Equation Model
                for the Michigan Study of Adolescent Life
                Transition and BIJU Data 130
Figure 5.1.   Hypothesized Latent Growth Curve Model of
                Perceived Math, Language Arts, and Science
                Ability 150
Figure 5.2.   Hypothesized Latent Growth Curve Model of
                Perceived Math, Language Arts, and Science Ability
                With Gender as a Time-Invariant Predictor 151
Figure 5.3.   Hypothesized Latent Growth Curve Model of
                Perceived Math, Language Arts, and Science
                Ability With Grades in Math, Language Arts, and
                Science as Time-Varying Predictors 152
Figure 6.1.   Sociomotivational Model of Persistence in Science
                and Technology 173
Figure 6.2.   Gender × Persistence Interactions 186

Figure 8.1.   Interaction of Adolescents' Gender and
                 Gender Role Attitudes on Male-Typed Career
                 Self-Efficacy Beliefs at Age 20 222
Figure 8.2.   Interaction of Adolescents' Gender and Mothers'
                 Gender Role Attitudes on Female-Typed Career
                 Self-Efficacy Beliefs at Age 20 223
Figure 10.1.   Gendered Factor Means for Beliefs About Key
                 Influences on Engineering Choice 281
Figure 11.1.   National Percentages of Female Graduate
                 Students and Faculty, 1991 and 2001 301
Figure 11.2.   Percentages of Male and Female Faculty by Rank
                 in Literature, Science, and the Arts
                 (Natural Sciences); Medicine (Basic Sciences);
                 and Engineering at the University of Michigan,
                 2000–2001 302
Figure 11.3.   Accumulation of Disadvantage: A Feedback Loop 309

Gender and Occupational Outcomes

GENDER AND OCCUPATIONAL OUTCOMES: AN INTRODUCTION

HELEN M. G. WATT

Why do men and women frequently end up in different kinds of careers? In particular, why are there fewer women in careers related to math, science, and technology, including the physical sciences, engineering, and information communication technology? Why, despite 25 years of research into gender differences for career choices related to math and science, does this phenomenon still appear robust across a range of different countries and cultural contexts? Although women have been making gains in entering traditionally male-dominated professions, gender differences persist. Women are both less likely to choose careers in these fields and more likely to leave them if they do enter (American Association of University Women, 1993, 1998; National Center for Education Statistics, 1997; National Science Foundation, 1999). In view of concentrated research into this question, numerous policy documents, and educational efforts—why do we see these patterns of gender participation in the 21st century?

A resurgence of interest in this question has been prompted in part by a general shortage of people entering the so-called "STEM" careers (in science, technology, engineering, and math) because women are an undertapped resource for filling the predicted shortfalls. Participation in advanced science and mathematics education has exponentially declined in the United States over the past 2 decades, to the point where there is grave concern about the viability of those disciplines to sustain economic growth and development (see Jacobs, 2005; see also National Science Board, 2003; National Science Foundation, 2002). Similar concern exists in Australia (Dow, 2003a, 2003b; National Committee for the Mathematical Sciences of the Australian Academy of Science, 2006) and many other Western nations, whereas Asian countries do not show the same systematic pattern (Jacobs, 2005). For example, a recent examination showed only 32% of bachelor's degrees in the United States were in science or engineering (National Science Foundation, 2004), and declines in undergraduate mathematics, engineering, and physical sciences enrollments through the 1990s declined 19%, 21%, and 13%, respectively (National Science Foundation, 2000).

At the same time, the association of high-status, high-salary careers with advanced participation in the STEM disciplines has continued to fuel the concern of researchers with an interest in gender equity. Ever since Lucy Sells (1980) voiced social concerns about lower female participation in math courses in her identification of math as the "critical filter" limiting access to many high-status, high-income careers, others have also pointed out that many females prematurely restrict their educational and career options by discontinuing their mathematical training in high school or soon after (Bridgeman & Wendler, 1991; Heller & Parsons, 1981; Lips, 1992; Meece, Wigfield, & Eccles, 1990). This has important ramifications for women's well-being, both from an economic or sociological standpoint as well as a psychological point of view. First, gender differences in earning potential are important because women are more likely than men to be single, widowed, or single heads of households and therefore likely to need to support themselves and other dependents financially without assistance from a partner or significant other (Meece, 2006). Second, women (and men) need to develop and deploy their talents and abilities in their work outside the home because this substantially impacts their general life satisfaction and psychological well-being (Eccles, 1987; Meece, 2006).

The result of the underrepresentation of women in STEM careers is that these careers tend to reflect the values of majority male professionals. This in turn reinforces the gender imbalance through girls' and women's perceptions regarding the culture of those careers. This is most noticeable in relation to the ways in which such careers accommodate—or fail to accommodate—the familial obligations women often carry. The culture associated with male-dominated professions may affect girls' and women's aspirations toward those careers in the first place, stunt their development and progression should they enter those careers, and deter them from persisting. The potential talent pool for STEM careers has often been regarded as a "pipeline" that starts in secondary school and runs through university and then into the workforce. Consideration of gender differences and gendered influences at each of these critical points in the pipeline is key to interventions designed to promote women's participation.

Of course, there are not only gender differences in STEM careers. Considerably fewer men than women are represented in the arts and humanities and in the helping professions such as nursing, social work, and teaching (e.g., Carrington, 2002; Richardson & Watt, 2006). There has been less concern about the underrepresentation of men in these professions, perhaps because the potential earnings and prestige at stake are lower than in STEM careers. However, it is certainly possible that boys and men are not pursuing their interests and abilities in those domains, which may have ramifications for their satisfaction and well-being.

INTERVENTIONS TO INCREASE WOMEN'S PARTICIPATION IN MALE-DOMINATED PROFESSIONS

Over the past 15 years, educators have implemented significant reforms in both the curricula and teaching practices of elementary and secondary mathematics and science to incorporate more collaborative, problem-focused, and authentic instruction (Meece & Scantlebury, 2006). This has been due to research suggesting that girls take an active role and respond favorably in individualized and cooperative learning environments (Eccles (Parsons), Kaczala, & Meece, 1982; Kahle & Meece, 1994). Similarly, at the other end of the pipeline, interventions have been designed and implemented to meet professional women's needs within STEM careers. One example is outlined and reported in chapter 11 of this volume.

It is not clear at the present time how such reforms will change young women's motivation, performance, development, or persistence. Despite a plethora of intervention efforts particularly targeting the secondary school years, most of these programs have not been formally evaluated. There has also been a lack of longitudinal rather than "one-shot" examinations, a lack of large-scale and representative samples rather than small and opportune groups, a lack of representation across diverse samples and sociocultural settings, and a lack of representation and integration of diverse theoretical perspectives. Previous research into the question of why women are less likely to end up in traditionally male-dominated spheres collectively points to the importance of factors such as gender differences in individuals' motivations, self-concepts, interests, values, and life-goals (e.g., Bong, 2001; Eccles, 1985; Ethington, 1991; Wigfield & Eccles, 1992); influences of family planning, parents, and biology (e.g., Benbow & Stanley, 1982; Eccles, Jacobs, & Harold, 1990; Jacobs & Eccles, 1992; Jodl, Michael, Malanchuk, Eccles, & Sameroff, 2001); and sociocultural affordances and constraints on women's career development (e.g., Lee, 2002; Siann & Callaghan, 2001; Willis, 1989).

One explanation that is important to outline relates to superior male mathematics abilities. It is difficult to find a more controversial topic in recent educational research than gender differences in mathematics performance. There is no dispute that in samples from the general population, male and female global mathematical performance is similar (e.g., Hyde, Fennema, Ryan, Frost, & Hopp, 1990; Kimball, 1989; Rosenthal & Rubin, 1982; Tartre & Fennema, 1995). Two comprehensive meta-analyses using approximately 100 research articles each (Friedman, 1989; Hyde, Fennema, & Lamon, 1990) found that in samples from the general population, boys' and girls' secondary school mathematical performance is similar. In the meta-analysis of Hyde, Fennema, and Lamon (1990), girls outperformed boys by a negligible amount on overall scores, understanding of mathematical concepts, and computation, whereas boys outperformed girls by a negligible amount on problem-solving tasks. The Friedman (1989) meta-analysis found that a 95% confidence interval for the relative superior mathematical performance of males to females covered zero.

Other researchers have focused on gender differences in spatial skills (Linn & Petersen, 1985) and gender differences among very high achieving students (e.g., the *Study of Mathematically Precocious Youth*; Lubinski, Benbow, & Sanders, 1993). It has been pointed out that differential variability renders comparisons of gendered mathematical performances problematic (Feingold 1992, 1993), and an influential United States study found that the ratio of male to female variability in "space relations" scores on the Differential Aptitude Test generally decreased from 1947 to 1980 (Feingold, 1992), although an interaction effect between year and grade showed this variance ratio decreased from grades 8 to 12 in 1947, was constant across grades from 1962 to 1972, and increased over grades in 1980. Such findings imply an imperative for seeking explanations additional to biology, because these changes are occurring "rather faster than the gene can travel" (Rosenthal & Rubin, 1982, p. 711). Gender differences in mathematical performance favoring males have also been identified among moderately selective and precocious samples, although Hyde, Fennema, and Lamon (1990) have cautioned against mean-level comparisons because of the different variability within gender groups being compared. Males are in fact overrepresented at both the high and low extremes of mathematical performance (e.g., Lubinski et al., 1993), which some have argued relates to boys being more often selected for remedial help and for gifted programs in mathematics (Willis, 1989). It is clear that continued research is needed into the antecedents and influences additional to biology on gendered participation in mathematics and other male-typed occupational pursuits.

IMPETUS FOR THE BOOK

It is time to take stock of what the research literature from diverse fields tells us. This will inform the design of future intervention efforts and enable researchers and educators to prioritize key "levers for change" (Roeser, 2006). To date, there has been no synthesis of the findings from across the different literatures specifically focused toward understanding gendered occupational outcomes. There is an absence of work drawing together the state of play from across different literatures and across a range of different cultural contexts. Although some books on gendered occupational outcomes are available, they have tended to focus on a narrower scope (e.g., math or science) and certainly do not represent the range of cultures, time points, data sets, and perspectives that are represented in the current volume.

A major impetus for our book was to draw together researchers from around the world who are each using multiwave longitudinal data to address the question of what factors contribute to gendered occupational outcomes, from a variety of perspectives and in a variety of cultural settings. A unique feature is our inclusion of studies that involve multiple waves of longitudinal data. Rather than speculating about how processes may unfold over time to produce certain outcomes, longitudinal studies allow us to draw strong conclusions regarding those processes and to tease apart and test out a range of theoretical models.

There is a growing imperative to explore gendered career outcomes across a range of cultural settings because this will facilitate a greater understanding of how career and life choices are made in contexts of varying gendered opportunity structures and levels of economic development (Roeser, 2006). To date, research into gendered career outcomes has been concentrated in the Western world, primarily the United States. However, even Western school populations are becoming more culturally diverse, creating a need to examine how explanatory models focusing on individual motivations, parental beliefs, and broader social and institutional influences operate across different ethnic, racial, and socioeconomic groups. Examining influences on women's career choices across a range of cultural contexts provides the opportunity to highlight distinctive contextual features that relate to culturally specific patterns and suggests circumstances that may be the most conducive to promoting and supporting women's development in STEM careers. For the most part, these issues have been largely unexamined in research on women's achievement-related decisions, and a global perspective and interdisciplinary approach is integral to this current endeavor. Our book includes large-scale longitudinal samples from the United States, Canada (Anglophile and Francophile), Australia, Turkey, Germany, Japan, and other countries of the European Union.

The volume is timely, providing implications to further the knowledge base on development, intervention, and policy concerning gender differences in occupational outcomes. The book has been designed to have broad appeal— to educators, counselors, psychologists, and researchers. The contributors represent an international team of experts from several fields of study, including developmental psychology, social psychology, cultural anthropology, human development, biology, education, and sociology, who investigate explanations for gendered occupational outcomes from diverse perspectives within different sociocultural contexts. Accordingly, the book will appeal to students and scholars in all of these areas. The chapters use a diverse range of current sophisticated techniques for analyzing longitudinal data—methodological and statistical advances enable research to shed new light on the persistent issue of gendered occupational representation. Consequently, we have asked all contributors to make a special effort to provide details on the methodologies they have used to conduct their studies. Further, the authors each discuss the intervention and policy relevance of their work.

OVERVIEW OF CHAPTERS

The book is structured into four broad sections. Part I addresses the question of math achievement and coursework as a critical filter and whether this limits women's access in particular to high-status careers in specific specialist domains. Part II contains chapters that primarily focus on the influences of individual factors in women's career choices and persistence in STEM fields, including motivations, self-concepts, values, and competing interests. Part III focuses on the importance of family considerations, parental influences, and biology. The final part (Part IV) considers broader social and institutional contextual constraints on women's career development. Findings from the 12 studies considered collectively are much more powerful than if they were taken individually, allowing us to reflect across the multiplicity of interacting influences shaping women's career outcomes, at levels of intensity ranging from individual characteristics through to national policies.

Part I: Mathematics as the Critical Filter?

Chapter 1 examines whether math achievement acts as a critical filter limiting later educational and occupational aspirations among Anglophile Canadian youth. The authors present evidence that early high school math achievement shaped the prestige dimension of their educational and occupational aspirations from Grade 9 up to 3 years following secondary school. High math achievers maintained high educational aspirations, whereas low math achievers' aspirations remained consistently low, even when general school achievement and perceived mathematical abilities were statistically controlled. Low math achievement in early high school also related to lower occupational aspirations and more rapid deterioration in occupational aspirations toward the end of high school compared with high achievement, which was related to only a gradual decline over the same period. These findings suggest that math achievement in early high school acts as a critical filter more than 20 years after Lucy Sells (1980) first proposed her hypothesis. In this sample, mathematical success at school was associated with trajectories of both educational and occupational aspirations. The findings signal two priorities for future research: How does math achievement affect subsequent actual educational and occupational outcomes, and which aspects of math study and achievement are influential?

It is interesting that there were no gender differences in the prestige level of the occupations to which the young men and women aspired, raising the important question of whether gender differences in occupational pursuits are more differences of kind. This has important implications for our thinking about gendered occupational outcomes—what gendered career "outcomes" should we be concerned with? Is it problematic if women are choosing careers that are equally prestigious and highly paid yet nonmathematical? I return to this question later in this chapter (p. 11).

Chapter 2 also investigates the math as a critical filter hypothesis, using longitudinal data from the 6-year U.S. *Longitudinal Study of American Youth* (see Miller, Kimmel, Hoffer, & Nelson, 2000), which spanned Grades 7 through 12. The authors examined which among the various math courses in the United States secondary curriculum predicted subsequent actual college choices for different kinds of majors (science, engineering, economics, law, medicine, liberal arts, and education) as well as the prestige dimension of occupational aspirations. In the United States, secondary students select which math courses they wish to study at school. The authors identify how participation in each of the different math courses related to college and occupational choices over and above measured mathematical achievement.

They found that mathematics coursework played an important role, with Algebra II acting as a critical filter for the career choices of males and calculus as a critical filter that screened females from science and engineering majors and into majors in liberal arts. In the U.S. curriculum, Algebra II is the first highly theoretical mathematics course that requires considerable abstract thinking and reasoning for problem solving (see chap. 2, this volume). The authors speculate that many males may first encounter serious difficulties with math in this course and start to rethink their career choices. They argue that Algebra II could lead males to doubt their abilities to successfully handle the mathematics needed for their desired occupations. Part of their hypothesis is that males may have had unrealistic career expectations beforehand, and as a result of their experiences in Algebra II may put these into a more realistic perspective. The fact that males nominated more prestigious career choices than females across the preceding middle and high school years and did not show further negative coursework effects following Algebra II provides support for this hypothesis.

For females, taking calculus in Grade 12 was strongly associated with college enrollment in science and engineering and negatively associated with majoring in liberal arts. It is possible that the females who were already planning to pursue STEM-related tertiary study were those who chose to undertake calculus in Grade 12 rather than calculus experiences having determined their college choices. The low percentage of females who undertook calculus in grade 12 and the importance of calculus for females' college major choices reflect the limited number of females entering STEM fields.

The findings raise several intriguing questions and provide an important step in the direction of identifying what math coursework experiences most shape young men's and women's educational and occupational aspirations. Future research should further examine the relationships between coursework sequencing in addition to the relationships this study has identified between discrete math courses and college and career choices. It is a strength of this chapter that actual college choices were included rather than educational aspirations; however, actual career choices remain a critical component for future research so we can understand how math filters eventual career choices or options young adults actually take up. One significant question raised by this chapter is, if the authors' hypotheses regarding the effects of Algebra II are correct, whether it is a bad thing that males' career aspirations become lower but more realistic as a result of their coursework experience.

The chapters in this first section together demonstrate that math continues to act as a critical filter, playing an important role in determining young women's and men's educational and occupational aspirations as well as their actual college majors. We therefore should be highly concerned about girls' and women's lower involvement in advanced math, which delimits their access to certain educational and occupational pursuits.

Part II: Psychological Processes and Gendered Participation in Math, Science, and Technology-Based Careers

The second section of the book follows naturally from the first: If math acts as a critical filter limiting women's (and men's) access to high-status, high-salary careers, what psychological processes and motivations lead to women's lower participation in STEM disciplines at critical points in the pipeline? Chapters in this section examine gendered STEM-related participation choices from senior high school enrollments through college majors, persistence, and the individual motivations and perceptions that shape these choices.

Chapter 3 describes a study of mine that investigated what motivates females and males among a sample of Australian youth to pursue sex-stereotyped careers. In this study, I included actual senior high enrollments and careers aspired to as outcome measures. In contrast to the first two chapters, I was not focused on the prestige dimension of young adults' career choices but rather on the extent to which their career aspirations involved math and English. The concentration of boys in "masculine" career types has caused less consternation than that of girls in non-STEM fields. Whether boys may not be pursuing their other areas of interest and potential fulfillment has been less a topic for research concern or public interest (an issue also posed in chap. 9, this volume). It is likely that researchers who are concerned with gender equity have focused on gendered participation in male- rather than female-dominated domains (also argued in chap. 7, this volume) because female underrepresentation in stereotypically male-dominated domains (such as math) leads to careers of lower status and salary for women.

In the State of New South Wales, Australia, the options for math coursework selection are quite different from those in the United States or Canada that are outlined in Part I of this volume. In New South Wales, math courses are ordered by level of difficulty rather than topic area, providing a naturally occurring metric to investigate the extent of boys' and girls' chosen math participation. In this setting, results confirmed the persistence of greater male participation in both math-related educational and occupational choices. Conversely, and consistent with gender stereotypes, greater female participation occurred for English-related educational and occupational choices. The operationalization of different levels of involvement in math and English career aspirations provides an important extension to existing research in the area. Findings of gender differences according to the math- and English-relatedness of careers aspired to brings us back to the question posed earlier in this chapter (p. 9): Is it possible that young women are aspiring to equally prestigious careers as young men but that their career choices are nonmathematical? The collective findings from chapters 1 and 3 suggest this may well be the case. This is an important ingredient that needs to be incorporated in thinking about gendered career choices and what career dimensions are most critical for gender equity researchers to examine. Is career prestige the most important dimension, or is it differences in the kinds of careers young men and women choose?

Chapters 3 and 4 draw on a prominent, productive, and highly influential theoretical framework developed to explain gendered math participation: the *expectancy-value model* developed by Eccles (Parsons) et al. (1983). Within it, success expectancies and the subjective valuation of success are the most proximal influences on achievement-related choices and behaviors, and these are in turn predicted by ability beliefs as well as perceived task demands. Chapter 3 findings imply that a focus on boys' perceptions of English, compared with girls', as being less useful through secondary school will likely promote greater male participation in English-related careers should their lower participation be considered to require attention. For math, key factors will be a focus on girls' liking for and interest in math, their self-perceptions of mathematical talent and expectations for success, and their valuation of the utility of math.

Chapter 4 examines gendered math and English participation choices for senior high enrollments within the United States and Germany. Predictions about processes linking gender to students' choices of advanced courses in high school were derived from both the Eccles (Parsons) et al. (1983) expectancy-value model outlined above and the internal/external frame of reference model (Marsh, 1986). A strength of the study examined in chapter 4 is the theoretical integration of both models to incorporate ipsative intraindividual processes in young women's and men's senior high enrollment choices. The authors found support for the merits of their combined model: Both self-concept and intrinsic value predicted high school course choices, and both internal and external comparison processes occurred.

This study included longitudinal data from two different educational systems, providing an in-depth investigation of how key contextual factors shape students' decision-making processes. The major relevant differences relate to the ways in which students are tracked and the freedom that they have to choose between courses. In the United States, all students attend high school, where within-school tracking usually starts at Grade 8 or 9 but where students have a great deal of freedom to choose between classes. Although it is possible to identify college-bound students from the courses they select, the distinction is far less clear than in the German system. From as early as age 10, German students are tracked into the different schools of the three-tiered secondary system. These differ greatly in the intensity and content of the curriculum, but within each, tracking is very unusual. The exception is the most academically competitive track—the *Gymnasium*—from which the German sample for this study was located. For the last 2 years of schooling in the *Gymnasium*, students have to select two, and only two, advanced elective courses, forcing even students who perform well across the board to specialize.

The authors argue that this process is likely to amplify gendered course participation through forcing ipsative decision making. This is in contrast to the United States system, in which high-achieving, college-bound youth may opt for several advanced courses in order to boost their chances of college acceptance—particularly advanced math and English classes, which are critical entrance criteria. Consistent with the authors' hypothesis, differences were more pronounced in the German sample, where high school course selection is based primarily on domain-specific self-concepts and intrinsic value rather than on achievement. The restriction to two advanced courses in Germany resulted in self-concepts and intrinsic value becoming paramount in the selection process, whereas in the United States, course choices were likely to be more ability driven, because high school coursework is one of the determinants for college admission. As a result, the authors caution that school systems that require early specialization can lead to the amplification of gendered course choices and may consequently increase the gender segmentation of the workforce.

Chapter 5 follows from the preceding two chapters, which demonstrate the importance of ability-related beliefs in students' gendered math and English choices. Chapter 5 examines the development of gendered self-concepts in math, English (or "language arts"), and science during high school. It explicitly illustrates the use of latent growth curve modeling within the framework of structural equation modeling. The author first introduces the basic concepts associated with latent growth curve modeling and then walks the reader through three related, increasingly complex applications designed to measure change. Application 1 tested for the extent of change in domain-specific self-concepts. Application 2 extended the multiple-domain model to include gender in order to identify gender differences in domain-specific self-concepts and possible gender differences in their rates of change over time. Application 3 tested for the influence of academic grades as concurrent time-varying predictors of change in self-concepts for math, English, and science. The chapter primarily demonstrates how the LGC modeling approach can be used to analyze the development of important psychological precursors to gendered occupational outcomes, enabling researchers interested in gendered processes to model directly how they unfold. The chapter additionally furthers understanding of how math, English, and science self-concepts develop through adolescence.

Chapter 6 examines gendered trajectories beyond high school for college students interested in studies and careers in science and technology (S&T) in Francophile Canada (Québec). The study adopted a sociomotivational framework incorporating contextual factors, (e.g., parent, teacher, and counselor) in addition to personal motivations, to examine gendered trajectories for persistence and graduation in S&T studies. Results supported the validity of a sociomotivational model. That is, youths' commitment to their studies, their self-determined motivation toward pursuing S&T studies, autonomy support from their parents in the process of choosing studies and a career, and the opportunities offered by their science teachers made unique contributions to the prediction of persistence. It is noteworthy that the motivational variables accounted for nearly twice as much variance in persistence as the social support variables and that persistence may result from the additive effects of motivation and parental and teacher support, even during early adulthood.

It is intriguing that as many girls as boys persisted in their S&T studies, and girls were more likely to start a career in the S&T field sooner after their graduation, commit and persist in their program, and leave the field only after having graduated from college. This profile of persistence reflected girls' higher levels of self-determination, academic involvement, and institutional attachment, identified in the authors' earlier research. Such motivational factors are likely to make girls' academic path less chaotic than that of boys. However, more girls than boys abandon S&T after having obtained their college diploma in this field. The authors argue that the girls who left S&T after having graduated probably had highly positive motivational dispositions without maintaining high intentions regarding careers in mathematics, physics, and computer science. They argue this on the basis that girls' motivational dispositions and support received from parents and teachers contributed weakly to whether they went on to pursue S&T studies. This was in contrast to boys, for whom associations were strong. Results show the critical importance of examining the moderating effects of gender not only in describing the development of S&T-related motivation and support from the family, school, and society, but also in examining the links between these sociomotivational factors and youths' academic and professional trajectories. The next exciting stage of the authors' longitudinal study is to follow participants into the labor market, providing data on actual career choices, which are very much needed in this field of research.

These chapters collectively highlight the importance of individuals' own psychological processes and motivations through different stages of the pipeline—their choice to specialize in STEM domains, persistence in educational training, and professional entry. These influences appear to operate differently for women than for men.

Part III: The Importance of Family Considerations, Family, and Biology in Gendered Career Choices

Chapters 7 through 9 focus on the importance of family-related influences on gendered occupational choices. Chapter 7 draws on longitudinal data from the United States to examine two hypotheses regarding why young women abandoned, 7 years later, occupational aspirations toward male-dominated fields that they had espoused during late adolescence. The authors' first hypothesis concerns the young women's attitudes toward math and science and the second hypothesis their desire for job flexibility that allows for a balance between work and family responsibilities. The findings show that the desire for a flexible job, high time demands of an occupation, and low intrinsic value of physical science were the best predictors of women changing their occupational aspirations out of male-dominated fields. Positive attitudes toward math and science predicted persistence in aspirations toward male-dominated careers, and job inflexibilities predicted desistence away from those careers.

These findings suggest that despite the women's movement and increased efforts to open occupational doors for women, concerns about balancing career and family, together with less positive attitudes toward science-related domains, continue to steer young women away from occupations in traditionally male-dominated fields even if that is where their abilities and ambitions lie. An examination of the women's actual careers and life circumstances at the second measurement occasion, when they were age 25, also would have been interesting. Future research could additionally include men as well as women to determine whether, and the extent to which, these influences identified among the women may be gender specific. Do the same factors deter both men and women who turn away from traditionally male-dominated careers, or only women?

Chapter 8 focuses on the role that parents play in their children's gender-typed occupational choices. The authors use the parent socialization model (Eccles (Parsons), Adler, & Kaczala, 1982) as a framework to analyze longitudinal data from the United States across a 13-year period. The theoretical model posits that characteristics of parents, family, and neighborhood as well as characteristics of the child shape parents' behaviors and their general beliefs about the world and specific beliefs about their child. The authors focus on how parents' general world beliefs (including their gender role beliefs and attitudes), as well as their child-specific beliefs (occupational expectations and aspirations for their children), shape the opportunities they provide for their children, the children's own motivations, and consequent future behaviors and choices.

The authors present three related studies to unpack their theorized relationships. The first examined the relation between parents' gender role beliefs and children's gender-typed occupational choices. The second study examined the relation between parents' expectations for their children's occupational prestige and the prestige of their children's actual occupations, and the third examined the relation between parents' gender-typed occupational expectations for their children and the gender-typing of their children's actual occupations.

The nature of parent influence differed for mothers versus fathers and according to the child's sex: Fathers' gender-typed occupational expectations were related to both their sons' and daughters' actual gender-typed occupational choices, but mothers' related only to sons' choices. From this, the authors conclude that fathers may play a more powerful role in shaping both their sons' and daughters' career choices than mothers. Parents' gender role beliefs were also more strongly related to their adult children's decisions to enter male- rather than female-typed occupations. Young adults made their career choices within the context of gender-typed parental expectations and within a gender-typed world of occupational opportunities. Together, these findings provide strong evidence for the important role of parents' beliefs and expectations in shaping their children's occupational choices from adolescence through young adulthood, up to 13 years later.

Chapter 8 signals as a clear priority for future research the examination of ways in which parents communicate their expectations to their children. The theoretical model on which the three studies were founded suggests that parents shift from sharing perspectives and providing exposure, opportunities, and role modeling at early ages to providing encouragement and guidance for activities that continue to be supportive of the child's developing interests in certain occupations. How these processes occur and the mechanisms by which they come to shape children's career choices in young adulthood are critical next steps.

Chapter 9 addresses the highly important and topical role of biological predispositions as a contributor to the causes of sex differences in occupational outcomes. Much evidence has focused on social contributors to these gendered outcomes, but it is also important to consider the role of biology. The authors describe evidence that sex hormones present during prenatal development affect a variety of psychological characteristics that may contribute to gendered occupational choices. Much of this evidence was from females with *congenital adrenal hyperplasia* (CAH), a condition caused by exposure to moderately elevated androgens during prenatal development. Compared with their unexposed female relatives, females with CAH were more male typical and less female typical in activity interests, some personal and social characteristics, aspects of social relationships, and some cognitive abilities (especially spatial abilities). In contrast, gender identity in females with CAH was female typical.

The authors caution that biology does not operate in a vacuum, and they highlight the necessity to understand the mechanisms through which hormones influence behavior. In particular, how do hormones alter individuals' selection and interpretation of their social environment? They emphasize that biology is not destiny, that social factors also affect psychological sex differences, that sex-differential representation in different occupations reflects social practices as well as individual characteristics, and that findings of hormonal influences on psychological characteristics related to gendered occupational outcomes do not provide justification for the unequal treatment of men and women.

Collectively, the chapters in this section show that biology, early and continuing parental influences, and individuals' own family intentions all contribute to women's lower participation in traditionally male-dominated occupational pursuits.

Part IV: Social and Institutional Constraints on Women's Career Development

Chapter 10 examines gendered occupational outcomes in the field of professional training and work in Turkey. The results of three empirical studies (the case of engineering students, the case of professorial workers, and the case of banking sector employees) informed the authors' work. They use historical and institutional data sources to supplement data from the three studies to present a multilayered and relational account of the gendered outcomes of professional employment and education, situating the phenomenon at macro sociohistorical, meso-organizational, and microindividual levels. They present Turkey as a complex and paradoxical example for the study of gender and occupations, with high levels of female representation in professional work in contrast to persistent gendered prejudices upholding a male-centered organization of work life.

Their first study of engineering students revealed that males believed women had lower interest in and were less suited to engineering, tacitly suggesting lower female representation in engineering fields as a matter of choice rather than an outcome of structural conditions. Their second study showed that professors of both genders mostly perceived the academic domain to be free from gender inequality and discrimination. However, male professors reported experiences of institutional barriers such as promotion procedures, and female professors reported experiencing barriers due to their family and child-care responsibilities. It is interesting that this situation was perceived as "normal" by both male and female professors. In their third study, case studies of three banking companies demonstrated both vertical and horizontal gender segregation, with women's employment heavily concentrated in customer relations such as marketing, investment, and stock exchange and at the middle ranks rather than senior or low rank positions. The exclusion of women from areas such as auditing was reinforced by a lack of organizational procedures for combating the sexual harassment they received in the field. However, the home offices were also not free from sexual harassment, and complicated grievance procedures combined with a culture of low awareness did not support the victims. The culture of long working hours further circumscribed women's development. Long hours are one of the main features of the male-centered organization of work life in the banking sector in Turkey; they are equated with strong commitment and provide networking opportunities that promote career advancement. This consequently serves as an exclusion mechanism for women having domestic and child-care responsibilities. The implications of this study were again that gender inequality is perceived as a matter of personal lifestyle rather than institutional culture. Although women have been encouraged to take up employment in the banking sector, there has been no accompanying reform of male dominated cultures and practices.

The authors describe the important symbolism of professional representation of women during the modernization of Turkey while gendered patterns of life in the private space remained intact and unquestioned. Absence of work–life balance supports at institutional and national levels has meant that professional Turkish women find themselves serving "double shifts" because of their disproportionately heavy domestic roles, which has negative effects on their careers. Unlike in the developed countries, where legal protectionism to combat gender discrimination in the workplace has been a long-standing tradition, in Turkey sex equality depends heavily on employers' initiative, willingness, and ideology. The authors conclude that although ideological state support has been an important medium for promoting sex equality, it should be incorporated within a progressive equal opportunities legislation. In addition, because it is individuals who can practice, promote or obstruct any action taken at a policy level, a strong personal awareness and critical understanding of the gendered nature of employment will need to be developed.

Chapter 11 outlines the impetus for and development of ongoing interventions by the University of Michigan's ADVANCE program, part of a nationwide effort by the National Science Foundation to increase the participation of women at the highest levels of science and engineering. Thus far, 19 universities have received multimillion dollars worth of grants to fund efforts toward institutional transformation—to increase the hiring and promotion of women faculty members and to improve the academic climates in which they work. Slow progress toward gender equity among faculty in science and engineering over the past 20 years, particularly at the highest ranks, has led researchers to investigate ways in which the climate of academic science might contribute both to women "leaking" from the academic pipeline and to their low status within the academy. It is a fair assumption that the relative absence of women at the end of the pipeline, their low status, and their low morale might all be important factors in the choices being made by girls and younger women to be less likely to pursue those careers. The authors discuss likely interactions among and cumulative effects of the interventions as well as their potential influence on young women still in the pipeline.

Specific interventions included invitations to individual faculty members to compete for grants to help bolster individual women's careers; invitations to departments to apply for grants to allow them to design their own new approaches to recruiting, retaining, and promoting women faculty; and the development of university-wide policies to address family friendly issues, particularly related to recruitment and the timeline available in which to obtain tenure. These interventions are intended to improve the recruitment, retention, and promotion of women faculty and to increase the visibility and authority of women scientists and engineers in leadership positions.

Viewing the university as a system allowed the researchers to approach the climate problems from multiple points of entry, intervening at several levels. Although it is too early to evaluate the combined effects of the interventions, if the experiments at this and the other 18 institutions involved succeed, climate improvement for women faculty in science and engineering will continue. The authors point out that institutions need to remain committed to the project over a long period to allow for meaningful change in the demographic makeup of departments and the development of a critical mass of tenured women faculty thereby guaranteed long and secure careers. They suggest that this "price" should be acceptable because the cost of continued underrepresentation of women in science and engineering is already known. Large-scale, systemwide, and long-term interventions such as these are critical to the understanding of how women's development at the far end of the pipeline may best be fostered and promoted. It is important to note that this intervention is being continually monitored and evaluated, and the evaluation findings will be invaluable in an area lacking in formal evaluation data.

The final chapter gathers women's employment and educational statistics from the United States, the European Union, and Japan to present an "equality profile" of these regions, selected because more than 90% of new technologies are patented via these countries' trilateral system. Because most efforts to remedy gendered participation in STEM-related fields have been through targeting female educational preparation, the author empirically tested whether equivalent educational preparation translated into equitable occupational outcomes for males and females across these three geographic regions. Equity measures included the Convention Against Elimination of Discrimination Against Women (CEDAW) reports, of which about 150 countries are signatories, for which CEDAW monitors progress in policy and practice. These reports are highly significant in monitoring policy and implementation of gendered occupational outcomes at the national level. On examination of these and other indicators, the author found that despite antidiscriminatory legislation and policies for equality, women experience gendered economic disadvantage throughout their working lives.

The author further analyzed differences between the levels of gender equity measures across the three regions by comprehensive review of international and national policy and legal initiatives and their corresponding effects on labor force demographics. She, like others in this volume, argues the paramount importance of women's participation in STEM fields because of the economic boundary that separates the technologically powerful and the technologically disadvantaged. Her recommendations include continued access strategies for women's employment in nontraditional careers alongside the transformation of workplaces to accommodate women's dual home–work responsibilities.

This chapter paints a portrait of women's opportunities and representation across a range of different countries and contexts, providing detailed statistics for a number of regions, which also help us to better interpret findings from the other chapters, which are situated across those settings. The author argues that women worldwide tend to perceive that higher levels of education help them to compete in the labor market but that higher levels of education may create greater pay inequality; that gender inequalities are most pronounced in high-level positions in the scientific world, whether academic, government, or private sectors; that hiring more women into the technical labor force may result from an impetus to reverse the shortages in this sector rather than a genuine concern with gender equity; and that women are penalized because of their combined responsibilities at work and in the home. As she eloquently states, these historical factors continue to deal women a losing hand in the labor market, especially as they age.

These chapters together analyze social and institutional barriers to women's development and success in male-typed occupational fields, emphasizing the need for explicit policy reform agenda and multipronged initiatives aimed at accommodating women's outside-work responsibilities while changing the values of the workplace culture. Until this can be achieved, it is small wonder that girls and young women elect to specialize in non-STEM occupations as they look forward to the situation at the further end of the pipeline.

IMPLICATIONS AND OUTLOOK

The present volume is the first book to draw together this range of perspectives, contexts, and time points to consolidate and expand existing knowledge about the internal and external forces that lead to gendered occupational outcomes. This approach is consistent with a developmental systems perspective, which examines individuals' development across different stages in the life span and within the contexts in which individuals are embedded (Roeser, 2006; Roeser, Peck, & Nasir, 2006). Individual, local, and distal social environments shape individuals' occupational choices, and more research is needed on these "embedded" contexts of life choices (Roeser, 2006). Collectively, the chapters highlight the range of key psychological, familial, biological, social, and institutional factors that together shape women's occupational entry and progression.

Most of the chapters focus on occupations in which women are underrepresented relative to men, reflecting our concern with gender equity and the fact that women are underrepresented in those high-status, high-salary careers. Our aim is to raise awareness about the complex interplay of internal and external forces that together shape women's occupational choices and behaviors; to inform policy, education, individuals' own choices; and to highlight the influences we each exert on others. This collection of chapters makes a far more powerful contribution than any single chapter could on its own, each focusing intensively on particular explanations situated within different contexts. The fact that each chapter makes use of longitudinal data and uses sophisticated analytic techniques also enormously strengthens the conclusions that we can draw.

The major messages we want readers to take from the book concern the continuing importance of math as a critical filter that limits access to traditionally male-dominated high-status, high-income careers; the critical role of girls' and women's own motivations and beliefs in steering them away from STEM-related domains; gender differences in biological predispositions that may contribute to gendered occupational outcomes; the enduring effects of parental influences; and the social and institutional constraints on women's career development. Administrators should find valuable information here to help them improve ways to attract girls and women into STEM-related domains and sustain their persistence during educational training. Legislators will appreciate the need to target both ends of the pipeline at once, working to both attract girls and women to the educational opportunities at its entry and also, at the career end, to sustain women's development in traditionally male-dominated occupations by enforcing explicit policies to change the often unfriendly and unsupportive workplace cultures that conflict with women's frequently held family responsibilities.

There is still more we need to know. I view the most important next steps for research in the field as continuing to draw together longitudinal studies from across different cultural settings and further exploring how multiple domains of individuals' lives jointly interact to produce occupational choices. Longitudinal research is necessary to really test out and tease apart how processes unfold over time and the long-term effects for different influences, which cannot be determined by single-shot or cross-sectional studies. Of course, long-term longitudinal studies are expensive, resource intensive, and take a long time to do, but more such studies, situated within a range of different settings, are needed. Cross-cultural research provides opportunities to contrast how different salient cultural features relate to different gendered outcomes. As one example, by contrasting the United States with the German segregated school system, the authors of chapter 4 are able to show that forced early specialization may amplify gender differences in students' course selections. Cross-cultural comparisons provide wonderful natural experiments for investigating how different structural features may shape different occupational outcomes for men and women. Research that incorporates multiple domains of individuals' lives further allows us to look at how these interact to shape young men's and women's career decisions. It is vital that we better understand what girls and women are choosing to do instead of pursuing traditionally male-dominated occupations and why they are choosing those other paths. To conduct research in this vein implies the need for large-scale, longitudinal, international, interdisciplinary, and collaborative programs of research, involving teams of experts from across different specializations. Our book takes important steps in this direction.

REFERENCES

American Association of University Women. (1993). *How schools shortchange girls*. Washington, DC: Author.

American Association of University Women. (1998). *Separated by sex: A critical look at single-sex education for girls*. Washington, DC: Author.

Benbow, C. P., & Stanley, J. C. (1982). Consequences in high school and college of sex differences in mathematical reasoning ability: A longitudinal perspective. *American Educational Research Journal, 19,* 598–622.

Bong, M. (2001). Role of self-efficacy and task-value in predicting college students' course performance and future enrollment intentions. *Contemporary Educational Psychology, 26,* 553–570.

Bridgeman, B., & Wendler, C. (1991). Gender differences in predictors of college mathematics performance and in college mathematics course grades. *Journal of Educational Psychology, 83,* 275–284.

Carrington, B. (2002). A quintessentially feminine domain? Student teachers' constructions of primary teaching as a career. *Educational Studies, 28*(3), 287–303.

Dow, K. L. (2003a). *Australia's teachers: Australia's future: Advancing innovation, science, technology and mathematics. Agenda for action.* Canberra: Commonwealth of Australia.

Dow, K. L. (2003b). *Australia's teachers: Australia's future: Advancing innovation, science, technology and mathematics. Main report.* Canberra: Commonwealth of Australia.

Eccles, J. S. (1985). A model of student enrollment decisions. *Educational Studies in Mathematics, 16,* 311–314.

Eccles, J. S. (1987). Gender roles and women's achievement-related decisions. *Psychology of Women Quarterly, 11,* 135–172.

Eccles, J. S., Jacobs, J. E., & Harold, R. (1990). Gender role stereotypes, expectancy effects, and parents' socialization of gender differences. *Journal of Social Issues, 46,* 183–201.

Eccles (Parsons), J., Adler, T. F., Futterman, R., Goff, S. B., Kaczala, C. M., Meece, J. L., et al. (1983). Expectancies, values, and academic behaviors. In J. T. Spence (Ed.), *Achievement and achievement motivation* (pp. 75–146). San Francisco, CA: Freeman.

Eccles (Parsons), J. S., Adler, T. F., & Kaczala, C. M. (1982). Socialization of achievement attitudes and beliefs: Parental influences. *Child Development, 53,* 310–321.

Eccles (Parsons), J. S., Kaczala, C. M., & Meece, J. L. (1982). Socialization of achievement attitudes and beliefs: Classroom influences. *Child Development, 53,* 322–339.

Ethington, C. A. (1991). A test of a model of achievement behaviors. *American Educational Research Journal, 28,* 155–172.

Feingold, A. (1992). The greater male variability controversy: Science versus politics. *Review of Educational Research, 62,* 89–90.

Feingold, A. (1993). Joint effects of gender differences in central tendency and gender differences in variability. *Review of Educational Research, 63,* 106–109.

Friedman, L. (1989). Mathematics and the gender gap: A meta-analysis of recent studies on sex differences in mathematical tasks. *Review of Educational Research, 59,* 185–213.

Heller, K. A., & Parsons, J. E. (1981). Sex differences in teachers' evaluative feedback and students' expectancies for success in mathematics. *Child Development, 52,* 1015–1019.

Hyde, J. S., Fennema, E., & Lamon, S. J. (1990). Gender differences in mathematics performance: A meta-analysis. *Psychological Bulletin, 107,* 139–155.

Hyde, J. S., Fennema, E., Ryan, M., Frost, L. A., & Hopp, C. (1990). Gender comparisons of mathematics attitudes and affect: A meta-analysis. *Psychology of Women Quarterly, 14,* 299–324.

Jacobs, J. E. (2005, Winter). Twenty-five years of research on gender and ethnic differences in math and science career choices: What have we learned? *New Directions for Child and Adolescent Development, 110,* 85–94.

Jacobs, J. E., & Eccles, J. S. (1992). The impact of mothers' gender-role stereotypic beliefs on mothers' and children's ability perceptions. *Journal of Personality and Social Psychology, 63*, 932–944.

Jodl, K. M., Michael, A., Malanchuk, O., Eccles, J. S., & Sameroff, A. (2001). Parents' roles in shaping early adolescents' occupational aspirations. *Child Development, 72*, 1247–1265.

Kahle, J., & Meece, J. L. (1994). Research on girls in science: Lessons and applications. In D. Gabel (Ed.), *Handbook of research on science teaching* (pp. 1559–1610). Washington, DC: National Science Teachers Association.

Kimball, M. M. (1989). A new perspective on women's math achievement. *Psychological Bulletin, 105*, 198–214.

Lee, J. D. (2002). More than ability: Gender and personal relationships influence science and technology involvement. *Sociology of Education, 75*, 349–373.

Linn, M. C., & Petersen, A. C. (1985). Emergence and characterization of sex differences in spatial ability: A meta-analysis. *Child Development, 56*, 1479–1498.

Lips, H. M. (1992). Gender- and science-related attitudes as predictors of college students' academic choices. *Journal of Vocational Behavior, 40*, 62–81.

Lubinski, D., Benbow, C. P., & Sanders, C. E. (1993). Reconceptualizing gender differences in achievement among the gifted. In K. A. Heller, F. J. Monks, & A. H. Pass (Eds.), *International handbook of research and development of giftedness and talent* (pp. 693–707). New York: Pergamon Press.

Marsh, H. W. (1986). Verbal and math self-concepts: An internal/external frame of reference model. *American Educational Research Journal, 23*, 129–149.

Meece, J. L. (2006). Introduction: Trends in women's employment in the early 21st century. *Educational Research and Evaluation, 12*, 297–303.

Meece, J. L., & Scantlebury, K. (2006). Gender and schooling: Progress and persistent barriers. In J. Worrell & C. Goodheart (Eds.), *Handbook of girls' and women's psychological health* (pp. 283–291). New York: Oxford University Press.

Meece, J. L., Wigfield, A., & Eccles, J. S. (1990). Predictors of math anxiety and its consequences for young adolescents' course enrollment intentions and performances in mathematics. *Journal of Educational Psychology, 82*, 60–70.

Miller, J. D., Kimmel, L., Hoffer, T. B., & Nelson, C. (2000). *Longitudinal study of American youth: Users manual.* Chicago: International Center for the Advancement of Scientific Literacy, Northwestern University.

National Center for Education Statistics. (1997). *Digest of education statistics, 1997* (NCES Publication No. 98-015). Washington, DC: Author.

National Committee for the Mathematical Sciences of the Australian Academy of Science. (2006). *Mathematics and statistics: Critical skills for Australia's future. The national strategic review of mathematical sciences research in Australia.* Canberra: Australian Academy of Science.

National Science Board, Committee on Education and Human Resources, Task Force on National Workforce Policies for Science and Engineering. (2003). *The science and engineering workforce: Realizing America's potential* (NSB 03-69). Washington, DC: Author.

National Science Foundation. (1999). *Women, minorities, and persons with disabilities in science and engineering: 1998.* Arlington, VA: Author.

National Science Foundation. (2000). *Women, minorities, and persons with disabilities in science and engineering.* Arlington, VA: Author.

National Science Foundation. (2002). *Higher education in science and engineering: Increasing global capacity.* Washington, DC: Author.

National Science Foundation. (2004). *Women, minorities, and persons with disabilities in science and engineering.* Arlington, VA: Author.

Richardson, P. W., & Watt, H. M. G. (2006). Who chooses teaching and why? Profiling characteristics and motivations across three Australian universities. *Asia-Pacific Journal of Teacher Education, 34*(1), 27–56.

Roeser, R. W. (2006). On the study of educational and occupational life-paths in psychology: Commentary on the special issue. *Educational Research and Evaluation, 12,* 409–421.

Roeser, R. W., Peck, S. C., & Nasir, N. S. (2006). Self and identity processes in school motivation, learning, and achievement. In P. A. Alexander, P. R. Pintrich, & P. H. Winne (Eds.), *Handbook of educational psychology* (2nd ed., pp. 391–424). Mahwah, NJ: Erlbaum.

Rosenthal, R., & Rubin, D. B. (1982). Further meta-analytic procedures for assessing cognitive gender differences. *Journal of Educational Psychology, 74,* 708–712.

Sells, L. W. (1980). Mathematics: The invisible filter. *Engineering Education, 70,* 340–341.

Siann, G., & Callaghan, M. (2001). Choices and barriers: Factors influencing women's choice of higher education in science, engineering and technology. *Journal of Further and Higher Education, 25*(1), 85–95.

Tartre, L. A., & Fennema, E. (1995). Mathematics achievement and gender: A longitudinal study of selected cognitive and affective variables [grades 6–12]. *Educational Studies in Mathematics, 28,* 199–217.

Wigfield, A., & Eccles, J. (1992). The development of achievement task values: A theoretical analysis. *Developmental Review, 12,* 265–310.

Willis, S. (1989). *"Real girls don't do maths": Gender and the construction of privilege.* Waurn Ponds, Victoria, Australia: Deakin University Press.

I

MATHEMATICS AS THE CRITICAL FILTER?

1

GENDER, MATHEMATICS ACHIEVEMENT, AND THE EDUCATIONAL AND OCCUPATIONAL ASPIRATIONS OF CANADIAN YOUTH

JENNIFER D. SHAPKA, JOSÉ F. DOMENE, AND DANIEL P. KEATING

Although some of the influences on women's career outcomes are encountered after entering the workforce (e.g., the "glass ceiling," balancing work and family responsibilities), other influential factors are established earlier in life, during childhood, adolescence, and young adulthood. This study focuses on perceptions of future aspirations—including occupational goals and expected level of educational attainment—as they change over the course of adolescence and young adulthood. More specifically, we used growth curve modeling to examine young men's and women's aspirations toward prestigious occupations and educational attainment over a 6-year period (spanning Grade 9 through to 3 years postsecondary) for a multicohort sample of 218 (129 female, 89 male) university-bound Canadian youth. Results indicated that low math achievers had lower occupational aspirations to begin with and experienced a more rapid deterioration in their aspirations near the end of high school, whereas high achievers experienced a more gradual, linear decline in occupational aspirations over time. For educational aspirations, high math achievers had very high aspirations through high school and afterward, whereas low math achievers' aspirations remained consistently low.

Previous research has demonstrated that these aspirations play an important role in eventual occupational choice and attainment. For example,

Schoon and Parsons (2002) found that the educational and occupational aspirations of 16-year-olds predicted whether at age 26 they were working in professional or managerial positions versus occupations requiring fewer skills and less education. Also, Farmer, Wardrop, and Rotella (1999) demonstrated that career-related aspiration levels in high school had a significant direct effect on entry into science versus nonscience careers 10 years later for both men and women (although the relationship was stronger for men). Finally, Marjoribanks (2003) demonstrated that high school educational aspiration levels predicted the amount of education that participants had attained at 20 years of age.

The study of career-related aspirations has two principal dimensions: (a) the field of study and type of occupation to which adolescents and young adults aspire and (b) the amount of education needed for and the *prestige level* of the aspired occupations (i.e., the social status or importance that is associated with different kinds of occupations; Gottfredson, 1996). A majority of the existing research on career-related aspirations has explored the former dimension of aspirations, addressing issues such as the individual and social factors involved in people's choice of gender-stereotyped occupational and educational paths (e.g., chaps. 3, 7, and 8, this volume; Hill, Ramirez, & Dumka, 2003; Jacobs, Chhin, & Bleeker, 2006) and women's experiences in considering careers in mathematics, science, and technology (e.g., Ciccocioppo et al., 2002; Farmer, 1997b; Packard & Nguyen, 2003; Schoon, 2001; Webb, Lubinski, & Benbow, 2002). The level of education and the prestige of career-related aspirations have received far less attention, with previous research yielding mixed conclusions about gender differences in the development of occupational and educational aspirations over time. This study is unique in that it focuses on this latter dimension of career-related aspirations, namely, the prestige level of occupation aspired to as well as the amount of education aspired to.

OCCUPATIONAL PRESTIGE AND EDUCATIONAL ASPIRATION LEVELS

The existing literature on the amount–prestige dimension of career-related aspirations (i.e., hopes and plans for one's future education and occupation) is sparse. Research has demonstrated that the occupational prestige levels and education levels to which youth aspire are directly influenced by numerous characteristics, including academic ability and achievement (Farmer, 1985; Hill et al., 2004; Marjoribanks, 1986; Mau & Bikos, 2000), parental and family influences (Buchmann & Dalton, 2002; Hill et al., 2004; Marjoribanks, 1986; Mau & Bikos, 2000; Schoon & Parsons, 2002; Wilson & Wilson, 1992), peer attitudes and social support (Buchmann & Dalton, 2002; Farmer, 1985;

Mau, 1995), school characteristics and attitudes toward school (Farmer, 1985; Marjoribanks, 1986; Mau & Bikos, 2000; Watson, Quatman, & Edler, 2002; Wilson & Wilson, 1992), self-concept and self-efficacy (Mau & Bikos, 2000; Rojewski, 1997), and socioeconomic status (Farmer, 1985; Mau & Bikos, 2000; McWhirter, Larson, & Daniels, 1996; Schoon & Parsons, 2002; Wilson & Wilson, 1992). Some authors have also found ethnicity–race to be important in the development of aspirations (McWhirter et al., 1996; Mau, 1995; Mau & Bikos, 2000; Wilson & Wilson, 1992), but Fouad and Byars-Winston's (2005) recent meta-analysis concluded that this factor exerts relatively little influence, for occupational aspirations at least.

Other studies have examined change in youths' aspiration levels over time. VanLeuvan (2004) traced the education level associated with aspired math, science, and other careers of female adolescents in the United States and found that significantly more students lowered their educational aspirations than increased them from Grade 7 to Grade 12 (although nearly as many maintained the same aspired education level over that time). However, Francis (2002) found the opposite in her qualitative study of British youth, where a greater number of 14- to 16-year-old girls aspired to careers requiring postsecondary education than 7- to 11-year-olds. Similarly, an American study of gifted students from Grade 4 through Grade 12 demonstrated that educational aspirations were higher for students in higher grades (Gassin, Kelly, & Feldhusen, 1993). Focusing specifically on occupational aspirations (coded according to the income associated with occupations that participants reported aspiring to), Armstrong and Crombie (2000) reported that for Canadian youth who had congruence between their occupational aspirations and occupational expectations, aspirations decreased between Grade 8 and Grade 9, then remained stable between Grade 9 and Grade 10. With an American sample, Watson et al. (2002) also found a significant effect of grade levels on students' occupational aspirations, operationalized as students' self-reported ideal and realistic career plans, coded according to the Naoko–Treas Socioeconomic Index (Naoko & Treas, 1994, cited in Watson et al., 2002): prestige levels of students' aspired occupations remained stable between Grade 6 and Grade 8 but then declined between Grade 8 and Grade 12. In contrast, Mau and Bikos (2000) found that educational and occupational aspiration levels both increased from Grade 10 to 2 years after high school in a large, nationally representative sample of American youth (although only by a small amount). In the Mau and Bikos study, occupational aspirations were defined by coding participants' expected occupation at age 30 into one of three categories: unskilled–semi-skilled, technical–semi-professional, or professional.

It would appear that although many predictors of youths' future aspirations have been identified, far fewer studies have traced the development of these aspirations over time. The developmental studies that do exist present a confusing picture, with some studies finding that aspirations generally decreased over time and others finding that they increased over time. Part of the problem, especially with the occupation-related findings, is inconsistency of measurement. However, it is also evident that there is substantial variation in the patterns of change between individuals (with VanLeuvan [2004] demonstrating that nearly as many participants maintained the same level of aspirations as changed them over time) and between time periods (Armstrong & Crombie [2000] and Watson et al. [2002] both found that there were some periods of stability and some periods of change in youths' aspirations through the high school years). Moreover, many of these studies have methodological weaknesses such as the use of a cross-sectional rather than longitudinal design (Watson et al., 2002), the absence of sufficient rigor (Francis [2002] failed to specify an analytical model–strategy for coding her data or making comparisons), or attempting to capture change through only two time points (Mau & Bikos, 2000; VanLeuvan, 2004).

Ideally, new research in this area should sample youths' aspirations at multiple time points to adequately capture periods of stability and change. Furthermore, researchers should use analytical strategies that can accommodate the substantial amount of within-group variation that appears to be present for career-related aspirations. Our study incorporated such a design. Specifically, we used a multicohort, multi-occasion design and analyzed data using growth-curve modeling (hierarchical linear modeling) techniques to elucidate more clearly youths' educational and occupational aspiration levels.

THE ROLE OF MATHEMATICS ACHIEVEMENT AND GENDER

In this section, we explore possible linkages between youths' career-related aspirations and women's occupational outcomes and examine the trajectories of youths' educational and occupational aspirations as a function of gender. Given historical gender differences in mathematics performance and the argument that mathematics functions as a "critical filter" in career development (see chap. 2, this volume; Sells, 1978), we also examine career-related trajectories as a function of early high school mathematics achievement. A number of researchers over the past few decades have proposed that performance in high school mathematics courses functions as a critical filter for students' future career paths by restricting low math achievers from being able to pursue higher levels of education or attaining higher prestige occupations later in life (e.g., Astin, 1968; Carnegie Commission on Higher Education, 1973; Sells, 1978; Sherman, 1982). That is, low math achievement early in high school may steer adolescents away from math courses that are prerequisites to obtaining the education required to attain many higher prestige careers, not only in the physical science and technology fields but also in health, commerce, and many social sciences.

Unfortunately, there is little research on the relationship between prior mathematics achievement and the development of aspirations in terms of their prestige in either the educational or occupational domains. Moreover, this limited body of literature is equivocal, with some studies concluding that mathematics achievement is an important contributor to the development of subsequent aspirations and other studies finding it to be nonsignificant. Farmer (1985), using path analysis to examine the effects of math-specific grade point average (GPA) on occupational aspiration levels in high school, found it to be a nonsignificant contributor in her final model. In Hill et al.'s (2004) structural equation modeling study of parental involvement on various aspects of schooling, math grades correlated with aspirations in Grade 6 and educational aspirations in Grade 9. However, math-specific achievement was only one component of their "school achievement" latent variable and, therefore, not a principal focus in their analyses. Buchmann and Dalton (2002) used logistic regression to examine the effects of a number of variables on educational aspiration levels of students who were approximately 13 years old in Austria, France, Germany, Greece, Hong Kong, Hungary, Korea, Norway, Spain, Switzerland, Thailand, and the United States. They found that math achievement predicted higher educational aspirations (i.e., attending university or higher) in all 12 countries. Other research (e.g., Marjoribanks, 1986; Mau & Bikos, 2000; Rojewski, 1997; Watson et al., 2002) has examined the relationship between overall academic achievement and aspirations, but those studies are less relevant to the question of whether mathematics, in particular, is a critical filter for career-related aspirations and occupational outcomes.

It has been commonly assumed that individuals who pursue occupations outside of intensive career paths in the fields of science and technology prefer occupations with fewer educational requirements that are, consequently, less prestigious. That is, gender differences in occupational outcomes may be the result of women having aspired to lower levels of education and lower prestige occupations when they were younger. Although this possibility is intuitively appealing, Eccles (1994) has suggested an alternative explanation: It may be the case that young women do not value math- and science-related careers as highly as their male counterparts and choose to pursue careers that are equally prestigious but are not as mathematics intensive (e.g., law, social sciences). If so, then no gender differences would be evident in the amount of education and prestige associated with young people's aspired career paths, despite the presence of gender differences in the types of career that are aspired to by young men and women.

Unfortunately, the existing literature examining the effect of gender on the prestige dimension of adolescents' aspirations presents a confusing picture, with some research indicating the absence of gender differences (Armstrong & Crombie, 2000; Gassin et al., 1993; Mau & Bikos, 2000; Watson et al., 2002), some research indicating that girls have lower aspirations than boys

(Mendez & Crawford, 2002; Wilson & Wilson, 1992), and some research indicating that girls have higher aspirations than boys (Marjoribanks, 1986; Mau, 1995; Rojewski, 1997). In addition, Farmer (1997a) found that for women who initially aspired to science-related careers but then shifted to nonscience interests a decade later, subsequent aspirations remained as prestigious as their original, science-related aspirations and as prestigious as the aspirations of women who persisted in science-related career paths over that time.

In contrast, two studies have found support for the notion that young women aspire to less education and lower prestige careers than their male counterparts. Specifically, Wilson and Wilson (1992) found that male high school students had higher educational aspirations than females. Similarly, in a study of American gifted students in Grades 6 to 8, Mendez and Crawford (2002) found that boys aspired to careers that were higher in prestige and required more education than girls. However, both of these studies measured aspirations at only a single point in time.

The issue is complicated further by three studies with conclusions that do not fit commonly held societal assumptions. Mau (1995) found that young women had higher educational aspirations than young men in a sample of middle school students in the United States. In a study where the prestige of occupations aspired to by 11- to 16-year-old Australian youth was classified according to the Australian National University's occupational classification system, Marjoribanks (1986) found that girls had lower occupational aspirations than boys but similar levels of educational aspirations. Finally, Rojewski (1997) analyzed American youths' occupational aspirations using the National Education Longitudinal Study of 1988 (n.d.) database and concluded that significantly more boys than girls aspired to "moderate prestige" careers in Grades 8 and 10, whereas there were more girls than boys in the "high prestige" and "low prestige" occupational aspiration groups during that time.

Evidently, the relationship between gender and the prestige dimension of career-related aspirations is complex and may differ by age. Whether gender has a direct influence on the development of educational and occupational aspiration levels over time remains an open question. Moreover, none of the studies described above examined the development of career-related aspirations (i.e., how they change over time), which would elucidate any age effects. The current study, by incorporating a multicohort, multi-occasion longitudinal design, sought to overcome this limitation of previous research.

With longitudinal data spanning 5 years, we used individual growth curve modeling to examine the trajectories of the occupational prestige level and educational aspirations of young, university-bound Canadians as a function of gender and prior mathematics achievement. Growth curve modeling was chosen for its superior ability (over traditional regression and analysis of variance techniques) in examining change over time (Alsaker, 1992). Traditional methods are less suited to detecting nonlinear change and are restrictive in their assumptions (Bryk & Raudenbush, 1987). In contrast, growth curve modeling enables the identification of nonlinear growth trajectories as well as the identification of factors that influence initial status, rate of growth, and acceleration in growth. These models also relax the assumption of independent observations by allowing for correlated errors (Bryk & Raudenbush, 1987; Rogosa & Saner, 1995) and, further, allow both fixed effects (assumed to be identical across people) and random effects (assumed to vary across people) to be examined in the same models (Singer, 1998).

Our primary aim was to track the development of career-related aspirations toward high-prestige occupations through high school and into young adulthood. We also made a number of specific hypotheses regarding the effects of prior mathematics achievement and gender on these trajectories. In accordance with the critical filter model of mathematics' influence on occupational outcomes, we hypothesized that the trajectories of youths' educational and occupational aspiration levels would vary as a function of prior math achievement, with youths who experienced low math achievement early in their high school career aspiring to less prestigious occupations and having lower expectations for their educational attainment.

We chose early math achievement (as opposed to current math achievement) for several reasons. First, given the literature on the potentially negative effects of moving from a smaller sized to a larger sized school setting (Eccles et al., 1993), we wanted to see the long-term impact of the first math course after the transition to high school (in Canada, high schools are typically much larger than elementary schools). Also, use of Grade 9 math achievement provided comparable math achievement data for all participants. For the participants in this study, Grade 9 math was a required course (after Grade 10, math is no longer required), and all students take the same course (after Grade 10, students have a number of different math courses available to them, ranging from accounting to calculus). For theoretical and pragmatic reasons, we therefore examined the trajectories of aspirations as a function of early (i.e., Grade 9) math achievement. Given our interest in the specific effects of math achievement, it was also necessary to control for the possible confounding effects of overall achievement levels. By including early overall GPA as a control variable in our models, it was possible to highlight the independent effect of math-specific achievement.

Regarding gender differences, our hypotheses were less clear cut. On the one hand, given the well-documented (albeit lessening) gender differences found in math participation (e.g., American Association of University Women [AAUW], 1990, 1998), we expected that the trajectories would vary as a function of the interaction between low math achievement and gender, with low-achieving young women having aspirations that decreased particularly sharply over time. However, the possibility that young women turn away from science and technology careers because of low valuation of those fields rather than a desire for less education or less prestigious jobs suggests the opposite: namely, that the trajectories of the occupational prestige and educational attainment levels that youth aspire to would be similar between genders.

METHOD

Participants and Procedures

Participants ($N = 218$) were drawn from an ongoing longitudinal study involving two public high schools (Grades 9 to 13) in Ontario, Canada. The two schools were chosen on the basis of their demographic similarity. Both schools were located in the same suburban area, were in the same school board jurisdiction, and the students were from predominantly middle or upper middle class White families. In previous work with this data set, several analyses were conducted to ensure the comparability of the two schools and demonstrated that students from the two schools did not differ on several key psychological and demographic variables (including those used in this study; Shapka & Keating, 2003). Only students who were enrolled in the regular (university-streamed) math classes were included in this study. We did not include students who were enrolled in basic or general levels of math. This means that our findings are not generalizable to students of all mathematic abilities.

Participants were followed over a 5-year period. Self-report information was collected at three time points: first when students were in Grades 9 ($n = 92$), 10 ($n = 81$), or 11 ($n = 45$); then 2 years later when they were in Grades 11, 12, or 13 (Grade 13 was a required university preparation year in Ontario at the time that data were collected, which increased the attrition for this grade because students had the option of graduating in Grade 12); and finally 3 years later when they were 1 to 3 years beyond secondary school. Together, observations span Grade 9 through 3 years post–secondary school. Data came from all three waves of self-report data as well as yearly data from high school student records.

In the first two waves of the study, data were collected using a questionnaire that was group administered to students during their first class of the day in the 1st year of participation (Time 1) and then again 2 years later (Time 2) within each school. The questionnaire included questions and scales aimed at identifying motivational and personality factors deemed to impact adolescent achievement. Most students were able to complete the questionnaire within the allocated hour. To ensure consistency, the vice principal at each school introduced the study and read the instructions over the school's public address system. Prior to completing the questionnaire, students completed a consent form in which they provided their name and signature to confirm their agreement to participate. Less than 2% of the students chose not to participate in the study ($n = 30$).

Participants for the third wave were those individuals for whom we had longitudinal data across Time 1 and Time 2 (i.e., who were still attending the same high school for both time periods and had been in attendance on both data collection days) and who had indicated that they would be willing to participate in future waves of the study ($n = 322$). Of the 264 students who were successfully contacted at Time 3, 129 females and 89 males completed the questionnaire, resulting in a total of 218 individuals who contributed data on three occasions. The resultant data set, therefore, comprised 654 observations, spread over three occasions collectively spanning Grade 9 through 3 years post–secondary school.

Attrition biases have been examined elsewhere (Shapka, 2002) and were examined separately for each point of departure (participants declining to be involved in future phases of the study, our being unable to locate participants at Time 3, or participants not returning the Time 3 questionnaire). The only attrition biases that were found were between those who returned their Time 3 questionnaires and those who did not. More specifically, the group who returned their questionnaires attained higher grades in math and science in Grades 11 and 12 (and this was similar for both genders). This means that our sample was likely more elite, which has implications for generalizability (mentioned in the Discussion section).

Measures

Outcome Variables

Occupational Prestige. At each wave of the study, participants were asked to state what career or occupation they expected to have in the future. The prestige levels of these occupational aspirations were then coded using the occupational prestige ranking system of the O*NET 98 database (O*NET OnLine, n.d.), a comprehensive database of occupational information maintained by the U.S. Department of Labor. This database provided comprehensive information on approximately 1,000 occupations found in North America on the basis of data gathered by the Bureau of Labor Statistics division of the Department of Labor and the Standard Occupational Classification system (Hubbard et al., 2000). One dimension that the original 1998 version of O*NET provided is the average "prestige" of an occupation within the United States, ranked on a scale from 1(*lowest*) through 5(*highest*). This prestige score is derived from several different factors, including average estimated wage for the occupation across the United States and types and amount of experience and education required for the occupation. As such, it encompasses more information than educational aspirations alone and differentiates between more and less prestigious occupations within any given level of educational attainment. Using data from all three phases of the study, a 3-point

TABLE 1.1

Average Levels of Occupational Prestige for Time Across all Participants

Outcome	Phase of data collection		
	Time 1	Time 2	Time 3
Occupational prestige[a]			
M	4.2	4.1	3.6
SD	0.86	0.83	0.94
Educational aspiration[b]			
M	3.0	3.2	3.1
SD	0.53	0.74	0.78

Note. $N = 218$. Both occupational prestige and education aspiration variables were found to be negatively skewed but not significantly so (skewness statistics were well below the standard error for each variable at each time point).
[a]The range for this variable was 1–5, with higher numbers representing higher levels of occupational prestige.
[b]The range for this variable was 1–4, with 1 representing high school graduation and 4 representing a graduate or professional degree.

trajectory of the prestige of each participant's occupational aspirations was created. Table 1.1 documents the average levels of these aspirations over the three time periods.

Educational Aspiration. The second outcome variable in this study was each student's level of educational aspiration as it changed over the course of the study. At each wave of data collection, students were asked to identify the highest level of education that they hoped to obtain. The responses were coded on a 4-point scale consisting of 1 = *high school diploma*, 2 = *community college diploma/certificate*, 3 = *university degree*, and 4 = *graduate or professional degree*. Using data from all three waves of the study, a trajectory was created for each participant, tracking how his or her educational aspirations changed over the course of high school and post–secondary school. Table 1.1 documents the average levels of educational aspiration for the entire sample across time.

Covariates and Grouping Variables

The grouping variables of interest were gender and level of early high school math achievement. Math achievement level was constructed by coding participants as "high" if they attained 75 % or better in math courses taken in Grade 9, their 1st year of high school. This information was obtained from school records. Seventy-five percent was chosen as the cutoff point because it represented the difference between a B and C+ letter grade. In addition, there appeared to be a natural break in the data at this point. The frequencies for the grouping variables can be seen in the third column of Table 1.2.

Prior to examining differences in trajectories as a function of Grade 9 math achievement and gender, the effects of several potentially confounding

TABLE 1.2
Descriptive Statistics for Grouping Variables and Covariates

Variable	M	SD	n
Parental education	2.89	0.89	218
Grade 9 grade point average	77.07	8.93	218
Gender			
Female			129
Male			89
Math achievement			
Low			78
High			132
Grade			
9			92
10			81
11			44

variables were partialed out. Below is a description of each of these covariates. The descriptive statistics are presented for all covariates in Table 1.2.

1. *Parental education*, which was constructed from an average of the highest level of education that participants' parents and/or step-parents had attained (elementary school, high school, some college/university, bachelor's degree, or a graduate/professional degree). Mother's and father's education levels were significantly correlated at both time points ($r = .85$, $p < .001$). This variable was included as a proxy for socioeconomic status.

2. *Perceived math competence* as it varied over the course of the study. To ensure that group differences were attributable to early math achievement and not to participants' current perceptions of their ability in math, this variable was included as a control variable. This variable was a composite of six questionnaire items assessing self-perceptions of math ability at each phase of the study. The items were standardized at each wave (because of inconsistent Likert scales across items) such that the overall mean and standard deviation were 0 and 1, respectively. The items included in this variable were essentially the same at all three waves of data collection, except that words relevant at the high school level were replaced with college-appropriate words when necessary (for example, the word *teacher* was replaced with *professor*). For psychometric properties and details on scale construction, see Shapka and Keating (2003).

3. *Overall GPA in Grade 9* as reflected by participants' average grade across that school year. This variable was included to ensure that the independent effects of math achievement were examined over and above their general achievement levels.

Analytic Technique

Standard hierarchical linear modeling techniques were used to develop two series of models to examine (a) how aspired occupational prestige changed over the 5-year period of the study and (b) how educational aspirations changed over the same period of time. Readers who are unfamiliar with the general principles and background theory behind the use of hierarchical linear modeling to examine growth and change over time are referred to Boyle and Willms (2001), Collins (2006), and Singer and Willet (2003). See also chapter 5, this volume.

All modeling was performed using HLM 5 (Raudenbush, Bryk, Cheong, & Congdon, 2001), with estimates performed using full maximum likelihood estimation, so that the fit statistics for nested models could be compared by examining change in the deviance statistics. All nondichotomous variables were grand mean centered in the models to facilitate interpretability. For each model, the intercept for the time variables (time and time squared) was set at Time 1, so that statistics for "intercept" refer to initial status, and the quadratic growth term describes the degree of acceleration. The Level 1 (within-person) factors included time and time squared (to allow for nonlinearity in the trajectories), self-perceived math competence (entered as a time-varying covariate), and the outcome variables (occupational prestige and educational aspiration). The Level 2 (between-person) variables included both grouping variables (gender and Grade 9 math achievement level), with parental education and Grade 9 GPA entered as covariates.

Occupational Prestige Trajectories

A series of models was run to identify the shape of participants' occupational prestige trajectories. First, an unconditional model, containing no predictor variables, was fitted. This null model indicated significant variation in the average levels of occupational prestige, $t(205) = 85.85, p < .001$. As can be seen from the variance components (Table 1.3), the total unexplained variance was 79%, with 27% (34% of the total variance) unexplained at the between-person level and 52% (66% of the total variance) at the within-person level. The high level of unexplained variation, at both the between- and within-person levels, revealed much room for improving the model through the inclusion of additional predictor variables.

Next, the two time variables (time and time squared) were included in the equation to explore the shape of the occupational prestige trajectories as a function of time. To allow for the possibility that the occupational aspirations of different individuals have growth trajectories that accelerate at different rates, the intercept, linear, and the quadratic components were all allowed

TABLE 1.3
Variance Components Analysis for Null, Unconditional, and Conditional Growth Models for Occupational Prestige

Outcome	Between-person variance		Within-person variance	
	τ	Percent reduction[a]	σ^2	Percent reduction[a]
Occupational prestige				
Null model	.27	—	.52	—
Unconditional growth model	.33	0	.41	21
Growth model with covariates	.31	6	.41	0
Growth model with covariates and main effects[b]	.30	3	.40	2
Main effect and interaction growth model	.30	0	.40	0

[a]Refers to percent reduction from amount of variance explained in preceding model.
[b]Gender, Grade 9 math.

to vary randomly in the models. The time-squared variable was significant (see Table 1.4 for parameter estimates), which meant that a quadratic (curvilinear) model was a better fit for the data than assuming that occupational aspirations change in a linear way over time. The fact that the coefficient for the linear term (time) was positive and fairly large and the nonlinear coefficient was negative and small indicated that the growth curve forms an inverted U shape, skewed to the right. As can be seen from Table 1.3, the addition of the time variables explained an additional 21% of the variance in the occupational prestige.

After identifying the shape of the trajectories, a third model was built through the addition of the time-invariant (parental education, Grade 9 GPA) and time-varying (self-perceived math competence) control variables. None of these fixed effects was significant but as a group explained 6% of the

TABLE 1.4
Parameter Estimates for the Unconditional Growth Curve Model for Occupational Prestige and Educational Aspirations

Outcome	Coefficient	SE	t	df
Occupational prestige				
Intercept	4.00***	0.19	21.16	615
Time	0.27	0.21	1.13	205
Time squared	−0.12*	0.05	−2.33	205
Educational aspiration				
Intercept	2.67***	0.17	15.73	416
Time	0.45*	0.20	2.19	205
Time squared	−0.08+	0.05	−1.69	205

$+p < .10.$ $*p < .05.$ $***p < .001.$

between-person variance, and on the basis of the change in the deviance statistic (which is based on a chi-square distribution), the variables as a group significantly increased the explanatory power of the model, $\chi^2(9, N = 598) = 41$, $p < .001$. Given the significance of all the control variables as a group, they were retained in subsequent models. This allowed the subsequent models to provide a purer estimate of the effect of the variables of interest (gender and math achievement), accounting for the influence of the three control variables.

Occupational Prestige as a Function of Gender and Math Achievement. The next model included gender as a between-person fixed effect as well as the dichotomized high versus lower Grade 9 math achievement variable (with "high" being defined as scores of 75% or better on Grade 9 math courses). In this model, the gender variable was not significant: Neither the intercept nor the time variables differed as a function of gender, suggesting that the trajectories of individuals' occupational prestige are similar for both males and females. The math achievement variable was significant in terms of the intercept, as well as time, and time squared (see Table 1.5 for parameter estimates). As can be seen in Figure 1.1, the intercept, slope, and curvature of the trajectories all differed as a function of experiencing high versus low math achievement. This pattern indicates that low-achieving students had lower occupational aspirations to begin with and experienced an accelerated decline in their aspiration levels near the end of high school. In contrast, high achieving Grade 9 math students experienced a more gradual, linear decline in occupational aspirations through high school and postsecondary.

TABLE 1.5
Parameter Estimates for the Main Effects Growth Curve Model
for Occupational Prestige

Predictor	Coefficient	SE	t	df
Intercept				
Grade 9 math achievement	1.09**	0.45	2.40	201
Gender	0.06	0.39	0.16	201
Parental education	−0.08	0.33	−0.39	201
Grade 9 grade point average	−0.01	0.02	−0.55	201
Time				
Grade 9 math achievement	−1.04*	0.52	−2.00	598
Gender	0.07	0.43	0.17	598
Parental education	0.04	0.25	0.14	598
Grade 9 grade point average	0.01	0.03	0.47	598
Time Squared				
Grade 9 math achievement	0.25*	0.13	1.85	201
Gender	−0.03	0.11	−0.34	201
Parental education	0.01	0.06	0.15	201
Grade 9 grade point average	−0.01	0.01	−0.16	201

$^*p < .05.$ $^{**}p < .01.$

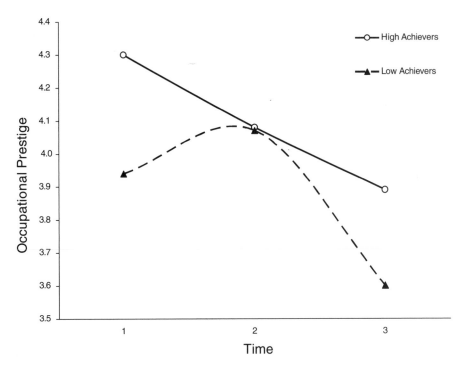

Figure 1.1. Level of occupational prestige through high school and postsecondary as a function of Grade 9 math achievement.

Finally, another model was fitted to investigate whether the impact of early high school math achievement on occupational prestige aspirations was different for males and females. Specifically, a variable representing the interaction of gender and math achievement was added to the existing variables in the model. This variable was not significant in terms of the intercept or the time variables and, on the basis of the deviance statistic, failed to improve the overall fit of the model $\chi^2(4, N = 598) = 4.98, p = .29$. Consequently, this final model was rejected, and it was concluded that the interaction between gender and math achievement does not significantly account for variation in occupational aspirations over time.

Educational Aspiration Trajectories

Models examining educational aspiration trajectories were developed in a similar fashion, starting with the null; then adding the variables representing change over time; then adding control variables; then adding the variables of interest (gender and math achievement); and finally, exploring the possibility of an interaction between gender and math achievement.

TABLE 1.6

Variance Components Analysis for Null, Unconditional, and Conditional
Growth Models for Educational Aspirations

Outcome	Between-person variance		Within-person variance	
	τ	Percent reduction[a]	σ^2	Percent reduction[a]
Educational aspiration				
Null model	.15	—	.27	—
Unconditional growth model	.04	73	.24	11
Growth model with covariates	.03	25	.23	4
Growth model with covariates and main effects[b]	.03	0	.21	9
Main effect and interaction growth model	.03	0	.21	0

[a]Refers to percent reduction from the amount of variance explained in the preceding model.
[b]Gender, Grade 9 math.

Initially, a null model with a constant term as the only predictor was run to partition the within- and between-person variability. This model suggested variation in average levels of educational aspirations over time for this group of individuals, $t(205) = 85.85$, $p < .001$. The variance components in Table 1.6 show that the total unexplained variance was 42%, with 15% (36% of the total variance) unexplained at the between-person level and 27% (64% of the total variance) at the within-person level. Although this represents less unexplained variance than in the occupational prestige series of models, it remained sufficient to warrant the inclusion of additional predictors.

The growth models were run next for this outcome. As can be seen in Table 1.4, the linear time variable was significant, but the quadratic time-squared variable was not quite significant ($p = .08$). However, it was decided to retain the quadratic term in subsequent models in order to explore the possibility that nonlinearity varied as a function of gender or of high versus low math achievement. The shape of the curve of educational aspirations was similar to the occupational prestige trajectory curve—a steep increase followed by a leveling off or slight decrease.

The next model that was fitted involved adding the three control variables to the existing model: the time-varying perceived math competence, as well as the time-invariant parental education and Grade 9 GPA. Similar to the occupational prestige trajectories, the fixed effects for each of these factors were not significant, but as a group they significantly improved the model, $\chi^2(9, N = 444) = 59.2$, $p < .001$, and accounted for an additional 1% of the total variance. In light of this significance, all three control variables were retained in the subsequent models.

Educational Aspirations as a Function of Gender and Math Achievement.
Next, gender and math achievement were added to the model to explore their
main effects on the trajectories of educational aspirations. As can be seen
from the parameter estimates in Table 1.7, both the intercept and the slope
differed significantly as a function of gender. These differences are presented
in Figure 1.2: Young women's educational aspirations were relatively linear
and slightly increased over high school and postsecondary, whereas young
men's aspirations appeared to climb steeply during high school but leveled
off afterward.

Math achievement was also significant in terms of the intercept and the
slope. The parameter estimates are presented in Table 1.7, and from Figure 1.3,
it is clear that for high math achievers, educational aspirations became high
early in high school and maintained this level, whereas for lower math achievers, educational aspirations remained consistently low across the same time
period.

As with occupational aspirations, the possible interaction of gender and
math achievement was explored in a final model, by adding a variable representing this interaction. This variable was not significant, nor did it improve
the predictive ability of model, with the deviance statistic being $\chi^2(4, N =
444) = 5.75, p = .22$. Consequently, it was concluded that the interaction
between gender and math achievement does not meaningfully influence the
trajectory of educational aspirations, and the interaction term was removed
from the model.

TABLE 1.7
Parameter Estimates for the Main Effects Growth Curve Model
for Educational Aspirations

Predictor	Coefficient	SE	t	df
Intercept				
Grade 9 math achievement	−0.91*	0.39	−2.34	199
Gender	0.81*	0.32	2.51	199
Parental education	0.28	0.20	1.47	199
Grade 9 grade point average	−0.01	0.02	0.07	199
Time				
Grade 9 math achievement	1.06*	0.44	2.34	444
Gender	−0.74*	0.37	−1.98	444
Parental education	−0.14	0.22	−0.65	444
Grade 9 grade point average	0.01	0.02	0.35	444
Time squared				
Grade 9 math achievement	−0.24*	0.11	−2.08	199
Gender	0.15	0.10	1.61	199
Parental education	0.02	0.06	0.42	199
Grade 9 grade point average	−0.01	0.01	−0.10	199

*$p < .05$.

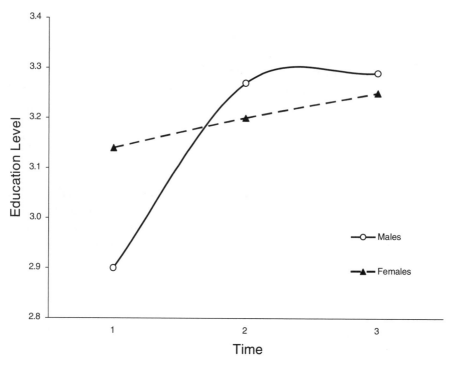

Figure 1.2. Level of educational aspirations through high school and postsecondary as a function of gender.

DISCUSSION

Math as a Critical Filter

As we hypothesized, early math achievement had a significant impact on the shape and slope of both the occupational and educational aspiration trajectories. For occupational aspirations (which, on average, declined for students over the course of the study), students who experienced a low grade in early high school math started out with lower expectations for their careers, and their aspirations declined at a more rapid pace from mid high school onward. Regarding educational aspirations, on average, expected level of education increased over the course of high school and postsecondary. However, the educational aspirations of individuals who experienced high math achievement in early high school increased dramatically through high school and leveled off afterward. In contrast, for students with low initial high school math achievement, educational aspirations decreased slightly over the course of high school but recovered to their initial levels by the end of high school, although they were well below those of the high achievers at that point (despite low achievers' edu-

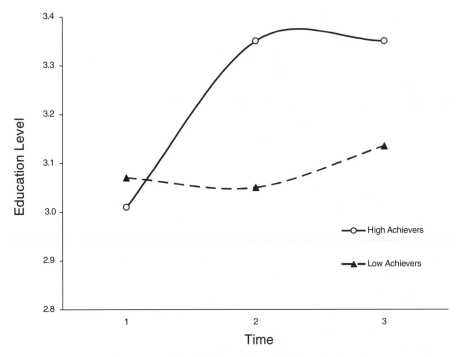

Figure 1.3. Level of educational aspirations through high school and postsecondary as a function of Grade 9 math achievement.

cational aspirations being slightly higher than high achievers' aspirations at the beginning of the study).

These findings provide support for our hypothesis that early math achievement has a substantial impact on youths' aspirations and their subsequent educational and occupational attainment. It appears that math acts as a "filter" by limiting students' future options—because many postsecondary programs require certain levels of high school mathematics performance. It is intriguing that the fact that educational aspiration levels were actually slightly higher for low math achievers than high math achievers during early high school suggests that the filtering effect of math on educational aspirations is not yet present at the beginning of high school but emerges over the course of the high school years. Overall, this study indicates that there is a filtering effect of mathematics on youths' aspirations for the future. The effect is similar for occupational aspirations, although the timing differs, with a more rapid decline seen between late high school and the years immediately following. Moreover, because both overall academic achievement and the perceptions students had about their math abilities were partialed out in all analyses, the specific effect of early math achievement was over and above the influence of these other factors. That is, our findings are not simply an artifact of being an inferior student (and having low grades in general) or of having low perceptions of math competence. With this in mind, our findings highlight the implications of math-specific achievement for subsequent career and educational aspirations. Furthermore, our results illustrate how long lasting and important earlier math experiences are and highlight the need to use longitudinal designs for understanding developmental phenomena.

Effects of Gender

The results concerning the main effect of gender were mixed, with significant gender differences being present for the trajectories of educational aspirations but not for occupational aspirations. Young women's educational aspirations increased slightly, and in a linear manner, through high school and postsecondary. In contrast, young men's aspirations were far more variable, being relatively low in early high school, then climbing sharply to be higher than young women's aspirations toward the end of high school, and remaining stable into the postsecondary years. It is interesting that although they followed very different trajectories, the educational aspirations of both genders appeared to converge after the completion of high school. These results suggest that the principal gender difference that exists in educational aspirations is not that young women are expecting to attain less education but that young men are more variable in the amount of education that they plan to pursue than young women. However, despite the fact that the main gender effect over time appears to be in the variability rather than absolute amount of educational aspirations, it must still be recognized that boys' aspirations were, on average, somewhat higher than girls' at the end of high school. Because this is the period of time when decisions about pursuing postsecondary education are finalized and pursued, the fact that girls' aspirations were lower at this specific time period remains troubling.

Our findings must be interpreted in light of the sample that was used in this study: We focused specifically on advanced-streamed, university-bound students. It may be the case that gender effects on the development of career-related aspirations are more prevalent in the general student population and, in particular, among those who do not intend to pursue postsecondary education. Our study is relevant to understanding the aspirations of youth who are academically facile and therefore have high potential to pursue advanced education and attain highly prestigious careers. However, future research needs to examine students across all achievement levels to determine whether gender emerges as a significant factor in the aspirations of less academically oriented students.

On the surface, the absence of a significant effect for gender on the occupational aspiration trajectories appears to be counterintuitive. However, it must be recognized that a majority of the literature on gender and aspirations has examined the type of career that youth aspire to rather than the prestige level of youths' aspired occupations. The present findings suggest that whatever gender differences exist do not occur at the level of prestige differences. That is, the developmental course of young women's occupational aspirations is similar to young men's. Indeed, these findings may be consistent with Eccles's (1994) proposal that young men and young women choose different career paths because of different interests and subjective values by indicating that differences in the prestige level of aspired occupations may be ruled out as an explanation for gender differences in career choice. However, the interplay of values, gender, and aspirations needs to be examined more fully before such conclusions can be established.

Absence of an Interaction Between Early Math Achievement and Gender

There were no significant Gender × Math interaction effects for either the occupational prestige outcome or the educational aspiration outcome, which suggests that the filtering effects of prior math achievement are equally important for both young men's and young women's futures. This pattern of results also implies that existing gender differences in students' math involvement (AAUW, 1990, 1998) and people's eventual career attainment (Farmer, Wardrop, Anderson, & Risinger, 1995) are due to factors other than math filtering effects being stronger for women. Researchers and policymakers should instead be exploring other reasons to explain the difference between men's and women's career outcomes. For example, there is some evidence that compared with young men, young women anticipate facing different kinds of barriers to achieving their career aspirations (Perrone, Sedlacek, & Alexander, 2001) and perceive the existence of a greater amount of barriers (e.g., McWhirter, 1997). The consequences of barriers such as the "glass ceiling" that continues to exist for women in a number of career fields or the need to balance work with child-rearing responsibilities (e.g., chap. 7, this volume) require closer examination and, if necessary, remediation. Gender differences have also been consistently found in self-perceptions of math competence and efficacy, and these have been found to predict vocational behavior (e.g., Bandura, Barbaranelli, Caprara, & Pastorelli, 2001; chaps. 3, 4, and 6, this volume; Hackett & Betz, 1981; Lapan, Boggs, & Morrill, 1989; Lent, Brown, & Hackett, 1994). It may be such aspects that interact with gender to influence career-related aspirations, rather than math achievement per se.

Implications for Policy

Before discussing the policy implications of these results, a word of caution must be raised. This study used a rather narrow sample (relatively high-achieving, university-bound youth) drawn from a single region of a single province in Canada. Therefore, any extrapolation to policy must be treated as tentative and understood as requiring confirmation through replication of the study, with samples drawn from other regions of Canada and containing a broader range of students.

Having said that, this study is consistent with previous literature (e.g., Armstrong & Crombie, 2000; Marjoribanks, 1986; Watson et al., 2002) indicating that the prestige associated with an occupation is both a distinct dimension of youths' aspirations and useful to attend to in understanding those aspirations. It may be beneficial to attend to this dimension of occupations in many different spheres of policy and program development, including developing curricula for career and vocational preparation courses, measuring the outcomes of agencies contracted to perform career and employment counseling, and informing governments' practices when tracking provincial and federal employment and labor trends. Unfortunately, there is no Canada-specific index for categorizing occupations in terms of their prestige. It may be important for the federal government to commit funding to develop such an index, using existing models from other countries (e.g., United States' O*NET system, Australia's ANU scale). Moreover, Statistics Canada and the Ministry of Human Resources and Social Development already track many of the factors that would contribute to such an index, making the task more one of combining existing data in a systematic way rather than having to collect large amounts of new information.

At the provincial and school board level, a major implication for policy development stems from the finding that regardless of gender, low math achievers experience more negative trajectories in terms of their future aspirations. This implies that over and above general GPA, achievement in early high school math courses functions as a useful predictor of individuals who are at higher risk of being filtered out of higher educational and occupational pathways. The accurate identification of such individuals is important in order to tailor programming to address the difference in trajectories, whether that takes the shape of (a) intervening to improve math performance to prevent them being filtered out from certain career paths, or (b) directing them toward career paths that although less prestigious and requiring less education can be equally lucrative and fulfilling, such as the skilled trades.

Finally, the few gender differences that were found in this study have implications for educational and career planning programs. Although the results may primarily be a function of differences in rates of maturation, they may also indicate a need to attend to gender in promoting the pursuit of higher education over the course of high school. Early in high school, there appears to be a need to find more creative and effective ways to engage boys in the process of thinking about and planning for their future education. By the end of high school and through into the beginning of postsecondary, the greatest need appears to be to address the slight gender gap favoring men. School administrators should avoid a "one size fits all" approach to program planning and counseling students about their future education.

Limitations and Future Directions

One limitation of this study is that we had only three waves of data collection with 2 and 3 years between them, respectively. These gaps in data collection make it difficult to examine how aspiration levels change between each grade of high school. Although we had multiple cohorts, unfortunately our sample was too small to use an accelerated growth model, which would have allowed us to look at grade by grade changes. Future replication of this work needs to examine yearly changes to allow for a more fine-grained analysis of career aspiration trajectories. That said, it is important to point out that our findings highlight the benefits of using growth curve modeling in studying youths' aspirations. Had these data only been reported for the effects at one or two points in time, the circumstances surrounding the group differences would remain ambiguous. The nonlinearity of students' occupational aspiration trajectories would not have been identified, and it would have been unclear as to how and when the trajectories of groups varied. By modeling these trajectories over time, we can clearly see the pathways that resulted in differential outcomes across educational transitions.

As noted, these results may generalize only to other university-bound students. In fact, for students whose career aspirations involve transitioning from high school straight into the work force, early math achievement might have little or no impact. Alternatively, given the strength of the effect of early low math achievement on the future aspirations of high-functioning high school students, it is possible that for lower achieving students, the filter effects of mathematics began even earlier and have already affected career aspirations by the time those students enter high school. This type of causal analysis requires longitudinal designs that begin in elementary school and track students across all streams of high school rather than only the university preparation stream. Such a study would also be better positioned to examine the influence of math participation on career aspiration trajectories. In contrast to our set of participants, many of whom took the higher level mathematics courses required by many university programs regardless of gender, a broader sample would be more likely to reflect the gender disparity in mathematics participation that has previously been documented (e.g., Acker & Oatley, 1993; Catsambis, 1994).

Another task for future work in this area is to examine math achievement in a more complex manner. For this study, we examined the aspiration trajectories as a function of high versus low math achievement. Future studies, with larger samples, should examine achievement as a continuous variable. In fact, this need is highlighted by the results of Watson et al.'s (2002) recent study, which suggested that the relationship between achievement and aspiration levels may not be linear, with "moderately high" academic achievers having higher aspirations than either "superior" or "below average" achievers.

The findings of the other studies in this volume should also be incorporated into future research on gender, math, and the prestige dimension of occupational aspirations. As described earlier, it may be useful to incorporate the self-efficacy and perceived competence variables that the authors of chapters 4 and 6 in this volume explore in future models of the trajectories of career-related prestige aspirations. Similarly, the links between job flexibility and gendered occupational prestige levels should be explored in greater detail because the authors of chapter 7 (this volume) found that the desire for job flexibility to accommodate family responsibilities was an important predictor of women's career choices. It is important to explore the possibility that desired job flexibility moderates the relationship between gender and the prestige dimension of occupational aspirations—specifically, gender may have a significant effect on aspirations for people who consider job flexibility important, but not for individuals who are unconcerned about flexibility. Finally, the study described in chapter 3 (this volume) suggests two avenues for future research. In light of the author's finding that students' values had a significant effect on the trajectories of the "math-relatedness" dimension of students' aspirations, it may be important to include values measures in future models of the prestige dimension of aspirations. Additionally, it may be fruitful to determine if there are relationships between these two dimensions (math relatedness and prestige) of career-related aspiration or if these are truly independent of each other.

It will be beneficial to replicate this study with students from other nationalities, because the links between gender, schooling and career development are influenced by a number of cultural and social-environmental factors (Buchmann & Dalton, 2002; Leong & Hartung, 2000). Examining the trajectories of the prestige dimension of career aspirations among youth from different cultural settings will establish whether the patterns that were found in this study are specific to Anglophone Canadians or are more general in nature.

Despite these limitations and the many questions that remain to be answered, our study has increased knowledge about adolescent and youth career-related aspirations and how these change over the course of high school and postsecondary. Specifically, math achievement in the 1st year of high school has important implications for subsequent change in occupation and educational aspirations for both girls and boys. Results imply that high school math does act as a critical filter to adolescents' and young adults' plans for high status careers. This highlights the need to target adolescents' disengagement from math during high school and, in particular, to research and promote the retention of girls in math, who remain at risk for nonparticipation (e.g., AAUW, 1990, 1998).

REFERENCES

Acker, S., & Oatley, K. (1993). Gender issues for science and technology. *Canadian Journal of Education, 18*, 255–272.

Alsaker, F. D., (1992). Modeling quantitative developmental change. In J. B. Asendorpf & J. Valsiner (Eds.), *Stability and change in development: A study of methodological reasoning* (pp. 88–115). Thousand Oaks, CA: Sage.

American Association of University Women. (1990). *Shortchanging girls, shortchanging America: Full data report.* Washington, DC: Author.

American Association of University Women. (1998). *Separated by sex: A critical look at single-sex education for girls.* Washington, DC: American Association of University Women Educational Foundation.

Armstrong, P. I., & Crombie, G. (2000). Compromises in adolescents' occupational aspirations and expectations from Grades 8 to 10. *Journal of Vocational Behavior, 56*, 82–98.

Astin, H. S. (1968). Career development of girls during the high school years. *Journal of Counseling Psychology, 15*, 536–540.

Bandura, A., Barbaranelli, C., Caprara, G. V., & Pastorelli, C. (2001). Self-beliefs as shapers of children's aspirations and career trajectories. *Child Development, 71*, 187–206.

Boyle, M. H., & Willms, J. D. (2001). Multilevel modeling of hierarchical data in developmental studies. *Journal of Child Psychology and Psychiatry, 42*, 141–162.

Bryk, A. S., & Raudenbush, S. W. (1987). Application of hierarchical linear models to assessing change. *Psychological Bulletin, 101*, 147–158.

Buchmann, C., & Dalton, B. (2002). Interpersonal influences and educational aspirations in 12 countries: The importance of institutional context. *Sociology of Education, 75*, 99–122.

Carnegie Commission on Higher Education. (1973). *Opportunities for women in higher education.* New York: McGraw-Hill.

Catsambis, S. (1994). The path to math: Gender and racial–ethnic differences in mathematics participation from middle school to high school. *Sociology of Education, 67*, 199–215.

Ciccocioppo, A., Stewin, L. L., Madill, H. M., Montgomerie, T. C., Tovell, D. R., Armour, M., et al. (2002). Transitional patterns of adolescent females in non-traditional career paths. *Canadian Journal of Counselling, 36*, 25–37.

Collins, L. M. (2006). Analysis of longitudinal data: The integration of theoretical model, temporal design, and statistical model. *Annual Review of Psychology, 57*, 505–528.

Eccles, J. S. (1994). Understanding women's educational and occupational choices: Applying Eccles et al. model of achievement-related choices. *Psychology of Women Quarterly, 18*, 585–609.

Eccles, J. S., Midgley, C., Wigfield, A., Miller Buchanan, C., Reuman, D., Flanagan, C., & Mac Iver, D. (1993). Development during adolescence: The impact of stage–environment fit on young adolescents' experiences in schools and in families. *American Psychologist, 48,* 90–101.

Farmer, H. S. (1985). Model of career and achievement motivation for women and men. *Journal of Counseling Psychology, 32,* 363–390.

Farmer, H. S. (1997a). Why women don't persist in their high school science career aspirations. In H. S. Farmer (Ed.), *Diversity and women's career development: From adolescence to adulthood* (pp. 62–80). Thousand Oaks, CA: Sage.

Farmer, H. S. (1997b). Women who persisted in their high school aspirations for careers in science or technology. In H. S. Farmer (Ed.), *Diversity and women's career development: From adolescence to adulthood* (pp. 37–61). Thousand Oaks, CA: Sage.

Farmer, H. S., Wardrop, J. L., Anderson, M. Z., & Risinger, R. (1995). Women's career choices: Focus on science, math and technology careers. *Journal of Counseling Psychology, 42,* 155–170.

Farmer, H. S., Wardrop, J. L., & Rotella, S. C. (1999). Antecedent factors differentiating women and men in science/nonscience careers. *Psychology of Women Quarterly, 23,* 763–780.

Fouad, N. A., & Byars-Winston, A. M. (2005). Cultural context of career choice: Meta-analysis of race/ethnicity differences. *Career Development Quarterly, 53,* 223–233.

Francis, B. (2002). Is the future really female? The impact and implications of gender for 14–16 year olds' career choices. *Journal of Education and Work, 15,* 75–88.

Gassin, E. A., Kelly, K. R., & Feldhusen, J. F. (1993). Sex differences in the career development of gifted youth. *School Counselor, 41,* 90–96.

Gottfredson, L. S. (1996). Gottfredson's theory of circumscription and compromise. In D. Brown & L. Brooks (Eds.), *Career choice and development* (3rd ed., pp. 179–232). San Francisco: Jossey-Bass.

Hackett, G., & Betz, N. E. (1981). The relationship of career-related self-efficacy expectations to perceived career options in college women and men. *Journal of Counseling Psychology, 28,* 399–410.

Hill, N. E., Castellino, D. R., Langford, J. E., Nowlin, P., Dodge, K. A., Bates, J. E., et al., (2004). Parent academic involvement as related to school behaviour, achievement, and aspirations: Demographic variations across adolescence. *Child Development, 75,* 1491–1509.

Hill, N. E., Ramirez, C. A., & Dumka, L. E. (2003). Early adolescents' career aspirations: A qualitative study of perceived barriers and family support among low-income, ethnically diverse adolescents. *Journal of Family Issues, 24,* 934–959.

Hubbard, M., McCloy, R., Campbell, J., Nottingham, J., Lewis, P., Rivkin, D., et al. (2000). *Revision of O*NET data collection instruments (revised version).* Retrieved February 1, 2007, from http://www.onetcenter.org/dl_files/Data_appnd.pdf

Jacobs, J. E., Chhin, C., & Bleeker, M. (2006). Enduring links: Parents' expectations and their young adult children's gender-typed occupational choices. *Educational Research and Evaluation, 12,* 395–407.

Lapan, R. T., Boggs, K. R., & Morrill, W. H. (1989). Self-efficacy as a mediator of investigative and realistic general occupational themes on the Strong–Campbell Interest Inventory. *Journal of Counseling Psychology, 36,* 176–182.

Lent, R. W., Brown, S. D., & Hackett, G. (1994). Towards a unifying social cognitive theory of career and academic interest, choice, and performance. *Journal of Vocational Behavior, 45,* 79–122.

Leong, F. T. L., & Hartung, P. J. (2000). Adapting to the changing multicultural context of career. In A. Collins & R. A. Young (Eds.), *The future of career* (pp. 212–227). Cambridge, England: Cambridge University Press.

Marjoribanks, K. (1986). A longitudinal study of adolescents' aspirations as assessed by Seginer's model. *Merrill-Palmer Quarterly, 32,* 211–230.

Marjoribanks, K. (2003). Family background, individual and environmental influences, aspirations and young adults' educational attainment: A follow-up study. *Educational Studies, 29,* 233–243.

Mau, W. C. (1995). Educational planning and academic achievement of middle school students: A racial and cultural comparison. *Journal of Counseling and Development, 73,* 518–526.

Mau, W. C., & Bikos, L. H. (2000). Educational and vocational aspirations of minority and female students: A longitudinal study. *Journal of Counseling and Development, 78,* 186–194.

McWhirter, E. H. (1997). Perceived barriers to education and career: Ethnic and gender differences. *Journal of Vocational Behavior, 50,* 124–140.

McWhirter, E. H., Larson, L. M., & Daniels, J. A. (1996). Predictors of educational aspirations among adolescent gifted students of color. *Journal of Career Development, 23,* 97–109.

Mendez, L. M. R., & Crawford, K. M. (2002). Gender-role stereotyping and career aspirations: A comparison of gifted early adolescent boys and girls. *Journal of Secondary Gifted Education, 13*(3), 96–107.

National Education Longitudinal Study of 1988. (n.d.). Retrieved August 1, 2007, from http://nces.ed.gov/surveys/nels88/index.asp

O*NET OnLine. (n.d.). Retrieved August 1, 2007, from http://online.onetcenter.org/cgi-bin/gen_search_page?5

Packard, B. W., & Nguyen, D. (2003). Science career-related possible selves of adolescent girls: A longitudinal study. *Journal of Career Development, 29,* 251–263.

Perrone, K. M., Sedlacek, W. E., & Alexander, C. M. (2001). Gender and ethnic differences in career goal attainment. *Career Development Quarterly, 50,* 168–178.

Raudenbush, S. W., Bryk, A. S., Cheong, Y. F., & Congdon, R. T. (2001). HLM 5: Hierarchical linear and nonlinear modelling (2nd ed.) [Computer software]. Chicago: SSI Scientific Software.

Rogosa, D., & Saner, H. (1995). Longitudinal data analysis examples with random coefficient models. *Journal of Educational and Behavioral Statistics, 20,* 149–170.

Rojewski, J. W. (1997). Characteristics of students who express stable or undecided occupational expectations during early adolescence. *Journal of Career Assessment, 5*, 1–20.

Schoon, I. (2001). Teenage job aspirations and career attainment in adulthood: A 17-year follow-up of teenagers who aspired to become scientists, health professionals, or engineers. *International Journal of Behavioral Development, 23*, 124–132.

Schoon, I., & Parsons, S. (2002). Teenage aspirations for future careers and occupational outcomes. *Journal of Vocational Behavior, 60*, 262–288.

Sells, L. W. (1978). Mathematics: A critical filter. *The Science Teacher, 45*, 28–29.

Shapka, J. D. (2002). *Math engagement, perceptions, and performance across high school and post-secondary education.* Unpublished doctoral thesis, University of Toronto, Toronto, Ontario, Canada.

Shapka, J. D., & Keating, D. P. (2003). Effects of a girls-only curriculum during adolescence: Performance, persistence, and engagement in mathematics and science. *American Education Research Journal, 40*, 929–960.

Sherman, J. A. (1982). Mathematics as a critical filter: A look at some residues. *Psychology of Women Quarterly, 6*, 428–444.

Singer, J. D. (1998). Using SAS PROC MIXED to fit multilevel models, hierarchical models, and individual growth models. *Journal of Educational and Behavioral Statistics, 24*, 323–355.

Singer, J. D., & Willett, J. B. (2003). *Applied longitudinal data analysis: Modeling change and event occurrence.* Oxford, England: Oxford University Press.

VanLeuvan, P. (2004). Young women's science/mathematics career goals from seventh grade to high school graduation. *Journal of Education Research, 97*, 248–268.

Watson, C. M., Quatman, T., & Edler, E. (2002). Career aspirations of adolescent girls: Effects of achievement level, grade, and single-sex school environment. *Sex Roles, 46*, 323–335.

Webb, R. M., Lubinski, D., & Benbow, C. P. (2002). Mathematically facile adolescents with math-science aspirations: New perspectives on their educational and vocational development. *Journal of Educational Psychology, 94*, 785–794.

Wilson, P. A., & Wilson, J. R. (1992). Environmental influences on adolescent educational aspirations: A logistic transform model. *Youth and Society, 24*, 52–70.

2

MATHEMATICS AS THE CRITICAL FILTER: CURRICULAR EFFECTS ON GENDERED CAREER CHOICES

XIN MA AND WILLIS JOHNSON

Murnane and Levy (1996) pointed out that "the most important problem U.S. schools face is preparing children for tomorrow's jobs" (p. 18). A successful school-to-work transition is highly contingent on academic training that students receive in school, in particular in the core areas of mathematics and science (see Hunt, 1997; Murnane & Levy, 1996). Students with limited academic preparation in high school are likely to face an extremely difficult path toward workplaces (Bishop, 1996; Wilson, 1996).

Mathematics preparation is important to the pursuit of high-status careers. As early as 1973, Sells referred to mathematics as the "critical filter" that effectively screens students for prestigious careers (Sells, 1973). She reported that 92% of the 1st-year female students entering the University of California at Berkeley had such an inadequate number of advanced mathematics courses that they would eventually lose more than 70% of career options available to them, most of which were prestigious ones. The situation was not much better near the turn of the century. The High School Transcript Study indicated that 10% of high school graduates had precalculus or calculus and 7% had advanced placement calculus (Finn, Gerber, & Wang, 2002). Stinson (2004) argued that mathematics has been an effective tool for social stratification.

Why is mathematics relevant to high-status careers? Newer forms of employment, many of which are in the high-technology sector, require a greater understanding of computerized data analyses, sophisticated mathematical models, and elaborate accounting systems (National Council of Teachers of Mathematics, 1991). More explicit than ever before is the statement made by the U.S. Department of Education (1997, 1999) that "mathematics equals opportunity": Advanced mathematics courses can put students "at a clear advantage" for educational and occupational opportunities (U.S. Department of Education, 1999, p. 1). Different types of mathematics pursued lead to careers of different prestige. Overall, "mathematics has become a critical filter for employment and full participation in our society" (National Council of Teachers of Mathematics, 1989, p. 4).

Some factors have been identified in the research literature as having critical influences on students' educational and occupational choices. Working on the basis of Bandura's (1977) self-efficacy theory, Betz and Hackett (1983) developed a theory of career self-efficacy that constitutes an important factor in career choices (for an overview of the social cognitive career theory, see also Lent, Brown, & Hackett, 1994). In this model, students' sense of career self-efficacy is partly informed by prior educational attainment. Focusing on mathematics-intensive career choices, these researchers have argued that *mathematics self-efficacy*, defined as beliefs about one's ability to perform mathematical tasks, is related to choice of careers in mathematics and science fields. Prior mathematics attainment is the major source of mathematics self-efficacy in the Betz and Hackett model. Using Walberg's (1981, 1986) model of educational productivity, Ma and Wang (2001) found that students' educational attainment was the best predictor of career aspirations among major productivity factors that Walberg derived from synthesizing a huge number of research studies.

Expectancies and values are also factors that have been shown to influence career choices. The expectancy-value model of academic choice (Eccles et al., 1983) addresses four groups of traits of an individual: (a) perception of the attitudes and expectancies of his or her socializers and his or her interpretations of past experiences; (b) task beliefs, broad goals, and general self-schemata; (c) subjective task values and expectancies for success; and (d) achievement-oriented behaviors such as persistence, choice, and performance. The relationship sequence of these groups is specified as (a) predicting (b), (b) predicting (c), and (c) predicting (d) (Eccles et al., 1983). Wilson-Relyea (1997) reported that with control for mathematics achievement, there was a significant direct effect of expectation to do well in mathematics on career choices for males but not females. Therefore, male choice of careers was related to the extent to which males expected success in the learning of mathematics. Values also have been demonstrated to have an effect on mathematics-related career choices for males and females (e.g., Watt, 2006).

There are individual differences in career aspirations and career choices (Signer & Saldana, 2001). Jensen (1997) found a relationship between socioeconomic status (SES) and choice of careers among both males and females. Individuals from advantaged socioeconomic backgrounds tended to choose advanced mathematics courses and, subsequently, careers that required intensive mathematics. Examining educational and occupational aspirations of high school seniors in northern California, Madsen et al. (2002) found that Latino/a youth had the lowest aspirations among all ethnic groups. The policy concern is that socially or racially advantaged students are filtered through to prestigious career options, whereas socially or racially disadvantaged students are filtered away from career options that come to correspond with high SES.

We expect that the mathematics coursework participation of high school students is also an indicator of educational and occupational aspirations. Shernoff and Hoogstra (2001) demonstrated a relationship between engagement in high school mathematics and science classes and choice of college mathematics and science majors. Nagy, Trautwein, Baumert, Köller, and Garrett (2006) also found that students' choices of specialized courses were related to their aspired field of college education (i.e., high school course choice mirrors choice of college major). Using data from the 1988 National Education Longitudinal Study, Hoogstra (2002) found that the number of advanced mathematics courses taken in high school was predictive of majoring in mathematics and science at the college level, and Kilpatrick (1988) emphasized the importance of taking calculus—the most advanced U.S. high school mathematics course—to planned higher education and future occupation, showing that taking calculus had a strong influence on individuals' choice of undergraduate majors leading to highly prestigious careers.

Among the influential factors on career choices that we have discussed, gender differences are most evident in mathematics coursework participation. Females take fewer advanced mathematics courses than males (e.g., Ma, 1997; Updegraff, Eccles, Barber, & O'Brien, 1996; Watt, 2005). There has been a historical pattern that females self-select themselves out of mathematics coursework (see Marion & Coladarci, 1993). Differences in mathematics coursework between males and females often become evident during the high school years (e.g., Kaufman, 1990; Ma, 1997). For example, Lee and Ware (1986) found that females took fewer mathematics courses, were less persistent in transition from course to course, and were more likely to leave college preparatory mathematics sequences.[1] In general, males spent more semesters in mathematics

---

[1]Research evidence has begun to emerge in the United States showing that males and females now take the same number of mathematics courses during high school (e.g., Chipman, 2004; De Lisi & McGillicuddy-De Lisi, 2002). Apart from the number of mathematics courses, the content of mathematics courses also needs to be taken into account when comparing males and females in mathematics coursework. Overall, more research evidence needs to be accumulated to challenge the traditional pattern of mathematics coursework in favor of males.

coursework than females, and more males than females engaged in advanced or accelerated mathematics courses (Doolittle, 1985). These differences occur even when males and females share equal achievement scores and class grades (Friedman, 1989).

Our search of the research literature for studies on the effects of mathematics coursework on career and major choices revealed a lack of empirical evidence, highlighting the significance of the present analysis. First of all, although we can infer indirectly from a number of existing studies that mathematics coursework can be critical for career and major choices (see chap. 1, this volume), the present analysis is pioneering in providing a direct assessment of mathematics curricular effects on students' choice of careers and majors. Secondly, we focus on differential behaviors of males and females in career and major choices in relation to mathematics coursework. Although many researchers expect such gender differences, the present analysis is among the first investigations that provide direct empirical evidence on this issue, and it holds good potential to fill some critical gaps in the research literature.

Among competing influences, we examine mathematics coursework as our major explanatory variable. Although mathematics coursework has not been emphasized as strongly as mathematics achievement in having significant influences on career and major choices (see chap. 1, this volume), it may be a critical precursor to mathematics achievement and may demonstrate effect patterns on career and major choices different from those of mathematics achievement. In fact, educational systems have more control over mathematics coursework participation through the use of educational policies to develop or change access patterns of students to mathematics courses. This means that although educators may not have direct control over students' career destinations, they can create an academic pathway for students, leading them to careers that use their mathematical potential. From this perspective, analytic results from mathematics coursework may actually bear more meaningful policy implications than those from mathematics achievement.

To meaningfully examine the effects of mathematics coursework on career and major choices, it is preferable to control for mathematics achievement, as we did in the present analysis. This means that we are able to examine the unique effects of coursework participation over and above mathematics achievement. Unfortunately, the lack of adequate measures of self-efficacy and expectancy-value in the data set we used prevents us from comparing the perspectives of self-efficacy and expectancy-value theories—a fruitful direction for future research.

Using data from the Longitudinal Study of American Youth (LSAY), a 6-year national panel study that spanned Grades 7 through 12 (Miller, Kimmel, Hoffer, & Nelson, 2000), we examined career choices after each completed mathematics course, beginning with the 7th grade, and college major choices in relation to each completed mathematics course in the 12th grade. Although the LSAY data are not current—they were collected from 1987 through 1993—they represent the most comprehensive education longitudinal data among all national databases on education. The large scale of the survey and the representative sample it produced add significant advantages to our analysis. We focus on gender discrepancies regarding whether change in career and major choices can be attributed to mathematics coursework. Our main research questions include the following:

1. What is the impact of each antecedent mathematics course on subsequent career choices from the 7th grade to the 12th grade, with control for antecedent career choices, antecedent mathematics achievement, and student characteristics?
2. Are there any differences in antecedent mathematics coursework effects on subsequent career choices between males and females from the 7th grade to the 12th grade?
3. What is the impact of each mathematics course in the 12th grade on choices of college or university major, with control for career choices and mathematics achievement in the 12th grade and student characteristics?
4. Are there any differences in mathematics coursework effects on college major choices between males and females?

We statistically control for confounding factors to specifically focus on mathematics coursework and its relationship to career and major choices. According to Best and Kahn (1998), "confounding variables are those aspects of a study or sample that might influence the dependent variable (outcome measure) and whose effect may be confused with the effects of the independent variable" (p. 161). We control for student characteristics (individual differences) in the examination of both career and major choices. In addition, antecedent career choices and antecedent mathematics achievement were considered as key confounding variables when examining the impact of antecedent mathematics courses on career choices.[2] For example, improvement in students' career choices may come from improvement in their mathematics achievement, which contaminates measurement of the impact of mathematics courses. Career choices and mathematics achievement in the 12th grade

---

[2]In this chapter, our focus is on mathematics coursework rather than mathematics achievement as it impacts students' choices of careers and majors. We used mathematics achievement mainly as a control variable to reduce confounding effects in our data analysis. Nevertheless, many aspects of our analytical results touch on the relationship between career choice and mathematics achievement. Female career choices were more likely to be influenced by mathematics achievement, a phenomenon that occurred in 3 out of 5 grade levels compared with 2 out of 5 grade levels for male career choices. However, common between males and females is that whenever the relationship between career choice and mathematics achievement occurred, it was negative. This finding implies that if one cannot do well in mathematics, one is not likely to commit to a career of high prestige such as engineering.

were identified as key confounding factors to mathematics coursework when examining the selection of majors for college or university. For example, students may select engineering as a major because it is their career choice, which contaminates measurement of the impact of mathematics courses.

METHOD

Data

We obtained data for the present analysis from the LSAY (see Miller et al., 2000). The LSAY started in the fall of 1987 with approximately 60 randomly selected 7th graders from each of 52 schools in a national probability sample. These 7th graders were studied for 6 years (from Grade 7 to Grade 12). Students took an achievement test on mathematics and science and completed a student questionnaire in each year. The present analysis used mathematics test and student questionnaire data across all 6 years (from Grade 7 to Grade 12). The LSAY sample contained 3,116 students in the 7th grade; 2,798 in the 8th grade; 2,748 in the 9th grade; 2,583 in the 10th grade; 2,409 in the 11th grade; and 2,215 in the 12th grade. The 29% attrition rate over 6 years was reasonable, and no selective data attrition has been identified (see Miller et al., 2000).

Measures of Mathematics Coursework

We derived mathematics coursework indicators from the LSAY composite variable measuring the highest mathematics course that each student took in each grade. The LSAY identified common mathematics courses offered in most U.S. schools, including low, average, and high 7th-grade and 8th-grade mathematics; basic mathematics; consumer mathematics; vocational mathematics; pre-algebra; Algebra I (also honors); Algebra II (also honors); geometry (also honors); trigonometry (also honors); analytic geometry; and calculus. Students in most U.S. schools are tracked into different mathematics curricula that can be classified as vocational track, general track, and academic (college preparatory) track. Usually, students in the vocational track take applied mathematics such as basic, consumer, and vocational mathematics; students in the general track take regular mathematics such as Algebra I, Algebra II, and geometry; and students in the academic track take advanced mathematics such as trigonometry, analytic geometry, and calculus. Often, mathematics performance, teacher suggestion, and parental request are major factors that determine the placement of students in mathematics curriculum tracks.

In total, students engaged in 5 different mathematics courses in Grade 7, 8 in Grade 8, 10 in Grade 9, 12 in Grade 10, 13 in Grade 11, and 9 in

TABLE 2.1
Effects of Mathematics Coursework in Grade 7 on Career Choice in Grade 8

Variable	Changes in R^2		Effects	
	Males	Females	Males	Females
Prior (Grade 7) career choice	.28	.21	0.49*	0.38*
Prior (Grade 7) mathematics achievement	.01	.06	−1.39	−6.58*
Student characteristics[a]	.02	.03		
Black				−145.11*
Mathematics coursework				
Low Grade 7 mathematics	—	—	61.54	22.60
Average Grade 7 mathematics	—	—	−11.76	−1.31
High Grade 7 mathematics			—	−0.64
Pre-algebra	—	—	−36.80	−1.53

Note. Dashes in cells indicate there were no changes in R^2.
[a]Student characteristics include age, father's socioeconomic status, mother's socioeconomic status, race–ethnicity (White, Black, Hispanic), both parents (vs. single parents), and number of siblings. Because the only statistically significant variable was whether the student was Black, the other variables are omitted from the table.
*$p < .05$.

Grade 12. We created a number of dummy variables that we referred to as "coursework indicators" at each grade level, with "no course" as the reference against which other courses were compared. At each grade level, we concentrated on courses studied by at least 10% of students in either gender group. This strategy allowed us to focus on "populated" courses for better policy implications. Tables 2.1 to 2.6 contain coursework indicators for Grades 7 to 12 after omitting "unpopulated" courses at each grade level. We selected one

TABLE 2.2
Effects of Mathematics Coursework in Grade 8 on Career Choice in Grade 9

Variable	Changes in R^2		Effects	
	Males	Females	Males	Females
Prior (Grade 8) career choice	.41	.51	0.60*	0.76*
Prior (Grade 8) mathematics achievement	—	.01	−2.08	−1.88
Student characteristics[a]	.02	.03		
Black			−179.65*	
Mathematics coursework				
Low Grade 8 mathematics	—		12.56	
Average Grade 8 mathematics	—	—	40.67	33.62
Pre-algebra	—	—	−14.33	−34.03
Algebra I	—	—	−18.19	23.64

Note. Dashes in cells indicate there were no changes in R^2.
[a]Student characteristics include age, father's socioeconomic status, mother's socioeconomic status, race–ethnicity (White, Black, Hispanic), both parents (vs. single parents), and number of siblings. Because the only statistically significant variable was whether the student was Black, the other variables are omitted from the table.
*$p < .05$.

TABLE 2.3
Effects of Mathematics Coursework in Grade 9 on Career Choice in Grade 10

Variable	Changes in R^2		Effects	
	Males	Females	Males	Females
Prior (Grade 9) career choice	.33	.35	0.47*	0.47*
Prior (Grade 9) mathematics achievement	.03	.02	−2.98*	−1.53
Student characteristics[a]	.02	.03		
Father's socioeconomic status				−26.18*
Number of siblings				22.67*
Mathematics coursework				
Basic mathematics	—	—	40.94	−8.55
Geometry	—	—	31.38	11.74
Pre-algebra	—	0.01	97.89	106.26
Algebra I	0.00	.01	−16.45	−52.99

Note. Dashes in cells indicate there were no changes in R^2. Empty cells indicate that the variable was not statistically significant for that gender.
[a]Student characteristics include age, father's socioeconomic status, mother's socioeconomic status, race–ethnicity (White, Black, Hispanic), both parents (vs. single parent), and number of siblings. Because the only statistically significant variables were father's socioeconomic status and number of siblings, the other variables are omitted from the table.
*$p < .05$.

TABLE 2.4
Effects of Mathematics Coursework in Grade 10 on Career Choice in Grade 11

Variable	Changes in R^2		Effects	
	Males	Females	Males	Females
Prior (Grade 10) career choice	.31	.27	0.57*	0.44*
Prior (Grade 10) mathematics achievement	.06	.02	−4.36*	−2.66*
Student characteristics[a]	.02	.03		
Mathematics coursework				
Geometry	.04	—	42.99	22.77
Algebra I	.04	.01	−63.04	−65.54
Algebra II	.01	.01	−64.58*	−32.43

Note. Dashes in cells indicate there were no changes in R^2. Empty cells indicate that the variable was not statistically significant for that gender.
[a]Student characteristics include age, father's socioeconomic status, mother's socioeconomic status, race–ethnicity (White, Black, Hispanic), both parents (vs. single parents), and number of siblings. Because none of these variables is statistically significant, they are omitted from the table.
*$p < .05$.

TABLE 2.5
Effects of Mathematics Coursework in Grade 11 on Career Choice in Grade 12

Variable	Changes in R^2		Effects	
	Males	Females	Males	Females
Prior (Grade 11) career choice	.46	.31	0.63*	0.55*
Prior (Grade 11) mathematics achievement	.01	.02	−1.68	−2.20*
Student characteristics[a]	0.02	0.01		
Both parents			−92.11*	
Mathematics coursework				
Geometry	—	—	13.18	36.42
Algebra I	0.01		113.32	.00
Algebra II	—	0.01	−21.59	−63.22
Analytic geometry	—	—	−20.08	−3.47

Note. Dashes in cells indicate there were no changes in R^2. Empty cells indicate that the variable was not statistically significant for that gender.
[a]Student characteristics include age, father's socioeconomic status, mother's socioeconomic status, race–ethnicity (White, Black, Hispanic), both parents (vs. single parent), and number of siblings. Because only both parents is statistically significant, other variables are omitted from the table.
*$p < .05$.

TABLE 2.6
Effects of Mathematics Coursework in Grade 12 on Likelihood of Majoring in Science

Variable	Changes in R^2		Odds ratio	
	Males	Females	Males	Females
Grade 12 Career choice	.03	.02	1.00*	1.00
Grade 12 mathematics achievement	—	.02	1.02	1.05*
Student characteristics[a]	0.02	0.04		
White				0.26*
Mathematics coursework				
Algebra II	—	.02	1.05	.00
Analytic geometry	—	—	1.45	1.02
Calculus	—	.01	1.22	3.16*

Note. Dashes in cells indicate there were no changes in R^2. Empty cells indicate that variable was not statistically significant for that gender.
[a]Student characteristics include age, father's socioeconomic status, mother's socioeconomic status, race–ethnicity (White, Black, Hispanic), both parents (vs. single parent), and number of siblings. Because the only statistically significant variable was whether the student was White, the other variables are omitted from the table.
*$p < .05$.

TABLE 2.7

Proportions of Males and Females Undertaking Selected
Mathematics Courses, Grades 7 to 12

	Grade and selected mathematics coursework (% of entire sample)					
Gender	Grade 7 (pre-algebra)	Grade 8 (Algebra I)	Grade 9 (geometry)	Grade 10 (Algebra II)	Grade 11 (analytic geometry)	Grade 12 (calculus)
Male	16	16	11	18	13	14
Female	16	18	12	19	12	11

mathematics course from each of Grades 7 to 12, and we have provided illustrative descriptive statistics on participation in these courses for males and females in Table 2.7.

Measures of Mathematics Achievement

The LSAY mathematics achievement test measured student performance in four domains: basic skills, algebra, geometry, and quantitative literacy. Basic skills measured student ability to understand number concepts and number operations; algebra measured student ability to solve problems typical of the first algebra course in high school; geometry measured student ability to solve geometric and measurement problems; and quantitative literacy measured student ability to understand percentages, probability concepts, data analysis, and statistical graphs. The LSAY staff computed mathematics achievement (for each year) as formula scores (from 1 to 100) that were adjusted for difficulty, reliability, and guessing through the use of item response theory (see Miller et al., 2000). Also using item response theory, they equated test scores to make these comparable across Grades 7 to 12. We used these mathematics achievement scores as control variables.

Measures of Career Choices and University Majors

Students were asked each year to write in the names of their first and second choice occupations that they expected to pursue. The LSAY staff applied the three-digit occupation codes used by the U.S. Bureau of the Census to students' responses as a way to quantify the prestige of their career choices (see U.S. Census Bureau, 2000). Because the same scale (from 1 to 988) was used year after year to measure the prestige of students' career choices, this index was comparable across grade levels (Grades 7 to 12). We used this index as a continuous dependent variable when we examined the effects of mathematics coursework on career choices. We have provided descriptive statistics of career choices from Grade 7 to Grade 12 for males and females in Table 2.8.

TABLE 2.8

Descriptive Statistics for Career Choice Prestige, Grades 7 to 12, by Gender

| Gender | Career choice prestige | | | | | |
	Grade 7	Grade 8	Grade 9	Grade 10	Grade 11	Grade 12
Male						
M	222.46	227.41	201.83	217.07	228.74	259.29
SD	265.17	261.54	254.97	258.04	275.79	277.82
Female						
M	181.67	174.78	188.86	185.89	192.66	202.66
SD	252.43	236.41	258.24	252.04	251.81	247.64

The LSAY also contained a question on the student questionnaire that asked students in Grade 12 what their major would be in college or university. There was a total of 95 university majors for students to choose from. We collapsed them into seven exhaustive categories of majors including science, engineering, economics, law, medicine, liberal arts, and education.[3] We created seven corresponding dummy variables with not attending college or university as the reference against which the seven majors were compared. We used these dummy variables as dependent variables when we examined the effects of mathematics coursework on the selection of university majors. We have provided descriptive statistics of major choices for males and females in Table 2.9.

Measures of Student Characteristics

We used student characteristics as control variables including gender, age, SES, race–ethnicity, number of parents (both parents vs. single parent), and number of siblings. Gender was used to group males (52%) and females (48%)

TABLE 2.9

Proportions of Males and Females for College Major Choices
Made in Grade 12

| Gender | Major choice (%) | | | | | | |
	Science	Engineering	Economics	Law	Medicine	Arts	Education
Male	16	23	21	7	13	24	7
Female	9	6	18	5	24	29	13

---

[3]*Science majors* in this chapter refers to natural science, computer science, and technological science. This definition fits well into the traditional notion of hard science (e.g., mathematics, physics, chemistry, and biology). Because we set aside engineering as a distinct category, this definition constitutes the rest of what is often referred to as STEM (science, technology, engineering, and mathematics).

for separate analyses. The unit of age was set as year, ranging from 8 to 16 in Grade 7. Parental SES was a composite of parental education, occupational prestige, and household income, including separate measures for fathers and mothers. These formed a standardized index with a mean of 0 and a standard deviation of 1. We created three dummy variables to represent race–ethnicity, denoting White (73%), Black (12%), and Hispanic (10%), with other racial–ethnic backgrounds (mainly Asian; 5%) as the reference. Number of parents was used as a dummy variable coded as both parents (78%) versus single parents (22%) as the reference. Number of siblings (from 0 to 10) was used as a continuous variable.

Statistical Procedures for Predicting Career Choices (Grades 8 to 12)

We used multiple regression techniques to estimate the effects of mathematics coursework on career choices. Cohen and Cohen (1983) discussed three methods to enter independent variables into a regression equation, including the simultaneous method, stepwise method, and block method. Regression using the block method is considered theoretically conservative, statistically rigorous, and practically suitable for explanatory studies because it ensures that the influence of preceding sets of independent variables is statistically controlled to obtain good validity for a follow-up set of independent variables (Cohen & Cohen, 1983). The present analysis used this type of regression technique.

Career choices in each grade were the dependent variable, and career choices and mathematics achievement in the previous grade were used as prior measures (covariates). Prior career choices were entered first into the equation, followed by prior mathematics achievement; the set of student characteristics; and, lastly, coursework indicators. The significance of independent variables was determined by the incremental change in R^2 (the variance explained in the dependent variable) for the set, over and above the R^2 for the set(s) entered earlier. This procedure was used to adjust the effects of mathematics coursework for prior career choices, prior mathematics achievement, and student characteristics.

One regression equation was estimated at each of Grades 8 through 12. For example, in the case of Grade 8, the equation regressed Grade 8 career choices on prior (Grade 7) career choices; prior (Grade 7) mathematics achievement; student characteristics; and coursework indicators (on an individual base) including low, average, and high 7th-grade mathematics, pre-algebra, and Algebra I. Because career choices in Grade 7 were used as one of the independent variables, coursework effects signified the impact of each course on how much the prestige level of students' career choices had changed from Grade 7 to Grade 8. This is appropriate given that the major interest of the present analysis was to examine the effects of mathematics coursework on changes in career choices. Note that coursework refers to those courses students chose to take in Grade 7 rather than Grade 8 because it is appropriate to assume that coursework in Grade 7 has some effect on career choices in Grade 8. Thus, the results of those regression analyses estimated how much change in career choices, if any, could be attributed to having completed a certain course at that stage. Multiple regression was performed for males and females separately.

Statistical Procedures for Predicting University Majors (Grade 12)

Because the choice of a college or university major was a dummy variable, we used logistic regression techniques to examine the effects of mathematics coursework on majoring in a certain domain (e.g., engineering). Following the same logic of block method, we used Grade 12 career choices, Grade 12 mathematics achievement, and student characteristics as control variables. We estimated one logistic regression for each major, regressing students' intentions to major in a certain domain on career choices in Grade 12, mathematics achievement in Grade 12, student characteristics, and coursework indicators entered in a block way. Logistic regression was also performed separately for males and females.

RESULTS

Mathematics Coursework and Subsequent Career Choices

Table 2.1 presents analytic results of the impact of mathematics coursework in Grade 7 on career choices in Grade 8 with control for career choices and mathematics achievement in Grade 7 and student characteristics. When prior (Grade 7) career choices were introduced into the model, they accounted for 28% of the variation for males and 21% for females in Grade 8 career choices. When prior (Grade 7) mathematics achievement was added to the model, it accounted for an additional 1% of the variation for males and 6% for females in Grade 8 career choices over and above the proportions accounted for by Grade 7 career choices. When student characteristics were added to the model, they accounted for an additional 2% of the variation for males and 3% for females in Grade 8 career choices over and above the proportions accounted for by career choices and mathematics achievement in Grade 7. These independent variables formed what we call the *base model*—the basis to which mathematics coursework indicators were introduced.

When coursework indicators were added to the base model, they accounted for less than 1% of additional variation in Grade 8 career choices over and above the proportions accounted for by career choices and mathematics achievement in Grade 7 and student characteristics. This indicates that mathematics coursework in Grade 7 had limited influence on career choices in Grade 8 once Grade 7 career choices, Grade 7 mathematics achievement, and student characteristics were controlled. This was the case for both males and females.

We now interpret statistically significant effects on career choices. Note that each effect controls for the effects of all other variables in the model (we do not continually reiterate this condition throughout the following text for economy of space). Students with a higher career choice index in Grade 7 continued to have a higher career choice index in Grade 8. Statistically, a 1-unit increase in the Grade 7 career choice index was accompanied by an increase of 0.49 units for males and 0.38 units for females in their Grade 8 career choice index. Antecedent mathematics achievement affected the subsequent career choices of females but not males. The effect was negative, suggesting that females with a higher score in mathematics achievement actually reported a lower score in career choice (a 1-unit increase in mathematics achievement in Grade 7 was associated with a decrease of 6.58 units in career choice in Grade 8). In comparison with males, females with similar mathematics achievement in Grade 7 showed inferior career choices in Grade 8. This unique female phenomenon is not alone in the research literature. Friedman (1989) reported that although males and females share similar achievement scores and classroom grades, females have a worse record of participation in mathematics courses than males.

Student characteristics did not have statistically significant effects on career choices in Grade 8 for males once career choices and mathematics achievement in Grade 7 were controlled. On the other hand, Black females showed lower career choices in Grade 8 than the reference students (mainly Asian females; the difference was 145.11 units). Mathematics coursework in Grade 7 had no statistically significant effects on career choices in Grade 8 for either males or females once career choices and mathematics achievement in Grade 7 and student characteristics were controlled. We omit some details in the following interpretation for economy of space: Specifically, the effects of prior career choices, prior mathematics achievement, and student characteristics are omitted because these variables functioned mainly as controls in investigating coursework effects.

Table 2.2 presents analytic results of the impact of mathematics coursework in Grade 8 on career choices in Grade 9 with control for career choices and mathematics achievement in Grade 8 and student characteristics. Mathematics coursework in Grade 8 had no statistically significant effects on career choices in Grade 9 for either males or females. Table 2.3 shows a similar phenomenon—mathematics coursework in Grade 9 had no statistically significant effects on career choices in Grade 10 for either males or females.

Table 2.4 indicates that mathematics coursework in Grade 10 had no statistically significant effects on career choices in Grade 11 for females. However, males who took Algebra II—the most advanced U.S. high school algebra course—in Grade 10 reported lower career choices in Grade 11 than males who did not take Algebra II in Grade 10 (the difference was 64.58 units). Finally, mathematics coursework in Grade 11 had no statistically significant effects on career choices in Grade 12 for either males or females (see Table 2.5).

Overall, antecedent mathematics coursework effects on subsequent career choices were minimal across middle and high school years once antecedent career choices, antecedent mathematics achievement, and student characteristics were controlled. The only coursework effect concerned Algebra II in Grade 10, which had a negative effect on career choices in Grade 11. In comparison, antecedent mathematics achievement showed strong effects on subsequent career choices. Specifically, antecedent mathematics achievement was a significant predictor of subsequent career choices for males for 2 out of 5 grade levels and females for 3 out of 5 grade levels. However, all these effects were negative, suggesting that students who scored higher in antecedent mathematics achievement actually reported lower subsequent career choices. Females were somewhat more likely to demonstrate this phenomenon than males.

Mathematics Coursework in Grade 12 on Selection of University Majors

Tables 2.6 and 2.10 to 2.15 present statistical results from the logistic regression analyses that examined the effects of mathematics coursework in Grade 12 on the likelihood that students would major in certain domains (e.g., science, engineering), with adjustments for career choices and mathematics achievement in Grade 12 and student characteristics. Logistic regressions

TABLE 2.10
Effects of Mathematics Coursework in Grade 12
on Likelihood of Majoring in Engineering

Variable	Changes in R^2		Odds ratio	
	Males	Females	Males	Females
Grade 12 career choice	—	.02	1.00	1.00*
Grade 12 mathematics achievement	.01	—	1.02*	1.00
Student characteristics[a]	.03	.01		
Mathematics coursework				
Algebra II	.01	—	0.53	1.23
Analytic geometry	—	.01	1.35	0.21
Calculus	.01	.03	1.65	9.39*

Note. Dashes in cells indicate there were no changes in R^2.
[a]Student characteristics include age, father's socioeconomic status, mother's socioeconomic status, race–ethnicity (White, Black, Hispanic), both parents (vs. single parent), and number of siblings. Because none of these variables is statistically significant, they are omitted from the table.
*$p < .05$.

TABLE 2.11
Effects of Mathematics Coursework in Grade 12 on Likelihood of Majoring in Economics

Variable	Changes in R^2		Odds ratio	
	Males	Females	Males	Females
Grade 12 career choice	—	—	1.00	1.00
Grade 12 mathematics achievement	—	—	0.99	0.99
Student characteristics[a]	.04	.03		
White			0.22*	
Hispanic			0.26*	
Mathematics coursework				
Algebra II	—	—	1.45	0.64
Analytic geometry	—	—	0.77	1.08
Calculus	—	—	0.74	1.40

Note. Dashes in cells indicate there were no changes in R^2.
[a]Student characteristics include age, father's socioeconomic status, mother's socioeconomic status, race–ethnicity (White, Black, Hispanic), both parents (vs. single parent), and number of siblings. Because the only statistically significant variable was whether the student was Hispanic or White, the other variables are omitted from the table.
*$p < .05$.

followed the same logic of analysis as the multiple regressions reported in the previous section (i.e., the order in which variables were entered into the model was the same). The interpretation of mathematics coursework effects was also similar. The only difference was that estimates were odds ratios rather than regression coefficients in the case of logistic analyses. Grade 12 career choices, Grade 12 mathematics achievement, and student characteristics were again statistically controlled.

TABLE 2.12
Effects of Mathematics Coursework in Grade 12 on Likelihood of Majoring in Law

Variable	Changes in R^2		Odds ratio	
	Males	Females	Males	Females
Grade 12 career choice	.10	.04	1.00*	1.00*
Grade 12 mathematics achievement	—	.05	1.00	1.00
Student characteristics[a]	.01	.06		
Mathematics coursework				
Algebra II	—	—	2.41	0.36
Analytic geometry	—	—	0.36	0.58
Calculus	—	—	0.30	0.26

Note. Dashes in cells indicate there were no changes in R^2.
[a]Student characteristics include age, father's socioeconomic status, mother's socioeconomic status, race–ethnicity (White, Black, Hispanic), both parents (vs. single parent), and number of siblings. Because none of these variables is statistically significant, they are omitted from the table.
*$p < .05$.

TABLE 2.13
Effects of Mathematics Coursework in Grade 12 on Likelihood of Majoring in Medicine

Variable	Changes in R^2		Odds ratio	
	Males	Females	Males	Females
Grade 12 career choice	.03	.11	1.00*	0.99*
Grade 12 mathematics achievement	—	.01	0.98	0.98*
Student characteristics[a]	.02	.01		
Age				1.70*
Mathematics coursework				
Algebra II	—	.01	0.73	1.90
Precalculus	—	—	1.39	0.86
Calculus	—	—	1.14	0.80

Note. Dashes in cells indicate there were no changes in R^2. Empty cells indicate that variable was not statistically significant for that gender.
[a]Student characteristics include age, father's socioeconomic status, mother's socioeconomic status, race–ethnicity (White, Black, Hispanic), both parents (vs. single parent), and number of siblings. Because the only statistically significant variable was age, the other variables are omitted from the table.
*$p < .05$.

Table 2.6 presents statistical results regarding students' majoring in science conditional on mathematics coursework in Grade 12. Males did not demonstrate any coursework effect on majoring in science after controlling for career choices and mathematics achievement in Grade 12 and student characteristics. However, females showed coursework effects related to calculus, the most advanced U.S. high school mathematics course. Females who took

TABLE 2.14
Effects of Mathematics Coursework in Grade 12 on Likelihood of Majoring in Liberal Arts

Variable	Changes in R^2		Odds ratio	
	Males	Females	Males	Females
Grade 12 career choice	.03	.02	1.00*	1.00*
Grade 12 mathematics achievement	.02	.01	0.98*	1.02
Student characteristics[a]	.02	.04		
Hispanic				5.75*
Mathematics coursework				
Algebra II	—	—	1.23	1.84
Analytic geometry	—	—	0.67	1.13
Calculus	.01	.03	0.55	0.22*

Note. Dashes in cells indicate there were no changes in R^2. Empty cells indicate that variable was not statistically significant for that gender.
[a]Student characteristics include age, father's socioeconomic status, mother's socioeconomic status, race–ethnicity (White, Black, Hispanic), both parents (vs. single parent), and number of siblings. Because the only statistically significant variable was whether the student was Hispanic, the other variables are omitted from the table.
*$p < .05$.

TABLE 2.15
Effects of Mathematics Coursework in Grade 12
on Likelihood of Majoring in Education

Variable	Changes in R^2		Odds ratio	
	Males	Females	Males	Females
Grade 12 career choice	—	—	1.00	1.20
Grade 12 mathematics achievement	—	.01	0.99	1.20*
Student characteristics[a]	.01	.03		
Mathematics coursework				
Algebra II	—	—	0.87	0.96
Analytic geometry	—	—	0.47	1.31
Calculus	.01	—	0.38	0.54

Note. Dashes in cells indicate there were no changes in R^2.
[a]Student characteristics include age, father's socioeconomic status, mother's socioeconomic status, race–ethnicity (White, Black, Hispanic), both parents (vs. single parent), and number of siblings. Because none of these variables is statistically significant, they are omitted from the table.
*$p < .05$.

calculus in Grade 12 were 3.16 times as likely to major in science as females who did not take calculus in Grade 12. We emphasize that this coursework effect was unique to females: Calculus functioned as a gatekeeper for females regarding majors in science. This reflects the notion of advanced mathematics as a critical filter in that calculus was highly effective in screening females for science majors at colleges and universities. In other words, without calculus, it was not likely that females would major in science. This was not true, however, for males. Calculus was not significantly predictive of majoring in science for males.

Table 2.10 shows mathematics coursework effects for majoring in engineering. There was a coursework effect for females, showing the same phenomenon as for the case of majoring in science. After controlling for career choices and mathematics achievement in Grade 12 and student characteristics, females who took calculus in Grade 12 were 9.39 times as likely to major in engineering as females who did not take calculus in Grade 12. Again, it was highly evident that calculus functioned as a critical filter to females majoring in engineering.

Table 2.11 shows our attempts to discern the 12th-grade mathematics courses that could possibly lead students to major in economics at colleges and universities; however, we discovered no significant coursework effects. That is, majoring in economics was not associated with mathematics coursework in Grade 12, nor were mathematics coursework effects evident in decisions to major in law (see Table 2.12) or medicine (see Table 2.13). All these conclusions were true for both males and females.

Table 2.14 shows mathematics coursework effects for majoring in liberal arts. Females who did not take calculus in Grade 12 were 4.55 times (1/0.22) as likely to major in liberal arts as females who took calculus in Grade 12. Conversely, females who took calculus in Grade 12 were not likely to major in liberal arts. Again, calculus functioned as a critical filter that screened females for college and university majors. Finally, Table 2.15 shows our examination of whether there were specific mathematics courses that could lead students to major in education. However, majoring in education was not associated with mathematics coursework in Grade 12 for either males or females.

Similar to the situation concerning mathematics coursework effects on career choices, mathematics achievement showed somewhat more effects on college major choices than did mathematics coursework: There were five significant achievement effects versus three significant coursework effects. Higher mathematics achievement was more likely to lead females to major in science and education (Tables 2.6 and 2.15) and males to major in engineering (Table 2.10). On the other hand, lower mathematics achievement was more likely to lead females to major in medicine (Table 2.13) and males to major in liberal arts (Table 2.14). We note that mathematics achievement affected college major choices of both males and females, a phenomenon quite different from that concerning mathematics coursework, which affected college major choices of females but not males.

DISCUSSION

Statistical results from our data analyses illustrate the effects of mathematics coursework on career and college major choices. We emphasize that these analytical results were adjusted vigorously for antecedent career choices, antecedent mathematics achievement, and student characteristics. We implemented this adjustment to rule out critical confounding factors to mathematics coursework. Needless to say, antecedent career choices are strongly related to subsequent career choices. Antecedent mathematics achievement, as a critical measure of prior educational attainment, is also critically important to career self-efficacy (see Betz & Hackett, 1983). In addition, individual differences exist widely in career aspirations (see Signer & Saldana, 2001). With control over or removal of effects for these critical influences, our confidence in making knowledge claims about the unique effects of mathematics coursework increases greatly. After control over antecedent career choices, antecedent mathematics achievement, and student characteristics, significant mathematics coursework effects bear highly creditable and important implications for education policy and practice. On the basis of our principal findings on mathematics coursework effects, we offer the following explanations as hypotheses rather than conclusions because we do not have data to examine our speculations. Further studies may fruitfully pursue this line of research and test these hypotheses.

Negative Mathematics Coursework Effect for Males:
Hypothesis of Stumbling Block

We identified a negative coursework effect on the career choices of males who took Algebra II in Grade 10, a period during which many students undertake this course. Compared with males not enrolled in Algebra II, males who completed Algebra II decided to pursue new occupations that were significantly lower in prestige. This suggests that males might have had some eventful experiences in Algebra II that made them consider the need to downgrade their career choices. Could Algebra II lead males to doubt that they could successfully handle the mathematics needed for their desired occupations? We expect that it could, because males did not experience any negative coursework effect before they reached Algebra II in Grade 10, nor did they demonstrate any negative coursework effects after Algebra II in other advanced courses.

We hypothesize that Algebra II is a stumbling block for males in their career choices. Part of our hypothesis is that males may have unrealistic career expectations before they reach the level of Algebra II. In support of this hypothesis, males did have constantly higher career choices scores than females across the entire middle and high school years, as shown in Table 2.8. Algebra II in Grade 10 may prompt males to put their career expectations into a more realistic perspective. The fact that males did not show further negative coursework effects in more advanced courses after taking Algebra II appears to endorse such thinking—Algebra II is a stumbling block for male career aspirations.

The fact that Algebra II did not show any negative coursework effect on career choices in Grade 11 does entice us to speculate that from the perspective of career aspirations, the later males undertake Algebra II, the more stable their career choices are. However, taking Algebra II in Grade 11 may seriously prevent males from pursuing more advanced mathematics courses—they simply have less time to advance to the level of calculus in Grade 12. We are not arguing for males to take calculus in Grade 12—rather, we think that they should be encouraged to advance to the calculus level, which may actually ameliorate their declines in occupational aspirations. Algebra II appears to function as a critical filter for the career choices of males.

Lack of Mathematics Coursework Effects for Females:
Hypothesis of Realistic Aspirations

There was a noticeable lack of mathematics coursework effects for females. For example, although Grade 10 Algebra II produced a negative coursework effect on the career choices of males, taking or not taking Algebra II had no effect on the career choices of females. In fact, females did not experience at all the "fall" from any mathematics course that they undertook during their entire middle and high school years. We hypothesize that females have more realistic career expectations based on a more accurate assessment of their mathematical abilities (see Crandall, 1969; Watt, 2005) and accordingly have made up their minds regarding their career choices. As a result, females have more stable career choices. This stability could explain the lack of mathematics coursework effects for females.

Females Choosing University Majors: Hypothesis of Calculus as a Powerful Critical Filter

Essentially, mathematics coursework effects on choice of college or university majors consistently highlighted one single mathematics course—calculus. Evidently, calculus functioned as a critical filter for female career choices. Females who undertook calculus in Grade 12 were highly likely to major in science and engineering and highly unlikely to major in liberal arts. Conversely, without calculus in Grade 12, females were not likely to major in either science or engineering but very likely to major in liberal arts. Calculus constrained females' choice of college majors more seriously than males'. Apparently, completing the most difficult, most advanced, and most rigorous course in school mathematics can promote females to think boldly about prestigious majors.

Our emphasis on the importance of calculus to female college major choices is perfectly in line with Kilpatrick (1988), who demonstrated that the study of calculus has a particularly strong influence on the choice of undergraduate majors that lead to careers of high prestige. College or university majors can indeed pave the way to corresponding occupations. To a large extent, choice of college majors is equivalent to choice of careers (see Schnabel & Gruehn, 2000). This is why we emphasize the important role of calculus. We hypothesize that calculus is a powerful career filter that critically screens females for prestigious occupations. The National Science Foundation has recently been emphasizing the importance of attracting many more high school graduates into what are often referred to as "STEM" fields (science, technology, engineering, and mathematics). Quite a few current National Science Foundation grants deal directly with this concern through research and development. We argue from the perspective of mathematics coursework that calculus is a powerful critical gatekeeper that can prevent females from entering the STEM fields.

Males Choosing University Majors: Hypothesis of Achievement as a Better Predictor

In general, we found that mathematics coursework in Grade 12 was unrelated to choice of college or university majors for males. On the other hand, mathematics achievement did show some influences on males' college major choices. Higher mathematics achievement was likely to lead males to major in engineering, whereas lower mathematics achievement was likely to lead males to major in liberal arts. On the basis of the contrast between coursework and achievement effects, we hypothesize that mathematics achievement is a better predictor of college or university majors for males. Although we did not have adequate measures to investigate explanations relating to the expectancy-value model of academic choice (see Eccles et al., 1983), we do suggest that expected success in desired college majors (on the basis of mathematics achievement) may also play a critical role in the college major choices of males. Higher mathematics achievement can indeed raise expectations for success, especially in majors that require mathematical skills. Although the same is true for females who were also influenced by mathematics achievement when making college major choices (higher mathematics achievement was likely to lead females to major in science and education, whereas lower mathematics achievement was likely to lead females to major in medicine),[4] the uniqueness in the male situation is that no mathematics coursework effects were evident. We suggest that the college major choices of males are more sensitive to mathematics achievement than mathematics coursework.

Retaining Students in Advanced Mathematics Courses

It has been a serious educational challenge in the United States and elsewhere to retain an adequate number of students in advanced mathematics courses. As shown in Table 2.7, 14% of males and 11% of females in the LSAY sample undertook calculus in Grade 12. Ma and Wilkins (2004) previously showed that these students were all high achievers in mathematics, defined by mathematics achievement at the beginning of middle school. Using the same data set (the LSAY) in an earlier study, Ma (1997) was able to show that during the senior years (Grades 11 and 12) of high school, attitude toward mathematics outweighed mathematics achievement in determining participation in advanced mathematics courses. He concluded that students avoided the study of advanced mathematics not because they did not have the mathematics ability required to succeed in advanced coursework but because they did not desire to pursue further studies in mathematics. Ma emphasized that this phenomenon was particularly noticeable for females because females performed as well as males in mathematics achievement but demonstrated more

---

[4]The fact that low mathematics achievement predicts the choice of medicine by females is perhaps counterintuitive, but it is not unusual. Females in high school tend to believe that medical schools do not require as much mathematics and science as, say, engineering schools, so it is not uncommon for them to opt for law or medicine as their choice of high-prestige major and career when they dislike or do not fare well in mathematics and science.

negative attitude toward mathematics than males. As a result, Ma argued that retaining students in advanced mathematics is as much an affective effort as a cognitive effort. These findings underscore those within the expectancy-value literature (see also chaps. 3 and 4, this volume).

The low percentage of females who undertook calculus in Grade 12 and the importance of calculus for females' college major choices are a worrisome indication that a limited number of females is likely to enter the STEM fields. Retaining many more females in advanced mathematics courses remains a critical educational challenge (see Updegraff et al., 1996; Watt, 2005). One effective method is to change females' attitude toward mathematics—to foster their appreciation of the role of mathematics in their life (Ma, 1997; Vida & Eccles, 2003; Watt, 2005, 2006). Among the new goals for mathematics education, the National Council of Teachers of Mathematics (1989) emphasized valuing mathematics as the very first goal. Fostering a positive attitude toward mathematics could hold the key to retaining both females and males in advanced mathematics coursework and eventually attract them to the STEM fields with careers of high prestige.

Policy Implications

Mathematics coursework participation through secondary school does demonstrate important although isolated effects on adolescents' and young adults' career and college major choices, and coursework effects differ in some key aspects between males and females. We wish to direct empirical and practical attention to the negative coursework effect for males undertaking Algebra II in Grade 10. These males became significantly discouraged from their aspired career choices subsequent to completing this course. This negative coursework effect was unique to males, who may need to be singled out for special focus: We suggest that educators pay close attention to the teaching and learning of males in Algebra II in Grade 10. Algebra II is the first highly theoretical mathematics course that requires considerable abstract thinking and reasoning for problem solving, and we expect that this course is where many males first encounter serious difficulties in mathematics and start to rethink their career choices, resulting in a decline in the prestige of their career choices. Stated differently, Algebra II is likely the critical filter for career choices of males. Males may need adequate support such as monitoring, tutoring, homework assistance, and frequent reviews to succeed in Algebra II.

The uneventful experiences of females in terms of the lack of mathematics coursework effects on their career choices suggest that females have considerable room to upgrade their career choices. We found that even higher achieving females shied away from higher status career choices. These females might seriously underestimate their potential to pursue careers of high prestige (see Bandura, Barbaranelli, Caprara, & Pastorelli, 2001; Crandall, 1969;

Eccles & Harold, 1992; Watt, 2006). We assert that the problem may be mainly affective—beliefs about and attitudes toward mathematics may be problematic among females (see Bandura et al., 2001; Crandall, 1969; Eccles & Harold, 1992; Ma, 1997; Watt, 2006). In addition, educators need to promote increased degrees of risk taking among females, especially among high achievers, to help them understand their potential to pursue prestigious careers. Female role models (those who succeed in careers of high prestige) may be an effective way to support females in setting higher standards for their career choices. Parents may also join this effort by cooperating with educators to encourage female students to appreciate their potential to succeed in prestigious careers.

As far as aspirations toward college or university majors are concerned, we suggest that educators pay close attention to calculus. As discussed earlier, calculus is the single most critical career filter for females in terms of secondary school coursework. If the goal is to attract more females into STEM fields, educators need to encourage more females to enter and complete the traditional mathematics course sequence of algebra, trigonometry, analytic geometry, and calculus because it is presently the best way to prepare students for STEM majors. Special affective and cognitive care needs to be made available to females as they pursue this traditional sequence of mathematics. Mathematics curricula may also need to incorporate alternative sequences to the traditional sequence, which is mainly theory-oriented mathematics. Alternatives may emphasize the advanced applied aspect of mathematics so that students who appreciate application-oriented mathematics can still pursue advanced mathematics coursework (see Vida & Eccles, 2003). Alternative modern advanced sequences may be (a) discrete mathematics, probability, and statistics; (b) mathematics related to logic and computing (oriented toward computer sciences); and (c) courses that emphasize advanced modern applications of mathematics in natural and social sciences. These course sequences prepare students for the study of disciplines such as accounting, finance, and computer sciences that are not considered traditional science areas but that nevertheless require intensive mathematical skills. We expect that these alternative mathematics course sequences may also attract students oriented toward the sequence of basic, vocational, and consumer mathematics. Such alternative course sequences may help open up many new doors for students, especially females, to pursue occupations of high prestige.

Ernest (2002) emphasized the importance of empowerment in mathematics education. One form of empowerment is sociopolitical: to focus on the utilitarian uses for mathematics. For students to consider themselves as members of the mathematics community, they need to see and appreciate how mathematics helps in the understanding of space, time, and events. They also need to see and appreciate how mathematics plays a role in obtaining personal success in life through role models. These appreciations should promote positive attitudes toward mathematics among students that will keep them in advanced mathematics courses and lead them to careers requiring high levels of mathematics.

We believe that mathematics achievement is a better "persuader" than mathematics coursework participation for males to pursue college or university majors leading to prestigious careers. Common sense indicates that taking more mathematics courses, especially advanced ones, is important for college entry requirements, but this does not appear to convince males to aspire toward prestigious college majors. Helping males improve their mathematics achievement is a more effective way to promote such college major choices than pushing them to take mathematics courses (for concerns about males' mathematics coursework participation, see Ma, 1997). Higher mathematics achievement does raise expectations for success in prestigious college majors that need intensive mathematical skills. This call for improving the mathematics achievement of males is in line with our earlier argument concerning Algebra II. Our key recommendation is that successful performance in mathematics (e.g., in Algebra II) is critical for males to aspire to the pursuit of prestigious careers and college majors.

CONCLUSION

As we have shown in the present analysis, mathematics coursework has isolated but important effects on the status of students' career and college major choices. Algebra II was identified as a critical filter for the career choices of males, whereas calculus was identified as a critical filter that screened females from STEM majors and into majors in liberal arts. Mathematics coursework had no identifiable impact on the career choices of females, and mathematics coursework was secondary to mathematics achievement in terms of the impact on college major choices of males. Overall, mathematics coursework does play a critical although isolated role related to the prestige dimension in the selection of adolescents' and young adults' intended careers and college majors and the processes by which these effects occur.

Longitudinal data are essential to unraveling the cognitive and affective processes that lead to gendered educational and occupational outcomes. Self-efficacy and expectancy-value theories emphasize that adolescents' and young adults' career and college major choices are a product of long-term interactions with significant others and long-term experiences with their learning environment. The importance of longitudinal studies is obvious in the present analysis in which we traced males' and females' changes in career and college major choices in relation to their mathematics coursework history through secondary school. Participation in mathematics courses was indeed related to gendered career and college major choices, which has important implications for policy and practice.

REFERENCES

Bandura, A. (1977). Self-efficacy: Toward a unifying theory of behavior change. *Psychological Review, 84*, 191–215.

Bandura, A., Barbaranelli, C., Caprara, G. V., & Pastorelli, C. (2001). Self-efficacy beliefs as shapers of children's aspirations and career trajectories. *Child Development, 72*, 187–206.

Best, J. W., & Kahn, J. V. (1998). *Research in education* (8th ed.). Needham Heights, MA: Allyn & Bacon.

Betz, M. E., & Hackett, G. (1983). The relationship of mathematics self-efficacy expectations to the selection of science-based college majors. *Journal of Vocational Behavior, 23*, 329–345.

Bishop, J. (1996). Singling the competencies of high school students to employers. In L. Resnick & J. Wirt (Eds.), *Linking school and work* (pp. 79–124). San Francisco: Jossey-Bass.

Chipman, S. F. (2004). Research on the women and mathematics issue: A personal case history. In A. M. Gallagher & J. C. Kaufman (Eds.), *Gender differences in mathematics: An integrative psychological approach* (pp. 1–24). New York: Cambridge University Press.

Cohen, J., & Cohen, P. (1983). *Applied multiple regression/correlation analysis in behavioral sciences*. Hillsdale, NJ: Erlbaum.

Crandall, V. C. (1969). Sex differences in expectancy of intellectual and academic reinforcement. In C. P. Smith (Ed.), *Achievement-related motives in children* (pp. 11–45). New York: Russell Sage Foundation.

De Lisi, R., & McGillicuddy-De Lisi, A. (2002). Sex differences in mathematical abilities and achievement. In A. McGillicuddy-De Lisi & R. De Lisi (Eds.), *Biology, society, and behavior: The development of sex differences in cognition* (pp. 155–181). Westport, CT: Ablex.

Doolittle, A. E. (1985, April). *Understanding differential item performance as a consequence of gender differences in academic background*. Paper presented at the Annual Meeting of the American Educational Research Association, Chicago.

Eccles, J. S., Adler, T. F., Futterman, R., Goff, S. B., Kaczala, C. M., Meece, J. L., & Midgley, C. (1983). Expectancies, values and academic behaviors. In J. T. Spence (Ed.), *Achievement and achievement motives* (pp. 75–146). San Francisco: Freeman.

Eccles, J. S., & Harold, R. D. (1992). Gender differences in educational and occupational patterns among the gifted. In N. Colangelo, S. G. Assouline, & D. L. Amronson (Eds.), *Talent development: Proceedings from the 1991 Henry B. and Jocelyn Wallace National Research Symposium on Talent Development* (pp. 3–29). Unionville, NY: Trillium Press.

Ernest, P. (2002). Empowerment in mathematics education. *Philosophy of Mathematics Education Journal, 15*, 1–16.

Finn, J. D., Gerber, S. B., & Wang, M. C. (2002). Course offerings, course requirements, and course taking in mathematics. *Journal of Curriculum and Supervision, 17*, 336–366.

Friedman, L. (1989). Mathematics and the gender gap: A meta-analysis of recent studies on gender differences in mathematical tasks. *Review of Educational Research, 59*, 185–231.

Hoogstra, L. A. (2002). Divergent paths after high school: Transitions to college and work (Doctoral dissertation, University of Chicago, 2002). *Dissertation Abstracts International, 63*, 330.

Hunt, J. B. (1997). *The national education goals report: Summary.* Washington, DC: National Education Goals Panel.

Jensen, J. A. (1997). Gender differences in the relationship of attitudinal and background factors to high school students' choice of math-intensive curriculum and careers (Doctoral dissertation, Northern Illinois University, 1997). *Dissertation Abstracts International, 58*, 162.

Kaufman, P. (1990). *The relationship between postsecondary and high school course-taking patterns: The preparation of 1980 high school sophomores who entered postsecondary institutions by 1984* (Rep. No. NCES-91-345). Berkeley, CA: MPR Associates.

Kilpatrick, J. R. (1988). Influences on choice of major: A causal model across gender (Doctoral dissertation, University of Toledo, 1988). *Dissertation Abstracts International, 49*, 232.

Lee, V. E., & Ware, N. C. (1986). *When and why girls "leak" out of high school mathematics: A closer look.* Princeton, NJ: Educational Testing Service.

Lent, R. W., Brown, S. D., & Hackett, G. (1994). Toward a unifying social cognitive theory of career and academic interest, choice, and performance. *Journal of Vocational Behavior, 45*, 79–122.

Ma, X. (1997). *A national assessment of mathematics participation in the United States: A survival analysis model for describing students' academic careers.* Lewiston, NY: Edwin Mellen.

Ma, X., & Wang, J. (2001). A confirmatory examination of Walberg's model of educational productivity in student career aspiration. *Educational Psychology, 21*, 443–453.

Ma, X., & Wilkins, J. (2004, April). *Mathematics coursework regulates growth in mathematics achievement.* Paper presented at the Annual Meeting of the American Educational Research Association, San Diego, CA.

Madsen, E. R., Brosnahan, A., Valdez, I., Donohue, S., McAllister, T., & Braverman, M. T. (2002). Survey explores influences on youth workforce preparation. *California Agriculture, 56*(2), 48–54.

Marion, S. F., & Coladarci, T. (1993, April). *Gender differences in science course-taking patterns among college undergraduates.* Paper presented at the Annual Meeting of the American Educational Research Association, Atlanta, GA.

Miller, J. D., Kimmel, L., Hoffer, T. B., & Nelson, C. (2000). *Longitudinal study of American youth: Users manual.* Chicago: International Center for the Advancement of Scientific Literacy, Northwestern University.

Murnane, R., & Levy, F. (1996). *Teaching the new basics: Principles for educating children to thrive in a changing economy.* New York: Free Press.

National Council of Teachers of Mathematics. (1989). *Curriculum and evaluation standards for school mathematics*. Reston, VA: Author.

National Council of Teachers of Mathematics. (1991). *Professional standards for teaching mathematics*. Reston, VA: Author.

Nagy, G., Trautwein, U., Baumert, J., Köller, O., & Garrett, J. (2006). Gender and course selection in upper secondary education: Effects of academic self-concept and intrinsic value. *Educational Research and Evaluation, 12*, 323–345.

Schnabel, K. U., & Gruehn, S. (2000). Studienfachwünsche und Berufsorientierungen in der gymnasialen Oberstufe [Aspired courses of college study and career orientations in the final years of *Gymnasium* schooling]. In J. Baumert, W. Bos, & R. Lehmann (Eds.), TIMSS/III: *Dritte Internationale Mathematik- und Naturwissenschaftstudie. Mathematische und naturwissenschaftliche Bildung am Ende der Schullaufbahn: Vol. 2. Mathematische und physikalische Kompetenzen am Ende der gymnasialen Oberstufe* (pp. 405–443). Opladen, Germany: Leske + Budrich.

Sells, L. W. (1973). High school mathematics as the critical filter in the job market. In *Proceedings of the Conference on Minority Graduate Education* (pp. 37–49). Berkeley: University of California.

Shernoff, D. J., & Hoogstra, L. (2001). Continuing motivation beyond the high school classroom. *New Directions for Child and Adolescent Development, 93*, 73–87.

Signer, B., & Saldana, D. (2001). Educational and career aspirations of high school students and race, gender, class differences. *Race, Gender and Class, 8*, 22–34.

Stinson, D. W. (2004). Mathematics as "gate-keeper": Three theoretical perspectives that aim toward empowering all children with a key to the gate. *Mathematics Educator, 14*(1), 8–18.

Updegraff, K. A., Eccles, J. S., Barber, B. L., & O'Brien, K. M. (1996). Course enrollment as self-regulatory behavior: Who takes optional high school math courses? *Learning and Individual Differences, 8*, 239–259.

U.S. Census Bureau. (2000). *Information on the Census 2000 special EEO file*. Washington, DC: Author.

U.S. Department of Education. (1997). *Mathematics equals opportunity*. Washington, DC: National Center for Education Statistics.

U.S. Department of Education. (1999). *Do gatekeeper courses expand education options?* Washington, DC: National Center for Education Statistics.

Vida, M., & Eccles, J. S. (2003, April). *Predicting mathematics-related career aspirations and choices*. Paper presented at the Biennial Conference of the Society for Research in Child Development, Tampa, FL.

Walberg, H. (1981). A psychological theory of educational productivity. In F. H. Farley & N. Gorden (Eds.), *Psychology and education* (pp. 81–108). Berkeley, CA: McCutchan.

Walberg, H. (1986). Synthesis of research on teaching. In M. C. Wittrock (Ed.), *Handbook of research on teaching* (pp. 214–229). Washington, DC: American Educational Research Association.

Watt, H. M. G. (2005). Explaining gendered math enrollments for NSW Australian secondary school students. *New Directions in Child and Adolescent Development, 110*, 15–29.

Watt, H. M. G. (2006). The role of motivation in gendered educational and occupational trajectories related to math. *Educational Research and Evaluation, 12*, 305–322.

Wilson, J. W. (1996). *When work disappears.* New York: Knopf.

Wilson-Relyea, B. J. (1997). Influences on the level of mathematics achieved by female adolescents: A test of a model of academic choice (Doctoral dissertation, University of Memphis, 1997). *Dissertation Abstracts International, 58*, 1194.

II

PSYCHOLOGICAL PROCESSES AND GENDERED PARTICIPATION IN MATH, SCIENCE, AND TECHNOLOGY-BASED CAREERS

3

WHAT MOTIVATES FEMALES AND MALES TO PURSUE SEX-STEREOTYPED CAREERS?

HELEN M. G. WATT

Why do females and males choose sex-stereotyped careers? Why is it that women are underrepresented in math-related careers? Are men underrepresented in English-related careers and if so, does it matter? There is a general consensus that more men are involved in highly math-related careers than women. This has prompted a large body of research directed toward understanding boys' and girls' mathematical participation. A prominent, productive, and highly influential theoretical framework developed to explain gendered math participation is the *expectancy-value model* developed by Eccles and her colleagues (e.g., Eccles (Parsons) et al., 1983; Wigfield & Eccles, 2000), which informs the present study. Ever since Lucy Sells (1980) first voiced concerns about female underparticipation in math courses, which then acts as a critical filter to limit their access to many high-status, high-income careers, researchers have argued that too many females prematurely restrict their educational and career options by discontinuing their mathematical education in high school (e.g., chaps. 1 and 2, this volume; Heller & Parsons, 1981; Meece, Wigfield, & Eccles, 1990) or soon after in postsecondary education, when fewer females

Thank you to Ray Debus and Mike Bailey from the University of Sydney, Australia, for their invaluable advice in the earlier stages of this research.

than males elect to study math (Bridgeman & Wendler, 1991; Lips, 1992). In the Australian context, the plethora of government policy documents and reports targeting girls' math education signals a general concern with girls' lower mathematical participation during school (for an earlier review of these curricular and professional development initiatives, see Leder & Forgasz, 1992). Because many girls do not share equally in the advantages that are afforded to the mathematically well prepared, I regard lower female participation in math as socially important from both a utilitarian "waste of talent" perspective and a social justice perspective.

The concentration of boys in "masculine" career types has caused less consternation. Whether boys may not be pursuing their areas of interest and potential fulfillment has been less a topic for research concern or public interest (an issue posed in chap. 9, this volume). Is it because female underrepresentation in stereotypically male-dominated domains (such as math) leads to lower status and salary for women that researchers who are concerned with gender equity have focused on gendered participation in male- rather than female-dominated domains (as argued in chap. 7, this volume)? Over the past decade, there has been an increasing trend in educational research, policy initiatives, and the media to target boys' educational needs. Such discussions have invariably focused on boys' academic achievement and boys' disaffection with schooling together with a call for positive male role models among teachers to bring out the best in boys (e.g., House of Representatives Standing Committee on Education and Training, 2002; Lingard, Martino, Mills, & Bahr, 2002; Martin, 2002). In Australia, there has been insistent and vocal concern regarding boys' education and participation in domains sex-typed as feminine, calling for more efforts to encourage boys' involvement in those domains. A major example of this is the Inquiry Into the Education of Boys (House of Representatives Standing Committee on Education and Training, 2002; O'Doherty, 1994). I argue from both social justice and human resource perspectives that we should be concerned with the educational opportunities and outcomes of both boys and girls. Further, I argue the importance of retaining attention to girls' academic well-being alongside current emphases focused on boys. This chapter consequently provides a detailed examination of gendered participation in adolescents' educational and occupational choices in two domains—math and English—commonly perceived as sex stereotyped. I then focus on understanding what motivates girls and boys to pursue sex-stereotyped careers in these two domains.

GENDERED EDUCATIONAL CHOICES

Courses studied through school, particularly in senior high, can have important implications for adolescents' further educational and career options (see chap. 4, this volume). If young women decide to opt out of senior high math (and young men out of English), they begin to limit certain types of career paths that are readily available to them. In the United States, gendered senior high math participation in terms of high-school course enrollments has been documented through the work of Eccles and her colleagues (e.g., Eccles, 1985; Eccles (Parsons), 1984; Updegraff, Eccles, Barber, & O'Brien, 1996), and in Australia other researchers have reviewed gendered trends in specialized math course taking (e.g., Leder, 1992; Leder, Forgasz, & Solar, 1996; Watt, 2006; Watt, Eccles, & Durik, 2006). However, the organizational structure of math courses in U.S. schools, where the majority of research in this area has been concentrated, does not lend itself as easily as does the New South Wales (NSW) Australian context to the study of gendered math enrollment choices. Senior high math participation in the United States has been primarily operationalized according to the number of senior high courses taken. In that context, a greater number of math courses does not necessarily imply participation in increasingly higher order and more complex mathematics. This is because courses are structured around topic areas rather than along an explicit underlying continuum of complexity. Although some topics are generally regarded as less difficult (e.g., general math, beginning algebra) and others as the most difficult (e.g., calculus, trigonometry), there is no formal classification of the difficulty levels for the various topic areas.

Ideally, what is required to assess level of senior high math participation is a context where students' course choices explicitly reflect the extent of their participation in increasingly complex and demanding mathematics. This permits a more fine-grained analysis of math participation than has been possible previously in the concentration of research in this area that has occurred in the United States. In NSW Australia, the extent of both mathematics and English participation can be effectively operationalized during senior high school years using a naturally occurring ordered metric. This provides an ideal location for studying gendered choices in terms of course enrollment.

In the State of NSW Australia, students attend secondary school in Grades 7 through 12. Syllabi exist for each of Grades 7 and 8, 9 and 10, and 11 and 12. In math, Grades 7 and 8 are focused largely on consolidation of material learned in Grades 3 through 6, whereas in Grades 9 and 10, students are streamed into levels of "advanced," "intermediate," or "standard" math on the basis of their demonstrated ability up to that point. In Grades 11 and 12, which lead up to a major external examination supplemented by within-school assessment results called the Higher School Certificate (HSC), students elect which subjects they wish to study. The HSC is a statewide series of externally set and assessed examinations undertaken in Grade 12 supplemented by within-school assessment tasks conducted through Grades 11 and 12. The combined assessment result determines access to university courses and to other educational programs. English is the only required HSC subject, although most students also elect to study math because this is perceived to be an important subject and is in fact an entry requirement for many tertiary courses. In addition to selecting which academic subjects they wish to study for the HSC, students also select the difficulty level within their chosen subjects that they wish to undertake. In math, the lowest difficulty level is "Maths in Practice" (MIP), followed by the still basic but more demanding "Maths in Society" (MIS), with the difficulty level increasing in unit value through "2-unit" (2U), "3-unit" (3U), and the most advanced "4-unit" (4U) math (MacCann, 1995).

In English, there is no formal classification into ordered course levels through Grades 9 and 10 as for math. However, a structure similar to the one for math exists for Grades 11 and 12 senior high English, when students select the level of English they wish to study. There are four courses from which students may choose, each of which is taken by groups of students who differ substantially in general academic ability. The least able students take "2-unit Contemporary" English, followed in ascending order of ability through "2-unit General," "2-unit Related," and "3-unit" English (MacCann, 1995). Unlike math, the latent "difficulty" metric in this case relates to the immediacy and relevance of course texts to current social context, with 2U Related and 3U English courses concerned primarily with classic literature and 2U Contemporary and 2U General courses focused on more contemporary works.

In general, within the NSW context, a greater proportion of boys than girls elects to study the highest 4U math course in senior years, and a greater proportion of girls than boys elects the lowest MIP and MIS courses. This is demonstrated by boys' and girls' HSC examination enrollments in each level of senior high school math (Figure 3.1A). Gendered enrollments depicted in Figure 3.1A span the entire period of this course structure, which was introduced in 1991 and continued until 2000. Within this time frame, a similar pattern of greater male participation in the most demanding Grade 12 math option in another Australian State, Victoria, has also been documented (Forgasz & Leder, 2001).

Conversely, statewide HSC English course enrollments show that greater proportions of girls than boys undertake the 2U Related and 3U courses in senior high, and higher proportions of boys than girls study the lowest Contemporary level (Figure 3.1B). Again, the lowest English Contemporary course was only introduced in 1991, so the statistics are presented from this point onward. Clearly, within the NSW Australian context there remains a robust gender imbalance toward more males in math and more females in English in senior high enrollments.

GENDERED OCCUPATIONAL CHOICES

Measures of the math and English relatedness of adolescents' career intentions provide an important extension to understanding achievement-related

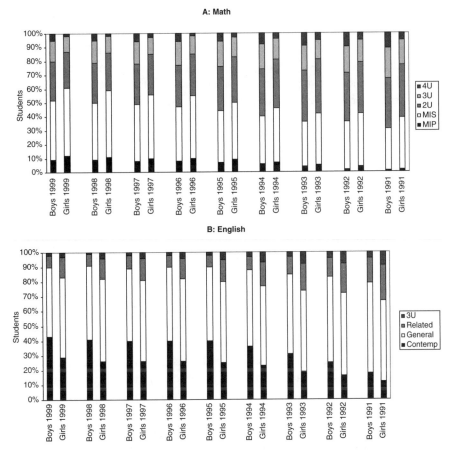

Figure 3.1. Gendered participation in senior high math (Panel A) and senior high English (Panel B) by course level in New South Wales, Australia, 1991–1999. 4U = 4-unit maths; 3U = 3-unit maths; 2U = 2-unit maths; MIS = Maths in Society; MIP = Maths in Practice; 3U = 3-unit English; Related = 2-unit Related English; General = General English; Contemp = Contemporary English. Adapted from Board of Studies (1991, 1992, 1993, 1994, 1995, 1996, 1997, 1998, 1999).

choices beyond the high school years. Although limited career opportunities as a consequence of limited participation in mathematics have been widely recognized, there has been little study of relationships between these two aspects of participation, and there has been an absence of empirical work establishing relationships between adolescents' math-related motivations and participation in the form of mathematical career relatedness. There has been little or no work in the area of English, and the current study is the first to classify career aspirations according to their "English relatedness." Math and English career relatedness were operationalized using O*NET 98 data (U.S. Department of Labor Employment and Training Administration, 1998; for full details see Watt,

2002). Although a U.S. reference, this is a comprehensive database based largely on data supplied by occupational analysts from sources such as the *Dictionary of Occupational Titles* (for an overview, see Osipow & Fitzgerald, 1996). To develop data for this database, analysts evaluated and refined existing occupational data and then applied these data to the O*NET 98 content model. No such comprehensive Australian database is available in published form, and given that there is sufficient cultural similarity and career transferability across the two countries, the database was considered an appropriate basis from which to perform career categorizations.

Categorizations were based on the math and English career content of students' nominated career plans. For mathematics, the definition used in O*NET 98 is "using mathematics to solve problems." For English, content descriptors *writing* and *reading comprehension* were selected as representing career English relatedness, respective definitions for which were "communicating effectively with others in writing as indicated by the needs of the audience" and "understanding written sentences and paragraphs in work related documents." As a result, two classifications of students' nominated career plans were formed: The first categorized plans into one of four levels, which O*NET 98 terminology names "high," "average," "any," or "no" mathematical content; the second categorized plans into one of "high," "average," "any," or "no" writing and reading comprehension content (hereafter referred to as "English" content). Example career classifications for math are science, accounting, and engineering ("high"); business, computing, and veterinary medicine ("average"); hospitality, fashion, and trades ("any"); and sports, music, and journalism ("none"). For English, examples are science, journalism, and law ("high"); business, accounting, and psychology ("average"); music, fashion, and aviation ("any"); and sports, hospitality, and trades ("none").

EXPLAINING GENDERED EDUCATIONAL AND OCCUPATIONAL CHOICES

Expectancy-value theory is one of the major frameworks for achievement motivation, initially developed to explain students' gendered choices and achievement in relation to math (for an overview of this framework, see Eccles, 2005a, 2005b; Eccles (Parsons) et al., 1983; Wigfield & Eccles, 2000). Within it, success expectancies and the subjective valuation of success are the most proximal influences on achievement-related choices and behaviors, and these are in turn predicted by ability beliefs as well as perceived task demands.

Success expectancies have been defined by Eccles (Parsons) et al. (1983) as beliefs about how well one will perform on an impending task, and these are distinguished conceptually from *ability beliefs*, which are defined as perceptions of one's current competence at a given activity. However, Eccles and colleagues have not been able to empirically distinguish these ability and expectancies constructs (Eccles & Wigfield, 1995; Wigfield & Eccles, 2000). Elsewhere, I have argued that this is likely to be due to ability perceptions having mostly been operationalized through broad questions that ask students to rate their performance in different domains (see Eccles & Wigfield, 1995). As a consequence, their responses may in part depend on evaluations of their performance and in part on evaluations of their aptitude (see Watt, 2002, 2004, 2006). It has been claimed that the concept of natural talent best represents the notion of ability as distinct from performance (Bornholt, Goodnow, & Cooney, 1994, based on Green, 1974). Empirical support for this distinction between talent and ability perceptions as commonly operationalized in the literature has been provided by Watt (2002, 2004). Because a student may feel she or he performs well on a certain task yet still not feel she or he has a talent or aptitude for it, talent perceptions are theoretically distinct from ability perceptions operationalized as competence beliefs. Higher order "self-perception" factors have also been validated for both math and English on the basis of component talent perceptions and success expectancies (for details, see Watt, 2002), and these are used in the present study rather than ability perceptions as measured in the expectancy-value framework.

Values relate to how a task meets individual needs (Eccles (Parsons) et al., 1983; Wigfield & Eccles, 1992), and here I focus on intrinsic and utility values. *Intrinsic value* refers to the enjoyment one gets from carrying out a given task, and *utility value* refers to how a task will be useful to an individual in the future (Wigfield & Eccles, 2000). The work of Eccles, Wigfield, and colleagues has demonstrated that expectancies and values predict achievement-related choices operationalized as course enrollment and also achievement (e.g., Eccles, 1985; Eccles, Adler, & Meece, 1984; Eccles (Parsons), 1984; Eccles (Parsons) et al., 1983; Meece, Eccles (Parsons), Kaczala, Goff, & Futterman, 1982; Meece et al., 1990; Wigfield, 1994; Wigfield & Eccles, 1992). Eccles and her colleagues have found values to emerge as powerful predictors of enrollment choices (e.g., Eccles, Adler, & Meece, 1984; Eccles (Parsons) et al., 1983; Updegraff et al., 1996), whereas expectancies better predict performance—findings that have also been supported by other researchers (e.g., Bong, 2001). Recent studies have additionally demonstrated a link between expectancies and enrollment choices (e.g., Simpkins, Davis-Kean, & Eccles, 2006; Watt, 2005).

There has been less empirical work within the expectancy-value framework connected with perceptions about the difficulty of a task (Eccles & Wigfield, 1995). Within the model, perceived task difficulty is posited to influence achievement-related outcomes through its influence on expectancies and values (Eccles (Parsons) et al., 1983; Wigfield & Eccles, 2000), although the researchers cited here have acknowledged that there has been little research directly addressing the relationship between perceived difficulty and task choice.

THE PRESENT STUDY

My goals in this study were, first, to use longitudinal data to establish the extent to which boys' math participation exceeded girls' and girls' English participation exceeded boys'—both for senior high course intentions and selections and for aspired careers. Second, I examine the nature and extent of gender differences in adolescents' prior achievement, self-perceptions, intrinsic values, utility values, and perceived task difficulty for both math and English. Finally, I model the influences of gender, self-perceptions, intrinsic and utility values, and perceived task difficulty on senior high and career math and English participation choices, taking into account adolescents' prior achievement in each domain.

METHOD

Sample and Setting

Participants ($N = 459$) spanned Grades 9 through 11 in a longitudinal design containing 43% girls and predominantly English-speaking background students (73%), with the largest ethnic subgroup being Asians (22%). Participants were from three upper middle class coeducational government secondary schools in northern metropolitan Sydney, matched for socioeconomic status according to the *Index of Education and Occupation* on the basis of census data (Australian Bureau of Statistics, 1991). Data were collected in February near the start of the Australian academic year from 1996 through 1998, when participants were in Grades 9 through 11. Achievement data were collected in the 1st year; intrinsic and utility values, self-perceptions, and perceptions of difficulty in the 2nd year; and participation choices for senior high and career intentions in all 3 years. At the final Grade 11 administration, course levels refer to the actual level students have selected rather than their aspired course levels. For English, some schools did not offer the 3U level until the final Grade 12, combining the 2U Related and 3U candidates through Grade 11. This was the case in schools involved in the present study, and consequently, Grade 11 actual HSC English courses did not include any 3U candidates.

Sixty-five percent of participants were present at all three time points, an additional 23% were present for two of the time points, and 12% participated only at the first time point. Table 3.1 shows the total numbers of participants who were present at each of the math and English administrations for each time point. People with missing data on all relevant variables for the present study were omitted, following which missing data were imputed for prior achievement, intrinsic and utility values, self-perceptions, and perceptions of difficulty, using *multiple imputation*—a methodology that accounts for

TABLE 3.1
Participation at Each Grade for Math and English

Grade	Total N	Math n	English n
9	459	415	429
10	418	393	387
11	368	358	360

the uncertainty in estimating missing data (Schafer, 1997). No imputations were made for missing data in educational and occupational choices that were measured at Grade 11 for the participants present at that wave (see Table 3.1). This resulted in reduced subsample sizes of 337 for the analysis predicting math course enrollments, 281 for math-related career plans, 351 for English course enrollments, and 273 for English-related career plans. Lower numbers for career plans were the result of a number of participants not knowing what careers they planned to pursue, and this "indecisive" group may be interesting to study in further research.

Instruments and Procedures

Questionnaires assessed students' self-perceptions (a composite of their comparative talent perceptions and success expectancies; for details, see Watt, 2002, 2004), values (intrinsic and utility values), and perceived task difficulty. These were measured at Grade 10—the year prior to students selecting senior high course levels. Items were those modified by Watt (2004) on the basis of those developed by Eccles and colleagues for success expectancies and values (see Wigfield & Eccles, 2000), and as discussed earlier, perceptions of talent were assessed instead of their perceptions of ability factor. Full details of modifications and good construct validity and reliability based on the present sample were reported by Watt (2002, 2004), and sample items are presented in Table 3.2. Correlations among constructs are summarized in Table 3.3. Prior achievement was measured using standardized Progressive Achievement Tests for math at Grade 9 (Australian Council for Educational Research, 1984) out of a possible total score of 28, and Tests of Reading Comprehension developed by the Australian Council for Educational Research (1987; Mossenson, Hill, & Masters, 1987, 1995) for English comprehension, out of a possible total score of 22.

Academic choices consisted of planned and actual senior high course levels as well as career intentions. Senior high plans were ascertained at Grades 9 and 10 by students checking boxes to indicate which levels of math and English they planned to study for Grade 11, and at Grade 11, students were asked which course levels they were actually studying. Career plans were assessed

TABLE 3.2

Sample Construct Items to Measure Student Perceptions

Construct	Sample item	Anchors
Self-perceptions		
Comparative talent perceptions	Compared with other students in your <u>class</u>, how <u>talented</u> do you consider yourself to be at math/English?	1 (*not at all*) to 7 (*very talented*)
Success expectancies	How well do you expect to do in your next math/English test?	1 (*not at all*) to 7 (*very well*)
Values		
Intrinsic value	How much do you <u>like</u> math / English, compared with your other subjects at school?	1 (*much less*) to 7 (*much more*)
Utility value	How <u>useful</u> do you believe math/English is?	1 (*not at all*) to 7 (*very useful*)
Task perceptions		
Perceived difficulty	How <u>complicated</u> is math/English for you?	1 (*not at all*) to 7 (*very complicated*)

Note. Underscorings appeared on the survey for emphasis.

using an open-ended question asking what career students intended pursuing; the mathematics and English relatedness of those plans was quantified as described earlier using O*NET 98 (U.S. Department of Labor Employment and Training Administration, 1998) into "none," "any," "average," and "high" for each of math and English.

The study was conducted with informed student and parent consent and approval of the school principals and formal university and departmental ethical bodies. Administration by the researcher was in the regular classroom to maximize ecological validity, with the exception of the final wave, which was administered to larger groups in each school's hall. The study formed part of my

TABLE 3.3

Pearson Correlations Among Prior Achievement, Perceived Difficulty, Intrinsic Value, Utility Value, and Self-Perceptions for Math and English

Factor	Prior achievement	Perceived difficulty	Intrinsic value	Utility value
Perceived difficulty	.02/−.18**			
Intrinsic value	.27**/.29**	−.44**/−.40**		
Utility value	.10*/.05	−.17**/−.03	.46**/.38**	
Self-perceptions	.24**/.33**	−.49**/−.55**	.57**/.63**	.32**/.22**

Note. Slashes separate correlations among constructs for math and English.
*$p < .05$. ** $p < .01$.

larger study investigating a broader range of perceptions about math and English (Watt, 2002).

Analyses

Gender differences in math and English participation choices at each grade were analyzed using dominance analysis (Cliff, 1993, 1996), summarized by the d statistic, which measures the extent to which one sample distribution lies above another. d is a point estimate of the population parameter δ (delta), where d is the difference in probabilities between any two randomly selected members, selected one from each group. d measures the probability that any selected member of group one will lie above any selected member of the second group. Proportions of each gender nominating courses and careers involving varying degrees of each of mathematics and English were of interest, so in randomly sampling girls and boys from each grade, d measures the probability that boys plan to pursue more highly mathematics-related careers than girls, minus the reverse probability. d then is the proportion of boys planning more highly math-related participation than girls, minus the reverse proportion; and conversely for English. This is a direct reflection of the overlap in the two sample distributions. The d statistic also makes no distributional assumptions, and so was appropriate to the present data (Cliff, 1993). Because the d distribution is asymptotically equivalent to the z distribution, to determine levels of statistical significance, d can be converted to a z score and compared with the appropriate critical value.

Initial explorations of gender differences in adolescents' prior achievement and motivations were tested separately for each of math and English using multivariate analysis of variance for Grade 9 achievement and Grade 10 self-perceptions, intrinsic and utility values, and perceived difficulty. Regression analyses then examined the influences of prior achievement, perceived difficulty, intrinsic and utility values, and self-perceptions on Grade 11 course selections and career intentions (prior multiple discriminant analyses established that one discriminant function explained 88% of the variability in Grade 11 math course selections, 94% in math-related career plans, 95% in English course selections, and 68% in English-related career plans; see Watt, 2002). Preliminary visual inspection of scatter plots indicated linear regression to be appropriate for relationships between boys' and girls' motivations and participation outcomes in all cases but one: A quadratic interaction of gender and utility value on math-related career plans appeared likely, and so this term was also modeled in the math regression analysis.[1]

---

[1]To model this effect, utility value was centered about zero, contrasts of −.5 and .5 represented boys and girls respectively, and Gender × Utility Value and Gender × Utility Value Squared were incorporated as predictors of math-related career choices.

RESULTS

Gender Differences in Participation

Robust gender differences were evident in both planned and actual senior high math participation, where boys planned to participate in the higher levels of mathematics more than girls through Grades 9 and 10 and, further, selected and undertook higher level math than girls at Grade 11 (see Figure 3.2A). Projected career intentions also showed boys planned to pursue math-related careers more than girls (Figure 3.2B). These differences were remarkably robust in terms of their consistency across successive years ($\rho = .60$, .73 for HSC math course choices between Grades 9 to 10 and Grades 10 to 11;

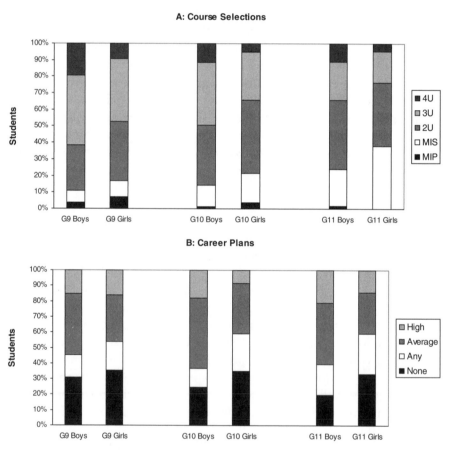

Figure 3.2. Gendered senior high planned and actual math course selections (Panel A) and gendered math-related career plans (Panel B). Grade 11 results in Panel A reflect students' actual course levels. G = grade; 4U = 4-unit maths; 3U = 3-unit maths; 2U = 2-unit maths; MIS = Maths in Society; MIP = Maths in Practice.

$\rho = .50, .49$ for math-related career plans). Differences in proportions favoring boys were statistically significant at each grade level for planned and actual senior high math course selections, with d ranging from .19 to .18 (see Table 3.3), indicating boys' HSC math choices were higher than girls' in 19% to 18% of paired comparisons. Significant d values favoring boys were also evident for math-related career plans, with d ranging from .21 to .23, except at Grade 9, where this effect did not achieve statistical significance (Table 3.4).

Conversely, for English, girls both planned and undertook significantly higher levels of English than boys, with d values ranging from $-.15$ through Grades 9 and 10 to $-.32$ by Grade 11 (see Table 3.3 and Figure 3.3A), indicating girls chose higher HSC levels of English than boys in 15% to 32% of paired comparisons. There was less stability in English course choices than was the case for math ($\rho = .45, .36$ for HSC English course choices between Grades 9 to 10 and Grades 10 to 11), although the second low correlation in particular is likely to relate to the fact that 3U English was not offered in participants' schools at Grade 11. Aspired careers were significantly more English-related for girls than for boys at the final time point (see Table 3.4 and Figure 3.3B), with a d value of $-.13$, although that gender difference was not statistically significant through earlier Grades 9 and 10. There was more stability in the English relatedness of career aspirations over time ($\rho = .57, .56$ for English-related career plans between Grades 9 to 10 and Grades 10 to 11).

Gender, Motivations, and Achievement

Boys rated their self-perceptions of mathematical talent and expected success significantly higher than girls did, $F(1, 440) = 24.36, p < .001$ (see Figure 3.4). This occurred despite equivalent levels of prior mathematical achievement for boys and girls, $F(1, 440) = .70, p = .40$ (boys: $M = 21.26, SD = 4.65$;

TABLE 3.4

Gender Differences in Academic Choices as Measured by the d Statistic for Senior High Courses and Career Choices Related to Math and English

Academic choices	Parameter estimate	Math			English		
		Grade 9	Grade 10	Grade 11	Grade 9	Grade 10	Grade 11
Senior high	d	.190*	.185*	.175*	−.149*	−.146*	−.324*
course	σ	.055	.056	.059	.055	.055	.045
level	z	3.455	3.304	2.966	−2.709	−2.655	−7.200
Career	d	.059	.225*	.207*	−.106	−.085	−.127*
choice	σ	.063	.061	.064	.062	.062	.064
	z	0.937	3.689	3.234	−1.710	−1.371	−1.984

Note. Positive values correspond to higher ratings for boys, negative values to higher ratings for girls.
*$p < .05$.

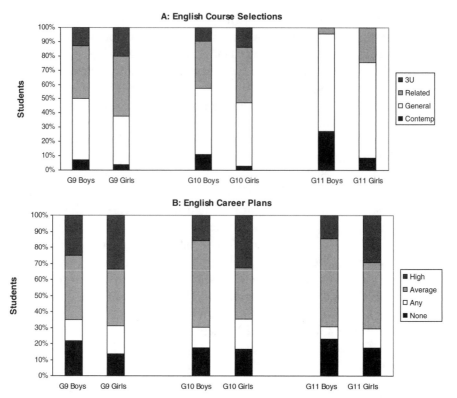

Figure 3.3. Gendered senior high planned and actual English course selections (Panel A) and gendered English-related career plans (Panel B). Grade 11 English course selections are actual rather than intended senior high selections. These schools did not offer 3-unit English commencement until Grade 12, explaining the lack of Grade 11 students electing the 3-unit level. G = grade; 3U = 3-unit English; Related = 2-unit Related English; General = General English; Contemp = Contemporary English.

girls: $M = 21.62$, $SD = 4.34$). Boys also rated their intrinsic value higher, $F(1, 440) = 15.36$, $p < .001$ (see Figure 3.4), and their perceptions about the difficulty of math lower than girls, $F(1, 440) = 5.61$, $p = .02$ (see Figure 3.4). Boys and girls rated the utility value of math similarly, $F(1, 440) = 1.77$, $p = .18$ (see Figure 3.4). For English, girls rated both their intrinsic and utility values statistically significantly higher than boys did, $F(1, 445) = 6.50$, $p = .01$, for intrinsic values; $F(1, 445) = 4.37$, $p = .04$, for utility values (see Figure 3.4), again despite equivalent English achievement scores, $F(1, 445) = 2.58$, $p = .11$ (boys: $M = 13.65$, $SD = 5.09$; girls: $M = 14.44$, $SD = 5.19$). Girls and boys held similar perceptions regarding the difficulty of English, $F(1, 445) = 1.12$, $p = .29$, and English-related self-perceptions, $F(1, 445) = .38$, $p = .54$.

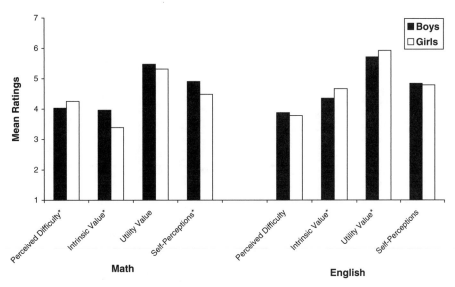

Figure 3.4. Gendered motivations related to math and English. $*F(1, 440)$, $p < .05$, for math; $F(1, 445)$, $p < .05$, for English.

Influences on Participation Choices

Multiple regression analyses modeled expectancy-value influences on math and English participation choices separately within each domain. The conceptual model that was empirically tested is represented diagrammatically in Figure 3.5. At the first step, the influence of gender on Grade 9 achievement was measured. This was followed by measurement of influences of gender and Grade 9 achievement on Grade 10 perceived difficulty; then gender, Grade 9 achievement, and Grade 10 perceived difficulty on each of Grade 10 self-perceptions, intrinsic value, and utility value; and finally the influences of gender, Grade 9 achievement, and Grade 10 perceived difficulty, self-perceptions, intrinsic value, and utility value on each of Grade 11 HSC course levels and Grade 11 aspired careers. The influence of Grade 11 course levels on Grade 11 aspired careers was also included. Paths with higher values, up to a value of ±1, denote the strongest relationships. For the goals of the present study, the paths of greatest interest were the ones that can impact on math and English participation in senior high and aspired careers: from intrinsic value, utility value, self-perceptions, perceived difficulty, prior achievement, and gender.

Math. Senior high math course levels selected by students at Grade 11 were influenced by prior mathematical achievement ($\beta = .31$), intrinsic value ($\beta = .20$), and self-perceptions related to math ($\beta = .15$; see Table 3.5). Students who had higher levels of prior achievement in math selected higher

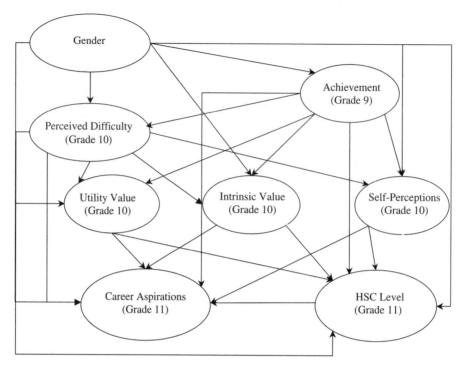

Figure 3.5. Conceptual model to predict participation choices. HSC = Higher School Certificate.

math course levels, and this was the strongest measured influence on their senior high enrollments. Students with higher intrinsic values ($\beta = -.20$) and self-perceptions of mathematical talent and success expectancies ($\beta = -.15$) also subsequently selected higher math course levels, even when their prior mathematical achievement was controlled.

Girls had lower math-related self-perceptions ($\beta = -.20$) and intrinsic value ($\beta = -.15$) than boys, and there was no gender effect on utility value. Prior achievement impacted positively on subsequent self-perceptions ($\beta = .21$) and intrinsic value ($\beta = .25$), although not utility value. Girls also perceived math as more difficult than boys ($\beta = .12$), and this in turn affected their lower math-related self-perceptions ($\beta = -.48$) and intrinsic ($\beta = -.43$) and utility ($\beta = -.14$) values, independent of their prior mathematical achievement. In this way, and as posited in the expectancy-value framework, task difficulty perceptions exerted weak negative indirect effects on senior high math participation choices, via their influence on self-perceptions and intrinsic value (indirect effects of $\beta = -.07$ and $\beta = -.09$, respectively), and did not themselves impact directly on math enrollment choices. Utility value did not affect senior high math enrollments, and, consequently, perceived difficulty did not exert an indirect effect on math enrollments via utility value.

TABLE 3.5
Summary of Regression Analyses Predicting Math-Related Educational and Occupational Participation

Dependent	Predictor	β	B	SE
Prior achievement (Grade 9; Adj. R^2 = .00)	Gender	.05	.46	.47
Perceived difficulty (Grade 10; Adj. R^2 = .01)	Gender	.12*	.25	.12
	Prior achievement	.01	.00	.01
Intrinsic value (Grade 10; Adj. R^2 = .27)	Gender	−.15**	−.50	.15
	Prior achievement	.25**	.09	.02
	Perceived difficulty	−.43**	−.66	.07
Utility value (Grade 10; Adj. R^2 = .02)	Gender	−.06	−.17	.14
	Prior achievement	.08	.02	.02
	Perceived difficulty	−.14**	−.17	.07
Self-perceptions (Grade 10; Adj. R^2 = .32)	Gender	−.20**	−.38	.09
	Prior achievement	.21**	.04	.01
	Perceived difficulty	−.48**	−.44	.04
Senior high math course enrollment (Grade 11; Adj. R^2 = .24)	Gender	−.09	−.16	.10
	Prior achievement	.31**	.07	.01
	Perceived difficulty	−.01	−.01	.06
	Intrinsic value	.20**	.12	.04
	Utility value	.02	.02	.05
	Self-perceptions	.15*	.15	.07
Math-related career plans (Grade 11; Adj. R^2 = .21)	Gender	−.05	−.10	.20
	Prior achievement	.03	.01	.02
	Perceived difficulty	.04	.04	.07
	Intrinsic value	.03	.02	.05
	Utility value	.09	.08	.06
	Gender × Utility Value	−.18	−.21	.14
	Gender × Utility Value Squared	.16	.07	.06
	Self-perceptions	.12**	.14	.09
	Senior high math course enrollment	.35*	.42	.08

*p < .05. **p <.01.

The extent to which students intended pursuing a math-related career was directly impacted only by level of senior high math course enrollment (β = .36). This emphasizes the importance of retaining girls in the math "pipeline" through senior high school, because other measured motivational influences exerted indirect effects through their influences on senior high math course enrollments.

The anticipated quadratic interaction of gender and utility value did not attain statistical significance (β = .16, p = .20), although this may have related to low power. Consequently, analysis of variance was used on the basis of a triad split for utility values (cut-offs at values of 5.00 and 6.00) to improve statistical power. This analysis identified an interaction effect of gender and math utility value as shown in Figure 3.6, $F(2, 334)$ = 4.72, p = .01 (boys: low M = 1.13, SD = .86; mid M = 1.79, SD = .95; high M = 1.70, SD = .90; girls: low M = 1.07,

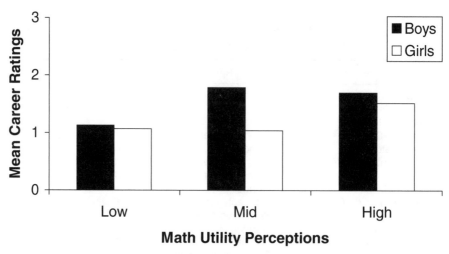

Figure 3.6. Math-relatedness of boys' and girls' career plans by level of math utility value.

$SD = 1.04$; mid $M = .89$, $SD = .81$; high $M = 1.52$, $SD = 1.00$). The interaction effect was due to boys with mid math utility values having math-related career plans that were statistically significantly higher than those of girls with mid utility values, $F(1, 103) = 26.39$, $p < .001$; boys and girls within each of the low, $F(1, 122) = .12$, $p = .73$, and high, $F(1, 165) = 1.35$, $p = .25$, utility value groups had similarly math-related career plans. Among boys, those with mid and high utility values planned similarly math-related careers, whereas those with low utility values planned significantly less math-related careers, $F(2, 221) = 10.52$, $p < .001$ (Tukey's honestly significant difference post hoc tests showed the low group differed from each of the mid and high groups with $p < .001$, and the mid and high groups were similar with $p = .79$). Among girls, those with low and mid utility values planned careers of similar math relatedness, whereas those with high utility values planned significantly more highly math-related careers than either the mid or low utility value groups, $F(2, 169) = 6.54$, $p = .002$ (Tukey's honestly significant difference post hoc tests showed the high group differed from each of the low [$p = .02$] and mid [$p = .002$] groups, and the low and mid groups were similar with $p = .63$). This implies that highly math-related career choices for girls were based on utility value only when this was high, whereas boys with both high and mid levels of utility value planned highly math-related careers.

English. A similar series of regressions was run for the English-related HSC and career outcomes. English senior high courses at Grade 11 were predicted by prior English achievement ($\beta = .33$), gender ($\beta = .29$), and intrinsic value ($\beta = .17$; see Table 3.6). Prior achievement and intrinsic values were the strongest measured influences on English course selections, with participants

TABLE 3.6
Summary of Regression Analyses Predicting English-Related Educational and Occupational Participation

Dependent	Predictor	β	B	SE
Prior achievement (Grade 9; Adj. R^2 = .02)	Gender[a]	.13*	1.31	.53
Perceived difficulty (Grade 10; Adj. R^2 = .04)	Gender	−.02	−.03	.10
	Prior achievement	−.22**	−.04	.01
Intrinsic value (Grade 10; Adj. R^2 = .16)	Gender	.04	.11	.13
	Prior achievement	.22**	.06	.01
	Perceived difficulty	−.30**	−.42	.07
Utility value (Grade 10; Adj. R^2 = .00)	Gender	.08	.19	.12
	Prior achievement	.04	.01	.01
	Perceived difficulty	.03	.04	.07
Self-perceptions (Grade 10; Adj. R^2 = .33)	Gender	−.12**	−.22	.08
	Prior achievement	.24**	.04	.01
	Perceived difficulty	−.47**	−.44	.04
Senior high English course enrollment (Grade 11; Adj. R^2 = .30)	Gender	.29**	.33	.05
	Prior achievement	.33**	.04	.01
	Perceived difficulty	.02	.01	.03
	Intrinsic value	.17**	.07	.03
	Utility value	.02	.01	.02
	Self-perceptions	.08	.05	.04
English-related career plans[b] (Grade 11; Adj. R^2 = .03)	Gender	.09	.19	.13
	Prior achievement	−.05	−.01	.02
	Intrinsic value	−.12	−.10	.07
	Utility value	.13*	.12	.06
	Self-perceptions	.14†	.17	.09
	Senior high math course enrollment	.11	.21	.13

Note. Preliminary analyses indicated a significant difference between the full sample and the regression analysis subsample on prior achievement, $F(1, 443) = 8.09$, $p = .005$, where the regression subsample scored higher; and a difference on utility values approached statistical significance, $F(1, 443) = 3.41$, $p = .066$, where the regression subsample scored lower. Controlling for prior achievement led to significant gender differences on self-perceptions, and nonsignificance on intrinsic values.
[a]The gender difference favoring boys for prior English achievement (β = .13) is not interpreted given the table note above and findings of no gender difference in the full sample.
[b]Perceived difficulty was excluded as a predictor at this step because it produced spurious effects—a direct positive effect (β = .18) and an indirect negative effect via self-perceptions (β = −.11) on English-related career plans—despite a nonsignificant bivariate Pearson correlation with English-related career plans ($r = .08$, $p = .22$).
†$p = .066$. *$p < .05$. **$p < .01$.

who had higher levels of prior English achievement and higher intrinsic values selecting higher levels of HSC English. Girls also chose higher English levels—with statistical control for prior achievement and motivational factors.

Gender differences were evident on English-related self-perceptions (β = −.12), with girls having higher self-perceptions related to English than boys (also see Table 3.6, note a). Prior English achievement positively predicted subsequent self-perceptions (β = .24) and perceptions of English as being less difficult (β = −.22). Difficulty perceptions affected intrinsic value (β = −.30) and self-perceptions ($\beta = -.47$), with lower perceptions regarding the difficulty of English promoting more positive interest and ability-related beliefs. Perceived difficulty had negative but weak flow-on effects to senior high course choices through its effect on intrinsic value ($\beta = -.05$), with higher difficulty perceptions influencing lower course levels. As posited in the expectancy-value theory, perceived difficulty did not impact directly on course choices, but indirectly through its relation to intrinsic values.

The English relatedness of participants' career plans was predicted equally by self-perceptions ($\beta = .14$) and utility value ($\beta = .13$; see Table 3.6, note b), with those students who believed themselves to be more talented in English, expected greater success in English, and perceived English as more useful aspiring toward careers involving more English-related skills. When student motivations were included in the model, there was no direct impact of level of HSC English to English-related career plans. Unlike math, then, English course level did not mediate the relations between adolescents' English-related motivations and their career plans.

DISCUSSION

Robust gender differences exist within the educational and occupational choices among this sample of Australian adolescents. Boys both planned and subsequently undertook higher levels of math in senior high school. Boys also planned more highly math-related careers. Conversely, girls planned and undertook higher levels of senior high English than boys and aspired to careers that were more English-related. These gendered educational and occupational choices were substantially explained by adolescents' motivations over and above their levels of math and English achievement.

Explaining Gendered Math Participation

Math-related self-perceptions and intrinsic values emerged as the key predictors of students' subsequent choices for math participation in senior high course selections. This finding is exactly as predicted by the expectancy-value model of Eccles and her colleagues (Eccles (Parsons) et al., 1983; Wigfield & Eccles, 2000). As with studies conducted by Eccles and her colleagues (see Eccles (Parsons) et al., 1983), no direct influence of task difficulty perceptions on choice outcomes was identified. Girls' perceptions of math as more difficult did, however, have flow-on effects to their lower math-related self-perceptions and intrinsic value, which in turn impacted on their lower senior high math course participation.

Math-related career plans were strongly impacted by adolescents' senior high math course level. There was also an interaction effect of gender and utility value. Girls who valued math as highly useful were more likely than other girls to aspire to highly math-related careers. Boys, on the other hand, who valued math as moderately to highly useful, were equally likely to aspire to highly math-related careers. For girls, then, valuing math as highly useful is likely to lead to the choice of a math-related career. For boys, moderate valuing of math is just as likely to lead to math-related career intentions. Perceptions of the utility of math are therefore more salient in girls' aspirations toward math-related careers. As argued by Eccles and her colleagues (e.g., Eccles, 1984; Eccles, Midgley, & Adler, 1984; Eccles (Parsons), 1984; Eccles (Parsons) et al., 1983; Ethington, 1991; Meece et al., 1990), values are indeed indicative of educational and occupational choices in math. Intrinsic value predicted senior high math participation, and the interaction of utility value with gender predicted math-related career plans. Different kinds of value were therefore relevant for different participation choices.

Previous analyses involving the current data have established that boys maintained higher intrinsic value for math as well as higher math-related self-perceptions than girls throughout adolescence (see Watt, 2004). Because the present study has identified the importance of these factors in math participation choices, for both senior high and planned careers, girls' lower perceptions are particularly problematic. Despite performing similarly, why is it that boys come to be more interested in and like math more than girls? How do girls come to perceive themselves as having less talent and to have lower expectations of mathematical success than boys?

Throughout adolescence, these boys and girls had similarly declining perceptions for the utility of math (see Watt, 2004). It may be most important to guard against girls' declining math utility values because of the different ways that utility value influenced math-related career plans for boys and girls. Because the usefulness of math emerged as a salient concern in girls' career choices, educators could fruitfully focus on explicating the high utility value of math (in general, in the workplace, and in the everyday world) to enhance the likelihood of girls pursuing highly math-related careers.

In the NSW Australian system, selecting what level of math to undertake in senior high school is the first point where students have a real choice regarding the difficulty level of math that they wish to pursue. Girls chose to opt out of more difficult levels of math at this first opportunity. Consistent with the notion of math as a critical filter, these choices in turn had strong implications for young adults' intentions to pursue math-related careers. Because senior high math enrollment selections exerted the strongest influence on math-related career plans, it appears that there should be particular concern about girls opting out of the math pipeline at that point.

Explaining Gendered English Participation

English-related intrinsic values emerged as a key predictor of choices for English participation in senior high course enrollments, with perceived difficulty exerting an indirect effect through its influence on intrinsic values (similar to math and consistent with expectancy-value theory). Unlike math, English-related self-perceptions did not predict HSC English course selections, and gender continued to significantly predict English senior high course levels when the motivation variables were included in the model. Thus, motivations and prior achievement did not fully explain the gender difference by which girls elect to participate more in English—so other factors must also be at play.

English-related career plans were impacted equally by English-related self-perceptions and utility values. Students who believed themselves more talented and likely to succeed in English and students who regarded English as more useful were those aspiring to highly English-related careers. Self-perceptions predicted aspired career but not senior high course level, and utility values demonstrated a relationship with English-related career plans uncomplicated by gender—boys and girls were both more likely to plan pursuing more highly English-related careers when they perceived English as more useful. The combination of English-related self-perceptions and utility values fully mediated the gender difference in adolescents' English-related career plans, with no remaining gender effect once these motivations were included in the analyses.

As was the case with math, and as predicted by expectancy-value theory, self-perceptions and values were most important in explaining adolescents' gendered English participation. Again, different types of value were important for different types of choice. As for math, English-related intrinsic values predicted English senior high course enrollments, whereas utility values influenced English-related career plans. Unlike math, English-related self-perceptions did not impact senior high course selections but did contribute to career plans. English-related self-perceptions and utility values impacted directly on career plans involving English rather than their influence operating through senior high English participation.

It is interesting to note that these findings suggest that the pipeline argument may be less relevant for explaining a continued pattern of lower English participation rates for boys relative to girls. To encourage boys to aspire to participate in English-related careers, it appears to be most important to directly target their ability-related beliefs and their conceptions regarding the utility of English. Because boys and girls demonstrated similar levels of English achievement, I suggest that it is a dangerous aim to enhance boys' ability-related beliefs at the expense of girls', leading to boys overestimating their English-related abilities relative to girls. On the basis of the findings of this study, I recommend targeting boys' lower English values, particularly their utility values.

It may also be less important to worry about boys' lower participation in senior high English courses because that does not subsequently determine the English relatedness of their aspired careers. If this were an issue of concern, however, it is boys' lower liking for and interest in English that would be most useful to address. That said, I reiterate that other factors are also at play in explaining boys' lower senior high English course enrollments. The other chapters in this volume elaborate on many additional important aspects to consider in understanding gendered participation choices, such as family influences, lifestyle goals, social contexts, and biological influences.

Previous analyses involving these data have demonstrated that girls have higher intrinsic and utility values for English than boys throughout secondary school, although boys and girls exhibit similar English-related self-perceptions over this period (see Watt, 2004). If it is a concern that boys are not pursuing English-related occupations that could lead to their potential personal satisfaction and fulfillment, findings from this study suggest that targeting boys' lower values for English throughout secondary school will foster their aspirations toward those careers.

CONCLUSIONS AND POLICY IMPLICATIONS

Operationalizing the extent of boys' and girls' math and English participation choices, both for senior high course selections and for career intentions, has enabled a more fine-grained analysis of the extent of gendered participation in these two traditionally sex-stereotyped domains. Across a sample of upper middle class secondary school students in metropolitan Sydney, Australia, it is clear that robust and persistent gender imbalances in math and English participation choices remain. The magnitude of these gender differences may be even greater among lower socioeconomic groups, where the push to excel academically may perhaps be less. A limitation of the study is its reliance on career intentions rather than actual future career choices, which is an important area of extension for future research.

Should similar participation of men and women in sex-stereotyped domains be the goal? Shapka, Domene, and Keating (2006) contended that the prestige of men's and women's occupations may be the more important dimension to consider rather than the type of occupation. Either way, the persistent gender imbalance in choices for math and English participation appears extraordinarily robust across contexts and time, and remains a social phenomenon, regardless of whether it is considered a social problem. To promote greater male participation in English-related careers, a focus on boys' lower utility values regarding English through secondary school promises to be the most fruitful direction. For math, given current shortages of people entering math-related careers in general, it is clearly important to target both boys' and girls' choices for math participation. Key to addressing this problem will be a focus on girls' liking for and interest in math, their self-perceptions of mathematical talent and expectations for success, and their valuation of the utility of math. Continued investigations into the origins and sources of gender differences in math- and English-related values and self-perceptions promise to shed further light on the resilient issue of gendered participation in sex-stereotyped careers.

REFERENCES

Australian Bureau of Statistics. (1991). *Index of education and occupation* (Catalogue No. 2912.0). Sydney, Australia: Author.

Australian Council for Educational Research. (1984). *Progressive achievement tests of mathematics*. Melbourne, Australia: Author.

Australian Council for Educational Research. (1987). *TORCH tests of reading comprehension*. Melbourne, Australia: Author.

Board of Studies. (1991). *1991 Higher School Certificate examination statistics*. Sydney, Australia: Author.

Board of Studies. (1992). *1992 Higher School Certificate examination statistics*. Sydney, Australia: Author.

Board of Studies. (1993). *1993 Higher School Certificate examination statistics*. Sydney, Australia: Author.

Board of Studies. (1994). *1994 Higher School Certificate examination statistics*. Sydney, Australia: Author.

Board of Studies. (1995). *1995 Higher School Certificate examination statistics*. Sydney, Australia: Author.

Board of Studies. (1996). *1996 Higher School Certificate examination statistics*. Sydney, Australia: Author.

Board of Studies. (1997). *1997 Higher School Certificate examination statistics*. Sydney, Australia: Author.

Board of Studies. (1998). *1998 Higher School Certificate examination statistics*. Sydney, Australia: Author.

Board of Studies. (1999). *1999 Higher School Certificate examination statistics*. Sydney, Australia: Author.

Bong, M. (2001). Role of self-efficacy and task-value in predicting college students' course performance and future enrollment intentions. *Contemporary Educational Psychology, 26*, 553–570.

Bornholt, L. J., Goodnow, J. J., & Cooney, G. H. (1994). Influences of gender stereotypes on adolescents' perceptions of their own achievement. *American Educational Research Journal, 31*, 675–692.

Bridgeman, B., & Wendler, C. (1991). Gender differences in predictors of college mathematics performance and in college mathematics course grades. *Journal of Educational Psychology, 83*, 275–284.

Cliff, N. (1993). Dominance statistics: Ordinal analyses to answer ordinal questions. *Psychological Bulletin, 114*, 494–509.

Cliff, N. (1996). Answering ordinal questions with ordinal data using ordinal statistics. *Multivariate Behavioral Research, 31*(3), 331–350.

Eccles, J. S. (1984). Sex differences in achievement patterns. In T. B. Sonderegger (Ed.), *Nebraska Symposium on Motivation: Vol. 32. Psychology and gender* (pp. 97–132). Lincoln: University of Nebraska Press.

Eccles, J. S. (1985). A model of student enrollment decisions. *Educational Studies in Mathematics, 16,* 311–314.

Eccles, J. S. (2005a, Winter). Studying gender and ethnic differences in participation in math, physical science, and information technology. *New Directions in Child and Adolescent Development, 110,* 7–14.

Eccles, J. S. (2005b). Subjective task value and the Eccles et al. model of achievement-related choices. In A. J. Elliot & C. S. Dweck (Eds.), *Handbook of competence and motivation* (pp. 105–121). New York: Guilford Press.

Eccles, J. S., Adler, T. F., & Meece, J. L. (1984). Sex differences in achievement: A test of alternate theories. *Journal of Personality and Social Psychology, 46,* 26–43.

Eccles, J. S., Midgley, C., & Adler, T. (1984). Grade-related changes in the school environment: Effects on achievement motivation. In J. G. Nicholls (Ed.), *Advances in motivation and achievement: The development of achievement motivation* (Vol. 3, pp. 283–331). Greenwich, CT: JAI Press.

Eccles, J. S., & Wigfield, A. (1995). In the mind of the actor: The structure of adolescents' achievement task values and expectancy-related beliefs. *Personality and Social Psychology Bulletin, 21,* 215–225.

Eccles (Parsons), J. S. (1984). Sex differences in mathematics participation. In M. W. Steinkamp & M. L. Maehr (Eds.), *Advances in motivation and achievement: Vol. 2. Women in science* (pp. 93–137). Greenwich, CT: JAI Press.

Eccles (Parsons), J., Adler, T. F., Futterman, R., Goff, S. B., Kaczala, C. M., Meece, J. L., et al. (1983). Expectancies, values, and academic behaviors. In J. T. Spence (Ed.), *Achievement and achievement motivation* (pp. 75–146). San Francisco: Freeman.

Ethington, C. A. (1991). A test of a model of achievement behaviors. *American Educational Research Journal, 28,* 155–172.

Forgasz, H. J., & Leder, G. C. (2001). The Victorian Certificate of Education—A gendered affair? *Australian Educational Researcher, 28*(2), 53–66.

Green, D. R. (1974). *The aptitude–achievement distinction.* Monterey, CA: McGraw-Hill.

Heller, K. A., & Parsons, J. E. (1981). Sex differences in teachers' evaluative feedback and students' expectancies for success in mathematics. *Child Development, 52,* 1015–1019.

House of Representatives Standing Committee on Education and Training. (2002). *Boys: Getting it right. Report on the inquiry into the education of boys.* Retrieved August 1, 2007, from http://www.aph.gov.au/house/committee/edt/eofb/report/fullrpt.pdf

Leder, G. C. (1992). Mathematics and gender: Changing perspectives. In D. A. Grouws (Ed.), *Handbook of research on mathematics teaching and learning* (pp. 597–622). New York: Macmillan.

Leder, G., & Forgasz, H. (1992). Gender: A critical variable in mathematics education. In B. Atweh & J. Watson (Eds.), *Research in mathematics education in Australasia 1988–1991* (pp. 67–95). University of Technology, Queensland: Mathematics Education Research Group of Australasia.

Leder, G. C., Forgasz, H. J., & Solar, C. (1996). Research and intervention programs in mathematics education: A gendered issue. In A. Bishop, K. Clements, C. Keitel, J. Kilpatrick, & C. Laborde (Eds.), *International handbook of mathematics education* (Vol. 2, pp. 945–985). Dordrecht, the Netherlands: Kluwer.

Lingard, B., Martino, W., Mills, M., & Bahr, M. (2002). *Addressing the educational needs of boys* (Rep. to Department of Education, Science and Training). Canberra, Australia: Commonwealth Department of Education, Science and Training.

Lips, H. M. (1992). Gender- and science-related attitudes as predictors of college students' academic choices. *Journal of Vocational Behavior, 40*, 62–81.

MacCann, R. (1995). Sex differences in participation and performance at the NSW Higher School Certificate after adjustment for the effects of differential selection. *Australian Journal of Education, 39*, 163–188.

Martin, A. J. (2002). *Improving the educational outcomes of boys: Final report to ACT Department of Education, Youth and Family Services.* Retrieved August 1, 2007, from http://www.decs.act.gov.au/publicat/pdf/Ed_Outcomes_Boys.pdf

Meece, J. L., Eccles (Parsons), J. S., Kaczala, C., Goff, S. B., & Futterman, R. (1982). Sex differences in math achievement: Toward a model of academic choice. *Psychological Bulletin, 91*, 324–348.

Meece, J. L., Wigfield, A., & Eccles, J. S. (1990). Predictors of math anxiety and its consequences for young adolescents' course enrollment intentions and performances in mathematics. *Journal of Educational Psychology, 82*, 60–70.

Mossenson, L., Hill, P., & Masters, G. (1987). *Tests of reading comprehension: Test booklet B.* Melbourne: Australian Council for Educational Research.

Mossenson, L., Hill, P., & Masters, G. (1995). *Tests of reading comprehension manual.* Burwood, Victoria: Australian Council for Educational Research.

O'Doherty, S. (1994). *Challenges and opportunities: A discussion paper* (Rep. to the Minister for Education, Training and Youth Affairs on the Inquiry into Boys' Education 1994 by the New South Wales Government Advisory Committee on Education, Training and Tourism). Sydney, Australia: Ministry of Education, Training and Youth Affairs.

Osipow, S. H., & Fitzgerald, L. F. (1996). *Theories of career development* (4th ed.). London: Allyn & Bacon.

Schafer, J. L. (1997). *Analysis of incomplete multivariate data.* London: Chapman & Hall.

Sells, L. W. (1980). Mathematics: The invisible filter. *Engineering Education, 70*, 340–341.

Shapka, J. D., Domene, J. F., & Keating, D. P. (2006). Trajectories of career aspirations through adolescence and young adulthood: Early math achievement as a critical filter. *Educational Research and Evaluation, 12*, 347–358.

Simpkins, S. D., Davis-Kean, P. E., & Eccles, J. S. (2006). Math and science motivation: A longitudinal examination of the links between choices and beliefs. *Developmental Psychology, 42*, 70–83.

Updegraff, K. A., Eccles, J. S., Barber, B. L., & O'Brien, K. M. (1996). Course enrollment as self-regulatory behavior: Who takes optional high school math courses? *Learning and Individual Differences, 8*, 239–259.

U.S. Department of Labor Employment and Training Administration. (1998). *O*NET: The occupational information network.* Washington, DC: U.S. Government Printing Office.

Watt, H. M. G. (2002). *Gendered achievement-related choices and behaviours in mathematics and English: The nature and influence of self-, task- and value perceptions.* Unpublished doctoral dissertation, University of Sydney, Sydney, Australia.

Watt, H. M. G. (2004). Development of adolescents' self perceptions, values and task perceptions according to gender and domain in 7th through 11th grade Australian students. *Child Development, 75*, 1556–1574.

Watt, H. M. G. (2005, Winter). Explaining gendered math enrollments for NSW Australian secondary school students. *New Directions for Child and Adolescent Development, 110*, 15–29.

Watt, H. M. G. (2006). The role of motivation in gendered educational and occupational trajectories related to math. *Educational Research and Evaluation, 12*, 305–322.

Watt, H. M. G., Eccles, J. S., & Durik, A. M. (2006). The leaky mathematics pipeline for girls: A motivational analysis of high school enrollments in Australia and the USA. *Equal Opportunities International, 25*, 642–659.

Wigfield, A. (1994). Expectancy-value theory of achievement motivation: A developmental perspective. *Educational Psychology Review, 6*, 49–78.

Wigfield, A., & Eccles, J. (1992). The development of achievement task values: A theoretical analysis. *Developmental Review, 12*, 265–310.

Wigfield, A., & Eccles, J. S. (2000). Expectancy-value theory of achievement motivation. *Contemporary Educational Psychology, 25*, 68–81.

4

GENDERED HIGH SCHOOL COURSE SELECTION AS A PRECURSOR OF GENDERED CAREERS: THE MEDIATING ROLE OF SELF-CONCEPT AND INTRINSIC VALUE

GABRIEL NAGY, JESSICA GARRETT, ULRICH TRAUTWEIN,
KAI S. CORTINA, JÜRGEN BAUMERT, AND JACQUELYNNE S. ECCLES

In the year 2000, women in the United States were one third as likely as their male counterparts to earn a bachelor's degree in math or computer science (National Science Foundation, Division of Science Resources and Statistics, 2004). In Germany, the imbalance in the gender ratio is even more pronounced (Statistisches Bundesamt, 2001). Educators, scientists, and politicians alike have long argued that this underrepresentation of women in the "hard" sciences is detrimental in numerous respects, among them the fact that it contributes critically to gender inequalities in income (Sells, 1980).

It is likely that many women entering college do not choose to study a hard science despite being qualified to do so. Gendered choices are also apparent prior to college entrance, however. Influenced by cultural norms surrounding gender, specific patterns of self-concept and intrinsic value are developed early in students' school careers, contributing to gendered high school course selection. The choice of high school courses, in turn, often determines students' fields of study at college and, consequently, their future occupations (e.g., Schnabel & Gruehn, 2000). Sells (1980) argued that the underrepresentation of females in advanced high school science courses is a "critical filter" that keeps them out of science- and math-related career paths (see also chap. 2, this volume). Following this reasoning, students' high school course choices can be seen as their first steps on their academic and occupational career paths. An understanding of the mechanisms that underlie gendered patterns of high school course enrollment can thus provide a deeper insight into gendered career paths (see also chap. 5, this volume).

In the present study, we focus on the role of domain-specific academic self-concepts and intrinsic values, which are assumed to mediate the effects of gender. To this end, we integrate two important theoretical models: Marsh's (1986) internal/external frame of reference model (I/E model) and Eccles et al.'s (1983) expectancy-value theory (EV theory). We also examine the effects of two different educational systems on gendered outcomes, comparing high school students' course choices in the United States and Germany. We argue that gendered outcomes may be accelerated or slowed by educational opportunities and constraints. More specifically, we show that ipsative processes that fuel gendered outcomes at the high school level are more pronounced when high school course selection is based primarily on domain-specific self-concepts and intrinsic value rather than on achievement. In Germany, students' self-concepts and values are likely to play a major role in explaining course choices, because these decisions primarily reflect students' preferences for different curricular domains. In the United States, in contrast, course choices are likely to be more ability driven, because which courses are taken in high school is one of the factors that determines college admission. In the following section, we first describe the I/E model (Marsh, 1986) and the EV model (Eccles et al., 1983) and integrate these two approaches. We then detail the impact of gender on self-concepts and intrinsic values. After describing the U.S. and German educational systems, we formulate several hypotheses regarding the effects of gender on course selection in these two countries. Finally, we present empirical results from two related large-scale studies, one in the United States and one in Germany.

INTERNAL/EXTERNAL FRAME OF REFERENCE MODEL, EXPECTANCY-VALUE THEORY, AND GENDER EFFECTS

The I/E model (Marsh, 1986) describes and explains the pattern of relationships that is usually found when academic achievement and domain-specific self-concepts in mathematics and verbal domains are studied. Academic self-concepts are closely connected to achievement in the same domain. In their review of 34 independent studies on the I/E model, Möller and Köller (2004) found a median correlation of $r = .47$ between math achievement and math self-concept and a median correlation of $r = .39$ between achievement in the first language and verbal self-concept. Second, math and verbal achievement are highly correlated. This was the case in 33 of the 34 studies reviewed by Möller and Köller (between $r = .31$ and $r = .94$, $Mdn = .63$). Third, math and verbal self-concepts tend to be only weakly related; Möller and Köller found a median correlation of $r = .10$.

The I/E model (Marsh, 1986) explains this seemingly paradoxical pattern of associations as the joint outcome of two comparison processes (see Figure 4.1). First, students compare their own achievement with the perceived achievement of other students. Thus, their classmates provide a frame of reference for a social comparison process that results in higher self-concepts among higher achieving students. Second, students compare their perceived achievement in one domain (e.g., verbal skills) with that in another domain (e.g., mathematics). This internal frame of reference results in a negative path from achievement in one domain to self-concept in the other; for instance, the better my achievement in math, the lower my verbal self-concept, controlling for verbal achievement (see the paths from achievement in one academic domain to self-concept in the other domain as illustrated in Figure 4.1). Because of the positive correlation between verbal and mathematical achievement and the negative cross-domain effects of achievement on self-concept, individuals' self-concepts in the math and verbal domain become decoupled. As a consequence, although individuals with high math achievement also tend to do well in the verbal domain, "people think of themselves as either 'math' persons or 'verbal' persons—but not both" (Marsh & Hau, 2004, p. 57).

Strong empirical support for the I/E model has been provided by both experimental (e.g., Möller & Köller, 2001) and longitudinal (e.g., Marsh & Yeung, 1997) studies, and its cross-cultural generalizability has been demonstrated by Marsh and Hau (2004). The particular strengths of the I/E model include the internal, ipsative-like processes of internal comparison. Clearly, the I/E model has important implications for studies on behavioral outcomes such as effort and persistence, on scholastic work, and on high school course

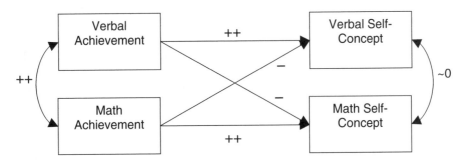

Figure 4.1. Path model predicted by the internal/external frame of reference model. Note that the effects of social comparisons on self-concept formation are not depicted in the figure because class-specific achievement means are not included. + and – signs represent the expected direction of association. ++ indicates that positive associations are assumed to be stronger than negative associations.

selection. However, it is only recently that studies have begun to explore this potential (see Köller, Baumert, & Schnabel, 2001; Marsh & Yeung, 1997).

Unlike the I/E model, Eccles's EV model (Eccles et al., 1983; Eccles, Wigfield, & Schiefele, 1998; Wigfield & Eccles, 2000) has always focused on explaining behavior and academic choices. It provides a useful theoretical framework for combining the influences of academic intrinsic values and expectancies of success as predictors of academic decision making. In the EV model, expectancy and task value are clearly separable components that have been demonstrated "to directly influence performance, persistence and task choice" (Eccles & Wigfield, 2002, p. 118). More generally, Eccles's EV theory considers the social and psychological factors that affect an individual's expectancies of success and task value.

Expectancies of success are defined as individuals' beliefs about how well they will perform on a future task (Eccles et al., 1998). Early writings on the EV model differentiated between self-concept and expectancy of success. However, on the basis of empirical studies in which the two components showed high intercorrelations, *self-concept* and *expectancy* have sometimes been collapsed into a single construct. In this study, we do not differentiate between the two constructs but use the terms synonymously. *Task value* is broken down into four components: intrinsic value, attainment value, utility value, and cost (Eccles et al., 1998). *Intrinsic value* is defined as the enjoyment a person gets from performing the activity or an individual's subjective interest in the subject. The key role of interest in learning is embedded in several motivational theories and has been highlighted in a large number of studies (see Krapp, 1999). *Attainment value* is defined as the personal importance of succeeding at a task; *utility value* indicates how well a task relates to goals; and, finally, *cost* is defined as the perceived negative consequences of engaging in the task, including performance anxiety, fear of failure, the effort necessary for success, and the opportunity cost of choosing that option. In empirical studies, the value component has been operationalized in several different ways (e.g., Jacobs, Lanza, Osgood, Eccles, & Wigfield, 2002; Watt, 2004). Although some researchers have focused on one specific component or treated the components separately, it is also common to use a combined measure that integrates, for instance, the attainment and utility components.

Expectancies and values are assumed to be influenced by task beliefs such as perceived competence, perceived difficulty of the task, and an individual's goals and self-schema. These, in turn, are influenced by social variables such as individuals' perceptions of others' attitudes and expectations, their affective memories, and their perceptions of their previous achievement. Task perceptions and interpretations of past outcomes are assumed to be influenced by socializers' beliefs and behaviors and by cultural milieu and historical time and place (Eccles & Wigfield, 2002; Wigfield, Eccles, & Pintrich, 1996).

There is some commonality between the I/E and the EV models. In both models, the outcomes (self-concept in I/E, educational choices in EV) are thought to be influenced by ipsative-like processes. These processes are clearly apparent in the internal comparison processes postulated by the I/E model. However, they are also inherent in the EV model, in which choices are assumed to be influenced by positive and negative task characteristics and to have associated opportunity costs in that one choice necessarily eliminates other options (Eccles & Wigfield, 2002). Moreover, academic interests play an important role in both models. This is clearly apparent in the EV model, where interest is an important part of the value component (intrinsic value). Less obviously, interest is also relevant to work on the I/E model, in that the self-concept component of the I/E model has often been measured with Marsh's Self-Description Questionnaire (Marsh & O'Neill, 1984), which contains items that tap interest (e.g., "I find many mathematical problems interesting and challenging") together with items focusing on ability (e.g., "I am quite good at mathematics"). More recent studies (e.g., Marsh, Trautwein, Lüdtke, Köller, & Baumert, 2005) have called for self-concept and interest to be separated because confirmatory factor analyses show these to be two clearly distinguishable factors—which have always been treated separately in the EV model.

What is the relationship between intrinsic value and self-concept? Is there a causal predominance of either construct? Although intensive research into these questions is still lacking, there is some indication that—at least in mathematics—the effect of self-concept on interest or intrinsic value is stronger than vice versa (e.g., Marsh et al., 2005). This is also in line with the original EV model proposed by Eccles et al. (1983), in which the value component was assumed to be influenced by self-concept. However, there is still a need for research on how, and under what conditions, self-concept and intrinsic value impact on each other. In Figure 4.2, we present our research model, which combines these I/E and EV perspectives.

Our research model posits that achievement has a positive influence on self-concept in the same domain and a negative effect on self-concept in the other domain. Self-concept is hypothesized to impact on intrinsic value, which in turn is believed to affect high school course choice. Moreover, we expect the paths relating neighboring constructs to be the strongest but do not necessarily expect that significant paths will be restricted to those relations.

We combine the I/E and EV models by using the two academic subject areas of mathematics and English (as in the I/E model) as well as self-concept and intrinsic value (as in the EV model) to predict high school course choice making. We believe that the effects of achievement and self-concept on academic choices are partially or wholly mediated by intrinsic values. Furthermore, we expect gender effects to be mediated—at least partially—by academic self-concept and intrinsic value. More specifically, gender is expected to have an impact on domain-specific self-concepts and intrinsic values that in turn

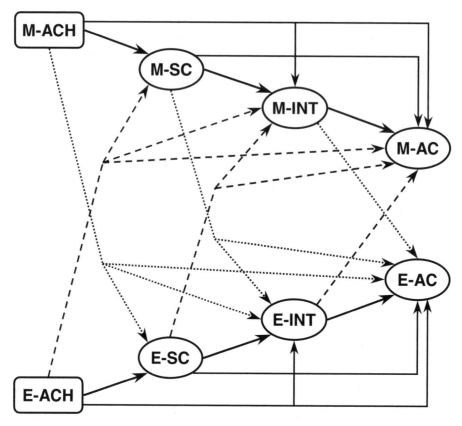

Figure 4.2. Research model combining the internal/external frame of reference model and the expectancy-value theory. Solid lines represent relations between constructs in one domain. Dashed and hatched lines highlight cross-domain relations. M = mathematics; ACH = achievement; SC = self-concept; INT = intrinsic value; AC = advanced course; E = English.

influence academic choices. Indeed, gender effects consistent with gender stereotypes (higher math self-concepts and values in males, higher language self-concepts and values in females) have been found in cross-sectional and longitudinal studies (e.g., Eccles, 1994; Eccles et al., 1998; Jacobs et al., 2002; Marsh et al., 2005; Trautwein, 2003; Watt, 2004).

THE U.S. AND GERMAN EDUCATIONAL SYSTEMS

Apart from gender, decision-making processes are also influenced by contextual variables (see Eccles et al., 1998). In fact, educational systems with their specific affordances and constraints are of particular interest for explaining differential decision-making processes (Schnabel, Alfeld, Eccles, Köller, & Baumert, 2002). Clearly, important academic decisions are not made in isolation from an individual's personal and cultural context. The data used in our study come from two samples of students: one in Germany and one in the United States. These two groups of students select school and college courses within two very different systems under different constraints.

The major relevant differences between the two systems are the ways in which students are tracked and the freedom that they have to choose among courses. In the United States, all students attend high school, where within-school tracking usually starts at Grade 8 or 9. However, there is no official age or grade level by which students and their families must decide on future educational pathways and the possibility of postsecondary education. It is possible to identify students who are on a "college-bound" track by the courses they select ("college preparatory"), although this distinction is less clear in the United States than it is in Germany. In addition, students in the United States have a great deal of freedom to choose among classes. Assuming they have taken the necessary prerequisite courses (i.e., have been on the "right" track), students are relatively free to choose between higher and lower level classes in each subject.

In Germany, in contrast, students are tracked into the different schools of the three-tiered secondary system from as early as age 10. The three most widespread secondary school types (*Hauptschule*, *Realschule*, and *Gymnasium*) differ greatly in the intensity and content of the curriculum, but within each school type, tracking is unusual. The exception is the most academically competitive track, the *Gymnasium*, in which course selection is an integral part of the last 2 years of schooling (Grades 12–13 in most states; Grades 11–12 in the others). For these 2 years, students must select two (and only two) advanced courses in addition to their core classes. Thus, even students who perform well across the board are forced to specialize. Although certain restrictions apply, students are free to choose from a wide range of academic subjects. Several prior studies have shown that course selection at *Gymnasium* is based on intrinsic values and academic self-concepts and is closely related to the fields of study chosen in college (e.g., Schnabel & Gruehn, 2000).

Taken together, the differences between the educational systems in the United States and Germany permit an in-depth investigation of how these contextual factors impact on the decision making processes of male and female students and thereby contribute to gendered educational and occupational outcomes. The basic–advanced course system embedded within the academic track of the German school system is likely to amplify gendered course choices through forcing ipsative-like decision making and, as a consequence, gendered career outcomes. This may be less the case in the United States, where students are comparatively freer to choose among different courses.

PURPOSE OF THE PRESENT STUDY

In view of the fact that academic choices in upper secondary school can open or close career paths in college and beyond (Eccles, 1994; Eccles, Vida, & Barber, 2004), the focus of this study is the relations among domain-specific achievement, self-concept, intrinsic value, and high school choices. We test three sets of hypotheses. First, we expect our combined I/E and EV model to improve predictions of academic decision-making outcomes. Based on the I/E model, we expect to find negative cross-domain effects from achievement in one domain on ability self-concept (and intrinsic value) in the other. On the basis of the finding that task values predict academic decision making (e.g., Eccles et al., 1983; Feather, 1988), we hypothesize that intrinsic value should prove as important or even more important than ability self-concept for predicting course enrollment.

Second, we predict that gender will have an effect on the intrinsic value and ability self-concept components of the model. We expect to find that girls report higher intrinsic value and ability self-concept in English and that boys report higher intrinsic value and ability self-concept in math. Although these effects may not be large, we hypothesize that they will mediate, either partially or fully, any gender differences found in course selection.

Third, we expect the overall model to hold for two different educational environments, namely those of Germany and the United States. Thus, we hypothesize that the model will fit the data in both systems. However, we also predict that the patterns of results will differ as a consequence of the affordances and constraints inherent in the two systems. Most important, *Gymnasium* students in Germany are obliged to select two advanced courses for their final 2 years at school; that is, the system requires them to engage in an ipsative-like decision-making process. In the United States, students are able to choose which classes, if any, to study at an advanced level. Theoretically, they might choose to undertake advanced classes in all subjects or in none. In other words, the system does not require them to specialize. We hypothesize that this difference will have clear effects on the I/E process and that the negative relation between English achievement and math ability self-concept (and math achievement and English ability self-concept) will be stronger for German students, whose course choices are restricted, than will be the case for U.S. students. However, we do expect to find ipsative-like processes in the U.S. sample as well. In addition, the *Gymnasium* being the college-bound track in Germany, all *Gymnasium* students who pass their final exams are granted access to further education. Their choice of advanced courses is irrelevant to college admission. Therefore, we assume that individual choices of advanced courses will be based more strongly on intrinsic value than is the case in the United States, where there are specific "college prep" classes in high school. In the United States, college-bound students must select high-level courses (particularly in math) if they hope to be considered for college admission. Therefore, we hypothesize that U.S. high school students will be motivated to select the highest level class that they feel they can succeed in, meaning that their choice will be based more strongly on achievement than is the case in Germany.

In short, we assume that the same basic model will fit the data for both educational systems but that the coefficients will vary. We expect the pattern of relationships among the constructs used in the following analyses—achievement, self-concept, and intrinsic value—to be largely invariant across the samples. However, the rationale behind students' course choices is likely to differ across the two systems, and we consequently expect the predictive power of the measures used for course enrollment to differ across the samples.

METHOD

Samples

The German sample was derived from a longitudinal study, whose German title translates to "Learning Processes, Educational Careers, and Psychosocial Development in Adolescence and Young Adulthood" (acronym for the German title: BIJU), conducted at the Max Planck Institute for Human Development in Berlin, Germany (Baumert et al., 1996). For the purposes of the present investigation, only students attending academic-track schools (*Gymnasium*) were included. Students attending the vocational track typically leave school after Grade 10 and do not have the opportunity to choose between core and advanced courses at school. The schools were located in four federal states and were randomly sampled in each participating state. The majority of the participants came from middle-class families. As is typically the case in German *Gymnasium* schools, working-class families were underrepresented.

The first data collection took place at the end of Grade 10 and the second in the middle of Grade 12. At each occasion of measurement, students participated in standardized assessments of several subjects and completed questionnaires covering a wide range of psychological constructs and socio-demographic variables. Our final sample of $N = 915$ participants (62% female) from 47 schools consists of those students who participated in the mathematics and English assessments. This group constitutes about half of the BIJU sample because students were randomly assigned to take either a math and a biology test or a math and an English test (also see Nagy, Trautwein, Köller, Baumert, & Garrett, 2006).

For the U.S. sample, data from $N = 1,416$ (54% female) adolescents were derived from the Michigan Study of Adolescent Life Transitions (MSALT; e.g., Eccles et al., 2004; Eccles, Lord, & Roeser, 1996). Eccles and her colleagues began collecting data in 1983, when participants were in Grades 5 and 6, in 10 school districts in southeastern Michigan. The majority of the participants in this ongoing study are White (87%) and come from working- or middle-class families in small communities surrounding Detroit, Michigan. To date, nine waves of data have been collected. The present study is based on the fifth and sixth waves. At the fifth wave, which was conducted in 1988, participants were high school sophomores. By the sixth wave, in 1990, they were high school seniors. Specific quantitative and qualitative information was gathered using mailed questionnaires.

Instruments

Because the MSALT and BIJU studies were not designed to be strictly comparable, different instruments were used to measure the constructs of intrinsic value, self-concept, and achievement in the two samples.

Math and English Achievement

In the BIJU study, standardized tests were used to assess both mathematics and English achievement. The items administered in the mathematics achievement test were taken from previous studies conducted by the International Association for the Evaluation of Educational Achievement—the First and Second International Mathematics Study and the Third International Mathematics and Science Study—and from an investigation carried out at the Max Planck Institute for Human Development (see Baumert, Gruehn, Heyn, Köller, & Schnabel, 1997). Thirty items were administered in Grade 10. Analyses based on item response theory demonstrated that a unidimensional Rasch model was appropriate for summarizing the test data. Item response theory was applied to compute test scores for all students. The standardized English test contained 52 items taken from the International Association for the Evaluation of Educational Achievement six-subject study, an earlier study conducted at the Max Planck Institute, and commercial English tests (see Baumert et al., 1997). Again, item response theory techniques were applied to compute test scores for all participants.

For the U.S. sample, participants' standardized mathematics and English test scores on the Michigan Educational Assessment Program, participation in which is mandatory for all state school students, were obtained from their school records at Grades 7 and 10. The tests have high content validity with respect to the subject-specific curriculum at particular grade levels in the State of Michigan, and scores have been shown to be highly reliable, with Cronbach's $\alpha \geq .85$ (Office of Michigan Merit Award Program, 2000). Despite the good overall psychometric quality, the distribution of Michigan raw scores pointed to ceiling effects, which typically lead to conservative underestimates of effect size. This should be kept in mind when interpreting the results. Nevertheless, supplementary analyses indicated that the deviation from the normal distribution was within the range in which the maximum likelihood estimation method usually used in structural equation modeling can be applied (Curran, West, & Finch, 1996).

Course Level

Course level in math and English was measured as a categorical outcome, with different numbers of categories in the German and U.S. samples. In Germany, there are two clearly defined course levels: basic and advanced. All students attended either basic or advanced courses in math and English. For the MSALT sample, we defined three course levels (low, intermediate, and high). For mathematics, remedial courses were designated as *low*, regular track course as *intermediate*, and courses identified as college preparatory (e.g., calculus and precalculus) as *high*. The same classification was applied for English.

Self-Concept and Intrinsic Value

In the BIJU study, domain-specific academic self-concepts in math and English were measured at the end of Grade 10 using an established German five-item self-concept scale (sample item: "Nobody's perfect, but I'm just not good at math"; Schwanzer, Trautwein, Lüdtke, & Sydow, 2005). Students responded to each item on a 4-point (*agree–disagree*) response scale. Intrinsic value at the end of Grade 10 was measured by means of a four-item scale with 5-point ratings (sample item: "How much do you look forward to mathematics [English] class?" rated from 1 = *not at all* to 5 = *very much*; Marsh et al., 2005). The scale primarily measures interest in the specific subject but also touches on the attainment value component (sample item: "How important is it for you to gain a deeper understanding of mathematics [English]?" rated from 1 = *not at all important* to 5 = *very important*). The wording of the items for the two subjects was strictly parallel except for the name of the subject itself (i.e., math or English). Effects of parallel wording were controlled by introducing residual correlations between school subjects. Because Items 1 and 4 of the intrinsic value measure had identical stems, these residuals were additionally allowed to correlate within each intrinsic value construct.

In the MSALT sample, self-concept and intrinsic value were measured by means of short but well-validated two-item scales, the general psychometric properties of which have been reported elsewhere (Eccles et al., 1983). Students responded on a 7-point scale. The wording of the subject-specific self-concept (sample item: "How good at math are you?") and intrinsic value scales (sample item: "How much do you like doing math?") was again strictly parallel except for the name of the subject itself (i.e., math or English). Effects of parallel wording were again controlled by including residual correlations in the same fashion as for the BIJU sample.

The reliabilities as well as the number of items of each scale are presented in Table 4.1. All scales exhibited good psychometric properties, with Cronbach's alphas ranging from .82 to .93. At the same time, some differences in reliabilities can be observed between the U.S. and German samples. To ensure that these differences did not affect the results, structural equation modeling was used to examine the predictive power of self-concept and intrinsic value on course choices because this approach explicitly incorporates measurement error in estimating the structural relationships under investigation.

Because different instruments were administered in the MSALT and BIJU studies, it would be ineffective to investigate whether the measures exhibit similar psychometric properties in the two cultures (e.g., Meredith, 1993) or to compare the means and standard deviations of the two samples. Because both sets of measures were theoretically derived, however, we assume that the instruments measure the same underlying constructs in both samples. The validity of the respective measures has been documented in numerous studies.

Statistical Analyses

It is critical to take into account the hierarchical nature of the present data in analyses. The present data are typical for educational research, with student samples being nested within schools. When data are clustered in this way, the assumption of independence of observations, crucial to all standard statistical procedures, is likely to be violated (Bryk & Raudenbush, 1992).

Preliminary analyses showed that there was no clustering effect for the MSALT data, with very low intraclass correlations coefficients for the measures used. A different picture emerged for the BIJU data, where considerable between-school differences in achievement were found. Because clustering

TABLE 4.1
Psychometric Properties of the Scales Analyzed

	MSALT		BIJU	
Variable	No. of items	Cronbach's α	No. of items	Cronbach's α
Math self-concept	2	.82	5	.86
English self-concept	2	.89	5	.92
Math intrinsic value	2	.91	4	.84
English intrinsic value	2	.93	4	.86

Note. MSALT = Michigan Study of Adolescent Life Transitions; BIJU = Bildungsverläufe und psychosoziale Entwicklung im Jugendalter (Learning Processes, Educational Careers, and Psychosocial Development in Adolescence).

only affected the results of the BIJU sample, we attended to the clustering effect in that sample only. Analyses were run using the Mplus 3.01 software (L. K. Muthén & Muthén, 2004). In the BIJU sample, we used the "complex" option and the "maximum likelihood estimator with robust standard errors" in Mplus (B. O. Muthén & Satorra, 1995) for continuous outcome variables. Thus, model fit and standard errors are not affected by the clustering effect. In the MSALT sample, parameters were estimated by maximum likelihood, and we used the "weighted least square estimator with robust standard errors" (B. O. Muthén, 1984) for models involving categorical outcome variables.

Almost all longitudinal studies must contend with the problem of missing data. It has been shown that popular approaches to missing data such as listwise and pairwise deletion or mean substitution of data might bias results (Allison, 2001). The imputation of missing data is highly preferable to most other approaches to this problem. We therefore used multiple imputation methodology to tackle the missing data problem. In contrast to single imputation strategies, this method accounts for uncertainty with respect to the missing values. Test statistics derived using multiple imputation are thus unbiased. Five imputed data sets were created for the MSALT and BIJU samples, respectively, using the NORM 2.03 software (Schafer, 1999). Analyses were performed separately for each data set. The results were combined using a formula proposed by Rubin (1987).

RESULTS

First, we describe gender differences in achievement, self-concept, intrinsic value, and course enrollment. We then test the effects of gender, achievement, and self-concept on intrinsic value. Finally, we test the full model, in which high school course selection is the dependent variable.

Gender Differences

Gender differences in the BIJU and MSALT data sets are summarized in Table 4.2. For continuous variables, gender differences are given in standard deviation units. The metric is similar to Cohen's d, with the exception that measurement error is controlled for self-report scales by using latent variables. Positive numbers indicate higher values for males.

In the MSALT sample, gender differences in school achievement were small. Although girls significantly outperformed boys in the math test ($p <$ .05), the difference was only $d = -.11$, and the gender difference for English was nonsignificant. A different pattern of results emerged for the BIJU sample. Substantial gender differences were found for math ($p < .01$), with male students outperforming female students by $d = .46$, but with females performing

TABLE 4.2

Gender Differences: Standard Deviations and Odds Ratios (Course Level)

Variable	MSALT	BIJU
	d values	
Math achievement	−.11*	.46**
English achievement	−.08	−.19†
Math self-concept	.16**	.60**
English self-concept	−.42**	−.11
Math intrinsic value	.03	.34**
English intrinsic value	−.49**	−.38**
	Odds ratios[a]	
Math course level	1.162/1.489*	2.773**
English course level	0.943/0.704**	0.451**

Note. Positive effect sizes indicate higher values for males. MSALT = Michigan Study of Adolescent Life Transitions; BIJU = Bildungsverläufe und psychosoziale Entwicklung im Jugendalter (Learning Processes, Educational Careers, and Psychosocial Development in Adolescence).
[a]For the MSALT sample, the first coefficient indicates the relative probability of males attending a low- rather than an intermediate-level course; the second coefficient reflects the relative probability of males attending a high- rather than an intermediate-level course.
†$p < .10$. *$p < .05$. **$p < .01$.

marginally better in the English test ($d = −.19$, $p < .10$). The relatively good math performance of males compared with females in German *Gymnasium* schools is largely attributable to the fact that more females than males attend the academic track (see Hosenfeld, Köller, & Baumert 1999). In other words, males attending *Gymnasium* schools are already a more selective group than their female counterparts.

For domain-specific self-concept, gender-differentiated patterns in line with gender stereotypes were found in both samples. Males reported higher math self-concept in both samples. Conversely, English self-concept was higher in females (although this difference was only significant in the MSALT sample). The gender differences in the intrinsic value scales were also consistent with typical gender stereotypes. Although there was no significant gender difference for math intrinsic value in the MSALT sample, a considerable difference ($d = −.49$) in favor of female students was found for English intrinsic value. In the BIJU sample, significant gender differences of considerable magnitude were found for both math and English intrinsic value. Boys reported higher math intrinsic value ($d = .34$), with the reverse pattern being observed for English ($d = −.38$).

We now turn to gender differences in course enrollment (see the last two rows of Table 4.2). Gender differences in course attendance are reported as odds ratios (ORs). In the BIJU sample, these statistics indicate the relative chance of a male student attending an advanced math or English course. An OR of 1 would indicate no gender differences in course enrollment. A coefficient of 2 would indicate that males are twice as likely as females to sign up for a specific advanced course, whereas an OR below 1 would indicate that females are more likely to enroll in the advanced course. In the MSALT sample, the ORs have to be interpreted somewhat differently. Because course level entailed three categories, two comparisons are given for each outcome: The first coefficient indicates the relative probability of males attending a low- rather than an intermediate-level course; the second coefficient reflects the relative probability of males attending a high- rather than an intermediate-level course.

As expected, in both samples, male and female enrollment rates in advanced and nonadvanced math and English classes differed significantly. In the BIJU sample, males were nearly 3 times as likely to enroll in an advanced math course than females (OR = 2.77, $p < .01$). Conversely, females were more likely to enroll in an advanced English course (OR = 0.45, $p < .01$). A similar picture emerged for the MSALT sample. Males were more likely to enter a high-level math course than females (OR = 1.49, $p < .05$) but less likely to attend a high-level English course (OR = 0.70, $p < .01$). It is interesting to note—and in line with our hypothesis—that the gender differences in the U.S. sample were less dramatic than in the German sample. Moreover, the U.S. gender differences were restricted to the comparison of high and intermediate course levels. No significant gender differences were observed with respect to students' relative enrollment rates in low- versus intermediate-level courses.

Gender, Achievement, Self-Concept, and Intrinsic Value

The analyses presented thus far have documented gender differences in achievement, academic self-concepts, and intrinsic value. In the next two sections, we extend these analyses to investigate the combined I/E and EV model in both data sets. We started by including all variables except course level in a structural equation model; analyses involving course level are reported in the next section.

In accordance with the I/E and the EV models, our model (see Figure 4.2) predicts that achievement will positively affect domain-specific self-concepts in the same domain. In turn, domain-specific self-concepts are expected to influence domain-specific intrinsic value in the same domain. Additionally, on the basis of the I/E model, we expected the beta coefficients of the cross-paths to be negative. Gender effects on all variables were freely estimated. Residuals of the corresponding latent constructs were allowed to correlate between domains, and residual correlations were introduced between the parallel items for math and English.

Results for the MSALT sample are presented in Figure 4.3A. The model had a satisfactory fit, $\chi^2(26, N = 1,416) = 155.90$, root-mean-square error of approximation (RMSEA) = .059, comparative fit index (CFI) = .986. Regression parameters linking the constructs within a single domain (i.e., the effect of achievement on self-concept and the effect of self-concept on intrinsic

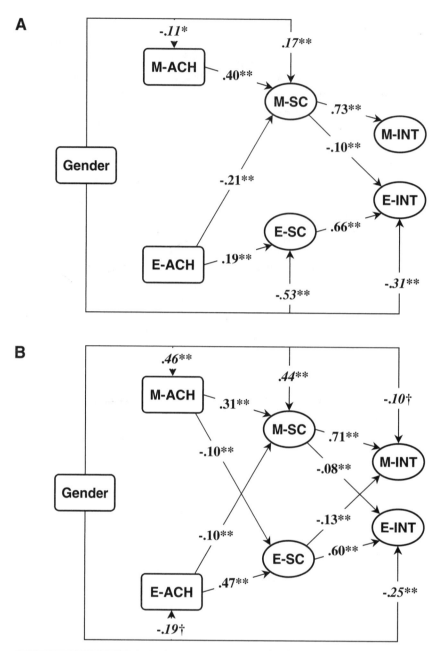

Figure 4.3. Path diagram of the structural equation model for the Michigan Study of Adolescent Life Transitions (Panel A) and BIJU (Panel B) data. Nonsignificant paths and correlations are not reported. Parameters printed in italics are y-standardized; all other coefficients are fully standardized. M = mathematics; ACH = achievement; SC = self-concept; INT = intrinsic value; AC = advanced course; E = English; BIJU = Bildungsverläufe und psychosoziale Entwicklung im Jugendalter (Learning Processes, Educational Careers, and Psychosocial Development in Adolescence). †*p* < .10. **p < .05. ***p < .01.

value) were positive and substantial. Moreover, in line with our theoretical expectations, the cross-domain paths from English achievement to math self-concept ($\beta = -.21$, $p < .01$) and from math self-concept to English intrinsic value ($\beta = -.10$, $p < .01$), were significant and negative. The other two cross-domain effects—the effect of math achievement on English self-concept and the effect of English self-concept on math intrinsic value—did not reach statistical significance. Gender effects on self-concept and intrinsic value were consistent with our findings reported above. Hence, gender differences in self-concept were still apparent after controlling for achievement, and gender differences in intrinsic value in English were still significant after controlling for achievement and self-concept.

The model also achieved a good fit in the BIJU sample, $\chi^2(164, N = 915)$ = 547.6, RMSEA = .051, CFI = .959; results are shown in Figure 3B. Regression parameters linking the constructs within a single domain were positive and substantial. Moreover, in line with our expectations, the cross-domain effects proved to be negative and statistically significant. Similar standardized cross-domain effects of achievement on self-concept were found for English and math. The effects of gender on the measures used were similar in magnitude to the zero-order differences, the exception being a slightly negative effect of gender on math intrinsic value after controlling for self-concept. This reversed effect is apparently due to a suppression effect and indicates that gender differences in math intrinsic value can be explained by differences in math self-concept.

Taken together, the findings of the structural equation modeling demonstrate the merits of combining features of the I/E and the EV models. In accordance with the EV model, the intrinsic value students attach to a subject is predicted by their self-concept in that domain. In line with the I/E model, students' domain-specific self-concepts are not only influenced by their individual achievement in that domain but are also negatively influenced by their achievement in the other domain. The latter effects indicate that students engage in intraindividual cross-domain comparisons. Negative intraindividual comparison processes were also discerned with respect to the effects of self-concept on intrinsic value. Not only do students develop intrinsic values in the domains where their self-concept is high, they also tend to lose intrinsic value for subjects in which they perceive themselves to be less competent than in other domains.

Course Enrollment

What are the determinants of students' course choices? Can gender differences in course enrollment be attributed to differences in domain-specific self-concepts and intrinsic value? These are the questions that we investigate in this section. For the BIJU sample, a series of logistic regression models with

TABLE 4.3

Logistic Regression Models Predicting Course Enrollment
in Math and English: Odds Ratios for the BIJU Sample

Variable	Mathematics: Course Level			English: Course Level		
	Model 1	Model 2	Model 3	Model 1	Model 2	Model 3
Gender[a]	2.09**	1.31	1.18	0.50**	0.53**	0.62*
Math achievement	1.80**	1.29*	1.28*	0.86†	1.09	1.11
English achievement	0.70**	0.85	0.86	1.24*	0.69**	0.66**
Math self-concept		4.50**	2.15**		0.59**	0.61*
English self-concept		0.65**	1.47		3.53**	2.31**
Math intrinsic value			3.33**			1.03
English intrinsic value			0.31**			2.26**
R^2	.17	.52	.65	.07	.38	.46

Note. BIJU = Bildungsverläufe und psychosoziale Entwicklung im Jugendalter (Learning Processes, Educational Careers, and Psychosocial Development in Adolescence).
[a]Female = 0; male = 1.
†$p < .10$. *$p < .05$. ** $p < .01$.

latent predictors (self-concept and intrinsic value) was run using Mplus 3.1. Because the course choice variable included three levels in the MSALT data set, multinomial regression models were specified for the MSALT sample.[1] All continuous predictors were standardized prior to the analyses. The resulting ORs can therefore be interpreted as the change in the relative probability of attending a low- or high-level course produced by a change of one standard deviation in the predictor variables.

We first document the results for the BIJU sample. In Table 4.3, the standardized regression coefficients from the latent logistic regression analyses are summarized. We start by describing the models for enrollment in advanced math courses. The first model included gender and school achievement as predictor variables. High math achievement increased the probability of attending an advanced math course (OR = 1.80, $p < .01$), whereas high English achievement (cross-domain effect) decreased the probability (OR = 0.70, $p < .01$). Relative to the bivariate analysis reported in Table 4.2, the inclusion of math and English achievement reduced the direct effect of gender on course enrollment in mathematics to some degree (OR = 2.09, $p < .01$). In Model 2, domain-specific self-concepts in math and English were added. Math self-concept proved to be a strong predictor of the choice of an advanced math course (OR = 4.50, $p < .01$). In addition, English self-concept was found to

---

[1]Unfortunately, it was not feasible to implement these models directly in a latent variable framework. In order to make the results comparable to those that used latent variables, a two-step strategy was implemented. In a first step, factor scores for the multiple indicator measures were estimated using LISREL 8.5 (Jöreskog, Sörbom, Du Toit, & Du Toit, 2000). In the second step, the estimated factor scores were used as predictors in subsequent multinomial regression models run in SPSS 11.5.

decrease the chance of enrolling in an advanced math course (OR = 0.65, $p <$ .01). In Model 2, gender differences were no longer significant. Similarly, the effects of school achievement were reduced, with only math achievement remaining significant (OR = 1.29, $p < .05$). Math and English intrinsic values were added as predictors in Model 3. The results show that the choice of an advanced math course was strongly influenced by the intrinsic value that students attached to the subject. High math intrinsic value positively predicted enrollment in an advanced math course (OR = 3.33, $p < .01$), whereas students high in English intrinsic value were less drawn to advanced math courses (OR = 0.31, $p < .01$). Moreover, intrinsic value partly mediated the effects of self-concept: The direct effect of English self-concept was no longer significant, and the effect of math self-concept was reduced (OR = 2.15, $p < .05$).

The pattern of results for English course enrollment in the BIJU sample was similar to that reported for math course enrollment. The first model revealed a significant effect of English achievement on enrollment in an advanced English course (OR = 1.24, $p < .05$). Math achievement exhibited only a small effect (OR = 0.86, $p < .10$). Model 1 also revealed that enrollment rates in advanced English courses were highly dependent on gender even after controlling for school achievement. As shown in Model 2, academic self-concepts were highly predictive of the subsequent choice of English courses. Students who were very confident in their English skills were likely to opt for an advanced English course (OR = 3.53, $p < .01$); those high in math self-concept were less likely to do so (OR = 0.59, $p < .01$). Thus, domain-specific self-concepts mediated the effects of school achievement. In fact, the effect of English achievement was reversed when this additional variable was introduced (OR = 0.69, $p < .01$), indicating a suppression effect. The gender effect decreased only moderately when self-concept measures were included in Model 2. In Model 3, math and English intrinsic value were added to the variable list. The inclusion of these variables reduced the effect of English self-concept. English self-concept (OR = 2.31, $p < .01$) and English intrinsic value (OR = 2.26, $p < .01$) proved to be the most powerful predictors. The effects of all other variables remained largely unaffected by the inclusion of the intrinsic values scales.

Taken together, gender, achievement, self-concept, and intrinsic value all contributed to predicting enrollment in advanced math and English courses. There was clear evidence for mediation effects. For instance, gender effects for math course enrollment were mediated by achievement and self-concept. Moreover, achievement effects were mediated by self-concept and intrinsic value. There were also several negative cross-domain effects, lending support to the hypothesis that ipsative-like comparison processes impact on course choices.

We next turn to our findings on course enrollment in the MSALT sample. As described above, analyses here were somewhat more complex because

TABLE 4.4
Multinomial Regression Models Predicting Course Enrollment in Math and English: Odds Ratios for the Michigan Study of Academic Life Transitions Sample

	Model 1		Model 2		Model 3	
Variable	Low	High	Low	High	Low	High
	Mathematics: Course level					
Gender[a]	1.00	1.46*	0.97	1.46*	0.99	1.48*
Math achievement	0.40**	2.61**	0.42**	2.00*	0.42**	1.96*
English achievement	0.85†	1.55	0.84†	1.69	0.84	1.70
Math self-concept			0.84†	1.88**	0.85	1.28
English self-concept			0.86†	1.23*	0.81†	1.38*
Math intrinsic value					0.99	1.63**
English intrinsic value					1.11	.87
R^2	.29		.33		.34	
	English: Course level					
Gender[a]	0.91	0.71*	0.95	0.77†	0.90	0.77†
Math achievement	0.75**	1.47**	0.78*	1.38**	0.77*	1.38**
English achievement	1.01	1.47**	0.98	1.42**	0.97	1.42**
Math self-concept			0.89	1.15†	0.96	1.13
English self-concept			1.05	1.34**	1.22	1.36**
Math intrinsic value					0.86	1.03
English intrinsic value					0.79*	0.98
R^2	.12		.14		.15	

Note. Low = low-level course; high = high-level course.
[a]Female = 0; male = 1.
†$p < .10$. *$p < .05$. **$p < .01$.

the three-level course categorization used for the MSALT study made it necessary to use multinomial regression analyses. Table 4.4 documents the results of regression models predicting course enrollment in Grade 12 by Grade 11 predictor variables. The two columns per model contain the ORs of being enrolled in a low versus intermediate and in a high versus intermediate course, respectively. Predictions regarding enrollment in math classes are summarized in the upper half of the table, and predictions regarding enrollment in English classes in the lower half of the table. Gender and achievement in mathematics and English were included as predictors in the first model. Math achievement had a strong impact on enrollment in an advanced math course. Low math achievement was associated with a high probability of attending a low-level math class (OR = 0.40, $p < .01$), whereas high math achievement was associated with a higher likelihood of choosing a high-level course (OR = 2.61, $p < .01$). A comparable pattern of results was found for English achievement, although the coefficients did not reach the significance level. Compared with the results without controlling for achievement (see Table 4.2), the inclusion of school achievement did not change the predicted gender effects on math outcomes. In Model 2, domain-specific self-concepts were added to the variable list. The findings for both variables are similar. Low math self-concept increased the probability of enrolling in a low-level math course ($p < .10$). High math and English self-concept increased the probability of attending a high-level math course. In Model 3, the intrinsic value scales were added. These additional variables did not change the influence of gender and achievement on math course enrollment. When controlling for intrinsic values, math self-concept no longer had an effect, whereas the effect of math intrinsic value on enrolling in a high-level math course reached statistical significance ($OR = 1.63$, $p < .01$).

Finally, we turn to the prediction of enrollment into English courses in the MSALT sample. In Model 1—in which achievement and gender were included as predictor variables—both math and English achievement predicted attendance of a high-level English course ($OR = 1.47$, $p < .01$). Enrollment in a low-level course was predicted by math achievement only ($OR = 0.75$, $p < .01$). Comparison with Table 4.2 reveals that the gender effect on course enrollment in English was only slightly affected by the inclusion of achievement scores. In Model 3, English self-concept turned out to be predictive of the choice of a high-level English course ($OR = 1.34$, $p < .01$). A similar effect was found for math self-concept ($OR = 1.15$, $p < .10$). The addition of self-concepts in Model 2 did not change the effects of the previous variables. Model 3 revealed that a high intrinsic value attached to English decreased the likelihood of choosing a low-level course ($OR = 0.79$, $p < .05$). The effects of gender, achievement, and self-concept remained stable after intrinsic value was included in Model 3.

To summarize the results for the MSALT data set, high math and English achievement, high math and English self-concept, and high intrinsic value predicted higher course levels chosen in the respective domains. The effect of achievement was partly mediated by self-concept and intrinsic value, highlighting the important role of these two variables in predicting course choices. It is interesting that although gender was associated with a distinct pattern of achievement, self-concept, and intrinsic value, gender effects on course choices were not mediated by these variables. In the multinomial regression models, no evidence was found for negative cross-domain effects on course enrollment, indicating that ipsative-like choice processes did not take place. This is probably adaptive in the U.S. school system, where adolescents who plan to attend college after high school are required to choose relatively demanding courses in both domains.

DISCUSSION

In this study, we examined a model to predict high school course choice that integrated the I/E model (Marsh, 1986) and Eccles et al.'s (1983) EV theory. We tested this model in two different educational systems, those of

Germany and the United States. Overall, the results supported most of our predictions. First, we found support for the merits of our combined I/E and EV model. On the one hand, we found evidence for internal comparison processes as posited in the I/E model. On the other hand, our assumption that self-concept and intrinsic value are both important predictors of course enrollment was confirmed. We also found gender to have a significant effect on self-concept and intrinsic value even after controlling for achievement.

Third, there were marked differences in the explanatory power of our model in the U.S. and German samples. As expected, self-concept and intrinsic value were more powerful predictors in the German sample, whereas achievement proved to be of specific predictive power in the U.S. sample. In addition, evidence for ipsative-like decision processes was much stronger in the German sample. Moreover, gender was more closely linked to course selection in Germany. Somewhat unexpectedly, however, gender effects on course selection were mediated by self-concept and intrinsic value in the German sample only. In the following, we discuss the main results of our study in more detail, before outlining its limitations and providing an outlook on future research.

Gendered Course Choice: The Impact of Educational Systems

Academic decision making is always situated within a specific educational context. In this study, we have argued that to fully understand boys' and girls' high school choices, attention must be paid to the specific affordances and constraints of the respective educational system (Schnabel et al., 2002). To examine context effects of this kind, we compared high school choices in the United States and in Germany. Our results indicate that characteristics of educational systems impact on whether and why young men and women enroll in high- or low-level math and English classes. Because these early specializations in specific fields foreshadow future academic choices and subsequent career opportunities, it is vital to consider such differences in educational opportunity structures if educational and occupational trajectories are to be better understood.

We found several marked differences between the U.S. and German samples in our study. First, in bivariate analyses, gender effects in course enrollment were more pronounced in the German sample than in the U.S. sample. In addition, although our combined EV and I/E framework helped to predict course choices, gender effects were substantially mediated by self-concept and intrinsic value in the German sample only; in a related vein, the negative cross-domain effects postulated by the I/E model were more pronounced in the German sample. Finally, relative to the German sample, achievement had more bearing on course choice in the U.S. sample. The finding that the achievement level in both domains investigated related positively to the level of the courses subsequently undertaken is especially intriguing because—given the skewed distribution of the achievement scores (see the Method section)—

the reported effect sizes are likely to be underestimated. This finding strengthens our interpretation that achievement is a key determinant of students' course choices in the United States.

How can these differences in the academic choice behavior of U.S. and German students be explained? In our view, the pattern of results can be traced back—at least in part—to some key characteristics of the respective school systems. In Germany, *Gymnasium* students are obliged to select two advanced courses, whereas high-achieving students in the United States are free to study several advanced classes. The choice of advanced courses is irrelevant to college admission in Germany, whereas it is important for U.S. students to have completed "college preparatory" courses.

Given these educational constraints, it is plausible that the need to choose two advanced courses triggers ipsative-like comparison processes in *Gymnasium* students, whereas high-achieving, college-bound youth in the United States, where success in advanced math and English classes is a critical entrance criterion, may opt for several advanced courses in order to boost their chances of college acceptance. In other words, the pattern of results implies that adolescents in Germany and the U.S. engage in different kinds of decision-making processes. In the United States, students applying to enter a high-prestige college will be likely to enroll in as many high-level courses as are possible and feasible at school. In Germany, because they are restricted to two advanced courses, *Gymnasium* students are forced to engage in a decision-making process in which self-concepts and intrinsic value become paramount.

Implications for Gendered Occupational Choices

In our view, the foundations for gendered occupational outcomes are often laid well before the end of high school or college. It is important for educators and policymakers to realize the extent to which educational structures may contribute to widening gender gaps (e.g., Lubinski & Benbow, 1992). High school course selection is a gateway to the field of study chosen at college and, consequently, to occupational outcomes (e.g., Schnabel & Gruehn, 2000).

Empirical evidence from Germany shows that the choice of advanced courses at secondary school is closely connected to the field of study at college (Schnabel & Gruehn, 2000; Watermann & Maaz, 2004). This certainly makes sense, to the extent that the decisions made at the high school and college levels are based on a similar rationale. At the same time, gender-differentiated patterns of course enrollment are likely to increase differences between young men and women, because advanced courses take up considerable time and resources over a two-year period and profoundly impact on achievement profiles by the end of college. Accordingly, gender differences in course enrollment are likely to increase gender differences in abilities, self-concepts, and intrinsic values at the end of high school, which in turn have an impact on the choice of college majors.

In contrast to the German system, the U.S. educational system fosters course choices that are primarily based on achievement. Because course level is an important factor in access to higher education, it seems reasonable to assume that males and females are both motivated to choose as many advanced courses as possible, irrespective of the domain. We anticipate that this selection rationale counteracts domain-specific gender achievement differences. Consequently, we expect gender differences in achievement at the end of high school to be less pronounced in the United States than in Germany. Policymakers may consider this a desirable outcome. However, it is important to note that minimizing gender differences in domain-specific achievement does not necessarily mean that gender differences in college major choices and/or occupational choices are minimized as well. Rather, it seems that U.S. students' decision-making processes at the end of high school and the predictive patterns of their subsequent choices of college majors are similar to those observed in the present study in the BIJU sample. From this perspective it seems that to a certain extent, the German educational system forces secondary school students to enter a decision-making process that is delayed until college in the United States. In support of this argument, when the MSALT data are used to predict college majors, the pattern of results is much more similar to the BIJU results than is the pattern obtained for the MSALT high school sample in the present study (e.g., Eccles & Vida, 2003; Garrett, Cortina, & Eccles, 2007).

Limitations and Outlook

In our view, the cross-national perspective on gender effects is an illuminating one. Specifically, this approach made it possible to show how educational contexts moderate the impact of gender effects. At the same time, however, the complexities surrounding the comparison of studies performed in different countries need to be addressed, especially when—as was the case in the current project—the two databases are not designed to be equivalent. First, it has to be reiterated that the instruments used are of high overall quality in both samples, but were not identical. Second, whereas the dependent variable—course choice—is a clear-cut zero-one variable in the German data, a category system had to be developed a priori to classify the course types in the MSALT data. Assuming that this classification is not perfectly reliable, the reported effect sizes for the MSALT data will slightly underestimate effects. Third, we compared two domains in both studies: math and English. Clearly, English has a somewhat different meaning in the German sample (where it is a foreign language) than in the U.S. sample. Testing the I/E model in a study with a large sample of German students, Möller, Streblow, Pohlmann, and Köller (2004) observed a similar relationship between math and German as between math and English. This suggests that we would be likely to obtain similar findings if we examined math and German rather than math and English. A more direct test of this hypothesis would be desirable, however.

Another limitation of our study is its use of intrinsic value as the only "value" component of the EV model—simply because of the scales that were available in both of the two studies. The other expectancy-value components of utility value, attainment value, and cost were not systematically examined. Further work is needed to evaluate whether these components improve the prediction of students' course choices and mediate the gender differences observed in course enrollment rates.

Finally, although we documented early consequences of gendered educational self-concepts and intrinsic values (course choice at high school), we were not able to describe the processes that led to differences in self-concept and intrinsic value in boys and girls more directly. EV theory (Eccles et al., 1983, 1998) gives a fuller account of how cultural norms surrounding gender contribute to the early development of specific patterns of self-concept and intrinsic value in school careers. Subsequent studies should expand the research design used in our study by assessing these variables longitudinally. This would give a more complete picture of the longitudinal processes of increasing subject specialization. An expanded longitudinal design would not only permit course choices to be studied as consequences of self-concepts and intrinsic values but also allow the ramifications of the courses chosen on the development of these constructs to be investigated.

CONCLUSION

In sum, our cross-national approach proved useful for explaining gender effects at the high school level. As our data show, school systems that require early specialization can lead to the amplification of gendered course choices. Given that early course choices have an impact on subsequent career decisions (e.g., Schnabel & Gruehn, 2000; Sells, 1980), compulsory early specialization may even increase the gender segmentation of the workforce. However, the impact of school contexts on individual decisions clearly warrants further comparative, longitudinal studies from several countries around the world to provide deeper insights into students' educational decisions and consequences of these decisions for individual careers. These studies would ideally use the same instruments for all samples and be longitudinal in design. We believe that our model, which encompasses key elements of two prominent and well-validated theoretical propositions, will serve as a fruitful vehicle in this endeavor.

REFERENCES

Allison, P. D. (2001). *Missing data* (Sage University Papers Series on Quantitative Applications in the Social Sciences, 07-136). Thousand Oaks, CA: Sage.

Baumert, J., Gruehn, S., Heyn, S., Köller, O., & Schnabel, K. U. (1997). *Bildungsverläufe und psychosoziale Entwicklung im Jugendalter (BIJU). Dokumentation—Band 1* [Learning Processes, Educational Careers, and Psychosocial Development in Adolescence. Documentation—Vol. 1]. Berlin, Germany: Max Planck Institute for Human Development.

Baumert, J., Roeder, P. M., Gruehn, S., Heyn, S., Köller, O., Rimmele, R., et al. (1996). Bildungsverläufe und psychosoziale Entwicklung im Jugendalter (BIJU) [Learning processes, educational careers, and psychosocial development in adolescence (BIJU)]. In K.-P. Treumann, G. Neubauer, R. Moeller, & J. Abel (Eds.), *Methoden und Anwendungen empirischer pädagogischer Forschung* (pp. 170–180). Münster, Germany: Waxmann.

Bryk, A. S., & Raudenbush, S. W. (1992). *Hierarchical linear models: Applications and data analysis methods.* Newbury Park, CA: Sage.

Curran, P. J., West, S. G., & Finch, J. F. (1996). The robustness of test statistics to non-normality and specification error in confirmatory factor analysis. *Psychological Methods, 1,* 16–29.

Eccles, J. S. (1994). Understanding women's educational and occupational choices: Applying the Eccles et al. model of achievement-related choices. *Psychology of Women Quarterly, 18,* 585–609.

Eccles, J. S., Adler, T. F., Futterman, R., Goff, S. B., Kaczala, C. M., Meece, J. L., & Midgley, C. (1983). Expectancies, values, and academic behaviors. In J. T. Spence (Ed.), *Achievement and achievement motivation* (pp. 75–146). San Francisco: Freeman.

Eccles, J. S., Lord, S. E., & Roeser, R. W. (1996). Round holes, square pegs, rocky roads, and sore feet: The impact of stage/environment fit on young adolescents' experiences in schools and families. In S. L. Toth & D. Cicchetti (Eds.), *Adolescence: Opportunities and challenges* (Vol. 7, pp. 49–93). New York: University of Rochester Press.

Eccles, J. S., & Vida, M. (2003, April). *Predicting mathematics-related educational and career choices.* Paper presented at the Biennial Meeting of the Society for Research on Adolescence, Baltimore.

Eccles, J. S., Vida, M., & Barber, B. L. (2004). The relation of early adolescent plans, and both academic ability and task value beliefs to subsequent college enrollment. *Journal of Early Adolescence, 24,* 63–77.

Eccles, J. S., & Wigfield, A. (2002). Motivational beliefs, values, and goals. *Annual Review of Psychology, 53,* 109–132.

Eccles, J. S., Wigfield, A., & Schiefele, U. (1998). Motivation to succeed. In W. Damon & N. Eisenberg (Eds.), *Handbook of child development* (5th ed., Vol. 3, pp. 1017–1095). New York: Wiley.

Feather, N. T. (1988). Values, valences, and course enrollment: Testing the role of personal values within an expectancy-value framework. *Journal of Educational Psychology, 80,* 381–391.

Garrett, J., Cortina, K. S., & Eccles, J. S. (2007). *When expectancies and values become majors: A longitudinal study on motivation in the transition to college*. Manuscript in preparation.

Hosenfeld, I., Köller, O., & Baumert, J. (1999). Why sex differences in mathematics achievement disappear in German secondary schools: A reanalysis of the German TIMSS-data. *Studies in Educational Evaluation, 25*, 143–161.

Jacobs, J. E., Lanza, S., Osgood, D. W., Eccles, J. S., & Wigfield, A. (2002). Changes in children's self-competence and values: Gender and domain differences across grades one through twelve. *Child Development, 73*, 509–527.

Jöreskog, K. G., Sörbom, D., Du Toit, S., & Du Toit, M. (2000). *LISREL 8: New statistical features* (2nd printing with revisions). Lincolnwood, IL: Scientific Software International.

Köller, O., Baumert, J., & Schnabel, K. U. (2001). Does interest matter? The relationship between academic interest and achievement in mathematics. *Journal for Research in Mathematics Education, 32*, 448–470.

Krapp, A. (1999). Interest, motivation, and learning: An educational–psychological perspective. *European Journal of Psychology of Education, 14*, 23–40.

Lubinski, D., & Benbow, C. P. (1992). Gender differences in abilities and preferences among the gifted: Implications of the math–science pipeline. *Current Directions in Psychological Science, 1*, 61–66.

Marsh, H. W. (1986). Verbal and math self-concepts: An internal/external frame of reference model. *American Educational Research Journal, 23*, 129–149.

Marsh, H. W., & Hau, K.-T. (2004). Explaining paradoxical relations between academic self-concepts and achievements: Cross-cultural generalizability of the internal/external frame of reference predictions across 26 countries. *Journal of Educational Psychology, 96*, 56–67.

Marsh, H. W., & O'Neill, R. (1984). Self Description Questionnaire III: The construct validity of multidimensional self-concept ratings by late adolescents. *Journal of Educational Measurement, 21*, 153–174.

Marsh, H. W., Trautwein, U., Lüdtke, O., Köller, O., & Baumert, J. (2005). Academic self-concept, interest, grades and standardized test scores: Reciprocal effects models of causal ordering. *Child Development, 76*, 397–416.

Marsh, H. W., & Yeung, A. S. (1997). Causal effects of academic self-concept on academic achievement: Structural equation models of longitudinal data. *Journal of Educational Psychology, 89*, 41–54.

Meredith, W. (1993). Measurement invariance, factor analysis and factorial invariance. *Psychometrika, 58*, 525–543.

Möller, J., & Köller, O. (2001). Dimensional comparisons: An experimental approach to the internal/external frame of reference model. *Journal of Educational Psychology, 93*, 826–835.

Möller, J., & Köller, O. (2004). Die Genese akademischer Selbstkonzepte: Effekte dimensionaler und sozialer Vergleiche [On the development of academic self-concepts: The impact of social and dimensional comparisons]. *Psychologische Rundschau, 55*, 19–27.

Möller, J., Streblow, L., Pohlmann, B., & Köller, O. (2004). *An extension to the internal/external frame of reference model to two verbal and numerical domains*. Manuscript submitted for publication.

Muthén, B. O. (1984). A general structural equation model with dichotomous, ordered categorical, and continuous latent variable indicators. *Psychometrika, 49*, 115–132.

Muthén, B. O., & Satorra, A. (1995). Complex sample data in structural equation modeling. In P. V. Marsden (Ed.), *Sociological methodology* (pp. 267–316). Washington, DC: American Sociological Association.

Muthén, L. K., & Muthén, B. O. (2004). *Mplus user's guide* (3rd ed.). Los Angeles: Author.

Nagy, G., Trautwein, U., Köller, O., Baumert, J., & Garrett, J. (2006). Gender and course selection in upper secondary education: Effects of academic self-concept and intrinsic value. *Educational Research and Evaluation, 12*, 323–345.

National Science Foundation, Division of Science Resources and Statistics. (2004). *Women, minorities, and persons with disabilities in science and engineering: 2004* (NSF 04-3174). Arlington, VA: Author.

Office of Michigan Merit Award Program. (2000). *Design and validity of the MEAP Test*. Lansing: Michigan Department of the Treasury.

Rubin, D. B. (1987). *Multiple imputation for nonresponse in surveys*. New York: Wiley.

Schafer, J. L. (1999). NORM for Windows 95/98/NT [Computer software]. University Park, PA: Penn State Department of Statistics.

Schnabel, K., Alfeld, C., Eccles, J. S., Köller, O., & Baumert, J. (2002). Parental influence on students' educational choices in the U.S.A. and Germany: Different ramifications—same effect? *Journal of Vocational Behavior, 60*, 178–198.

Schnabel, K. U., & Gruehn, S. (2000). Studienfachwünsche und Berufsorientierungen in der gymnasialen Oberstufe [Aspired courses of college study and career orientations in the final years of *Gymnasium* schooling]. In J. Baumert, W. Bos, & R. Lehmann (Eds.), *TIMSS/III: Dritte Internationale Mathematik- und Naturwissenschaftstudie. Mathematische und naturwissenschaftliche Bildung am Ende der Schullaufbahn: Vol. 2. Mathematische und physikalische Kompetenzen am Ende der gymnasialen Oberstufe* (pp. 405–443). Opladen, Germany: Leske + Budrich.

Schwanzer, A., Trautwein, U., Lüdtke, O., & Sydow, H. (2005). Entwicklung eines Instruments zur Erfassung des Selbstkonzepts junger Erwachsener [Development of a questionnaire on young adults' self-concept]. *Diagnostica, 51*, 183–194.

Sells, L. W. (1980). Mathematics: The invisible filter. *Engineering Education, 70*, 340–341.

Statistisches Bundesamt. (2001). *Bildung und Kultur. Studierende an Hochschulen* [Education and culture. Students in higher education] (Series 11, No. 4.1). Stuttgart, Germany: Metzler-Poeschel.

Trautwein, U. (2003). *Schule und Selbstwert* [Schools and self-esteem]. Münster, Germany: Waxmann.

Watermann, R., & Maaz, K. (2004). Studienneigung bei Absolventen allgemein bildender und beruflicher Gymnasien [Aspirations to higher education among graduates from traditional and vocational *Gymnasium* schools]. In O. Köller, R. Watermann, U. Trautwein, & O. Lüdtke (Eds.), *Wege zur Hochschulreife in Baden-Württemberg: TOSCA—Eine Untersuchung an allgemein bildenden und beruflichen Gymnasien* (pp. 403–450). Opladen, Germany: Leske + Budrich.

Watt, H. M. G. (2004). Development of adolescents' self-perceptions, values, and task perceptions according to gender and domain in 7th- through 11th-grade Australian students. *Child Development, 75,* 1556–1574.

Wigfield, A., & Eccles, J. S. (2000). Expectancy-value theory of achievement motivation. *Contemporary Educational Psychology, 25,* 68–81.

Wigfield, A., Eccles, J. S., & Pintrich, P. R. (1996). Development between the ages of 11 and 25. In D. C. Berliner & R. C. Calfee (Eds.), *Handbook of educational psychology* (pp. 148–185). New York: Macmillan Library.

5

TESTING FOR TIME-INVARIANT AND TIME-VARYING PREDICTORS OF SELF-PERCEIVED ABILITY IN MATH, LANGUAGE ARTS, AND SCIENCE: A LOOK AT THE GENDER FACTOR

BARBARA M. BYRNE

Self-perceived ability has been identified as having a compelling influence on gendered career outcomes. One prime example is that of self-perceived ability in math and language arts (e.g., chap. 3, this volume), as well as science (e.g., chap. 6, this volume). The question of why and how this phenomenon occurs continues to be an enigma of enormous interest. In the process of seeking answers to this intriguing developmental query, researchers have identified gender differences in self-perceived ability related to each of these subject areas at various time points along the continuum from elementary school through college. However, a review of the literature to date reveals scant information on the extent to which these differences vary across time within the parameters of the continuum.

One methodological ploy that can be effective in addressing this issue is the use of latent growth curve (LGC) modeling within the framework of structural equation modeling (SEM). As such, all postulated longitudinal structures are tested on the basis of the analysis of mean and covariance structures. The focus of this chapter, in broad terms, is to exemplify the SEM approach to LGC

I extend my sincere thanks to Gail Crombie for making these data available to me for the purposes of demonstrating the latent growth curve models in this chapter.

modeling in testing for change over time. More specifically, I demonstrate the strategy involved in testing for predictors of change in self-perceived ability in math, language arts, and science from Grade 8 through Grade 10. Gender is examined as a time-invariant predictor, and academic grades related to each of the three subject areas are examined as time-varying predictors. To further test for possible gender effects in the prediction of self-perceived ability from academic grades, the latter predictor model is tested separately for adolescent males and females. This illustration of LGC on an identified predictor of gendered occupational outcomes—self-concept of ability—adds to understanding how self-concepts develop through adolescence. It also illustrates how this approach can be used to model how other important psychological precursors to gendered occupational outcomes may develop.

This chapter is written in a didactic mode that embraces a nonmathematical, rather than a statistically oriented, approach to the topic. Working within the framework of SEM, I introduce the basic concepts associated with LGC modeling and then walk the reader through three related, albeit increasingly complex, applications designed to measure change across a 3-year span. I am hopeful that this pedagogical journey through these three applications of LGC modeling will both encourage and enable more researchers to use this strategy in the measurement of change as it relates to gender differences in self-perceptions of ability.

MEASURING CHANGE IN INDIVIDUAL GROWTH OVER TIME: THE GENERAL NOTION

In answering questions of individual change related to one or more domains of interest, a representative sample of individuals must be observed systematically over time and their status in each domain measured on several temporally spaced occasions (Willett & Sayer, 1994). However, several conditions may also need to be met to undertake LGC modeling within the SEM framework. First, the outcome variable representing the domain of interest must be of a continuous scale. Second, although the time lag between occasions can be either evenly or unevenly spaced, both the number and the spacing of these assessments must be the same for all individuals. Third, when the focus of individual change is structured as an LGC model, with analyses to be conducted using an SEM approach, data must be obtained for each individual on three or more occasions. Finally, the sample size must be large enough to allow for the detection of person-level effects (Willett & Sayer, 1994). Moreover, when analyses entail SEM, a methodology grounded in large-sample theory that assumes data to be multivariate normal, sample size requirements become even more critical. Accordingly, one would expect minimum sample sizes of not less than 200 at each time point (see Boomsma, 1985; Boomsma & Hoogland, 2001).

In presenting a logically ordered introduction to the topic of LGC modeling as it relates to the issue of gender, models illustrated in this chapter are presented as three separate applications. In Application 1, I describe components of the hypothesized multiple-domain LGC model under test. This model (Model 1) includes the three output variables of perceived ability in math, language arts, and science and serves as the preliminary model in determining the validity of testing for gender as a viable predictor in explaining change. On the basis of findings that support predictive inquiry, I then move on to Application 2, which extends the multiple-domain model to include the time-invariant (i.e., fixed) predictor variable of gender, in order to examine gendered changes in self-concept over time. Finally, in Application 3, I extend the multiple-domain model of Application 1 to include predictors that are time varying. As such, both the outcome variables (self-perceived math, language arts, and science ability) and the predictor variables (math, language arts, and science grades) are specified in the hypothesized model and tested separately for adolescent males and females. This final model examines gendered developmental trajectories for self-concept while controlling for individuals' concurrent changes in achievement.

The Example Data

The three applications presented in this chapter are based on three waves of data comprising individuals' self-ratings of perceived academic ability in Grades, 8, 9, and 10 for 601 adolescents. More specifically, the data represent subscale scores related to self-perceived ability in math, language arts, and science. Consistent with most longitudinal research, some subject attrition occurred over the 3-year period; 101 cases were lost, thereby leaving 500 cases (246 males, 254 females) with complete data. Although it is possible to address this issue of "missingness" by basing analyses on a multiple-sample missing-data model that involves three time-specific groups (see Byrne & Crombie, 2003; Duncan & Duncan, 1994), this approach is most easily applied to relatively simple models. Because the time-varying model presented in Application 3 of this chapter represents a very complex model, it does not lend itself easily to analyses using this multiple-sample approach. Thus, in the interest of simplicity, expediency, and space, I considered it best to base analyses for all three applications on complete data (although the pattern of results tested in Applications 1 and 2 also replicated across complete and multiple-sample data analyses).

Instrumentation

The Perceived Math Ability subscale, taken from the Student Attitude Questionnaire (see Eccles, 1983; Jacobs & Eccles, 1992), is designed to measure children's beliefs and attitudes about mathematics. Measurements of self-perceived ability in language arts and science were based on items from the Math subscale, with "math" modified to "language arts" and "science" for these two additional domains. The three 7-point Likert-scaled items included in each subscale assess students' perceptions of how good they are at math (language arts, science) (a) in an absolute sense (1 = *not at all good*, 7 = *very good*), (b) relative to other students in their class (1 = *the worst*, 7 = *the best*), and (c) relative to other school subjects (1 = *much worse*, 7 = *much better*). Moderately high internal consistency reliability (*Mdn* α = .84) for the Math subscale has been reported (Eccles, Adler, & Meece, 1984; Fuligni, Eccles, & Barber, 1995; Jacobs & Eccles, 1992; Parsons, Adler, & Kaczala, 1982). For the present sample, similarly high median coefficient alpha values over the 3-year period were obtained for the Math (.91), Language Arts (.88), and Science (.92) subscales, and test–retest reliability, measured over a 1-month period for a randomly selected subsample of 62 students, was found to be .91, .88, and .92, respectively.

Procedure

Working within a classroom setting, trained researchers administered the questionnaires to small groups of 10 to 25 students during the months of April and May for each of 3 years, spanning Grades 8, 9, and 10. Data collection at this time of the year ensured that students were at least 80% of the way through the school year and thus had a good sense of their ability in each of the targeted subject areas.

APPLICATION 1: TESTING FOR VALIDITY OF A MULTIPLE-DOMAIN LATENT GROWTH CURVE MODEL

Willett and Sayer (1994) have noted that the basic building blocks of the LGC model consist of two underpinning submodels that they term *Level 1* and *Level 2* models. The Level 1 model can be thought of as a "within-person" regression model that represents individual change over time with respect to time-varying factors that are measured on each occasion—for example, academic grades and self-perceived ability in math, language arts, and science. In contrast, the Level 2 model can be viewed as a "between-person" model that focuses on interindividual differences in change with respect to these outcome variables—for example, differential changes for boys versus girls.

Modeling Intraindividual Change

The first step in building an LGC model is to examine the within-person growth trajectory. In the present case, this task translates into determining, for each individual, the direction and extent to which his or her score in self-perceived ability in math, language arts, and science changes from Grade 8 through Grade 10. Of critical import in most appropriately specifying and testing the LGC model, however, is that the shape of the growth trajectory be known a priori. If the trajectory of hypothesized change is considered to be linear (for a description and illustration of tests for linearity related to LGC models, see Byrne & Crombie, 2003), then the specified model will include two growth parameters: (a) an intercept parameter representing an individual's score on the outcome variable at Time 1 and (b) a slope parameter representing the individual's rate of change over the time period of interest. On the basis of our work here, because the growth metric was centered at the initial time-point (Grade 8), the intercept represents a "typical" adolescent's self-perceived ability in math, language arts, and science at the end of Grade 8, and the slope represents the rate of change in these values over the 3-year transition from Grade 8 through Grade 10.

Of the many advantages in testing for individual change within the framework of a structural equation model, over other longitudinal strategies, two are of primary importance. First, this approach is based on the analysis of mean and covariance structures and, as such, distinction is made between observed and unobserved (or latent) variables in the specification of models. Second, the methodology allows for both the modeling and estimation of measurement error. With these basic concepts in hand, I turn now to Figure 5.1, which represents the model of best fit to the data for Application 1 (Model 1a).[1]

For readers who may not be familiar with the symbols associated with structural equation models, a brief explanation is in order. By convention, circles (or ellipses) represent unobserved factors, squares (or rectangles) represent observed variables, single-headed arrows ($\rightarrow$) represent the impact of one variable on another, and curved double-headed arrows ($\overset{\curvearrowright}{\curvearrowleft}$) represent covariances or correlations between pairs of variables. In building a model for study, researchers use these symbols in one of four basic configurations, each of which represents an important component in the analytic process. Let us now examine these four configurations as they relate to the LGC model (Model 1a) shown in Figure 5.1. For simplicity, I limit specifics in the text to only the first of the three constructs (i.e., self-perceived ability in math); however, interpretations are comparable for all three constructs.

Focus first on the three rectangles at the bottom of the path diagram. The labels "Perceived Math Ability1" through "Perceived Math Ability3" represent the observed scores on self-perceived math ability collected at each of three time points. The "E" associated with each of these observed variables represents

---

[1]As will be reviewed later, the originally hypothesized model (Model 1) was modified to address misspecification in the model; Model 1a represents this modified model.

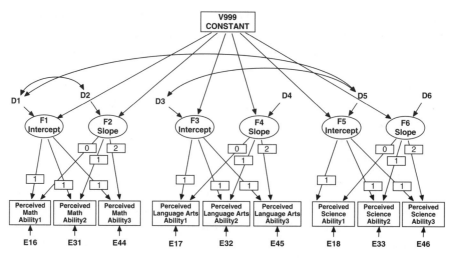

Figure 5.1. Hypothesized latent growth curve model of perceived math, language arts, and science ability. From "Modeling and Testing Change Over Time: An Introduction to the Latent Growth Curve Model," by B. M. Byrne and G. Crombie, 2003, *Understanding Statistics: Statistical Issues in Psychology, Education, and the Social Sciences, 2,* p. 191. Copyright 2003 by Lawrence Erlbaum Associates. Reprinted with permission.

random measurement error.[2] The two variables enclosed in circles represent the unobserved Intercept and Slope factors; they are designated as Factor 1 (F1) and Factor 2 (F2), respectively. Factors 3 and 4 relate to self-perceived ability in language arts, and Factors 5 and 6 to self-perceived ability in science. The "D" associated with each of these factors represents a residual term. In more general models, these variables represent residual error associated with the regression of unobserved factors on other unobserved factors in the model. Specific to the LGC model, however, these residuals represent individual differences in the intercept and linear growth trajectories, respectively. Finally, the rectangle labeled "Constant" is specially designated as variable V999 within the framework of EQS (Bentler, 2005), the SEM program used for all analyses of the present data.[3] It provides the mechanism by which a covariance structure is transformed into a mean and covariance (or *moment*) structure.

We turn now to the symbols used to connect each of these observed and unobserved variables—again with respect to self-perceived ability in math

---

[2]The labeling system applied in Figures 5.1, 5.2, and 5.3 is consistent with the notation of the EQS program. Accordingly, the numeral associated with each error term is consistent with the location of the related variable in the data set. For example, the variable "Perceived Math Ability" is the 16th variable in the data set; hence an error term labeled "E16."

[3]The rationale underlying the labeling of V999 is that relative to the measured variables in the program input file, the constant is always considered last (Byrne, 2006).

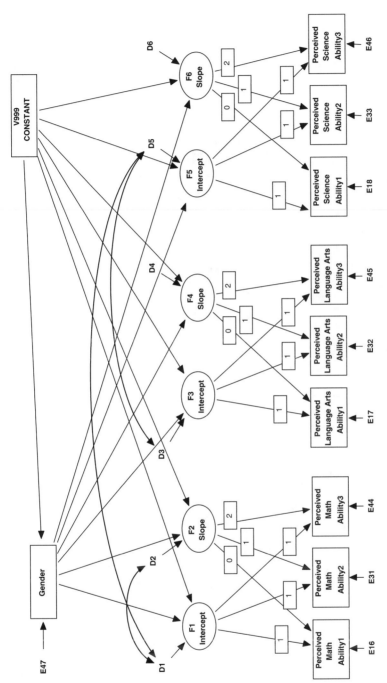

Figure 5.2. Hypothesized latent growth curve model of perceived math, language arts, and science ability with gender as a time-invariant predictor. From "Modeling and Testing Change Over Time: An Introduction to the Latent Growth Curve Model," by B. M. Byrne and G. Crombie, 2003, *Understanding Statistics: Statistical Issues in Psychology, Education, and the Social Sciences, 2,* p. 197. Copyright 2003 by Lawrence Erlbaum Associates. Reprinted with permission.

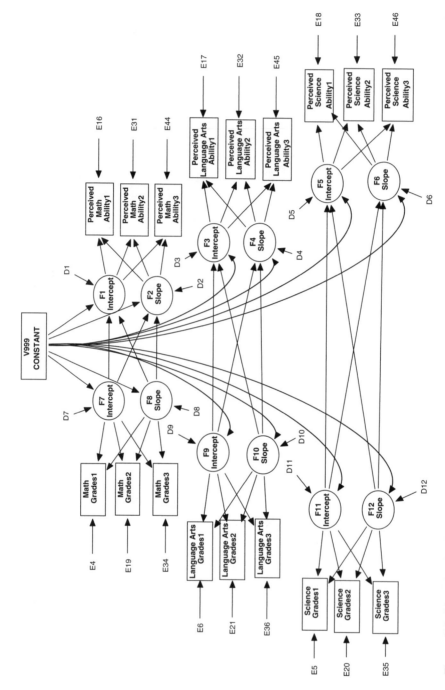

Figure 5.3. Hypothesized latent growth curve model of perceived math, language arts, and science ability with grades in math, language arts, and science as time-varying predictors.

only. Although each single-headed arrow represents a regression coefficient, its interpretative meaning varies according to whether or not it leads from a source variable. As such, the arrows leading from F1 and F2 to the three observed variables represent the regression of self-perceived math ability scores onto both the Intercept and Slope at each of three time points. The arrows leading from the constant to each of the Intercept and Slope factors represent the average intercept (or starting point of the growth curve) and rate of linear growth coefficient, respectively. In contrast, the arrows leading from the Es to the observed variables, and from the Ds to the two Intercept and Slope factors, represent the influence of error as described earlier. The double-headed arrow linking D1 with D2 represents a covariance between these two residuals. Likewise, D3,D4 and D5,D6 were specified in Model 1, and details related to these parameters are outlined later in the chapter. The validity of these hypothesized relations is assumed in the specification of an LGC model, given that each paired intercept and slope relates to the same construct. Explanation regarding the numerical values assigned to the regression paths leading from the Intercept and Slope factors to the observed variables is provided later in the testing of this model.

Recall that our primary focus in this application is to model intraindividual change. Within the framework of SEM, this focus is captured by what is termed the *measurement model*, the portion of a model that incorporates only linkages between the observed variables and their underlying unobserved factors. Of primary interest in any measurement model is the strength of the factor loadings or regression paths linking the observed and unobserved variables. (For a nonmathematical elaboration on fundamental concepts and applications related to SEM, in general, readers are referred to Byrne, 1998, 2001; for LGC models in particular, see Byrne, 2006.) Accordingly, the only parts of the model in Figure 5.1 that are relevant in the modeling of intraindividual change are the two factors (Slope, Intercept), the regression paths linking the three observed variables to these factors, and the measurement errors associated with the observed variables (Perceived Math Ability1 through Perceived Math Ability3). These same descriptions, of course, apply also to the other two constructs in the model—perceived ability in language arts and perceived ability in science.

In preparation for a transition from the modeling of intraindividual change to the modeling of interindividual change, it is important to review briefly the basic concepts underlying the analyses of mean and covariance structures in SEM. When population means are of no interest in a model, analysis is based on covariance structure parameters only; as such, all scores are considered to be deviations from their means and, thus, the constant term (represented as α in a regression equation) equals zero. Given that mean values play no part in the specification of the Level 1 (or within-person) portion of the LGC model, only the analysis of covariance structures is involved. In moving to Level 2 (the between-person portion of the model), however, interest focuses on mean values associated with the Intercept and Slope factors; these values derive from an analysis of mean structures. Because both levels are involved in the modeling of interindividual differences in change, analyses are based on both mean and covariance structures.

Modeling Interindividual Differences in Change

Level 2 effects demonstrate that over and above hypothesized linear change in self-perceived math, language arts, and science ability over time, trajectories will necessarily vary across different adolescents as a consequence of different intercepts and slopes. Within the framework of SEM, this portion of the model reflects the "structural model" component that in general portrays relations among unobserved factors and postulated relations among their associated residuals. Within the more specific LGC model, however, this structure is limited to the regression paths linking the constant (V999) to the Intercept and Slope factors. Limiting ourselves once again to only self-perceived ability in math, this structure includes the regression paths F1, V999 and F2, V999, along with their related residuals, as reflected in the upper tier of the model shown in Figure 5.1. The specification of these parameters, then, makes possible the estimation of interindividual differences in change. The key element in this specification is the constant term because it provides the mechanism for transforming the covariance structure of the measurement (Level 1) model into the mean structure needed for analysis of the structural (Level 2) model. More specifically, in modeling and testing mean and covariance structures, as is the case here, analysis must be based on the moment matrix, which is made possible by the inclusion of the constant in the model specification. This variable is always taken as an independent variable that has no variance and no covariance with other variables in the model.

Within the usual framework of SEM specification, the model in Figure 5.1 would convey the notion that both the Intercept and Slope factors are predicted by the constant but with some degree of error as captured by the residual terms (D1 and D2); furthermore, these residuals are hypothesized to covary (D1,D2). However, in the special case of an LGC model, as noted earlier, the residuals call for a somewhat different interpretation. Specifically, they are residuals in the sense that they represent individual differences in the intercept and slope parameters. These differences derive from deviations between the individual growth parameters and their respective population means (or average intercept and slope values).

Within the context of this first application, as it relates to self-perceived math ability for example, interest focuses on five parameters that are key to determining between-person differences in change: two factor means (F1,V999; F2,V999), two factor residual variances (D1; D2), and one residual covariance

(D1,D2). The factor means represent the average population values for the Intercept and Slope and answer the question, "What is the population trajectory of true change in self-perceived math ability from Grades 8 through 10?" The factor residuals represent deviations of the individual Intercepts and Slopes from their population means, thereby reflecting population interindividual differences in the initial (Grade 8) self-perceived math ability scores, and the rate of change in these scores, respectively. Addressing the issue of variability, these key parameters (D1; D2) answer the question, "Are there interindividual differences in the growth trajectory of self-perceived math ability in the population?" Finally, the residual covariance (D1,D2) represents the population covariance between any deviations in initial status and rate of change and answers the question, "Is there any evidence of interindividual differences in the association between initial status and rate of change in self-perceived math ability across the time from Grade 8 through Grade 10?"

Testing for Interindividual Differences in Change

The Hypothesized Model

In reviewing the hypothesized LGC model in Figure 5.1, we observe numerical values assigned to the paths flowing from the Intercept and Slope factors to the observed variables, but no such values associated with those linking the constant to these factors. The paths with assigned values represent fixed parameters that will not be estimated. The "1"s specified for the paths flowing from the Intercept factor to each of the observed variables indicate that each is constrained to a value of 1.0. This constraint reflects the fact that the intercept value remains constant across time for each individual (Duncan, Duncan, Stryker, Li, & Alpert, 1999). That is, the observed mean values for self-perceived ability in math, language arts, and science at Time 1 are assumed to remain constant across the three time points. The values of 0, 1, and 2 assigned to the Slope parameters represent Years 1, 2, and 3, respectively. These constraints address the issue of model identification, a complex topic that goes beyond the boundaries of the present chapter (for further elaboration of this concept, see Bollen, 1989; Byrne, 1998, 2001, 2006); they also ensure that the second factor can be interpreted as a slope. Three important points are of interest with respect to these fixed slope values. First, technically speaking, the first path (assigned a zero value) is really nonexistent and, therefore, has no effect. Although it would be less confusing to simply eliminate this parameter, it has become customary to include this path in the model, albeit with an assigned value of zero (Bentler, 2005). Second, these values represent equal time intervals (1 year) between measurements; had data collection taken place at unequal intervals, the values would need to be calculated accordingly (e.g., 6 months = .5). Third, although the choice of fixed values assigned to the Slope factor loadings is arbitrary, it is important to realize that the Intercept factor is tied to a time scale (Duncan et al., 1999). Thus, any shift in fixed loading values on the Slope factor will necessarily modify the scale of time bearing on the Intercept factor, which in turn will influence interpretations related to the Intercept factor mean and variance. Finally, the fact that no numerical values have been assigned to the paths flowing from the constant to each of the factors indicates that these parameters will be freely estimated. These parameters are typically unknown and, as noted earlier, represent the average intercept (or starting point) and average linear growth coefficients.

Statistical Analyses

All analyses were conducted using Version 6.1 of the EQS program (Bentler, 2005). In testing each of the three hypothesized models, goodness-of-fit to the sample data was based on the comparative fit index (CFI; Bentler, 1990) and the root-mean-square error of approximation (RMSEA; Browne & Cudeck, 1993). The CFI ranges in value from 0 to 1.00, with a value of .90 serving as the rule-of-thumb lower limit cut-off point of acceptable fit. The RMSEA takes into account the error of approximation in the population and asks the question, "How well would the model, with unknown but optimally chosen parameter values, fit the population covariance matrix if it were available?" (Browne & Cudeck, 1993, pp. 137–138). This discrepancy, as measured by the RMSEA, is expressed per degree of freedom, thus making it sensitive to model complexity; values less than .05 indicate good fit, and values as high as .08 represent reasonable errors of approximation in the population. Although we report the chi-square statistic in our summaries of model fit, its known sensitivity to sample size necessarily precludes its use as an appropriate measure of goodness-of-fit (see Jöreskog & Sörbom, 1993).

Preanalysis of the data revealed the distribution of scores to be approximately multivariate normal (mean skewness = −0.63; mean kurtosis = 0.17; Mardia's normalized estimate = 12.85. Mardia's normalized estimate of multivariate kurtosis behaves in large samples as a unit normal variable with values less than 10.00, suggesting evidence of multivariate normality; Bentler, 2005). These analyses also revealed evidence of one multivariate outlier; this case was deleted from all subsequent analyses.

Results

Goodness-of-fit statistics related to the initially specified model (Model 1; not shown here) revealed an extremely poor fit to the data, $\chi^2(30) = 255.84$ (CFI = 0.81; RMSEA = 0.12). A review of the z-values associated with the residual covariance between the Intercept and Slope factors representing self-perceived language arts and self-perceived science abilities (D3,D4; D5,D6) found them to be statistically nonsignificant; in the interest of parsimony, these parameters were subsequently deleted from the model.

Another aspect of assessing model fit in SEM, however, is the identification of misspecified parameters; that is, parameters that were constrained to zero (i.e., not estimated) but if freely estimated would lead to a statistically significant improvement in overall model fit to the data. Each SEM program has its own internal mechanism for pinpointing these misfitting parameters; in EQS, the process is based on the Lagrange Multiplier Test, which takes a multivariate approach to the testing of these constraints. A review of these Lagrange Multiplier Test statistics identified two between-domain residual covariances (D1,D5; D3,D5) that if freely estimated would lead to a better fitting model in the sense that it would represent the sample data more appropriately. Given the substantive reasonableness of these residual covariances, together with Willett and Sayer's (1996) caveat that in multiple-domain LGC models, covariation among the growth parameters across domains (as reflected in their residual terms) should be considered, Model 1 was modified to address these concerns. Specifically, this model (Model 1a) was respecified such that the two nonsignificant within-domain residual covariances were deleted and the two between-domain residual covariances were freely estimated. Goodness-of-fit related to this respecified model yielded an excellent fit to the data, $\chi^2(30) = 91.39$ (CFI = 0.95; RMSEA = 0.06). Results presented in Table 5.1 are based on this final model (Model 1a).

Turning, first, to the factor score means, we see that all are statistically significant, except for the slope related to self-perceived language arts ability. Findings related to the Intercepts reveal the average scores for both self-perceived language arts ability (4.89) and self-perceived science ability (4.76) to be slightly lower than those for self-perceived math ability (5.12). However, although the average change in adolescents' self-perceived math ability decreased over a 3-year period from Grade 8 to Grade 10 (as indicated by the value of −0.16), the average change in self-perceived science ability increased (0.12); the change in self-perceived language arts ability was negligible (−0.02), as indicated by its statistical nonsignificance.

Turning next to the residual variance associated with the intercept and slope for each self-perceived ability domain (i.e., the "D"s), we observe all parameters to be statistically significant. These findings reveal strong interindividual differences both in the initial scores of self-perceived ability in math, language arts, and science at Time 1, and in their change over time, as the adolescents progressed from Grade 8 to Grade 10. Such evidence of interindividual differences provides powerful support for further investigation of variability related to the growth trajectories. In particular, the incorporation of predictors into the model can serve to explain their variability.

In reviewing results related to the within-domain residual covariance between the intercept and slope for self-perceived math ability, we find the

TABLE 5.1
Parameter Estimates for Multiple Domain Model (Model 1a)

Variable	Perceived math ability			Perceived language arts ability			Perceived science ability		
	Parameter	Estimate	z-value	Parameter	Estimate	z-value	Parameter	Estimate	z-value
Factor means									
Intercept	F1,V999	5.12	92.56	F3,V999	4.89	107.51	F5,V999	4.76	92.56
Slope	F2,V999	−0.16	−5.10	F4,V999	−0.02	−0.55	F6,V999	0.12	4.12
Factor residuals									
Intercept	D1	1.32	10.33	D3	0.48	9.25	D5	0.62	9.62
Slope	D2	0.25	4.48	D4	0.09	3.18	D6	0.09	3.04
Factor residual covariances									
Intercept/Slope (within domain)	D1,D2	−0.29	−3.95						
Intercept/Slope (between domains)	D1,D5	0.52	9.91	D3,D5	0.21	5.93			
Error variances									
Year 1 (Grade 8)	E16	0.22	2.18	E17	0.66	11.33	E18	0.86	12.31
Year 2 (Grade 9)	E31	0.68	11.17	E32	0.66	11.87	E33	0.79	12.37
Year 3 (Grade 10)	E44	0.99	7.58	E45	0.56	6.05	E46	0.59	5.76

Note. $\chi^2(30) = 91.39$; comparative fit index = .95; root-mean-square error of approximation = .06. z-values > 1.96 indicate statistical significance (*p* < .05).

estimate, as expected, to be statistically significant. The negative value of −0.29 ($r = -.48$) suggests that for adolescents whose self-perceived scores in math ability were high in Grade 8, their rate of increase in scores over the 3-year period from Grade 8 through Grade 10 was lower than it was for adolescents whose self-perceived math ability scores were lower at Time 1.

The first Table 5.1 entry for between-domain residual covariances (D1,D5), shows a strong association between the intercepts of self-perceived ability in math and science (0.52; $r = .57$). Given the commonly perceived link between the subject areas of math and science, this finding would seem to be quite reasonable. Although the residual covariance between the intercepts for self-perceived language arts and science ability (0.21) was also moderately strong ($r = .38$), this finding is of a more curious nature because students who do well in language arts do not necessarily do well in science.

Finally, as is evidenced in Table 5.1, all error variances were found to be statistically significant. In general, although error variability associated with self-perceived language arts and science abilities appears to be relatively consistent across time (i.e., homoscedastic), those associated with self-perceived ability in math are less so. These findings suggest that whereas self-perceived ability in language arts and science remained relatively stable at least from Grade 8 through Grade 9, this pattern did not hold with respect to math, which by contrast was substantially more unstable.

APPLICATION 2: TESTING FOR GENDER AS A TIME-INVARIANT PREDICTOR OF CHANGE

As noted earlier, provided with evidence of interindividual differences, we can then ask whether, and to what extent, one or more predictors might explain this heterogeneity. For our purposes here, we ask whether statistically significant heterogeneity in the individual growth trajectories (i.e., intercept and slope) of self-perceived ability in math, language arts, and/or science can be explained by gender as a time-invariant predictor of change. As such, two questions might be, "Do self-perceptions of ability in math, language arts, and/or science differ for adolescent boys and girls at Time 1 (Grade 8)?" and "Does the rate at which self-perceived ability in math, language arts, and/or science change over time differ for adolescent boys and girls?" To answer these questions, the predictor variable "gender" must be incorporated into the Level 2 (structural) part of the model. This predictor model (Model 2) represents an extension of Model 1a and is shown schematically in Figure 5.2.

Of import regarding the path diagram displayed in Figure 5.2 are the newly added components. The first of these is the regression path leading from the constant to the predictor variable of gender. Essentially, this path represents the mean on the variable of gender. The second set of new components contains the regression paths that flow from gender to the Intercept and Slope factors associated with each self-perceived ability domain. These regression paths are of primary interest in Model 2 as they hold the key in answering the question of whether the trajectories of self-perceived ability in math, language arts, and/or science differ for adolescent boys and girls. Also worthy of note is the fact that with the addition of a predictor variable to the model, interpretation of the residuals necessarily changes; these residuals now represent variation remaining in the Intercepts and Slopes after all variability in their prediction by gender has been explained (Willett & Keiley, 2000). Rephrased within a comparative framework, note that for Model 1a, in which no predictors were specified, the residuals represent deviations between the factor Intercepts and Slopes, and their population means. In contrast, in Model 2, which specifies a predictor variable, the residual variances represent deviations from their conditional population means. These residuals represent the adjusted values of factor Intercepts and Slopes after partialing out the linear effect of the predictor of change (Willett & Keiley, 2000).

Results

Findings related to the analysis of Model 2 are summarized in Table 5.2. As reported in the table note, goodness-of-fit statistics related to this predictor model indicated an exceptionally good fit to the data. Consistent with Table 5.1, the first two rows of Table 5.2 present the average factor Intercept and Slope estimates for each outcome variable. These values exhibit a similar pattern to those reported in Table 5.1.

Lines 3 and 4 in Table 5.2 yield information that is essentially of most interest in the analysis of Model 2. These estimates represent the regression of individual change on gender. Turning first to results for self-perceived math ability, we see that gender was found to be a statistically significant predictor of both initial status (0.55) and rate of change (−0.15). Given a coding of 0 for females and 1 for males, these findings suggest that although self-perceived ability in math was, on average, higher for boys than for girls at Time 1 by 0.55, the rate of change in this perception for boys, from Grade 8 through Grade 10, was slower than it was for girls by a value of 0.15, leading to increasingly convergent self-perceived math ability for boys and girls. In this study, however, it was not determined whether in fact they actually do converge.

Results related to self-perceived language arts ability revealed gender to be a significant predictor of initial status, with boys exhibiting significantly lower perceptions of language arts ability than girls (−0.37). On the other hand, rate of change was indistinguishable between boys and girls as indicated by their nonsignificant estimates. Girls' higher language arts ability self-perceptions were therefore maintained over time.

TABLE 5.2
Parameter Estimates for Time-Invariant Predictor Model (Model 2)

Variable	Perceived math ability			Perceived language arts ability			Perceived science ability		
	Parameter	Estimate	z-value	Parameter	Estimate	z-value	Parameter	Estimate	z-value
Factor means									
Intercept	F1,V999	4.85	63.81	F3,V999	5.07	80.96	F5,V999	4.65	65.13
Slope	F2,V999	−0.09	−2.05	F4,V999	0.03	0.71	F6,V999	0.12	2.79
Factor regression of individual	F1,Gender	0.55	5.09	F3,Gender	−0.37	−4.11	F5,Gender	0.23	2.29
Change on gender	F2,Gender	−0.15	−2.28	F4,Gender	−0.09	−1.57	F6,Gender	0.01	0.22
Factor residuals									
Intercept	D1	1.25	10.07	D3	0.44	8.84	D5	0.59	9.43
Slope	D2	0.25	4.40	D4	0.08	3.02	D6	0.09	3.11
Factor residual covariances									
Intercept/Slope (within domain)	D1,D2	−0.26	−3.80						
Intercept/Slope (between domains)	D1,D5	0.47	9.56	D3,D5	0.21	6.29			
Error variances									
Year 1 (Grade 8)	E16	0.22	2.24	E17	0.67	11.64	E18	0.86	12.32
Year 2 (Grade 9)	E31	0.67	11.19	E32	0.66	12.04	E33	0.79	12.41
Year 3 (Grade 10)	E44	0.98	7.57	E45	0.57	6.17	E46	0.58	5.71

Note. $\chi^2(33) = 95.70$; comparative fit index = 0.95; root-mean-square error of approximation = 0.06. z-values > 1.96 indicate statistical significance ($p < .05$).

Finally, gender once again served as a significant predictor of self-perceived science ability in Grade 8, with boys showing higher scores on average by a value of 0.23. As was the case for self-perceived language arts ability, however, rate of change was indistinguishable across gender, with boys maintaining consistently higher science ability self-perceptions than girls.

APPLICATION 3: TESTING FOR ACADEMIC GRADES AS A TIME-VARYING PREDICTOR OF CHANGE

In contrast to analyses based on a time-invariant predictor, those based on a time-varying predictor allow for the modeling of change as it relates to both the outcome and predictor variables and then for examining whether changes over time in the two variables are related (Willett & Keiley, 2000). For example, with the present data, the question can be raised, "Do self-perceptions of ability in math, language arts, and science increase more rapidly over the period from Grade 8 to Grade 10 for adolescents if their academic grades in these subject areas are also increasing rapidly over the same period of time?" In other words, what is being asked here is whether the rate of change in self-perceived ability in math, language arts, and science is predicted by associated changes in grades related to math, language arts, and science.

To determine the extent to which change in an outcome variable depends on change in a time-varying predictor, within the framework of SEM, individual growth is modeled in both the outcome and predictor variables simultaneously. Related to the present sample data, this means that a model is specified in which self-perceived math, language arts, and science ability (the outcome variables) and grades in math, language arts, and science (the predictor variables) are parameters in the model. The next step, then, is to test the extent to which individual growth parameters representing change in the outcome variables can be predicted by individual growth parameters representing change in the predictor variables (see Willett & Keiley, 2000). A schematic representation of this model is shown in Figure 5.3. It is important to note that in the interest of visual clarity, correlated error and residual terms are not shown here.

In examining this model, you will quickly recognize that the right side of the model (i.e., the outcome variables) replicates the initial multiple domain LGC model presented in Figure 5.1. The major difference here is that the predictor variables, which are presented on the left side of the figure, have also been modeled. Of key importance in this model, however, are the four regression (or structural) paths leading from each set of predictor variables to each set of outcome variables, respectively. Results bearing on these path coefficients serve to answer questions related to the effectiveness of the predictor variables in bringing about change in the outcome variables. For example, the regression path relating to the question posed at the beginning of this application is the one leading from the slope associated with math grades (F8) to the slope associated with self-perceived math ability (F2).

In this application, the area of interest is the extent to which prediction of change in self-perceived ability by academic grades may vary for adolescent males and females. Thus, the model shown in Figure 5.3 was tested separately for each gender. These results are presented in Table 5.3 and 5.4. In the interests of space, only results related to the key parameters are presented in this table.

Results

In examining reported findings in Table 5.3, you will note that they are presented first for males, then for females. To facilitate perusal of these results, all statistically significant parameters are presented in bold type. Before exploring the individual components of the table, it is important to note, first, that this predictor model fitted the data well for each of males, $\chi^2(112) = 224.00$ (CFI = 0.96; RMSEA = 0.06), and females, $\chi^2(113) = 209.11$ (CFI = 0.98; RMSEA = 0.06). Establishing a well-fitting model for a longitudinal specification such as the one under study here necessarily entails a number of within- and across-domain residual and error covariances, some of which may vary across the groups. In the present case, one additional residual covariance (D1,D2) was specified for males, thereby accounting for the difference in degrees of freedom.

Turning first to factor means results for males, note that the average intercept of the predictor variables of math, language arts, and science grades are all statistically significant, as are the average slope values related to these academic areas. These analyses all control for students' concurrent grades. The negative signs associated with the slope estimates are indicative of substantial decrease in the average rate of change from Grade 8 through Grade 10. A review of results related to the average intercepts and slopes for the outcome variables, on the other hand, shows only the intercepts for self-perceived ability in math and language arts, and only the slopes for self-perceived ability in language arts and science to be statistically significant. These findings suggest that for adolescent males, self-perceptions related to math ability, on average, were substantial and underwent no statistically significant change through to Grade 10; self-perceived language arts ability was also strong and tended to become substantially stronger with progression across Grades 8 to 10. Self-perceived science ability, although somewhat weaker than for math and language arts, on average, increased significantly from Grade 8 to Grade 10.

We turn now to the key parameters of interest here—the regression paths flowing from the Intercept and Slope factors for grades in math, language arts, and science to the Intercept and Slope factors for self-perceived ability in these academic areas; only the parameters found to be statistically significant are considered. First, all paths flowing from the intercept for grades in math, language

TABLE 5.3

Parameter Estimates for Time-Varying Predictor Model (Model 3): Males

Variable	Math grades			Language arts grades			Science grades		
	Parameter	Estimate	z-value	Parameter	Estimate	z-value	Parameter	Estimate	z-value
Factor means									
Intercept	**F7,V999**	**74.62**	**93.08**	**F9,V999**	**72.53**	**106.75**	**F11,V999**	**74.17**	**106.89**
Slope	**F8,V999**	**−2.66**	**−6.13**	**F10,V999**	−1.72	**−4.26**	**F12,V999**	−1.25	**−3.47**
Perceived math ability				Perceived language arts ability			Perceived science ability		
Factor means									
Intercept	**F1,V999**	**1.34**	**2.86**	**F3,V999**	**1.45**	**2.24**	F5,V999	−0.35	−0.58
Slope	F2,V999	−0.37	−1.26	**F4,V999**	**1.18**	**2.73**	**F6,V999**	**1.21**	**3.06**
				Prediction of perceived ability from academic grades					
Regression Paths									
Intercept → Intercept	**F1,F7**	**0.06**	**8.96**	**F3,F9**	**0.04**	**4.97**	**F5,F11**	**0.07**	**8.67**
Slope → Slope	**F2,F8**	**0.07**	**6.10**	F4,F10	0.01	0.52	**F6,F12**	**0.06**	**3.84**
Intercept → Slope	F2,F7	0.00	1.05	**F4,F9**	**−0.02**	**−2.87**	**F6,F11**	**−0.01**	**−2.58**
Slope → Intercept	F1,F8	−0.00	−0.03	F3,F10	−0.03	−1.60	F5,F12	−0.03	−1.39

Note. z-values > 1.96 indicate statistical significance ($p < .05$). Estimates in boldface represent statistically significant values. $\chi^2(112) = 224.00$; comparative fit index = .96; root-mean-square error of approximation = .06.

TABLE 5.4
Parameter Estimates for Time-Varying Predictor Model (Model 3): Females

Variable	Math grades			Language arts grades			Science grades		
	Parameter	Estimate	z-value	Parameter	Estimate	z-value	Parameter	Estimate	z-value
Factor means									
Intercept	**F7,V999**	**78.06**	**108.88**	**F9,V999**	**78.94**	**133.29**	**F11,V999**	**78.59**	**123.65**
Slope	**F8,V999**	**−3.53**	**−8.37**	**F10,V999**	−1.83	**−4.91**	**F12,V999**	**−2.11**	**−6.05**
	Perceived math ability			Perceived language arts ability			Perceived science ability		
Factor means									
Intercept	**F1,V999**	**−2.27**	**−3.44**	**F3,V999**	**1.98**	**2.68**	F5,V999	−0.63	−0.84
Slope	F2,V999	0.75	1.95	**F4,V999**	1.31	**2.76**	F6,V999	0.18	0.39
	Prediction of perceived ability from academic grades								
Regression Paths									
Intercept → Intercept	**F1,F7**	**0.09**	**11.09**	**F3,F9**	**0.04**	**4.24**	**F5,F11**	**0.07**	**7.24**
Slope → Slope	**F2,F8**	**0.06**	**4.34**	F4,F10	−0.01	−0.58	**F6,F12**	**0.04**	**2.37**
Intercept → Slope	F2,F7	−0.01	−1.86	**F4,F9**	**−0.02**	**−2.77**	F6,F11	0.00	0.03
Slope → Intercept	**F1,F8**	**−0.05**	**−2.03**	F3,F10	0.01	0.33	F5,F12	−0.01	−0.25

Note. z-values > 1.96 indicate statistical significance ($p < .05$). Estimates in boldface represent statistically significant values. $\chi^2(113) = 209.11$; comparative fit index = .98; root-mean-square error of approximation = .06.

arts, and science are shown to be significant predictors of self-perceived ability in each of these three subject areas. Given that the intercept represents the average mean value across the three-year period considered in this study, these results suggest that for adolescent males, grades in math, language arts, and science serve as significant predictors of their self-perceptions of ability in these subject areas from Grade 8 through Grade 10. Second, as indicated by the paths leading from the slope for academic grades to the slope for self-perceived academic ability, the rate of change in math and science grades appears to be significantly related to the rate of change in self-perceived math and science ability. In other words, the rate at which grades in math and science change over the years from Grade 8 through Grade 10 is paralleled by a concomitant rate of change in self-perceptions of ability in math and science; the same pattern of change, however, was not evident for language arts. Finally, the statistically significant and negative paths flowing from the intercepts of grades in language arts and science to the slopes of self-perceived ability in these subject areas suggest that the higher the initial grades in these subject areas, the slower the rate of change in the self-beliefs related to these areas. These findings would seem to echo the same effect noted earlier with respect to the between-domain residual covariance between language arts and science.

For adolescent females, results for the factor means of both the intercepts and slopes related to grades in math, language arts, and science basically mirror those of adolescent males. Notable exceptions, however, are the higher values of both the intercepts and slopes for adolescent girls compared with their male counterparts. Likewise, the results replicate across gender groups with respect to the intercepts for self-perceived ability in math and language arts, with average scores for girls being higher than for boys. Of interest here is the finding that once grades are taken into account, girls exhibit higher levels of self-perceived math ability than boys, which runs counter to the results reported earlier for a model in which grades were not controlled (see Application 2). In both instances, however, rate of change in these self-perceptions of math ability was greater for girls than for boys. Indeed, Table 5.3 shows that whereas rate of change increased for girls (0.75), it decreased for boys (−0.37). The results differ across gender with respect to the slope for self-perceived ability in science. Although no significant effects were found for adolescent girls, the slope factor was statistically significant for adolescent boys. This result suggests that regardless of grades in science, boys tend to develop increasingly more positive self-perceptions of their ability in science as they progress from Grade 8 to Grade 10.

In reviewing only the statistically significant regression paths for adolescent females, again, results are similar to those for adolescent males. With the exception of the negative regression path leading from the intercept mean for grades in science to the slope mean for self-perceived ability in science, which was significant for males but not for females, all other significant paths exhibited a pattern that was similar across gender. This means that rate of growth related negatively to ability level for boys, but not for girls. Lower ability boys, therefore, are exhibiting greater increases in their self-perceived science ability from Grades 8 to 10. Or put differently, higher ability boys exhibit slower increases in their self-perceived science abilities.

CONCLUSION

On the basis of findings from both the time-invariant and time-varying predictor LGC models, it can be concluded that gender definitely plays an important role in influencing adolescents' self-perceptions of ability in math, language arts, and science. From the time-invariant model, for both math and science, self-perceived ability at initial status (Grade 8) was higher for boys than for girls, and conversely, girls had higher initial self-perceived language arts abilities. During the period from Grade 8 through Grade 10, however, rate of change in self-perceptions of math was slower for boys than for girls, with girls beginning to "catch up." Although gender convergence for math cannot be precisely determined in the present study, there is some evidence of a possible trend in this regard, a finding that has found mixed support in the literature. Jacobs, Lanza, Osgood, Eccles, and Wigfield (2002) in the United States, for example, have reported gender convergence for self-perceived math competence; whereas Watt (2004) in Australia has found that boys retain higher math talent perceptions by the same magnitude throughout secondary school. Nonsignificant findings in the present study preclude any conclusions being drawn with respect to both language arts and science ability.

From the time-varying model, it seems evident that overall, academic grades are strong and important predictors of self-perceptions of ability for both adolescent males and females, at least for the subject areas of math, language arts, and science. Indeed, the only statistically significant gender difference found here related to the science domain. Specifically, for adolescent males, the higher the mean grade in science, the slower the change in self-perception of ability in this subject area; there was no such relation for adolescent females.

Although LGC modeling, within the framework of SEM, can provide a host of data-analytic opportunities, applications of this methodological approach to longitudinal analyses are indeed scarce in the literature. This state of affairs is likely a function of three possible factors: (a) insufficient knowledge of basic concepts and application related to the SEM methodology; (b) insufficient expertise in the specific application of LGC modeling, a situation undoubtedly arising from a dearth of applied examples in the literature; and (c) unavailability of data capable of meeting the statistical demands of LGC modeling as outlined earlier in this chapter. I am therefore hopeful that my didactic approach to the presentation of these three models has not only provided a window into the world of SEM and the types of inquiry that become possible in the analysis of longitudinal data but also that it has stimulated readers to venture forth in using this methodology. I should note also that LGC modeling can be performed through the hierarchical linear modeling framework (Bryk & Raudenbush, 1992), and each of the two approaches to LGC modeling has its own advantages and disadvantages, leading Schnabel, Little, and Baumert (2000) to tag them the "unequal twins" (p. 12). For a review of their differential features and applications in general, readers are referred to Little, Schnabel, and Baumert (2000). For examples of the hierarchical linear modeling approach to LGC modeling pertinent to the impact of gender on children's academic self-perceptions in particular, see Jacobs et al. (2002) and Watt (2004). Both approaches to LGC modeling enable researchers interested in the gendered "processes" underlying career outcomes to model such development directly, thereby increasing our understanding of the manner by which these processes unfold.

REFERENCES

Bentler, P. M. (1990). Comparative fit indexes in structural models. *Psychological Bulletin, 107*, 238–246.

Bentler, P. M. (2005). *EQS 6 structural equations program manual*. Encino, CA: Multivariate Software.

Bollen, K. A. (1989). *Structural equations with latent variables*. New York: Wiley.

Boomsma, A. (1985). Nonconvergence, improper solutions, and starting values in LISREL maximum likelihood estimation. *Psychometrika, 52*, 345–370.

Boomsma, A., & Hoogland, J. J. (2001). The robustness of LISREL modeling revisited. In R. Cudeck, S. du Toit, & D. Sörbom (Eds.), *Structural equation modeling: A festschrift in honor of Karl Jöreskög* (pp. 139–168). Lincolnwood, IL: Scientific Software.

Browne, M. W., & Cudeck, R. (1993). Alternative ways of assessing model fit. In K. A. Bollen & J. S. Long (Eds.), *Testing structural equation models* (pp. 445–455). Newbury Park, CA: Sage.

Bryk, A. S., & Raudenbush, S. W. (1992). *Hierarchical linear models*. Newbury Park, CA: Sage.

Byrne, B. M. (1998). *Structural equation modeling with LISREL, PRELIS, and SIMPLIS: Basic concepts, applications, and programming*. Mahwah, NJ: Erlbaum.

Byrne, B. M. (2001). *Structural equation modeling with AMOS: Basic concepts, applications, and programming*. Mahwah, NJ: Erlbaum.

Byrne, B. M. (2006). *Structural equation modeling with EQS: Basic concepts, applications, and programming* (2nd ed.). Mahwah, NJ: Erlbaum.

Byrne, B. M., & Crombie, G. (2003). Modeling and testing change over time: An introduction to the latent growth curve model. *Understanding Statistics: Statistical Issues in Psychology, Education, and the Social Sciences, 2*, 177–203.

Duncan, T. E., & Duncan, S. C. (1994). Modeling incomplete longitudinal substance use data using latent variable growth curve methodology. *Multivariate Behavioral Research, 29,* 313–338.

Duncan, T. E., Duncan, S. C., Stryker, L. A., Li, F., & Alpert, A. (1999). *An introduction to latent variable growth curve modeling.* Mahwah, NJ: Erlbaum.

Eccles, J. S. (1983). Expectancies, values, and academic behaviors. In J. T. Spence (Ed.), *Achievement and achievement motives* (pp. 75–146). San Francisco: Freeman.

Eccles, J. S., Adler, T. F., & Meece, J. L. (1984). Sex differences in achievement: A test of alternate theories. *Journal of Personality and Social Psychology, 46,* 26–43.

Fuligni, A. J., Eccles, J. S., & Barber, B. L. (1995). The long-term effects of seventh-grade ability grouping in mathematics. *Journal of Early Adolescence, 15,* 58–89.

Jacobs, J. E., & Eccles, J. S. (1992). The impact of mothers, gender-role stereotypic beliefs on mothers, and children's ability perceptions. *Journal of Personality and Social Psychology, 63,* 932–944.

Jacobs, J. E., Lanza, S., Osgood, W., Eccles, J., & Wigfield, A. (2002). Changes in children's self-confidence and values: Gender and domain differences across grades one through twelve. *Child Development, 73,* 509–527.

Jöreskog, K. G., & Sörbom, D. (1993). *LISREL 8: Structural equation modeling with the SIMPLIS command language.* Chicago: Scientific Software International.

Little, T. D., Schnabel, K. U., & Baumert, J. (2000). *Modeling longitudinal and multilevel data: Practical issues, applied approaches, and specific examples.* Mahwah, NJ: Erlbaum.

Parsons, J. E., Adler, T. F., & Kaczala, C. M. (1982). Socialization of achievement attitudes and beliefs: Parental influences. *Child Development, 53,* 310–321.

Schnabel, K. U., Little, T. D., & Baumert, J. (2000). Modeling longitudinal and multilevel data. In T. D. Little, K. U. Schnabel, & J. Baumert (Eds.), *Modeling longitudinal and multilevel data: Practical issues, applied approaches, and specific examples* (pp. 9–13). Mahwah, NJ: Erlbaum.

Watt, H. M. G. (2004). Development of adolescents' self-perceptions, values, and task perceptions according to gender and domain in 7th- through 11-grade Australian students. *Child Development, 75,* 1556–1574.

Willett, J. B., & Keiley, M. K. (2000). Using covariance structure analysis to model change over time. In H. E. A. Tinsley & S. D. Brown (Eds.), *Handbook of applied multivariate statistics and mathematical modeling* (pp. 665–694). San Diego, CA: Academic Press.

Willett, J. B., & Sayer, A. G. (1994). Using covariance structure analysis to detect correlates and predictors of individual change over time. *Psychological Bulletin, 116,* 363–381.

Willett, J. B., & Sayer, A. G. (1996). Cross-domain analyses of change over time: Combining growth modeling and covariance structure analysis. In G. A. Marcoulides & R. E. Schumacker (Eds.), *Advanced structural equation modeling: Issues and techniques* (pp. 125–157). Mahwah, NJ: Erlbaum.

6

A SOCIOMOTIVATIONAL ANALYSIS OF GENDER EFFECTS ON PERSISTENCE IN SCIENCE AND TECHNOLOGY: A 5-YEAR LONGITUDINAL STUDY

SIMON LAROSE, CATHERINE F. RATELLE, FRÉDÉRIC GUAY, CAROLINE SENÉCAL, MARYLOU HARVEY, AND EVELYNE DROUIN

Over the past 30 years, Canada, and particularly the province of Québec, have seen the number of available jobs in science and technology (S&T) increase exponentially. From 1971 through 1996, 3 times more jobs were created in S&T than in all other occupational fields combined (Conseil de la science et de la technologie, 1998). During these same years, Québec postsecondary S&T programs recorded relatively high attrition rates among their students. Nearly 1 in 2 students admitted into college biology and physics technical programs, and 1 in 3 students admitted into college and university science programs, did not obtain a diploma across all S&T sectors combined, even after a 10-year follow up (Ministère de l'Éducation, du Loisir et des Sports du Québec, 2005). The rapid growth of the scientific workforce coupled with the low rates of persistence in postsecondary S&T training programs has evidently created a problem of recruitment for S&T employers. This problem is all the more worrying when we consider the significant gender gap in leading-edge sectors such as technological physics, mathematics, and engineering (where the male:female ratio is approximately 5 to 1) and technical biology (where the male:female ratio is approximately 1 to 5). In addition to the lack of specialized workers, the S&T sector must deal with an unequal representation of women and men as well as the social and economic consequences often associated with these inequalities.

171

This chapter presents some highlights of the Québec Scientific Career Project (QSCP), an ongoing longitudinal study using a sociomotivational framework intended to describe the academic and professional trajectories of youths interested in studies and careers in S&T and to examine the unique role of personal factors (e.g., motivation and gender) and contextual factors (e.g., parent, teacher, and counselor) involved in these trajectories. Specifically, three questions are examined: (a) What are the individual differences in the trajectories of persistence for youth newly admitted in college S&T programs; (b) what are the unique contributions of motivational, familial, and pedagogical factors in predicting these trajectories of persistence; and (c) do these factors have similar contributions for young men and women? This chapter is divided into four sections. Section 1 presents the sociomotivational model that underlies our project and describes the main longitudinal studies that have attempted to predict persistence in S&T, focusing particularly on gender discrepancies. The methodology of the QSCP is described in Section 2. Section 3 presents the results to address the three main questions, and Section 4 concludes with a discussion of the most important findings.

SOCIOMOTIVATIONAL MODEL OF PERSISTENCE IN SCIENCE AND TECHNOLOGY

The theoretical framework of the QSCP is based on a systemic model developed in a research program on science persistence among postsecondary students conducted at Laval University, Québec City, Québec, Canada. This program draws on three distinct theoretical perspectives of motivation: self-efficacy theory, which emphasizes people's beliefs about their capability to organize and perform behaviors (Bandura, 1991); self-determination theory, which gives a central role to the satisfaction of needs for competence and autonomy in the development of intrinsic motivation (Deci & Ryan, 1991, 2000); and the sociomotivational model of self, which proposes notions of structure, involvement, and autonomy support as determinants of motivation and individual adaptation (Connell & Wellborn, 1991). This systemic model adapted to the science context is illustrated in Figure 6.1.

In the model, scientific motivation is viewed as the central mechanism of academic and professional trajectories. Scientific motivation is defined by four personal concepts: feelings of competence and efficacy (e.g., "I feel that I can succeed in math and science"), self-determination (e.g., "I have chosen to study S&T for pleasure and knowledge"), academic involvement (e.g., "I am willing to sacrifice time in order to succeed in math and science courses"), and attachment to the scientific community (e.g., "I feel accepted and supported by members of the scientific community"). This model presumes that scientific motivation is built through the development of significant interactions

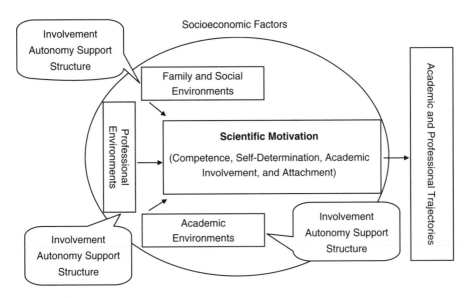

Figure 6.1. Sociomotivational model of persistence in science and technology.

in social, academic, and professional environments. These environments can be characterized by three elements: structure, involvement, and autonomy support. Youths who evolve in social contexts in which members expose them to scientific resources and opportunities to experiment with science in a practical way (structure); openly and respectfully discuss their choices of programs, courses, and career (involvement); and accept and value these choices without exerting pressure (autonomy support) should be more motivated toward science disciplines and careers. Such need-satisfying environments would facilitate their interests toward science as well as their adjustment, success, and professional integration into this field. The model also suggests that the contributions of these different environments and scientific motivations on career trajectories can be moderated by social and economic contexts. For instance, the underfunding of some industrial sectors and the transfer of North American production plants to Asia could have a negative impact on youths' interest and motivation to pursue studies and careers in S&T despite evident encouragement from family, academic, and professional environments.

Although this model does not make any prediction regarding the contribution of motivational and contextual variables as a function of students' gender, a few hypotheses can be proposed on the basis of a number of empirical studies. On the one hand, girls have been found to have lower feelings of competence and efficacy for science and math than boys, especially in late adolescence (Pajares, 2005). On the other hand, compared with boys, girls have also been found to show greater self-determination in their choices of studies and careers (Vallerand, 1997), to be more involved in their academic work (Larose & Roy, 1994), and to display stronger feelings of belonging to their school (Lightbody, Siann, Stocks, & Walsh, 1996). Moreover, studies on socialization in science and math suggest that parents, and sometimes teachers, do not treat boys and girls in the same way (Hyde, Fennema, Ryan, Frost, & Hopp, 1990; Jacobs, Davis-Kean, Bleeker, Eccles, & Malanchuk, 2005; Pajares, 2005). Often, because of expectations and stereotyped beliefs, parents tend to provide more math-supportive environments for their sons than for their daughters by spending more time working on math and science activities with sons and holding higher perceptions of their sons' than their daughters' math abilities (Jacobs et al., 2005). At the same time, a pioneer work from Youniss and Smollar (1985) indicated that parents exercise less control over their daughters' choices of studies and careers than their sons' and are more involved with their daughters during this process through "meaningful" conversations. Thus, although some dimensions of the model could be considered to be more detrimental to girls' persistence in science than boys' (e.g., weaker feelings of competence and fewer structure opportunities offered by parents), other dimensions might reinforce it (e.g., less controlling relationships with parents, greater self-determination in choices of studies, closer links with the academic community, and higher academic involvement). However, the speculative nature of these predictions must be recognized because few studies have sought to determine whether the links between sociomotivational variables and academic and professional trajectories are moderated by student gender (Hyde & Durik, 2005). On the basis of the model and questions described above, we next present a review of longitudinal studies that have sought to define the factors involved in academic and professional persistence in S&T and highlight their implications for modeling persistence and for the direction of our research program.

LONGITUDINAL STUDIES OF PERSISTENCE IN SCIENCE AND TECHNOLOGY

Before reviewing the studies on persistence in S&T, three clarifications are in order. First, persistence in S&T has been viewed as a continuous, temporal process that includes youths' intentions as well as behaviors (Tinto, 1987). Thus, on the basis of this perspective, we reviewed studies that attempted to predict (a) youths' aspirations, interests, and choices related to pursuing studies in S&T; (b) participation in advanced mathematics and/or science courses in high school; (c) persistence and graduation in postsecondary programs that lead to careers in S&T; and (d) career attainment in S&T. Second, to accurately determine the sociomotivational mechanisms leading to persistence in S&T, it is important to refer to longitudinal studies that have controlled for exogenous variables such as previous academic achievement in math and science and parent education and incomes. We therefore reviewed only longitudinal studies that controlled for such variables. Thus, retrospective studies such as that by Seymour and Hewitt (1997) were not included in this review, even though they generated valuable information on possible determinants of persistence in S&T. Third, only studies that covered the periods of adolescence and early adulthood were reviewed because the primary goal of the QSCP is to identify the determinants that come into play following the youths' choice to pursue studies in S&T.

Research by Eccles and her colleagues has generated a body of knowledge that is useful for understanding the mechanisms responsible for persistence in S&T. Much of this research has derived from the use of a large-scale longitudinal study, the Michigan Study of Adolescent Life Transitions (MSALT), whose initial goal was to test the validity of the expectancy-value model (Eccles, Roeser, Vida, Fredricks, & Wigfield, 2006). This model emphasizes the central role of expectations for success and the value that individuals attach to various options in predicting academic and professional trajectories. Using MSALT, Linver, Davis-Kean, and Eccles (1994) analyzed the growth trajectories of math interests from Grades 7 through 12 and found that higher maternal education predicted a less acute decline in math interest for boys taking less advanced mathematics courses, whereas higher maternal expectations at Grade 7 (i.e., expecting the child to succeed in math) predicted a sharpened decline in math interest for girls taking more advanced mathematics courses, suggesting a deleterious effect of maternal expectations for girls involved in more competitive learning contexts.

Using the same longitudinal sample, Alfeld-Liro, Frome, and Eccles (1996) studied young women who expressed male-typed occupational aspirations in Grade 12 and found that 65% of these women had changed their aspirations to female-typed or neutral jobs 2 years after high school (see also chap. 7, this volume). Women in high school who were uncertain about their career, who felt less competent regarding math and science, and who believed that math and science would not be useful in their career were more likely to change their aspirations while in college. These findings were obtained while controlling for mother's and father's education level, father's job status, and family income. In addition, mothers of young women who maintained male-typed aspirations had significantly higher job status than mothers of young women whose aspirations changed, suggesting that the presence of a female model in the social network could foster young women's aspirations toward nontraditional careers.

Again using MSALT, Updegraff, Eccles, Barber, and O'Brien (1996) found that girls were less likely than boys to follow an honors math trajectory (which contains more advanced math courses) and that girls who do engage in such a trajectory were less likely to pursue their math education than boys (see also Watt, 2005, 2006). Updegraff et al. also found that after controlling for gender and math aptitude, utility and interest in math in Grade 10 were found to predict the number of math classes taken by students between Grades 10 and 12, a finding that has been replicated among Australian youth (Watt, 2005). However, these variables explained only 12% of the variance in number of math courses taken, which suggests, as shown by one study (see Ma, 2001), that other motivational or contextual variables such as positive career expectations and parental support play an important role in predicting the participation in advanced mathematics.

From a prospective study involving Grade 12 Canadian students, Fortier (1994) found that 12th-grade students who chose to enroll in college science, physics (technical), or biology (technical) programs had a different motivational profile 6 months earlier than those who opted for other occupational domains. In particular, after having controlled for previous achievement in science, it was found that perceptions of competence in science, self-determined motivation to pursue studies in science, and students' gender (more boys than girls) had direct effects on the choice to go into scientific fields, whereas autonomy support from parents and high school science teachers (i.e., encouraging personal choices and not pressuring them regarding these choices) had indirect effects through students' feelings of autonomy and self-determined motivation. Moreover, two differences emerged from the predictive profiles characteristic of young men and women. First, although autonomy support from science teachers had a negative direct effect on women's choices to study S&T fields, it did not have a direct effect for men. Second, feelings of competence toward science were more strongly associated with women's choice to study S&T fields than with men's.

Using a subsample from a 10-year longitudinal study, Farmer, Wardrop, Anderson, and Risinger (1995) compared the cognitive, behavioral, and contextual dimensions for students who aspired to pursue S&T careers in high school and who had persisted in this direction 10 years later with those who had shared the same aspirations but had not persisted. Some interesting findings emerged. First, gender (more males) and race (more Caucasians) were predictive of persistence. Second, socioeconomic status and English grade point average were not related to persistence, whereas science grade point average was linked to persistence for men. Third, high levels of aspiration for science-related careers were found to be a moderate predictor of persistence, but again, only for men. Fourth, taking elective math courses in high school was linked to persistence, but only for women. Finally, parent, counselor, and societal positive encouragement toward undertaking and achieving in math and science courses and selecting S&T as a field of interest were not associated with persistence. Parts of these findings were replicated among highly selective students (see Strenta, Elliott, Adair, Matier, & Scott, 1994) and among college students who declared a major in engineering on enrolling (Schaefers, Epperson, & Nauta, 1997).

Using data from Britain's National Child Development Study, Schoon (2001) examined the psychosocial factors involved in the job aspirations and career attainment of 7,649 teenagers who aspired to become scientists, health professionals, or engineers. First, engineering and natural sciences were found to be clearly preferred by men, although the latter field was less male-dominated than engineering. However, an equal proportion of men and women opted for health professions, which strongly contrasted with the gender inequalities observed in the Province of Québec (i.e., approximately 80% of those who chose health professions were women). Second, scientific occupational attainment at age 33 was significantly predicted by gender (more men in engineering and more women in health professions), ability in math, perceived competence, and job aspirations at age 16. These contributions were shown to be unique because all independent variables were entered simultaneously in a logistic regression equation. Third, personality factors at age 16 predicted occupational attainment at age 33—specifically, engineers were previously described by their teachers as even-tempered and scientists as timid. Finally, coming from a professional background increased the chances of becoming a health professional in adulthood, whereas coming from a family where the father did not pursue higher education increased the chances of becoming an engineer.

With the sociomotivational model in mind, a number of conclusions can be made with respect to the findings reported in these longitudinal studies. First, the academic and professional trajectories of boys and girls are different. Girls are more drawn to health and non-math-related fields, whereas boys are more likely to choose engineering, math, and physics. Moreover, girls who aspire to nontraditional careers will often change their mind along the way. The lower interest and value they attach to math, as well as the scarcity of tangible support from family and social environments, seem to play an important role in their decision. Second, academic performance is still an important predictor of academic and professional trajectories in S&T, but it does not explain everything. Apart from performance, feelings of competence, and self-determination, expectations and values related to these fields of study play a crucial role. Third, involvement (e.g., presence of positive expectations) and autonomy support (e.g., absence of control or pressure on students' choices) from family and school seem to contribute to persistence in S&T, in particular through their effects on motivation. Moreover, few studies have considered "structured opportunities" in the area of scientific education. Exposure to scientific activities and resources in the context of meaningful relationships (with parents and teachers) and opportunities to experiment with S&T outside the classroom might allow youths to better clarify their career plans because these opportunities offer new ways for youths to compare their career representations with reality. Last, although boys seem to persist more than girls in S&T, few studies have examined whether the effects of motivational and contextual factors differ according to gender, with the exception of studies by Schaefers et al. (1997)

and Fortier (1994). The former concluded that models are the same for girls and boys, whereas the latter suggests that feelings of competence in science and autonomy support from science teachers play a greater role among girls than boys. Overall, the moderating role of gender in the relation between motivation and persistence is still an issue that requires more in-depth research (Hyde & Durik, 2005).

THE QUÉBEC SCIENTIFIC CAREER PROJECT

Our research project differs in many ways from past research on persistence in S&T. First, it examined the role of motivational, familial, and pedagogical factors in predicting persistence by drawing on a theoretical model that has received empirical support (see Bandura, 1991; Connell & Wellborn, 1991; Deci & Ryan, 1991). Second, it used a large sample of students newly admitted into college S&T programs and surveyed them over a 5-year period. It also controlled for academic grades at admission and parents' socioeconomic status. Finally, this is one of the few studies that has examined the moderating effect of gender on the relationships between motivation, support from parents and teachers, and persistence in S&T.

Overview of the Québec Scientific Career Project Methodology

Table 6.1 describes the design and procedure of the longitudinal study and the principal constructs assessed in the QSCP. This project began in Spring 2000 (Time 1) when 46 Québec Francophone colleges (almost all the

TABLE 6.1
Overview of the Québec Scientific Career Project Design
and of the Constructs Examined in This Chapter

Construct	Time 1 ($n = 725$)	Time 2 ($n = 408$)	Time 3 ($n = 427$)	Time 4 ($n = 611$)
Scientific motivation	X	X		
Parental support		X		
Teacher support		X		
Persistence	X	X	X	X
Program switch		X	X	X
Graduation			X	X
Science achievement	X			
Socioeconomic status	X			

Note. Xs in cells indicate that the variable was collected at the specified time. Time 1 = end of high school for all student participants, May 2000. For students following a normative trajectory (i.e., no program switch and no delay): Time 2 = second semester in college (March 2001); Time 3 = sixth semester in college or second semester at university (March 2003); Time 4 = sixth semester at university (March 2005).

public colleges in Québec) were invited to participate in a longitudinal study on persistence in S&T. Twenty-four of the colleges allowed us to invite students who had received and accepted the enrollment offer into an S&T program to participate in the project. A stratified random sample was then selected in each of these colleges: 10% of students in science, 5% of students in biology (technical), and 5% of students in physics (technical) were invited to participate in the project. Science includes all 2-year college programs leading to science, mathematics, and engineering university programs. Technical programs in biology and physics are 3 years long and prepare students for the labor market. Biology includes programs such as nursing, radiation oncology, biomedical laboratory, and diagnostic imaging. Physics includes programs such as civil and electronic engineering technology, computer science, and industrial design.

Seven hundred twenty-five students (approximately 40% of the target sample: 354 young men and 371 young women; mean age 17.3 years) agreed to participate in the study and completed a questionnaire at Time 1. Fifty-five percent had been admitted into a science program, 20% into a biology (technical) program, and 25% into a physics (technical) program. The majority of these students (76%) came from two-parent families whose mean income varied between $30,000 and $50,000 per year for fathers and between $20,000 and $30,000 per year for mothers (Canadian dollars). In more than 50% of families, fathers and/or mothers had attended college or university. Of the 725 students who participated at Time 1, 408 answered a second questionnaire at Time 2 (56%), 427 at Time 3 (59%), and 611 completed a phone interview and answered a fourth questionnaire at Time 4 (84%). Data on persistence in S&T, graduation, and program changes were collected several times during the study from all 725 students. The higher number of participants who completed the questionnaire between Time 2 and Time 4 can be explained by a change in follow-up strategies (i.e., more personalized contacts) and by the fact that new research funds were obtained. Attrition analyses between Time 1 and other measurement times showed that compared with other students, those participating at all the measurement times were more often women, $\chi^2(1, N = 408) = 9.53$, $p < .01$; reported better high school science grades, $F(1, 422) = 2.77$, $p < .01$; and displayed higher levels of self-determination in choosing to study S&T, $F(1, 422) = 6.55$, $p < .01$. However, the size of these effects was small, accounting for less than 2% of the total variance of those variables (Cohen, 1977).

To answer the research questions presented in the previous section, we first describe the trajectories of persistence between Time 1 and Time 4, and then examine the predictive relations between these trajectories and scientific motivation measured at Times 1 and 2, and parent and teacher support measured at Time 2 (see Table 6.1). In examining these relations, high school science grades as well as parents' socioeconomic status (Time 1) are controlled.

Trajectories of persistence for all 725 students are described. The prediction model is tested on the 408 students who completed all the measures.

Assessment, Findings, and Comments

This section presents the results of statistical analyses designed to answer the questions raised in the first part of this chapter. For each question, we specify the nature of methods used to assess the variables, the type of statistical analyses chosen to answer the question, and the obtained results, which are then discussed in the last part of this chapter.

1. What Are the Individual Differences in Trajectories of Persistence of Youths Newly Admitted in College S&T Programs?

To describe the trajectories of persistence for young men and women newly admitted into college S&T programs, colleges' official data on the students' academic paths since their admission (i.e., program change, dropping out, and graduation) were combined with data from interviews conducted at Time 4 (i.e., 5 years after initial admissions). These interviews lasted 15 to 20 minutes and allowed us to validate college information and obtain details on students' particular trajectories.

Sixty-four percent of the sample had not left the general field of S&T since their admission, whether they had changed program or graduated. Of these students, 57% had obtained a diploma in science, physics (technical), or biology (technical) and were pursuing university studies in S&T (e.g., mechanical engineering, computer science); 25% had obtained a diploma in physics (technical) or biology (technical) and had started a career in this field; 12% had changed program and were pursuing studies in another S&T program; and 6% were continuing with their original S&T program (all in a technical program).

Moreover, many trajectories reflected students' lack of persistence in S&T (36% of the sample): 43% of these students obtained a diploma in science, physics (technical), or biology (technical) but subsequently left the S&T field to pursue college or university studies in another field (e.g., psychology) or to work (e.g., tourism); 37% changed programs in college and were pursuing studies in fields unrelated to S&T (e.g., humanities); 13% dropped out of college; and 7% left postsecondary studies to pursue a high school vocational diploma.

We then assessed whether persistence rates (i.e., leaving vs. not leaving S&T) varied according to gender and as a function of college programs (science, physics [technical], and biology [technical]). Although more women persisted in biology (technical) and more men persisted in physics (technical; see Table 6.2), these differences were not statistically significant. Moreover, there

TABLE 6.2

Percentages of Men and Women Who Have Persevered
in Science and Technology

Field of study	Men	Women	$\chi^2(1)$	p
Sciences	66	61	0.87	.20
Biological technology	53	72	2.78	.08
Physics technology	64	55	0.84	.24

was no direct relation between persistence and college program at admission, $\chi^2(2, N = 725) = 1.47, p > .05$.

However, a closer examination of the gender differences with respect to trajectories of persistence (and nonpersistence) revealed a slightly different picture. Among persistent students, the distribution of men in the four trajectories described above differed from that of women, $\chi^2(3, N = 464) = 10.99, p < .05$. Although equal proportions of men and women graduated and continued with S&T at university (58% vs. 56%) or still continued with their original program (6% vs. 4%), twice as many women as men started a career in S&T after graduation (32% vs. 17%) and twice as many men as women changed programs along the way (16% vs. 8%). Among the nonpersistent students, the distributions within trajectories also varied according to gender, $\chi^2(3, N = 261) = 16.93$, $p < .01$. Although equal proportions of men and women changed programs in college to fields unrelated to S&T (37% for both genders), more women left the S&T field after graduating from college (54% vs. 32%) and more men dropped out of school (20% vs. 6%) or went back to high school after college to complete a professional degree (11% vs. 3%).

To sum up, these data suggest that the overall rates of persistence in S&T do not vary according to gender but that the trajectories of persistence (or nonpersistence) are different for women and men. On the one hand, persistent women seem to complete their studies and career plans more quickly than persistent men, who are more undecided and tend to change programs along the way. On the other hand, nonpersistent women seem to complete their initial study program before leaving the S&T field, whereas the nonpersistent men's trajectory is more characterized by dropout.

2. What Are the Unique Contributions of Motivational, Familial, and Pedagogical Factors in Predicting These Trajectories of Persistence?

Table 6.3 presents a summary of the measures selected to assess motivational, familial, and pedagogical variables as well as their psychometric qualities. Most constructs were assessed through validated scales, subjected to cross-cultural adaptations. The "scientific motivation" construct was assessed through feelings of competence, institutional attachment, academic involve-

TABLE 6.3

Psychometric Measures Used to Conceptualize Motivational, Family, and Teacher Factors Specified in the Sociomotivational Model of Persistence

Construct	Dimensions and item example	Scales and authors	αs		No. of items
			T1[a]	T2	
Scientific motivation	Competence and self-efficacy ("I feel confident about achieving well in S&T")	Perceived Competence Scale in sciences (Losier, Vallerand, & Blais, 1993)	.87	.85	4
	Self-determination ("I am pursuing studies in S&T for the pleasure and satisfaction of learning new things")	Self-Determination index of the Academic Motivation Scale (Vallerand, Blais, Brière, & Pelletier, 1989)	.81	.84	20
	Academic involvement ("I have been very efficient in the use of study time lately")	Academic Adjustment Scale of the SACQ (Baker & Siryk, 1984)	.80	.90	24
	Institutional attachment ("I feel that I fit in well as part of this S&T program")	Attachment Scale of the SACQ	.85	.90	15
Parental support	Autonomy ("My parents allowed me to have my own point of view regarding my choice of program")	Items adapted from Paulson, Marchant, and Rothlisberg (1994) and Robinson et al. (1995)		.88	8
	Involvement ("My parents showed me enthusiasm regarding my choice of program")	Scale adapted from Barnes and Olson (1985)		.90	10
	Structure ("My parents and I have conversations on different scientific issues and controversies")	Home scale[b]		.85	28
Teacher support	Autonomy ("Students' ideas and suggestions are used during classroom discussions")	Independence and Differentiation subscales of the ICEQ (Fraser, 1990)		.70	10
	Involvement ("The teacher takes a personal interest in each student")	Personalization subscale of the ICEQ		.81	5
	Structure ("The teacher gives examples of S&T careers")	Home scale[b]		.89	6

Note. S&T = science and technology; T1 = Time 1; T2 = Time 2; SACQ = Student Adaptation to College Questionnaire; ICEQ = Individualised Classroom Environment Questionnaire.

[a]The parental support and teacher support scales were administered only at Time 2.
[b]Scales developed specifically for the study described in the chapter.

ment, and self-determination scales. They were completed by students twice, at the end of their last year of high school (when they accepted the offer of admission into college, Time 1) and during their second semester in college (Time 2). These two measurement times were chosen to determine whether motivational dispositions after 1 year in college added to the contribution of motivational dispositions at the end of high school in predicting persistence. This is in line with studies showing that motivation fluctuates significantly between high school and college (Ratelle, Guay, Larose, & Senécal, 2004). Measures of parental and teacher support included structure (i.e., offering informative supervision to students by exposing them to scientific activities and discussing scientific issues and controversies with them), autonomy support (i.e., acknowledging students' perspectives, encouraging independent thinking, and providing opportunities to make choices), and emotional involvement (i.e., spending time with students, being interested and attentive to their needs, providing emotional resources). These measures were completed at Time 2 because they largely referred to the college experience.

A multivariate gender effect was detected on the measures previously described, $F(14, 350) = 3.71$, $p < .01$ (see Table 6.4 for descriptive statistics). Univariate analyses showed that women reported stronger feelings of institutional attachment and academic involvement in both high school and college; were more self-determined with regard to their decision to pursue studies

TABLE 6.4
Descriptive Statistics of the Sociomotivational Measures by Gender

Measure	Male students		Female students		$F(1, 340)$
	M	SD	M	SD	
Motivation in high school					
Competence	5.09	1.42	4.77	1.51	9.09**
Self-determination	6.42	5.29	6.59	5.29	0.17
Academic involvement	7.23	1.15	7.54	1.02	6.89**
Attachment	6.56	1.54	6.88	1.42	8.32**
Parental support					
Structure	0.54	0.32	0.62	0.35	1.88
Autonomy support	2.85	0.53	2.94	0.47	5.45*
Involvement	4.07	0.65	4.31	0.52	12.08**
Teacher support					
Structure	2.94	0.86	2.99	0.95	0.01
Autonomy support	2.67	0.43	2.61	0.46	2.43
Involvement	4.30	0.79	4.40	0.82	0.59
Motivation in college					
Competence	5.03	1.25	4.99	1.33	0.06
Self-determination	7.08	5.69	8.58	5.91	7.71**
Academic involvement	5.77	1.17	6.24	1.14	18.69**
Attachment	7.01	1.18	7.40	1.10	13.04**

*$p < .05$. **$p < .01$.

in S&T in college; and perceived more involvement and autonomy support from their parents. Men reported stronger feelings of science competence and efficacy, but only in high school.

A logistic regression analysis was conducted to estimate the contribution of motivational, familial, and pedagogical factors in predicting persistence in S&T (leaving vs. not leaving the S&T field). This analysis included five steps. In Step 1, average high school science grades and parents' socioeconomic status (estimated on the basis of mothers' and fathers' educational levels and incomes) were entered as control variables. The four scales measuring scientific motivation in high school (competence, self-determination, academic involvement, and attachment) were entered in Step 2 to assess whether motivational dispositions at admission predicted persistence. The parental support scales (structure, autonomy support, and involvement) were then entered in the analysis (Step 3) followed by the teacher support scales (Step 4) to test whether parents' and teachers' practices helped youths to persist beyond the contribution of initial motivational dispositions, history of performance in science, and family resources (socioeconomic status). Parent scores were entered before teacher scores because of the greater stability of parental figures in youths' academic paths. In Step 5, the motivation scales at Time 2 were entered to test whether the changes in motivational dispositions during the transition from high school to college improved the prediction of academic persistence in S&T after 5 years.

Table 6.5 describes the results of the logistic regression analysis. The model accounted for 28% of the variance in persistence. At every step, the variables made a unique and significant contribution to the prediction of persistence (see R^2 column). However, some variables made more important contributions than others. In particular, students who had higher high school grades in science were more likely to persist in S&T. Moreover, students who displayed high levels of academic involvement at admission were also more likely to persist 5 years later. Autonomy support from parents and the structure offered by college S&T teachers also predicted persistence over and above motivational and academic dispositions at admission. Last, changes in motivation, and particularly in feelings of self-determination, clearly contributed to the prediction of persistence. These results confirm the important role played by scientific motivation, structure, and autonomy support in predicting students' persistence in S&T. They also suggest that changes in self-determination between high school and college are an important process in the decision to leave or to persist in the S&T field.

3. Do Sociomotivational Factors Have Similar Contributions for Young Men and Women?

To answer our third question, a first series of univariate analyses of variance was conducted using motivational, familial, and pedagogical variables

TABLE 6.5
Summary of a Logistic Regression Analysis for Predicting Persistence
in Science and Technology

Predictor	Odds ratio	R^2 unique (%)	R^2 total (%)
Control variables (Step 1)			
Achievement in science	1.20*	2.6*	
Parents' socioeconomic status	0.94	0.0	2.6*
Motivation in high school (Step 2)			
Competence	0.80	0.6	
Self-determination	1.06	2.1	
Academic involvement	1.30**	3.8**	
Attachment	1.07	1.1	7.6**
Parental support (Step 3)			
Structure	1.29	1.4	
Autonomy support	1.44*	3.0*	
Involvement	0.67	0.24.6**	
Teacher support (Step 4)			
Structure	1.38*	2.8*	
Autonomy support	0.40	0.1	
Involvement	1.25	1.5	4.4**
Motivation in college (Step 5)			
Competence	0.98	1.1	
Self-determination	1.13**	6.1**	
Academic involvement	1.10	0.1	
Attachment	0.94	1.5	8.8**

*$p < .05$. **$p < .01$.

as dependent variables and gender (2), study program (3), and persistence (2) as factors. Given our goal here, only the Gender × Persistence and Gender × Persistence × Program effects are reported. None of the triple interaction effects was significant. However, Gender × Persistence interaction effects were found on motivational variables measured in college (i.e., competence, self-determination, academic involvement, and attachment). These interaction effects are illustrated in Figure 6.2. In all cases, differences in scientific motivation between persistent and nonpersistent students were greater among men than women, which suggests that the development of motivation in college plays a more determining role in predicting men's persistence in S&T than women's.

CONCLUSIONS

This chapter has presented highlights of the QSCP, a longitudinal study on the determinants of persistence in S&T. Drawing on a sociomotivational model of persistence that emphasizes the interaction between, on the one hand, feelings of competence, autonomy, involvement, and institutional attachment

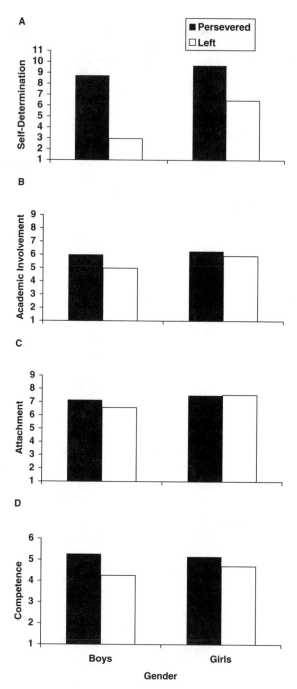

Figure 6.2. Gender × Persistence interactions. A: Self-determination in college, $F(1, 399) = 4.27$, $p < .01$. B: Academic involvement in college, $F(1, 399) = 9.28$, $p < .005$. C: Attachment in college, $F(1, 401) = 4.22$, $p < .05$. D: Competence in college, $F(1, 400) = 3.25$, $p < .05$.

and, on the other, individuals' familial, social, academic, and professional contexts, we have described the trajectories of persistence for students admitted into college S&T programs (Question 1) and explored the links between these trajectories, gender, and sociomotivational profiles (Questions 2 and 3).

Trajectories of persistence were obviously different for young men. Although there were as many women as men who persisted, we found women to be more likely to start a career in the S&T field sooner after their graduation, to commit and persist in their program, or to leave this field only after having graduated from college. Moreover, fewer women than men completely abandoned school or returned to high school after college to complete a professional degree (e.g., a vocational curriculum, such as mechanics). These distinctive profiles of men and women suggest that women who enroll in S&T put a lot of effort into it and value effort, persistence, and graduation very highly even in cases when the academic field is not suitable for particular individuals. This profile of persistence reflects women's higher levels of self-determination, academic involvement, and institutional attachment, which have been reported in past motivational research (Larose & Roy, 1994; Vallerand, 1997) as well as in the QSCP. These motivational factors are likely to protect women against the potentially negative effects of low feelings of self-efficacy and competence toward science and consequently make their academic path less chaotic than that of men.

Following the identified trajectories of persistence, we tested the validity of the sociomotivational model of persistence in S&T by assessing the predictive role of sociomotivational profiles measured during the 1st year of the study (Question 2) on trajectories of persistence measured over a 5-year period. We showed that sociomotivational variables predicted persistence in S&T over and above high school academic performance and parents' socioeconomic status. These variables accounted for nearly 26% of the variance in persistence. In particular, youths' involvement in their studies, their self-determined motivation toward pursuing S&T studies, autonomy support from their parents in the process of choosing studies and a career, and the structure opportunities offered by their science teachers (e.g., links between theory and S&T careers) made unique contributions to the prediction of persistence. Motivational variables (i.e., self-determination and academic involvement) accounted for nearly twice as much variance in persistence as social variables (parental and teacher support). These results corroborate those of several longitudinal studies (Fortier, 1994; Ma, 2001; Schaefers et al., 1997) and support the validity of a sociomotivational model of academic persistence. Moreover, our findings suggest that persistence might result from the additive effect of motivation and parental and teacher support, even at college age.

In examining moderating effects related to students' gender (Question 3), our findings suggest that scientific motivation after 1 year in college contributed more strongly to men's persistence than to women's. Indeed, young men who persisted after the 5-year follow-up displayed, at the end of their 1st year of college studies, stronger feelings of competence, self-determination, academic involvement, and institutional attachment than those who did not persist—differences that were not significant among young women. It may be useful to speculate on the processes accounting for these differences. First, perhaps women's scientific motivation comes into play earlier in their integration into S&T, particularly when they choose to pursue studies in this field. This hypothesis is consistent with Fortier's (1994) results, which indicate that feelings of competence and self-efficacy measured in high school were more important for predicting women's choice to pursue studies in S&T than for boys. These feelings are important predictors of one's decision to study in the S&T field, although we find that they partly lose their predictive power among women who have already made this choice. Indeed, it is reasonable to believe that as women progressively integrate the S&T path, the stronger and more homogenous their feelings of competence and self-efficacy are and the less discriminating those feelings become in predicting their academic and professional trajectories.

Second, women's persistence in S&T may be based more on ecological variables such as the stereotypes conveyed by parents, and sometimes teachers, regarding the role of women in science as well as their talent in this field (Hyde et al., 1990); family and school support regarding scientific education (Hill, Pettus, & Hedin, 1990); competition characteristic of S&T courses, which makes relationships more impersonal and often turns out to be more unpleasant for women than for men (Seymour & Hewitt, 1997); and the exclusion of women from group and mentoring experiences (Strenta et al., 1994). Such an explanation is in line with what some researchers refer to as the "chilly climate" hypothesis used to clarify the ecological variables at work in women's persistence in S&T (Hall, 1982; see also chap. 11, this volume).

Third, it is possible that the effects of scientific motivation on persistence are mediated by the lower levels of academic performance of young men relative to young women during the 1st year of college studies (Ministère de l'Éducation, du Loisir et des Sports du Québec, 2005). Low levels of academic performance could reduce boys' scientific motivation, which could lead to their decision to leave the S&T field. This last hypothesis is consistent with assertions of the self-efficacy theory, which specifies that feelings of self-efficacy and competence (an indicator of motivation) fluctuate in particular through graded mastery experiences (Bandura, 1986, 1997).

Finally, these results could also be explained by the fact that more young women than men abandon S&T after having obtained their college diploma in this field. Women who leave S&T after having graduated probably have highly positive motivational dispositions without maintaining high intentions regarding careers in mathematics, physics, and computer science. Their motivational dispositions as well as the support received from parents and teachers allow them to complete their academic project and thus meet the expectations of social and academic environments for graduation. However, these factors contribute weakly to whether they pursue studies in the S&T field.

The results presented in this chapter suggest that the feelings of self-determination, competence, academic involvement, and institutional attachment of young women who enter college S&T programs are quite different from young men's. Women do not follow the same academic and professional trajectories and are not highly influenced by their motivational dispositions in deciding to leave this field. One important implication of these results is that future research should consider the moderating effects of gender not only in describing the development of motivation and support from the family, school, and society in S&T education but also in examining the links between these sociomotivational factors and the academic and professional trajectories of youth. A second important implication is that school staff must recognize that high school academic performance in science is not the only factor involved in postsecondary persistence in S&T. Fostering student scientific motivation and involving parents and teachers in the vocational process should also prevent students from leaving S&T.

The next stage of the QSCP will be to follow participants when most of them will be entering the labor market. This will allow us to describe the quality of their professional integration and correlate it with sociomotivational profiles measured since the beginning of the project.

REFERENCES

Alfeld-Liro, C., Frome, P. M., & Eccles, J. S. (1996, March). *Factors that distinguish young women who continue or discontinue male-typed occupational aspirations two years after high school.* Paper presented at the Biennial Meeting of the Society for Research on Adolescence, Boston.

Baker, R. W., & Siryk, B. (1984). Measuring adjustment to college. *Journal of Counseling Psychology, 31*, 179–189.

Bandura, A. (1986). *Social foundations of thought and action: A social cognitive theory.* Englewood Cliffs, NJ: Prentice-Hall.

Bandura, A. (1997). *Self-efficacy: The exercise of control.* New York: Freeman.

Bandura, A. (1991). Human agency: The rhetoric and the reality. *American Psychologist, 46*, 157–162.

Barnes, H., & Olson, D. H. (1985). Parent–adolescent communication and the circumplex model. *Child Development, 56*, 438–447.

Cohen, J. (1977). *Statistical power analysis for the behavioral sciences.* San Diego, CA: Academic Press.

Connell, J. P., & Wellborn, J. G. (1991). Competence, autonomy, and relatedness: A motivational analysis of self-system processes. In M. R. Gunnar & L. A. Sroufe (Eds.), *The Minnesota Symposia on Child Psychology: Self processes and development* (pp. 43–77). Hillsdale, NJ: Erlbaum.

Conseil de la science et de la technologie. (1998). *Des formations pour une société de l'innovation: Avis* [Educational training for a society of innovation: Recommendations]. Québec, Canada: Gouvernement du Québec.

Deci, E. L., & Ryan, R. M. (1991). A motivational approach to self: Integration in personality. In R. Dienstbier (Ed.), *Nebraska Symposium on Motivation: Vol. 38. Perspectives on motivation* (pp. 237–288). Lincoln: University of Nebraska Press.

Deci, E. L., & Ryan, R. M. (2000). The "what" and "why" of goal pursuits: Human needs and the self-determination of behavior. *Psychological Inquiry, 11,* 227–268.

Eccles, J. S., Roeser, R., Vida, M., Fredricks, J., & Wigfield, A. (2006). Academic and motivational pathways through middle childhood. In L. Balter & C. S. Tamis-LeMonda (Eds.), *Child psychology: A handbook of contemporary issues* (2nd ed., pp. 325–355). New York: Psychology Press: New York.

Farmer, H. S., Wardrop, J. L., Anderson, M. Z., & Risinger, R. (1995). Women's career choices: Focus on science, math, and technology careers. *Journal of Counseling Psychology, 42,* 155–170.

Fortier, M. S. (1994). *Une analyse motivationnelle de la poursuite d'études en sciences* [A motivational analysis of persistence in science studies]. Montréal, Canada: Université du Québec à Montréal.

Fraser, B. J. (1990). *Individualised Classroom Environment Questionnaire*. Victoria: Australian Council for Educational Research.

Hall, R. M. (with Sandler, B. R.). (1982). *The classroom climate: A chilly one for women?* Washington, DC: Association of American Colleges, Project on the Status and Education of Women.

Hill, O. W., Pettus, W. C., & Hedin, B. A. (1990). Three studies of factors affecting the attitudes of Blacks and females toward the pursuit of science and science-related careers. *Journal of Research in Science Teaching, 27,* 289–314.

Hyde, J. S., & Durik, A. (2005). Gender, competence and motivation. In A. J. Elliot & C. S. Dweck (Eds.), *Handbook of competence and motivation* (pp. 375–391). New York and London: Guilford Press.

Hyde, J. S., Fennema, E., Ryan, M., Frost, L. A., & Hopp, C. (1990). Gender comparisons of mathematics attitudes and affect: A meta-analysis. *Psychology of Women Quarterly, 14,* 299–324.

Jacobs, J. E., Davis-Kean, P., Bleeker, M., Eccles, J. S., & Malanchuk, O. (2005). "I can, but I don't want to": The impact of parents, interests, and activities on gender differences in math. In A. M. Gallagher & J. C. Kaufman (Eds.), *Gender differences in mathematics: An integrative psychological approach* (pp. 246–263). New York: Cambridge University Press.

Larose, S., & Roy, R. (1994). *Le réseau social: un soutien potentiel à la transition secondaire—collégial. Rapport de recherche* [Social network: A potential support during the transition from high school to college. Research report]. Québec City, Québec, Canada: Cégep de Sainte-Foy.

Lightbody, P., Siann, G., Stocks, R., & Walsh, D. (1996). Motivation and attribution at secondary school: The role of gender. *Educational Studies, 22,* 13–25.

Linver, M. R., Davis-Kean, P. E., & Eccles, J. S. (1994, March). *The slippery slope: Predicting trajectories of males' and females' mathematics grades, interest, and self-concept in junior high and high school.* Presented at the Biennial Meeting of the Society for Research on Adolescence, Baltimore.

Losier, G. F., Vallerand, R. J., & Blais, M. R. (1993). Construction et validation de l'Échelle des peceptions de compétence dans les domaines de vie [Development and validation of the Perceptions of Competence in Life Domains Scale]. *Science et Comportement, 23,* 1–16.

Ma, X. (2001). Participation in advanced mathematics: Do expectation and influence of students, peers, teachers, and parents matter? *Contemporary Educational Psychology, 26,* 132–146.

Ministère de l'Éducation, du Loisir et des Sports du Québec. (2005). *Banques de données sur les Cheminements Scolaires au Collégial* (CHESCO) [Database on student college trajectories (CHESCO)]. Québec, Québec, Canada: Author.

Pajares, F. (2005). Gender differences in mathematics self-efficacy beliefs. In A. M. Gallagher & J. C. Kaufman (Eds.), *Gender differences in mathematics: An integrative psychological approach* (pp. 294–315). Cambridge, England: Cambridge University Press.

Paulson, S. E., Marchant, G. J., & Rothlisberg, B. A. (1994). *Constructs underlying students' perceptions of parents, teachers, and schools.* Chicago: Midwestern Educational Research Association.

Ratelle, C. F., Guay, F., Larose, S., & Senécal, C. (2004). Family correlates of trajectories of academic motivation during a school transition: A semi parametric group-based approach. *Journal of Educational Psychology, 96,* 743–754.

Robinson, C. C., Mandleco, B. L., Frost-Olsen, S., Bancroft-Andrews, C., McNeilly, M. K., & Nelson, L. (1995). *Authoritative, authoritarian, and permissive parenting practices: Psychometric support for a new measure.* Indianapolis, IN: Society for Research in Child Development.

Schaefers, K. G., Epperson, D. L., & Nauta, M. M. (1997). Women's career development: Can theoretically derived variables predict persistence in engineering majors? *Journal of Counseling Psychology, 44,* 173–183.

Schoon, I. (2001). Teenage job aspirations and career attainment in adulthood: A 17-year follow-up study of teenagers who aspired to become scientists, health professionals, or engineers. *International Journal of Behavioral Development, 25,* 124–132.

Seymour, E., & Hewitt, N. M. (1997). *Talking about leaving: Why undergraduates leave the sciences.* Boulder, CO: Westview Press.

Strenta, C. A., Elliott, R., Adair, R., Matier, M., & Scott, J. (1994). Choosing and leaving science in highly selective institutions. *Research in Higher Education, 35,* 513–547.

Tinto, V. (1987). *Leaving college: Rethinking the causes and cures of student attrition.* Chicago: University of Chicago Press.

Updegraff, K. J., Eccles, J. S., Barber, B. L., & O'Brien, K. M. (1996). Course enrollment as self-regulatory behavior: Who takes optional high school math courses? *Learning and Individual Differences, 8,* 239–259.

Vallerand, R. J. (1997). Toward a hierarchical model of intrinsic and extrinsic motivation. In M. P. Zanna (Ed.), *Advances in experimental social psychology* (Vol. 29, pp. 271–360). New York: Academic Press.

Vallerand, R. J., Blais, M. R., Brière, N. M., & Pelletier, L. G. (1989). Construction et validation de l'échelle de motivation en éducation (EME) [Construction and validation of the School Motivation Scale (EME)]. *Revue Canadienne des Sciences du Comportement, 21*, 323–349.

Watt, H. M. G. (2005). Explaining gendered math enrollments for NSW Australian secondary school students. *New Directions for Child and Adolescent Development, 110*, 15–29.

Watt, H. M. G. (2006). The role of motivation in gendered educational and occupational trajectories related to math. *Educational Research and Evaluation, 12*, 305–322.

Youniss, J., & Smollar, J. (1985). *Adolescent relations with mothers, fathers, and friends.* Chicago: University of Chicago Press.

III

THE IMPORTANCE OF FAMILY CONSIDERATIONS, FAMILY, AND BIOLOGY IN GENDERED CAREER CHOICES

7

IS THE DESIRE FOR A FAMILY-FLEXIBLE JOB KEEPING YOUNG WOMEN OUT OF MALE-DOMINATED OCCUPATIONS?

PAMELA M. FROME, CORINNE J. ALFELD, JACQUELYNNE S. ECCLES, AND BONNIE L. BARBER

Although women made tremendous gains in entering traditionally male-dominated professions during the 20th century, gender differences have persisted through the turn of the millennium in adult occupational pursuits (National Center for Education Statistics [NCES], 2002). By the end of the 1990s, women were earning more bachelor's degrees than men but were still underrepresented in many traditionally male-dominated occupational fields, such as engineering (18%), physical science, (37%), mathematical and computer science (34%), chemistry (26%), and law (27%; Bureau of Labor Statistics [BLS], 1998; NCES, 1997, 2000). In the mid-1990s, women represented 46% of the nation's labor force but only 9% of engineers, 29% of computer and math scientists, and 22% of physical scientists (NCES, 2000). Many women were still concentrated in traditionally "feminine" occupations with low status and low pay (BLS, 1998). For example, women were less represented in higher

This research has been funded by grants from the National Institute of Mental Health, the National Science Foundation (NSF), and the National Institute of Child Health and Human Development to Jacquelynne S. Eccles and by grants from the NSF, the Spencer Foundation, and the W. T. Grant Foundation to Jacquelynne S. Eccles and Bonnie L. Barber. We thank the following people for their assistance on the Michigan Study of Adolescent and Adult Life Transitions project: Andrew Fuligni, Amy Arbreton, and Debra Jozefowicz.

paying fields, such as engineering and computer systems analysis, and more likely to work in lower paying occupations such as primary and secondary school teaching (74%) and social work (65%; BLS, 1999). Although these statistics are informative, they do not shed light on possible reasons behind this pattern. Specifically, they do not tell us about young women who at one time aspired to occupations in these fields but changed their occupational aspirations to other fields. This article investigates a cohort of young women who, when they graduated from high school in 1990, held "male-dominated" job aspirations (occupations held by 30% or fewer women). Seven years later, the majority of these women aspired to either "female-dominated" jobs (occupations made up of 70% or more women) or "neutral" jobs (occupations made up of 31% to 69% women). What happened along the way to steer these women out of traditionally male-dominated occupational domains?

Not only are females less likely to choose careers in male-dominated fields (Jacobs, Chhin, & Bleeker, 2006; Watt, 2006), but when they do, they are more likely than males to drop out of these fields (Mau, 2003; National Science Foundation, 1999). At each successive educational level, girls are more likely than boys to opt out of math and science. This pattern of women leaving male-dominated occupations, which has been called the "leaky pipeline" (NCES, 1997; Oakes, 1990), has been repeatedly found in studies that have examined gendered occupational aspirations in the traditionally male-dominated fields of mathematics, physical science, and engineering. This "leak" of women from the pipeline toward male-dominated fields suggests that some women who once aspired to such careers did not fulfill their aspirations. This pattern can be both personally dissatisfying and economically costly in terms of personal and societal investment in these women's training (Carr, 1997; Oakes, 1990; U.S. Department of Labor, Women's Bureau, 1997).

In this study, we use longitudinal data to investigate several alternative hypotheses to explain the female exodus from male-dominated occupational aspirations. We draw on these data to tease apart some of the many hypotheses that have been put forth in the literature.

ALTERNATIVE HYPOTHESES

Why do women not actually enter male-dominated fields after indicating an initial interest? During the past several decades, there has been much interest in the underrepresentation of women in traditionally male occupational fields, and several theories have been proposed to explain this phenomenon. Such explanations include lack of encouragement from parents (Eccles, 1993), lack of "girl-friendly" instructional settings (e.g., American Association of University Women, 1993; Casserly, 1980; Eccles, Wigfield, & Schiefele, 1998), the "chilly climate" for women in nontraditional fields (Hall & Sandler, 1984; Seymour, 1995), low high school enrollment in math and science courses

(Farmer, Wardrop, Anderson, & Risinger, 1995; Nagy, Trautwein, Baumert, Köller, & Garrett, 2006; Sells, 1978, Watt, 2005), negative attitudes toward math (Eccles, 1987, 1994; Eccles (Parsons), Adler, & Meece, 1984), low self-perceptions of skills and future efficacy in math and science (Eccles, 1987; Eccles et al., 1985), and lifestyle and occupational values that are perceived to be incompatible with careers in male-dominated fields (Betz & Hackett, 1983; Eccles, 1987; Eccles, Barber, & Jozefowicz, 1998; NCES, 1997).

In this chapter, we focus on two major explanations: (a) young women's attitudes toward math and science and (b) their desire for an occupation that will allow them to combine a career with a family. We chose these two particular issues because our longitudinal data set of young adults lent itself to examining them in depth. For the first hypothesis, attitudes toward math and science, we include both self-perceptions of ability in and intrinsic value of these areas. For the second hypothesis, desire for a "family-flexible" occupation, we include concerns about combining a career and raising children and the demandingness of occupations in terms of educational requirements and time (number of hours typically worked annually for certain occupations).

Attitudes Toward Math and Science: Perception of Lack of Ability and/or Intrinsic Value

Some researchers have suggested that women's underrepresentation in male-dominated fields is due to the fact that women do not feel smart enough in or do not value math and physical science. Intrinsic value (or interest value) is one of the three major components of task value in the expectancy-value theory of achievement motivation (Eccles & Wigfield, 1995; Meece, Eccles (Parsons), Kaczala, Goff, & Futterman, 1982). These ideas originated in theories that propose that self-concept of ability and values relate to behavioral intentions and behaviors (Bandura, 1977; Betz & Hackett, 1983; Eccles et al., 1983). For example, the Eccles et al. (1983) expectancy-value model proposes that both self-concepts of ability and intrinsic values predict achievement choices.

Research supports these theories: There are gender differences in self-concept of ability (and the related construct, expectancy for success) and value of these areas, and these differences predict gender differences in subsequent achievement-related behaviors. For example, research has shown that from early adolescence through college, boys have higher ability self-concepts in math and assign math higher intrinsic values than do girls (Eccles et al., 1983; Jacobs, Lanza, Osgood, Eccles & Wigfield, 2002; Watt, 2004). In addition, girls tend to underestimate their abilities in math even when objective test scores show no gender differences in ability (Betz & Hackett, 1983; Eccles et al., 1983; Frome & Eccles, 1995; Updegraff, Eccles, Barber, & O'Brien, 1996), although some researchers have suggested that girls may be more realistic about (rather than underestimating) their math abilities (e.g., Crandall, 1969; Watt, 2005). Finally, women's ability self-concepts and interests are typically highest in more traditional "feminine" fields, such as the helping and people-oriented professions (Eccles, 1987; Eccles et al., 1989; Jozefowicz, Barber, & Eccles, 1993; Lips, 1992; Marini, 1978), whether or not these fields reflect their true ability profiles.

The higher a high school girl's self-concept of science and math ability, the greater the likelihood that she will aspire to a career in math or science (Hollinger, 1983). This pattern has also been found in other domains. Success expectancies and intrinsic values in math and biology have been found to predict college students' majors and intentions to take these courses in the future (Sullins, Hernandez, Fuller, & Tashiro, 1995). Self-concepts of ability in sports, math, and English are related to the amount of free time spent in these activities (Eccles et al., 1998). Finally, self-efficacy in traditionally male occupations is related to the amount of intrinsic value placed on and consideration of these occupations (Betz & Hackett, 1983; Larose, Ratelle, Guay, Senécal, & Harvey, 2006; Nagy et al., 2006). Jacobs et al. (2002) found that changes in self-concept of ability in a domain over time explained a large share of the changes in students' valuing of the domain over time. In addition to gender differences in self-concept of ability, there are also gender differences in interest in math and physical science. Researchers have found that girls show less interest than boys do in math (Watt, 2004; but see also Jacobs et al., 2002; NCES, 1997) and science (Jozefowicz et al., 1993). Further, 12th-grade boys have reported enjoying science more than 12th-grade girls (NCES, 1997).

These gender differences in ability self-perceptions and intrinsic values are important because they relate to students' achievement-related decisions. Self-concept of ability and expectancies for success in math are significantly related to intentions to take future math courses, the number of math courses actually taken, and aspirations to a career in math or science (Eccles et al., 1985; Feather, 1988; Updegraff et al., 1996; Watt, 2006). A positive attitude toward math and high self-concepts of ability in math and science are related to majoring in science in college and aspiring to a career in math or science (Ware & Lee, 1988), and college women's career goals relate significantly to their valuing of math (Eccles, 1994). Self-efficacy in traditionally male occupations is related to the amount of intrinsic value placed on and consideration of these occupations (Betz & Hackett, 1983; Larose et al., 2006; Nagy et al., 2006). These findings lead to our first hypothesis: Females' lower intrinsic value of and lower self-concept of ability in these areas may explain why many talented women eventually decide not to choose careers in these fields (Eccles, 1987; Nash, 1979).

Combining a Career With a Family

For many women, occupational choice involves weighing the perceived costs and benefits to family life (Eccles, 1987; Novack & Novack, 1996; Hayes & Watt, 1998). It has been suggested that one reason why women choose traditionally "female" professions is that these occupations allow women to combine work and family roles more easily than "male" professions (chap. 10, this volume; Eccles, 1994; Ware & Lee, 1988). One reason for this is that unlike male-dominated occupations, female-dominated (such as nursing or teaching elementary school) or neutral (such as teaching high school) occupations may appear more flexible (BLS, 1993; Farmer, 1997). High school girls are also more likely than boys to plan to make sacrifices in their professional life for the needs of their family (Jozefowicz et al., 1993). Ware and Lee (1988) found that female college students who placed a high priority on future family and personal life were less likely than their female peers to choose a major in science and were less academically oriented in general. The authors concluded that these women viewed scientific achievement and academic interests as incompatible with family life (Ware & Lee, 1988).

These findings lead to our second hypothesis: Females who believe that occupational flexibility is important when trying to combine a career with childcare may be more likely to change their aspirations out of male-dominated occupations because of the association of those occupations with lack of flexibility. Society's expectations for women's adult lives, combined with many women's knowledge that they will be expected to be the primary caretaker of the home and children, may serve to funnel women into fields perceived to be more flexible and "disposable" for the sake of family. Does this desire for occupational flexibility predict whether young women drop out of traditionally male-dominated fields after high school?

Job Content and Flexibility

In addition to examining women's (a) self-concept of ability and interest in math and science and (b) perceived cost to family life as barriers to women choosing occupations in male-dominated fields, it is also important to examine characteristics of the occupations themselves. In addition to exploring women's beliefs and perceptions, we also examined objective characteristics of the occupations: (a) the amount of math and physical science content of the job and (b) the occupational flexibility of the job (measured in two ways: the years of education required for the job and the average number of hours worked annually for that job). In line with the hypotheses that we have outlined here, we predicted that young women would be more likely to drop out of male-dominated occupations that (a) contained a high level of math and physical science content and (b) were low in occupational flexibility.

FOCUS OF THIS STUDY

We were interested in exploring alternative hypotheses about why young women with male-dominated career aspirations drop out of these pursuits in young adulthood. Although we are not proposing that male-dominated occupations are superior to female-dominated or neutral occupations, we do believe it is important to determine which factors serve to constrict the vocational options that young women perceive to be available to them, particularly because of the possible emotional, economic, and human capital losses associated with not fulfilling one's aspirations (Carr, 1997; Eccles, 1994; Oakes, 1990).

We studied a group of women who had aspired to male-dominated occupations in 12th grade and examined their occupational career aspirations 7 years later, when they were 25 years old. Eighty-three percent of the women in our sample who had held male-dominated occupational aspirations in 12th grade switched to female-dominated or neutral occupational aspirations 7 years later. Was it the math and physical science content that deterred them, the potential conflict of the demands of such occupations with their future roles as wives and mothers, or something else altogether? We examined the predictive strength of (a) intrinsic value placed on math and physical science, (b) self-concept of ability in math and physical science, (c) the desire for an occupation with enough flexibility to easily mesh future work and family roles, (d) the amount of math and physical science content of a job, (e) the educational requirements to obtain a specific occupation, and (f) the time demands of the specific male-dominated occupational aspiration.

METHOD

Data were collected as part of a larger multiple-wave longitudinal investigation (the Michigan Study of Adolescent Life Transitions). The first wave of data used in this study was collected in 1990 when the participants were in 12th grade (hereafter referred to as "12th grade"). The second wave of data used here was when the participants were on average 25 years old (hereafter referred to as "age 25"). Because of attrition between the waves and missing data, the sample size of women who had aspired to male-dominated occupations in 12th grade and who had job aspiration data at age 25 dropped from 208 to 104. Only the 104 who remained in the sample across both waves and for whom we had data for all of the variables used in the analyses are used in our longitudinal analysis.

Sample

Participants were 104 women from 12 low- to middle-income communities located within a 50-mile radius of a large industrial midwestern city in Michigan. Ninety-three percent of the participants were European American, 1% were African American, 4% were Asian American, and 2% were of other races–ethnicities. By age 25, 6% of the young women in the study had a high school diploma, 4% had obtained some post–high school vocational training,

25% had some college but no degree, 6% had an associate's degree, 43% had a bachelor's degree, 14% had 1 or 2 years of graduate school, and 2% had a master's degree. The distribution of race–ethnicity and education in the attrited sample was similar to that for the complete sample, and correlations between the variables for the attrited sample were similar to those in the Grade 12 full sample.

Measures

Occupational aspirations were measured at both time points: At 12th grade, participants were asked, "If you could have any job you wanted, what job would you like to have when you are 30?"; and at age 25, participants were asked, "What job would you most like to have when you are 30?" (underscoring in original). These open-ended responses were coded according to the U.S. Census occupational codes. Each occupation was further coded as either male dominated, neutral, or female dominated on the basis of the percentage of incumbents of that occupation who were women according to the 1990 Census (see Tables 7.1 to 7.3 for the categories that the occupations fell into). Occupations that were made up of 30% or fewer women were categorized as "male dominated," occupations made up of 31% to 69% women were categorized as "neutral," and occupations with 70% or more women were categorized as "female dominated." Male-dominated occupations included engineer, architect, and pilot; neutral occupations included accountant, manager, and pharmacist; female-dominated occupations included bookkeeper, nurse, and secretary. Unfortunately, because of our small sample size, it was not possible

TABLE 7.1
Numbers of Young Women Who Aspired to Male-Typed Occupations

Male-typed occupation	12th grade		Age 25	
	n	%	n	%
Airplane pilots and navigators	2	3	1	1
Automobile body and related repair persons	1	1	0	0
Engineers, architects, and surveyors	11	11	6	6
Executives, administrators, and managers	16	15	1	1
Health-related professional specialty (dentist, doctor, veterinarian)	32	31	3	3
Lawyers and judges	21	20	4	4
Mathematical and computer scientists	1	1	0	0
Natural scientists (e.g., geologist)	3	3	2	2
Protective service (e.g., police, detective)	4	5	1	1
Sales (securities and financial services, manufacturing and wholesale)	1	1	1	1
Writers, authors, entertainers, and athletes	12	12	0	0
Total	104	100	19	18

TABLE 7.2
Numbers of Young Women Who Changed to Neutral Occupational Aspirations by Age 25

	Age 25	
Neutral occupation	n	%
Administrative support, including clerical (supervisor, general office)	3	5
Advertising and related sales (advertiser, marketing)	5	9
Computer programming	2	4
Executives, administrators, and managers (manager and administrator; manager, medicine and health; administrator, education and related fields)	13	23
Health-related professional specialty (physicians' assistant)	2	4
Management related (accountant and auditor, financial officer, management analyst, buyer)	9	16
Natural scientists (biological and life scientist)	2	4
Sales supervisor and proprietor	1	2
Social, recreation, and religious workers (social worker)	2	4
Teachers, college and university	1	2
Teachers, except college and university (educational and vocational counselor; high school teacher; teacher, not elsewhere classified)	8	14
Writers, authors, entertainers, and athletes (artist, author, designer, editor, public relations specialist)	9	16
Total	57	55

to further analyze occupations by prestige level (see Nakeo & Treas, 1994). Tables 7.1 to 7.3 show the distribution of job aspirations in our sample across each of these categories at 12th grade and age 25.

Self-concept of ability in and intrinsic value of math and physical science were measured in 12th grade. Two items were used to measure self-concept of

TABLE 7.3
Numbers of Young Women Who Changed to Female-Typed Occupational Aspirations by Age 25

	Age 25	
Female-typed occupation	n	%
Administrative support, including clerical (secretary, clerk)	4	4
Health related technical (dental hygienist, health technologist and technician, radiology technician)	4	4
Health-related professional specialty (dietician, physical therapist, registered nurse, speech therapist)	12	12
Health-related service (health aide)	1	1
Homemaker	2	2
Religious worker	1	1
Teachers, except college and university (elementary school teacher, special education teacher)	4	4
Total	28	27

ability in each of math ($\alpha = .84$) and physical science ($\alpha = .86$). One item measured participants' interest in each of math and physical science. Beliefs about the importance of a family-flexible occupation were also measured in 12th grade by a five-item scale ($\alpha = .84$). These items tapped the value the respondent placed on having a career that accommodated fulfilling family responsibilities, such as a flexible working schedule or being able to take time off for family responsibilities (Jozefowicz et al., 1993). All of the items were created by Eccles and her colleagues and all were answered on 7-point Likert scales (see Appendix 7.1 for actual scale items).

To code the level of the math and physical science content in an occupation, the occupational aspirations of the sample were divided into three groups. The first group included occupations in which one's key or central tasks would involve math or physical science, the second included occupations in which one may perform tasks in math or physical science from time to time or in which training for this occupation may involve coursework in these areas, and the third group included occupations in which neither one's occupational tasks or training would involve math or physical science. Examples of occupations with a high level of math and physical science included engineer, chemist, and accountant; examples of occupations with a medium level of math and physical science included dentist, health manager, and health technician; examples of occupations with a low level of math and science included lawyer, counselor, and office clerk.

Job demandingness was measured using two items. The first item was the normative amount of education held by occupational incumbents, according to the 1990 Census. For each occupation, the mode for level of education of the incumbents was coded as follows: 1 = *less than high school*, 2 = *high school*, 3 = *some college*, 4 = *bachelor's degree*, 5 = *PhD or professional degree*. The second item, time demands, was the average number of hours worked annually by full-time occupational incumbents, according to the 1990 Census. The 1990 Census was used because that was the time when the participants were completing the survey in 12th grade. Because census information was given in categories divided by gender and age group, we used the averages listed for women aged 30 to 34, the age range most likely to have young children.

ANALYSES AND RESULTS

The focus of our study is the subsample of 104 young women who indicated male-dominated occupational aspirations in the 12th grade and were still in the study with complete data at age 25. This main subsample was divided into two groups, the "stable" group (those young women who continued to have male-dominated occupational aspirations at age 25) and the "change" group (those young women who had male-dominated occupational aspirations in their senior year of high school but who switched their occupational aspirations to female-dominated or neutral by age 25). Nineteen young women were in the "stable" group (18%) and 85 in the "change" group (82%: 55% changing to "neutral" and 27% to "female-dominated" occupations).

We used logistic regression, which regresses a categorical outcome variable on continuous independent predictors, to analyze the data. We tested the predictive strength of young women's self-concepts of ability in math and physical science, the intrinsic value they placed on math and physical science, the importance they placed on job flexibility, the typical amount of education required for the job they aspired to, and the typical number of hours worked annually for the job to which they aspired on the outcome variable of either stability (0) or change (1) from male-dominated occupational aspirations.

Math and physical science self-concepts of ability were each included in analyses separate from math and physical science interests, because incorporating self-concept and interest in the one model resulted in suppression effects due to their high intercorrelation within each subject area ($r = .76$ in math, $r = .78$ in physical science), producing estimates for both constructs that were positive rather than negative (.04 for interest in math and .29 for self-concept of ability in physical science). We therefore estimated one model containing the self-concept of ability in math and self-concept of ability in physical science variables but excluding the interest variables, and another model containing the interest in math and interest in physical science variables but excluding the self-concept of ability variables. Our estimates for self-concept of ability and interest effects should therefore not be interpreted as unique effects because they were not simultaneously estimated. Correlations among all variables are presented in Table 7.4.

We used a stepwise method of entering the predictors into the model in order to examine the effects of each type of predictor separately as well as together in the full model. We were looking not only for which variables significantly predicted the outcome but also for the relative strength of each of the predictors.

In the self-concept of ability model (see Table 7.5), a lower desire for a family-flexible job was the only significant predictor of maintaining a male-dominated occupational aspiration. There was a trend such that both a higher self-concept of ability in math and a lower number of hours worked annually predicted maintaining male-dominated occupational aspirations. The overall model was significant.

In the intrinsic value model (see Table 7.6), the strongest predictor of maintaining a male-dominated occupational aspiration was a lower number of hours worked annually. Other significant predictors of maintaining a male-dominated occupational aspiration were a higher intrinsic value placed on

TABLE 7.4
Correlations of Outcome and Predictor Variables

Variable	1	2	3	4	5	6	7	8	9
1. Change (0) versus stable (1)	1.00								
2. Self-concept of ability in math	-.27**	1.00							
3. Self-concept of ability in physical science	-.19*	.36***	1.00						
4. Intrinsic value of math	-.22*	.76***	.25**	1.00					
5. Intrinsic value of physical science	-.29**	.25**	.78***	.23*	1.00				
6. Math/physical science content of job	-.25**	.26**	.49***	.25**	.48***	1.00			
7. Desire for flexible job	.20*	.13	-.03	.13	-.08	.07	1.00		
8. Education required	.06	-.06	.20*	-.11	-.06	.19	-.02	1.00	
9. Annual hours	.20*	-.17	.27**	-.28**	.16	.17	.04	.68***	1.00

Note. N = 104. *p < .05. **p < .01. ***p < .001.

TABLE 7.5
Statistics for the Final Logistic Regression Model—
Includes Self-Concept of Ability

Predictor	Standardized β (B)	$p > \chi^2$	SE	Wald's χ^2	Exp(B)[a]
12th-grade self-concept of ability in math	−.36 (−.41)	.08	.24	1.18	0.66
12th-grade self-concept of ability in physical science	−.12 (−.14)	.57	.25	0.32	0.87
Level of math/physical science in job aspiration	−.19 (−.49)	.24	.41	1.40	0.62
12th-grade beliefs about the importance of a family-flexible occupation	.41 (.61)	.02	.25	5.81	1.83
Educational requirements for job aspiration	−.13 (−.32)	.57	.56	0.33	0.72
Number of hours need to work annually for job aspiration	.43 (.00)	.09	.00	2.86	1.00

Note. N = 104; R^2 = .19. Testing global null hypothesis: χ^2(6) = 21.68, p = .002.
[a]Odds ratio.

physical science and a lower desire for a family flexible job. The overall model was significant.

In sum, the analyses demonstrate that in this sample, a higher desire for a family-flexible job, having aspired to a job with high occupational time demands, and a lower intrinsic value placed on physical science spurred young

TABLE 7.6
Statistics for the Final Logistic Regression Model—Includes Intrinsic Value

Predictor	Standardized β (B)	$p > \chi^2$	SE	Wald's χ^2	Exp(B)[a]
12th-grade intrinsic value of math	−.14 (−.12)	.47	.17	0.53	0.88
12th-grade intrinsic value of physical science	−.43 (−.44)	.05	.23	3.8	0.64
Level of math and physical science in job aspiration	−.10 (−.26)	.55	.44	0.35	1.62
12th-grade beliefs about the importance of a family-flexible occupation	.33 (.49)	.04	.24	4.13	1.63
Educational requirements for job aspiration	−.24 (−.57)	.34	.60	0.92	0.56
Number of hours need to work annually for job aspiration	.51 (.00)	.05	.00	3.70	1.00

Note. N = 104; R^2 = .19. Testing global null hypothesis: χ^2(6) = 22.06, p = .001.
[a]Odds ratio.

women to change their aspirations away from male-dominated occupational fields. The most consistently strong, significant predictor was the desire for a job that allowed for the flexibility for these women to have a family.

DISCUSSION

What are the factors that lead young women to change their aspirations out of male-dominated occupations? In our sample, which we acknowledge may not be representative of the general population, we tested two alternative hypotheses: attitudes toward math and physical science (involved in many male-dominated occupations) and desiring a family-flexible job. We found that desire for a family-flexible job, having aspired toward a job involving high time demands, and having a low intrinsic value for physical science led to change away from a male-dominated occupational aspiration. On the other hand, young women who had placed less importance on having a family-flexible job, aspired toward a job that involved lower time demands, and placed high intrinsic value on physical science were less likely to "leak out" of the math and physical science pipeline.

These findings support previous research that has found that self-concepts and value predict occupational aspirations and behaviors, such as college majors (Eccles et al., 1983, 1985; Feather, 1988; Sullins et al., 1995; Updegraff et al., 1996; Watt, 2005, 2006). In sum, it seems that both factors, a desire for an occupation that will allow them to combine a career with a family as well as attitudes toward math and science, influence whether women keep their male-dominated job aspirations.

Our findings add to the existing literature by examining several types of attitude in one longitudinal analysis and by using objective measures of time demandingness and educational requirements of occupational choices to show the combination of factors that may lead young women to abandon their initial job aspirations toward male-dominated professions. Others have found similar patterns: Holland and Eisenhart (1990) found that as young women get older, they are more likely to conclude that it is harder to place a career in a male-dominated field second to a family than is the case for a career in a female-dominated or neutral field. They may begin to feel the very real pressure of societal expectations for their adult lives as they continue to make choices about their courses and career paths (Novack & Novack, 1996; Spade & Reese, 1991; Subotnik & Arnold, 1996). Information that young women gather regarding the flexibility of a job schedule and the ability to combine certain occupations with family responsibilities may lead them to conclude that combining work and family will be difficult in traditionally male-dominated fields (Gottfredson, 1981).

Tomlinson-Keasey (1990) discussed the fact that young women are not as likely as men to plan for a specific career because they feel that they need to take their relationships into account in making their career decisions. However, early career planning and having specific career goals lead to a higher probability of achieving those goals. One reason why many educated women may feel ambivalent about motherhood versus career advancement is that although raising children is a priority for many women, work and family are still not easily compatible in our society. Lubinski and Benbow (2006) recently found that among high-ability individuals, a gender difference in the number of hours willing to work has already begun to emerge by age 33, suggesting that women do not achieve the same level of career success as men in their lifetimes, despite similar levels of potential, because they are not willing to work the 50- to 70-hour work weeks that are typical for individuals at the cutting edge of their discipline.

It is unfortunate and unacceptable that after the turn of the new millennium, many male-dominated professions are still inflexible in practice, even if not in official policy, or at least are perceived to be inflexible. Girls and young women are not able to follow through with their professional plans because of the barriers (e.g., lack of affordable child care, lack of schedule flexibility) that still exist—despite the rhetoric. The reality is that it is difficult for women to pursue and be successful in the same types of careers as men if women want to have a family and to be the primary caregiver for their children. Baruch and Barnett (1986) reported that women in dual-career couples assume major responsibility for their families and household, and the pattern of returning home from work and beginning to take care of family has been named women's "second shift" (Hochschild, 1989). Young women today see these patterns among their role models and may expect that they will experience the same division of labor (Spade & Reese, 1991).

Probably because they learn early that they need to be flexible if they want to have children, girls have been found to be interested in a greater number of different careers than boys and also to show more gender-role flexibility, whereas the aspirations of boys tend toward careers that are higher in prestige and require higher levels of education (Mendez & Crawford, 2002; Shapka, Domene, & Keating, 2006). Further support for our interpretation comes from Meinster and Rose (2001), who found that high school girls' career interests became increasingly traditional from their freshman through to their senior year in high school. Hallett and Gilbert (1997) found that among college women who planned to be part of a dual-career couple, those who expected to share roles with their spouses had higher self-esteem, higher levels of instrumentality, and higher commitment to a lifelong career than those who expected to have a more conventional dual-career marriage with traditional divisions of household labor.

Our findings illustrate the continued circumscription of occupational aspirations among a cohort of young women moving into adulthood in the 1990s. Future long-term research will examine the socioeconomic and mental health consequences of these changes. Carr (1997) found that midlife women who fell short of their career goals showed lower levels of "purpose in life" and higher levels of depression than women who had attained their earlier career goals, even after controlling for a variety of confounding factors. In future research, it would be beneficial to test our hypotheses on a larger sample because this would allow us greater certainty in our findings as well as the ability to test for interacting predictors in influencing young women's decisions to opt out of male-dominated career choices.

CONCLUSION

On the basis of our findings, we suggest several types of intervention to target young women's "leak" from the pipeline toward male-dominated occupations:

1. Go beyond encouraging girls to take high-level courses in math and physical sciences and show them real role models who are living proof that many male-dominated careers are compatible with family goals, such as families where child-rearing and housework are shared equally between both parents, or examples of women in male-dominated occupations whose jobs have enough flexibility for them to be successful at both their job and their family roles (i.e., find the exceptions to the "rule" and publicize them widely). This could be done by universities and corporations offering orientations and internship positions to school-aged girls in their communities and by occupationally oriented high school student organizations such as Future Business Leaders of America organizing events where women currently working in male-dominated fields speak to groups of students about balancing their career and family.
2. Continue to press employers to provide child care and a flexible working schedule without compromising other benefits or promotions (and encourage fathers to take advantage of these opportunities).
3. Conduct interventions with fathers that focus on taking equal responsibility for child care and household duties. Research is currently being conducted to evaluate such interventions (e.g., McBride & Lutz, 2004).
4. Continue work on developing methods and interventions to target girls' and women's underestimation of their abilities in math and physical science and the lower value that they place on these domains relative to males.

APPENDIX 7.1
ITEMS USED TO MEASURE SELF-CONCEPT OF ABILITY IN AND INTRINSIC VALUE OF MATH AND PHYSICAL SCIENCE

SELF-CONCEPT OF ABILITY IN MATH ($\alpha = .84$)

How good at math are you? (1 = *not at all good*, 7 = *very good*)
How good do you think you would be in a career requiring good math skills? (1 = *not at all good*, 7 = *very good*)

INTRINSIC VALUE OF MATH

How much do you like doing math? (1 = *a little*, 7 = *a lot*)

SELF-CONCEPT OF ABILITY IN PHYSICAL SCIENCE ($\alpha = .86$)

How good at physical science are you? (1 = *not at all good*, 7 = *very good*)
How good do you think you would be in a career requiring good physical science skills? (1 = *not at all good*, 7 = *very good*)

INTRINSIC VALUE OF PHYSICAL SCIENCE

How much do you like doing physical science? (1 = *a little*, 7 = *a lot*)

IMPORTANCE OF A FAMILY-FLEXIBLE OCCUPATION
($\alpha = .84$; 1 = *not at all*, 7 = *a lot*)

Please indicate how much you would like a job with each characteristic:
"Has a flexible working schedule you can adjust to meet the needs of your family"
"Does not require you to be away from your family"
"Leaves a lot of time for other things in your life"
"Allows you to be at home when your children are out of school (like teaching)"
"Makes it easy to take a lot of time off for family responsibilities"

REFERENCES

American Association of University Women. (1993). *How schools shortchange girls*. Washington, DC: Author.

Bandura, A. (1977). Self-efficacy: Toward a unifying theory of behavioral change. *Psychological Review, 84*, 191–215.

Baruch, G. K., & Barnett, R. C. (1986). Role quality, multiple role involvement, and psychological well-being in midlife women. *Journal of Personality and Social Psychology, 51*, 578–585.

Betz, N. E., & Hackett, G. (1983). The relationship of mathematics self-efficacy expectations to the selection of science-based college majors. *Journal of Vocational Behavior, 23*, 329–245.

Bureau of Labor Statistics. (1993). *Employment and earnings.* Washington, DC: U.S. Government Printing Office.

Bureau of Labor Statistics. (1998). *Occupational outlook handbook.* Washington, DC: U.S. Government Printing Office.

Bureau of Labor Statistics. (1999, April). *Highlights of women's earnings in 1998.* Washington, DC: U.S. Government Printing Office.

Carr, D. (1997). The fulfillment of career dreams at midlife: Does it matter for women's mental health? *Journal of Health and Social Behavior, 38*, 331–344.

Casserly, P. (1980). An assessment of factors affecting female participation in advanced placement programs in mathematics, chemistry, and physics. In L. H. Fox, L. Brody, & D. Tobin (Eds.), *Women and the mathematical mystique* (pp. 138–163). Baltimore: Johns Hopkins University Press.

Crandall, V. C. (1969). Sex differences in expectancy of intellectual and academic reinforcement. In C. P. Smith (Ed.), *Achievement-related motives in children* (pp. 11–45). New York: Russell Sage Foundation.

Eccles, J. S. (1987). Gender roles and women's achievement-related decisions. *Psychology of Women Quarterly, 11*, 135–172.

Eccles, J. S. (1993). School and family effects on the ontogeny of children's interests, self-perceptions, and activity choices. In R. Dienstbier (Ed.), *Nebraska Symposium on Motivation: Vol. 40. Developmental perspectives on motivation* (pp. 145–208). Lincoln: University of Nebraska Press.

Eccles, J. S. (1994). Understanding women's educational and occupational choices: Applying the Eccles et al. model of achievement-related choices. *Psychology of Women Quarterly, 18*, 585–609.

Eccles, J. S., Adler, T. F., Futterman, R., Goff, S. B., Kaczala, C. M., Meece, J. L., & Midgley, C. (1983). Expectancies, values and academic behaviors. In J. T. Spence (Ed.), *Achievement and achievement motives* (pp. 75–146). San Francisco: Freeman.

Eccles, J. S., Adler, T. F., Futterman, R., Goff, S. B., Kaczala, C. M., Meece, J. L., & Midgley, C. (1985). Self-perceptions, task perceptions, socializing influences, and the decision to enroll in mathematics. In S. F. Chipman, L. R. Brush, & D. M. Wilson (Eds.), *Women and mathematics: Balancing the equation* (pp. 95–121). Hillsdale, NJ: Erlbaum.

Eccles, J. S., Barber, B., & Jozefowicz, D. (1998). Linking gender to educational, occupational, and recreational choices: Applying the Eccles et al. model of achievement-related choices. In W. B. Swann, J. H. Langlois, & L. A. Gilbert (Eds.), *Sexism and stereotypes in modern society: The gender science of Janet Taylor Spence* (pp. 153–192). Washington, DC: American Psychological Association.

Eccles, J. S., & Wigfield, A. (1995). In the mind of the actor: The structure of adolescents' achievement task values and expectancy-related beliefs. *Personality and Social Psychology Bulletin, 21*, 215–225.

Eccles, J. S., Wigfield, A., Flanagan, C. A., Miller, C., Reuman, D. A., & Yee, D. (1989). Self-concepts, domain values, and self-esteem: Relations and changes at early adolescence. *Journal of Personality, 57*, 283–310.

Eccles, J. S., Wigfield, A., & Schiefele, U. (1998). Motivation. In N. Eisenberg (Ed.), *Handbook of child psychology* (Vol. 3, 5th ed., pp. 1017–1095). New York: Wiley.

Eccles (Parsons), J. S., Adler, T., & Meece, J. L. (1984). Sex differences in achievement: A test of alternate theories. *Journal of Personality and Social Psychology, 46*, 26–43.

Farmer, H. S. (1997). Women's motivation related to mastery, career salience, and career aspiration: A multivariate model focusing on the effects of sex role socialization. *Journal of Career Aspiration, 5*, 355–381.

Farmer, H. S., Wardrop, J. L., Anderson, M. Z., & Risinger, R. (1995). Women's career choices: Focus on science, math, and technology careers. *Journal of Counseling Psychology, 42*(2), 155–170.

Feather, N. T. (1988). Values, valences, and course enrollment: Testing the role of personal values within an expectancy-valence framework. *Journal of Educational Psychology, 80*, 381–391.

Frome, P., & Eccles, J. S. (1995, March). *Underestimation of academic ability in the middle school years.* Poster presented at the Biannual Meeting of the Society for Research on Child Development, Indianapolis, IN.

Gottfredson, L. S. (1981). Circumscription and compromise: A developmental theory of occupational aspirations. *Journal of Counseling Psychology Monograph, 28*(6), 545–579.

Hall, R. M., & Sandler, B. R. (1984). *Out of the classroom: A chilly campus climate for women?* Washington, DC: Association of American Colleges.

Hallett, M. B., & Gilbert, L. A. (1997). Variables differentiating university women considering role-sharing and conventional dual-career marriages. *Journal of Vocational Behavior, 50*, 308–322.

Hayes, A., & Watt, H. M. G. (1998). Work and family life: Contemporary realities, current expectations and future prospects. *Australian Journal of Early Childhood, 23*, 33–39.

Hochschild, A. R. (1989). *The second shift.* New York: Viking.

Holland, D. C., & Eisenhart, M. A. (1990). *Educated in romance: Women, achievement, and college culture.* Chicago: University of Chicago Press.

Hollinger, C. L. (1983). Self-perception and the career aspirations of mathematically-talented female adolescents. *Journal of Vocational Behavior, 22*, 49–62.

Jacobs, J. E., Chhin, C. S., & Bleeker, M. M. (2006). Enduring links: Parents' expectations and their young adult children's gender-typed occupational choices. *Educational Research and Evaluation, 12*, 395–407.

Jacobs, J. E., Lanza, S., Osgood, D. W., Eccles, J. S., & Wigfield, A. (2002). Changes in children's self-competence and values: Gender and domain differences across grades one through twelve. *Child Development, 73*, 509–527.

Jozefowicz, D. M., Barber, B. L., & Eccles, J. S. (1993, March). *Adolescent work-related values and beliefs: Gender differences and relation to occupational aspirations*. Paper presented at the Biennial Meeting of the Society for Research in Child Development, New Orleans, LA.

Larose, S., Ratelle, C. F., Guay, F., Senécal, C., & Harvey, M. (2006). Trajectories of science self-efficacy beliefs during the college transition and academic and vocational adjustment in science and technology programs. *Educational Research and Evaluation, 12*, 373–393.

Lips, H. M. (1992). Gender- and science-related attitudes as predictors of college students' academic choices. *Journal of Vocational Behavior, 40*, 62–81.

Lubinski, D., & Benbow, C. P. (2006). Study of mathematically precocious youth after 35 years: Uncovering antecedents for the development of math–science expertise. *Perspectives on Psychological Science, 1*, 316–345.

Marini, M. M. (1978). Sex differences in the determination of adolescent aspirations: A review of the research. *Sex Roles, 4*, 723–751.

Mau, W. C. (2003). Factors that influence persistence in science and engineering career aspirations. *Career Development Quarterly, 51*, 234–243.

McBride, B. A., & Lutz, M. M. (2004). Intervention: Changing the nature and extent of father involvement. In M. E. Lamb (Ed.), *The role of the father in child development* (pp. 446–475). Hoboken, NJ: Wiley.

Meece, J. L., Eccles (Parsons), J., Kaczala, C. M., Goff, S. B., & Futterman, R. (1982). Sex differences in math achievement: Toward a model of academic choice. *Psychological Bulletin, 91*, 324–348.

Meinster, M. O., & Rose, K. C. (2001). Longitudinal influences of educational aspirations and romantic relationships on adolescent women's vocational interests. *Journal of Vocational Behavior, 58*, 313–327.

Mendez, L. M. R., & Crawford, K. M. (2002). Gender-role stereotyping and career aspirations: A comparison of gifted early adolescent boys and girls. *Journal of Secondary Gifted Education, 8*(3), 96–107.

Nagy, G., Trautwein, U., Baumert, J., Köller, O., & Garrett, J. (2006). Gender and course selection in upper secondary education: Effects of academic self-concept and interest. *Educational Research and Evaluation, 12*, 323–345.

Nakeo, K., & Treas, J. (1994). Updating occupational prestige and socioeconomic scores: How the new measures measure up. *Sociological Methodology, 24*, 1–72.

Nash, S. C. (1979). Sex role as a mediator for intellectual functioning. In M. A. Wittig & A. C. Petersen (Eds.), *Sex-related differences in cognitive functioning: Developmental issues* (pp. 263–302). New York: Academic Press.

National Center for Education Statistics. (1997). *Findings from the condition of education 1997, No. 11. Women in mathematics and science* (NCES 97-982). Washington, DC: Author.

National Center for Education Statistics. (2000). *Entry and persistence of women and minorities to college science and engineering education* (NCES 2000-601). Washington, DC: Author.

National Center for Education Statistics. (2002). *Digest of education statistics 2002*. Washington, DC: Author.

National Science Foundation. (1999). *Women, minorities, and persons with disabilities in science and engineering: 1998* (NSF 94-333). Arlington, VA: Author.

Novack, L. L., & Novack, D. R. (1996). Being female in the eighties and nineties: Conflicts between new opportunities and traditional expectations among White, middle class, heterosexual college women. *Sex Roles, 35*, 57–77.

Oakes, J. (1990). Opportunities, achievement, and choice: Women and minority students in science and mathematics. *Review of Research in Education, 16*, 153–339.

Sells, L. (1978). Mathematics—A critical filter. *The Science Teacher, 45*, 28–29.

Seymour, E. (1995). The loss of women from science, mathematics, and engineering undergraduate majors: An explanatory account. *Science Education, 79*, 437–473.

Shapka, J. D., Domene, J. F., & Keating, D. P. (2006). Trajectories of career aspirations through adolescence and young adulthood: Early math achievement as a critical filter. *Educational Research and Evaluation, 12*, 347–358.

Spade, J., & Reese, C. (1991). We've come a long way, maybe: College students' plans for work and family. *Sex Roles, 24*, 309–321.

Subotnik, R. F., & Arnold, K. D. (1996). *Remarkable women: Perspectives on female talent development*. Cresskill, NJ: Hampton Press.

Sullins, E. S., Hernandez, D., Fuller, C., & Tashiro, J. S. (1995). Predicting who will major in a science discipline: Expectancy-value theory as part of an ecological model for studying academic communities. *Journal of Research in Science Teaching, 32*, 99–119.

Tomlinson-Keasey, C. (1990). The working lives of Terman's gifted women. In H. Y. Grossman & N. L. Chester (Eds.), *The experience and meaning of work in women's lives* (pp. 213–244). Hillsdale, NJ: Erlbaum.

Updegraff, K. A., Eccles, J. S., Barber, B. L., & O'Brien, K. M. (1996). Course enrollment as self-regulatory behavior: Who takes optional high school math courses? *Learning and Individual Differences, 8*, 239–259.

U.S. Department of Labor, Women's Bureau. (1997). *Fair pay clearinghouse: Wages and occupational data on working women*. Retrieved from http://gatekeeper.dol.gov/dol/wb/public/programs/lw&occ.htm

Ware, N. C., & Lee, V. E. (1988). Sex differences in choice of college science majors. *American Educational Research Journal, 25*, 593–614.

Watt, H. M. G. (2004). Development of adolescents' self-perceptions, values, and task perceptions according to gender and domain in 7th- through 11th-grade Australian students. *Child Development, 75*, 1556–1574.

Watt, H. M. G. (2005). Explaining gendered math enrolments for NSW Australian secondary school students. *New Directions in Child and Adolescent Development, 110*, 15–29.

Watt, H. M. G. (2006). The role of motivation in gendered educational and occupational trajectories related to maths. *Educational Research and Evaluation, 12*, 305–322.

8

GENDER-TYPED OCCUPATIONAL CHOICES: THE LONG-TERM IMPACT OF PARENTS' BELIEFS AND EXPECTATIONS

CHRISTINA S. CHHIN, MARTHA M. BLEEKER, AND JANIS E. JACOBS

Recent research has shown that men are much more likely than women to pursue college degrees in engineering and computer sciences (Cooper & Weaver, 2003). This finding was further corroborated by a report from the National Science Foundation (2002) showing that women constitute less than 24% of the science and engineering labor force in the United States. In addition, men are more likely than women to be employed in construction, protective service, maintenance, farming, fishing, and forestry occupations, whereas women are more highly concentrated in health care and education occupations (U.S. Census Bureau, 2000). Together, these findings indicate that men and women still choose gender-typed occupations.

It is important to note, however, that the occupational choices men and women make are not necessarily made independently. There can be a number of explanations for the continuing gender difference in occupational

This research was made possible by grants from the National Science Foundation, the Spencer Foundation, and the William T. Grant Foundation to Jacquelynne S. Eccles and Bonnie Barber. The views and opinions expressed in this chapter are of the individual authors and do not represent the views and opinions of the authors' affiliations or employers. This chapter is dedicated to Janis E. Jacobs. She was one of the leading scholars and researchers in the field of gender and achievement. Her valuable insights and contributions will be missed.

215

choices, including societal norms, availability of occupations, and individual constraints. The desire to have family-flexible careers can also shape gender-typed occupational expectations (chap. 7, this volume).

This chapter presents three studies that provide evidence for the important role of parents' beliefs and expectations in shaping their children's occupational choices from adolescence through young adulthood. Gender differences in the occupational choices of men and women can be seen beginning with the occupational interests and aspirations of children and adolescents. For example, in one recent study, adolescent boys reported science and technology careers as their top occupational choices, whereas adolescent girls reported artistic and health professions as theirs (Lupart, Cannon, & Telfer, 2004). It is important to examine whether these gender-typed occupational aspirations of adolescents are actually related to later occupational choices in young adulthood and what role parents' beliefs and expectations play in these choices.

THEORETICAL PERSPECTIVE

Over the past 20 years, Eccles and her colleagues have highlighted the important role that parents play in their children's achievement choices using the parent socialization model (Eccles (Parsons), Adler, & Kaczala, 1982) as a framework (see Jacobs & Eccles, 2000). Specifically, characteristics of the parents, family, and neighborhood as well as characteristics of the child shape parents' behaviors and both their general beliefs about the world and their specific beliefs about their children. In this chapter we focus on two of the constructs in the Eccles (Parsons) et al. (1982) parent socialization model: (a) parents' general beliefs and behaviors and (b) parents' child-specific beliefs. In connection with the first construct, we focus on the relation between parents' gender role attitudes and their children's gender-typed occupational choices. According to the parent socialization model (Eccles (Parsons) et al., 1982), parents' general world beliefs, including their gender role beliefs and attitudes, can shape perceptions of their children and the opportunities they provide for their children. These general beliefs and behaviors that parents exhibit can, in turn, shape children's own future behaviors and choices. In connection with the second construct, we focus on the relation between parents' "child-specific beliefs" (i.e., parents' occupational expectations and aspirations for their children) and their children's actual occupational choices.

According to the parent socialization model (Eccles (Parsons) et al., 1982), the expectations that parents have regarding their children's future careers are expected to influence children's motivation to pursue those fields. Over time, children develop their own levels of interest in these careers and integrate these interests or values into their self-systems. Ultimately, the values that are incorporated into their self-beliefs will affect their future task choices. It is important to note that the influences between self-beliefs and values are bidirectional. Parents' roles may shift in this process from providing exposure, opportunities, and role-modeling of careers at early ages to providing encouragement and guidance for activities that continue to be supportive of children's developing interests in certain occupations.

We have tested and found support for both of these components of parent influence in the domain of educational achievement during childhood and adolescence (e.g., Jacobs, 1991; Jacobs & Eccles, 1985, 1992; Jacobs, Finken, Griffin, & Wright, 1998). By young adulthood, most individuals have achieved their highest level of education and entered the workforce; therefore, it is important to examine the parent socialization model (Eccles (Parsons) et al., 1982) during this next phase of life. We begin by highlighting research related to the role of parents' general beliefs and then discuss the role that parents' child-specific beliefs have in the development of children's actual occupational choices in young adulthood.

THE ROLE OF PARENTS' GENERAL BELIEFS AND BEHAVIORS

Previous research has suggested that parents' general beliefs and the goals they set for their children may reflect gender stereotypes (Jacobs, 1991; Jacobs & Eccles, 1992). This research suggests that parents' gender stereotypes directly impact perceptions of their children's abilities, resulting in more positive perceptions for children favored by the stereotypes (e.g., daughters for social skills, sons for math and sports skills; Jacobs, 1991; Jacobs & Eccles, 1992). Parents' perceptions, in turn, influence their children's performance and self-perceptions of abilities in each domain, even after controlling for previous performance. Judging from results from previous studies (Jacobs, 1991; Jacobs & Eccles, 1992), it is likely that parents' general beliefs and expectations for their children's future occupations will affect children's own beliefs and future expectations for their occupations.

Research examining the role of parents' gender stereotypes has found that parents generally endorse the cultural stereotype that mathematics achievement is more natural for boys than for girls (Eccles, Freedman-Doan, Frome, Jacobs, & Yoon, 2000). Despite an absence of gender differences in mathematics grades, parents who endorse this stereotype tend to underestimate girls' mathematics abilities and overestimate boys' abilities. Over time, girls' own self-perceptions come to reflect parents' stereotypes, and girls feel less efficacious about their math ability and lower their evaluations of the usefulness of math in the future. Girls may also spend fewer years studying mathematics and advanced science in high school than boys. These findings from Eccles et al. (2000) suggest that parents' general beliefs, in this case their gender stereotypes, can significantly shape their children's educational choices and, in the future, their occupational choices in a gender-typed manner.

In contrast, daughters of parents who hold more egalitarian gender role attitudes maintain a high level of math and science achievement across the transition to adolescence compared with daughters whose parents have more traditional gender role attitudes (Updegraff, McHale, & Crouter, 1996). These findings suggest that parents' gender stereotypes and gender role attitudes can undoubtedly shape children's experiences, beliefs, and attitudes (Eccles et al., 2000). In this chapter, we take a closer look at the relation between parents' general beliefs and their children's gendered occupational choices by examining the effect of parents' gender role attitudes on their children's gender-typed occupational choices.

THE ROLE OF PARENTS' CHILD-SPECIFIC BELIEFS

In addition to parents' general beliefs, parents' child-specific beliefs and expectations can shape their children's future beliefs and choices. This component of the Eccles (Parsons) et al. (1982) parent socialization model has been tested and supported by research spanning from childhood to adolescence. For example, in a longitudinal study of children from Grades 2 through 6, parents' occupational expectations for their children were positively related to children's own reports of their occupational expectations (Helwig, 1998). Similarly, parents' educational expectations for their adolescent children were positively related to adolescents' own reports of their educational expectations, especially for parents with higher levels of education (Raty, Leinonen, & Snellman, 2002). These findings suggest that children are aware of their parents' beliefs and expectations about their future education and careers beginning at a very young age and that parents' expectations play an important role in shaping children's own expectations and, possibly, future occupational choices.

Beyond adolescence, a recent study examined the relationships among mothers' earlier perceptions of their children's math abilities during adolescence and their children's math and science achievement beliefs and career choices 12 years later in young adulthood (Bleeker & Jacobs, 2004). The findings from that study showed that mothers' earlier predictions of their adolescent children's abilities to succeed in math careers were significantly related to their children's career choices in math and science during young adulthood, even after controlling for actual math abilities during adolescence. Young adult women whose mothers reported low perceptions of their abilities to succeed in math careers were substantially (66%) less likely to choose careers in the male-dominated areas of physical science and computing than careers in nonscience areas (Bleeker & Jacobs, 2004). It is interesting that mothers' perceptions had only a minimal relation to young adult men's occupational choices. These findings suggest that parents' child-specific beliefs and expectations can certainly play an important role in shaping children's—especially girls'—decisions to have a gender-typed or non-gender-typed occupation.

RESEARCH QUESTIONS

Research has shown that parents play an important role in shaping their children's occupational choices through their general beliefs about the world (i.e., gender role attitudes) and through the specific beliefs and expectations that they have for their children. Little research, however, has been conducted to examine the long-term relationship between parents' beliefs and expectations and children's occupational choices in young adulthood. To help fill this gap, in this chapter, we present data from three different longitudinal studies. In the first study, we examined the effect of parents' gender role attitudes on children's actual gender-typed occupational choices in young adulthood. In the second study, we examined the relation between the prestige level of parents' occupational expectations for their children during adolescence and the prestige of children's actual occupational choices in young adulthood. In the third study, we examined the relation between parents' expectations for their children having a gender-traditional or gender-nontraditional occupation during adolescence and the gender typing of children's subsequent actual occupational choices in young adulthood.

DESCRIPTION OF DATA SET

The data used in our research are part of a large, longitudinal investigation (Michigan Study of Adolescent Life Transitions; MSALT) that was designed to examine children's and parents' achievement attitudes during adolescence and young adulthood (Eccles, Wigfield, Reuman, & Mac Iver, 1987). During the 1st year of MSALT data collection in 1983, children were members of 143 sixth-grade math classrooms located in 12 school districts in primarily White middle- and working-class suburbs outside a large Midwestern city in the United States. School districts were selected to ensure a broad representation of schooling philosophies and procedures. All students and their parents within each classroom were invited to participate, and 80% of the students and 62% of the parents participated.

Although families in the school districts were not ethnically diverse, they were diverse in social class. Mothers' and fathers' highest levels of education ranged from grade school to advanced professional degrees, with the majority having attended a few years of college or technical school. Mothers' and fathers' annual incomes ranged from under $10,000 to over $80,000; the average for mothers was $25,000, and the average for fathers was $55,000.

During the beginning waves of data collection, adolescents completed questionnaires that asked about their relationships with parents, academic perceptions, and career efficacy. Parent questionnaires were mailed to the homes of families who agreed to participate. Each parent completed a separate questionnaire and returned it in a prepaid envelope. Questionnaire items assessed parents' beliefs about relationships with their adolescent children, perceptions of their children's abilities, and expectations for their children's future educational and occupational attainments.

After high school, the adolescents were surveyed again as they were entering young adulthood, at the ages of 20, 24, and 28. Surveys were mailed to participants' homes and returned in prepaid envelopes. In these surveys, the young adult children were asked to provide demographic information, including their current education and career statuses. In addition, the questionnaires assessed the adult children's perceptions of their accomplishments and relationships with their parents. On completion of the mailed surveys, participants were paid an honorarium.

Parents were not surveyed after high school until their children reached age 28. To obtain a reliable and valid sample of midlife parents, contact attempts were made with families of the original target children who met two inclusion criteria: (a) At least one parent of the target child must have participated at least once while their child was in high school, and (b) the target child must have participated in the study at age 20 or 24. Under these inclusion criteria, of the 1,406 families who originally participated in MSALT, 1,107 families were deemed eligible for participation in this last year of data collection. Of the 1,107 families, contact information was obtained for 699 sets of parents; 536 sets of parents and 885 children agreed to participate in the last year of data collection.

Participation from parents was solicited by telephone by trained interviewers. Completion of the telephone interview required only one parent's participation, and the survey asked parents to provide demographic information about career, marital status, and age. Parents were also asked to provide short answers to questions about their young adult children. On completion of the telephone interview, parent questionnaires (one for mothers and one for fathers) were mailed to the homes of those who had agreed to participate and returned in a prepaid envelope. Parent questionnaires assessed pride and perceptions about their young adult children's successes and choices with regard to careers, education, and relationships. Parents were also paid an honorarium for participation.

STUDY 1: PARENTS' GENDER ROLE ATTITUDES AND CHILDREN'S OCCUPATIONAL CHOICES

Previous research has shown that parents' gender stereotypes can shape their children's beliefs and choices during adolescence (e.g., Jacobs, 1991; Jacobs & Eccles, 1992). In a study using the MSALT data set (Chhin, Bleeker, & Jacobs, 2006), we examined in more detail the role of parents' general beliefs in shaping their children's occupational choices in young adulthood. Specifically, we examined (a) the relations among mothers' gender role attitudes when their children were age 12, adolescents' gender role attitudes at age 17, and reports of gender-typed career self-efficacy beliefs (i.e., male-typed and female-typed careers) at age 20 and (b) the relation between mothers' and adolescents' gender role attitudes at ages 12 and 17, respectively, and gender-typed career choices (i.e., male-typed, female-typed, or gender neutral careers) at age 28. The measure of gender role attitudes included items such as, "Babies and young children are likely to suffer if the mother works," and "It is usually better for everyone involved if the man is the breadwinner outside the home and the woman takes care of the children." In addition, young adult children at age 20 reported on how well they thought they would do in a variety of careers. On the basis of young adults' responses to the questions, separate measures of male-typed and female-typed career self-efficacy beliefs were created. Examples of careers that were included in the measure Self-Efficacy for Male-Typed careers were electrician, scientist, and military/protective service, whereas Self-Efficacy for Female-Typed Careers included careers such as clerical worker, child care worker, and human services worker.

In the first set of analyses, two regression equations were computed for each type of career self-efficacy belief (male typed and female typed) at age 20. Both regression equations included adolescents' gender, family income, mothers' education level, adolescents' gender role attitudes (at age 17), the interaction of adolescents' gender and adolescents' gender role attitudes, mothers' gender role attitudes (when children were age 12), and the interaction of adolescents' gender and mothers' gender role attitudes as predictors. All variables were entered at once, allowing us to measure the unique contribution of each variable.

We found a significant interaction between adolescents' gender and traditional gender role attitudes reported at age 17 ($\beta = .16, p < .01$) for male-typed career self-efficacy beliefs at age 20. The interaction indicates that girls' traditional gender role attitudes were negatively related to male-typed career self-efficacy beliefs; however, boys' traditional gender role attitudes seemed to have little or no relationship to their self-efficacy beliefs (see Figure 8.1). The interaction of mothers' gender role attitudes and adolescent gender, however, was not significantly related to children's reports of male-typed career self-efficacy at age 20. In contrast, the analysis examining young adult children's career self-

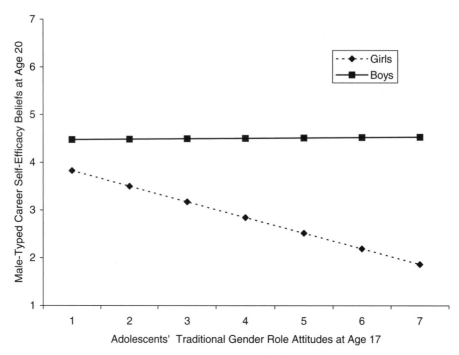

Figure 8.1. Interaction of adolescents' gender and gender role attitudes on male-typed career self-efficacy beliefs at age 20. Traditional Gender Role Attitudes scale: 1 = *less traditional;* 7 = *very traditional;* Male-Typed Career Self-Efficacy Beliefs scale: 1 = *low self-efficacy;* 7 = *high self-efficacy.*

efficacy beliefs for female-typed careers revealed an interaction between adolescent gender and mothers' reports of traditional gender role attitudes when their children were age 12 ($\beta = -.11$, $p < .05$). The interaction indicates that as mothers' traditional gender role attitudes increased, their sons' reports of female-typed career self-efficacy decreased, whereas their daughters' reports of female-typed career self-efficacy increased (see Figure 8.2). Together, these findings suggest that adolescents' gender role attitudes played a more important role in forming their self-efficacy beliefs for male-typed careers, whereas mothers' gender role attitudes played a more important role in forming young adult children's self-efficacy beliefs for female-typed careers.

In the second set of analyses, we examined the relation between mothers' and adolescents' gender role attitudes during adolescence and young adult children's actual gender-typed occupational choices using logistic regressions. The predictors in the model included family income and mothers' education level as controls and adolescents' gender, adolescents' gender role attitudes at age 17, interaction of gender and adolescents' gender role attitudes, mothers' gender

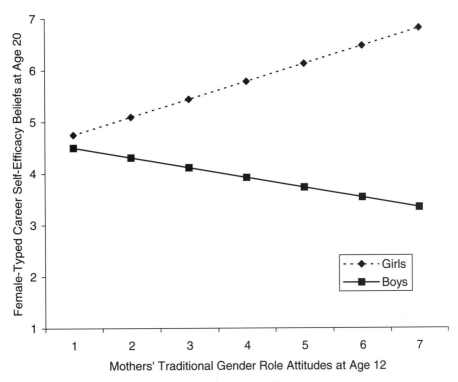

Figure 8.2. Interaction of adolescents' gender and mothers' gender role attitudes on female-typed career self-efficacy beliefs at age 20. Traditional Gender Role Attitudes scale: 1 = *less traditional;* 7 = *very traditional;* Female-Typed Career Self-Efficacy Beliefs scale: 1 = *low self-efficacy;* 7 = *high self-efficacy.*

role attitudes when their children were age 12, and the interaction of adolescents' gender and mothers' gender role attitudes. In addition, two new predictors, the young adults' level of education and parent status (0 = *not a parent/no children;* 1 = *parent/have children*) were included to control for the possible effect that these variables may have on young adults' career choices. The outcomes examined in the logistic regressions were having a female-typed, gender neutral, or male-typed career at age 28; all outcomes were dichotomous (0 = *did not have the job;* 1 = *had the job*).

The only significant effect of gender role attitudes was found for young adult children's male-typed occupational choices. Specifically, there was a significant interaction between gender and gender role attitudes, Exp(*b*) = 2.11, *p* < .01. This interaction indicates that men were 84.45% more likely to have a male-typed job than women. This gender difference was influenced by traditional gender role beliefs; in fact, men who reported more traditional gender role attitudes at age 17 were 67.85% more likely to have a male-typed job than women who reported more traditional gender role attitudes at age 17. In addition, a significant interaction of adolescent gender and mothers' gender role attitudes was also found, $Exp(b) = 1.37$, $p < .05$, suggesting that sons with mothers who reported more traditional gender role attitudes were 57.81% more likely to have male-typed careers at age 28 than sons with mothers who had less traditional gender role attitudes.

Together, the results from this first study provide evidence for the long-term relations of parents' gender role attitudes and their children's future beliefs and occupational choices. Specifically, we see that mothers' gender role attitudes can have a differential impact on sons' and daughters' gender-typed career self-efficacy beliefs and on their gender-typed occupational choices.

STUDY 2: PARENTS' GENERAL OCCUPATIONAL EXPECTATIONS AND CHILDREN'S OCCUPATIONAL CHOICES

Although many studies have shown that parents are powerful agents shaping the goals, choices, and behaviors of their children (Schulenberg, Vondracek, & Crouter, 1984; Trusty, 1998), most studies have not been able to examine the long-term relations between parents' earlier occupational expectations and aspirations for their children and their children's actual occupational choices later in life. In a second study, we helped fill this gap in the literature by examining the long-term relations between parents' career expectations and their children's actual career choices (Chhin, Jacobs, Bleeker, Vernon, & Tanner, 2007). Specifically, we examined the relation between the prestige of the career that parents expected of their children at age 15 and the prestige of the career that the children actually obtained at age 28. Occupational prestige was coded using the National Opinion Research Council coding system (Nakao & Treas, 1994). These codes can range from 0 to 100, with higher values representing greater occupational prestige (e.g., physician = 97.16; elementary school teacher = 78.50; bus driver = 29.75). Linear regressions were conducted with family income included as a covariate, and the child's gender and the prestige of parents' expected occupations for their children were included as predictors. The occupational prestige of the young adults' actual occupation at age 28 was the outcome. Regression analyses were conducted separately for mothers and fathers.

Results showed that both mothers' and fathers' career prestige expectations for their children at age 15 were positively related to the actual prestige of their children's career at age 28 ($\beta_{Mothers} = 3.23$, $p < .01$, $\beta_{Fathers} = 3.40$, $p < .001$). It is interesting that there were no significant differences between parents' occupational prestige expectations for their sons and daughters at age 15. In addition, mothers' and fathers' expectations for the prestige of their children's future careers were significantly correlated ($r = .57$, $p < .0001$). Descrip-

TABLE 8.1
Parents' Occupational Prestige Expectations and Children's Occupational Choices

Occupational prestige	M	SD
Mother's expectations when child was age 15		
Sons	71.11	18.17
Daughters	67.13	19.69
Father's expectations when child was age 15		
Sons	68.57	16.75
Daughters	71.10	17.72
Child's actual occupational prestige at age 28		
Sons	57.45	19.17
Daughters	56.95	18.49

Note. Occupational prestige: 0 = low, 100 = high. No significant differences were found between sons and daughters or between mothers and fathers.

tive information about parents' expectations for their children's occupational prestige and the prestige of their young adult children's actual occupations can be seen in Table 8.1.

These results suggest that if parents expected their adolescent children to have a prestigious career, their children were more likely to meet their parents' expectations and obtain a prestigious career in young adulthood. These results support the Eccles (Parsons) et al. (1982) model of parent socialization, which argues that parents' child-specific beliefs and expectations are related to their children's later behaviors and choices. The findings from this second study suggest that both mothers' and fathers' expectations for their adolescents' career choices are far-reaching; the level of prestige that parents expected for their child's career was significantly related to their child's actual career choice several years later.

STUDY 3: PARENTS' GENDER-TYPED OCCUPATIONAL EXPECTATIONS AND CHILDREN'S OCCUPATIONAL CHOICES

In Study 2, we showed that parents' general occupational expectations (i.e., the prestige of the occupation) for their children were related to their children's actual career choices at age 28. Building on these findings, in Study 3 we examined the long-term relations between parents' gender-typed career expectations for their children and their children's actual gender-typed career choices (Jacobs, Chhin, & Bleeker, 2006). Specifically, we examined the relations between parents' gender-typed occupational expectations for their children at age 15 and children's reports of their own gender-typed occupational expectations or aspirations at age 17. In addition, we examined the long-term relation between parents' occupational expectations for their children at age 17 and their children's actual occupational choices at age 28. Both parents' and children's gender-typed occupational expectations and occupational choices were categorized as gender traditional or gender nontraditional on the basis of data from the 1980 U.S. Census Bureau's (2000) classification of occupation by sex. Examples of gender-traditional occupations for men or gender-nontraditional occupations for women included engineer, construction worker, and doctor; gender traditional occupations for women or gender-nontraditional occupations for men included nurse, homemaker, and teacher; and gender neutral occupations included psychologist, writer, and factory worker. Chi-square analyses were conducted separately by both parent and child gender to examine these relations.

We found that parents' gender-typed career expectations were strongly related to their adolescent children's career expectations 2 years later but that this relation varied depending on the gender of both the parent and the adolescent (see Table 8.2). Specifically, significant relations were found between mothers' gender-typed occupational expectations and daughters' own gender-typed occupational expectations, $\chi^2(1, N = 116) = 10.16, p < .001$, and between mothers' gender-typed occupational expectations and sons' own gender-typed occupational expectations, $\chi^2(1, N = 89) = 4.37, p < .05$. In comparison, the results for fathers revealed a significant relation between fathers' gender-typed occupational expectations and daughters' own expectations, $\chi^2(1, N = 68) = 5.92, p < .05$, but not for sons' gender-typed occupational expectations. These

TABLE 8.2
Relations Between Parents' and Children's
Gender-Typed Career Expectations

	n (%)	
Children's expectations	Gender-traditional career	Gender-nontraditional career
Mothers' expectations when child was age 15		
Daughters' at age 17		
Gender-traditional career	20 (54.1)	17 (45.9)
Gender-nontraditional career	19 (24.1)	60 (75.9)
Sons' at age 17		
Gender-traditional career	62 (83.8)	12 (16.2)
Gender-nontraditional career	9 (60.0)	6 (40.0)
Fathers' expectations when child was age 15		
Daughters' at age 17		
Gender-traditional career	9 (47.4)	10 (18.4)
Gender-nontraditional career	9 (52.6)	40 (81.6)
Sons' at age 17		
Gender-traditional career	44 (80.0)	11 (20.0)
Gender-nontraditional career	10 (62.5)	6 (37.5)

findings suggest that parents' earlier gender-typed occupational expectations were similar to those held by their adolescent children 2 years later; however, both mothers' and fathers' expectations were related to daughters' gender-typed career expectations, whereas only mothers' expectations were related to sons' gender-typed career expectations.

After establishing the short-term links between parents' and adolescents' gender-typed occupational expectations, we wanted to extend these findings to examine the relations between parents' earlier gender-typed occupational expectations and the gender-typing of their young adult children's actual occupation 11 years later. Not surprisingly, we found significant gender differences in the children's actual careers at age 28, with many more women in gender-nontraditional careers and more men in gender-traditional careers, $\chi^2(1, N = 971) = 80.07$, $p < .001$ (see Table 8.3). The findings from this study also indicated that mothers' gender-typed occupational expectations for their daughters at age 17 were significantly related to their daughters' actual gender-typed occupations at age 28, $\chi^2(1, N = 95) = 7.48$, $p < .01$. In comparison, mothers' expectations of their sons' gender-typed occupations at age 17 were not significantly related to their sons' actual occupations at age 28. Similar to the results found for mothers, fathers' expectations of their daughters' gender-typed occupations at age 17 were significantly related to their actual occupational choices at age 28, $\chi^2(4, N = 60) = 5.92$, $p < .05$. In addition, fathers' expectations for their sons at age 17 were significantly related to their sons' occupational choices at age 28, $\chi^2(1, N = 56) = 7.47$, $p < .01$. More descriptive information on these findings can be seen in Table 8.4.

The findings from this study indicate that both mothers' and fathers' gender-typed occupational expectations for their children at age 17 were related to children's actual occupational choices 11 years later at age 28. In contrast to the first set of analyses examining the relation between parents' and children's gender-typed occupational expectations, fathers' occupational expectations significantly predicted both daughters' and sons' gender-typed career choices at age 28, whereas mothers' occupational expectations only predicted daughters' career choices at age 28. In sum, the results from this study suggest that parents' gender-typed career expectations have a significant bearing on their children's

TABLE 8.3
Young Adults' Gender-Typed Career Choices at Age 28

	n (%)		
Gender	Female-typed career	Gender neutral career	Male-typed career
Women	219 (38.4)	187 (32.8)	164 (28.8)
Men	29 (7.2)	101 (25.2)	271 (67.6)

Note. $\chi^2(1, N = 971) = 80.07$, $p < .001$.

TABLE 8.4
Relation Between Parents' Earlier Career Expectations and the Child's Actual Career at Age 28

Child's career at age 28	n (%)	
	Gender-traditional career	Gender-nontraditional career
Mother's expectations when child was age 17		
Daughter's		
Gender-traditional career	11 (34.4)	21 (65.6)
Gender-nontraditional career	7 (11.1)	56 (88.9)
Son's		
Gender-traditional career	37 (74.0)	13 (26.0)
Gender-nontraditional career	17 (68.0)	8 (32.0)
Father's expectations when child was age 17		
Daughter's		
Gender-traditional career	10 (47.6)	11 (52.4)
Gender-nontraditional career	7 (17.9)	32 (82.1)
Son's		
Gender-traditional career	34 (85.0)	6 (15.0)
Gender-nontraditional career	8 (50.0)	8 (50.0)

own gender-typed career expectations during adolescence, and on their actual gender-typed career choices in young adulthood. Fathers' gender-typed career expectations appear to play a more important role in their sons' occupational choices than do mothers' gender-typed career expectations. These findings further highlight the importance of parents' gender-typed expectations on their children's future beliefs, expectations, and career choices.

DISCUSSION

Using the parent socialization model (Eccles (Parsons) et al., 1982) as a framework, this chapter has focused on the role of parents' general and child-specific beliefs in shaping children's future occupational choices. Specifically, parents' gender role beliefs and expectations for their children's future occupational attainment were used to predict children's actual gender-typed occupational choices during young adulthood. Our chapter has highlighted some of our new findings related to the role of parents in shaping children's occupational choices over a 13-year time span from adolescence through young adulthood. In general, findings from the three studies show that parents' beliefs and expectations reported when their children were adolescents play an important role in shaping their children's gender-typed occupational choices during young adulthood.

In our first study (Chhin et al., 2006), the important role of parents' gender role beliefs, as outlined in the parent socialization model (Eccles (Parsons) et al., 1982) and supported by previous research (e.g., Zeldin & Pajares, 2000), is apparent, with mothers' earlier gender role beliefs relating to children's later self-efficacy beliefs. The results from Study 1 suggest that mothers' gender role attitudes may be more important for young adult children's female-typed career self-efficacy beliefs than for male-typed career self-efficacy beliefs. One explanation for this finding may be due to mothers being more familiar with and having more experience with female-typed careers than male-typed careers. Mothers, therefore, may be better able to reinforce female-typed career self-efficacy beliefs in their children, especially if they have more traditional gender role attitudes. In addition, mothers with traditional gender role attitudes may be more likely to promote their daughters' female-typed career self-efficacy beliefs, whereas mothers with less traditional gender role attitudes may be more laissez-faire about their sons' and daughters' gender-typed career self-efficacy beliefs.

In Study 1, we also found a significant relation between both adolescents' and mothers' reported gender role attitudes and young adult children's actual male-typed occupational choices. An explanation for adolescents' and mothers' gender role attitudes relating significantly to young adults' decisions to enter male-typed careers (but not female-typed or gender neutral careers) may be due to male-typed careers being more prestigious than either female-typed or gender neutral careers (Lips, 2005). Historically, because of the more prestigious nature of male-typed occupations, more barriers have been in place for women to enter male-typed occupations than for men to enter less prestigious, female-typed occupations (Hartung, Porfeli, & Vondracek, 2005). In addition, more prestigious male-typed careers may also be less family flexible, further placing greater constraints on women entering these occupations (chap. 7, this volume). Therefore, both parents' and children's gender role attitudes may play a much stronger role in children's decisions to enter male-typed occupations.

In Study 2 (Chhin et al., 2007), mothers' and fathers' occupational prestige expectations for their children at age 15 were found to be positively related to the prestige of their children's actual occupation at age 28. The results of this study also support the Eccles (Parsons) et al. (1982) model of parent socialization, which argues that the messages parents provide to children about their expectations relate to children's later occupational choices. Although we did not examine the process by which parents' occupational expectations for their children are related to later occupational choices, previous research using the Eccles (Parsons) et al. (1982) model has found evidence that parents' expectations are related to children's behaviors and choices through provision of opportunities, and through the encouragement of behaviors and choices consistent with their expectations (e.g., Eccles, 1993; Jacobs & Eccles, 1992). In addition to the role of parents' expectations, it is important to note that the child's characteristics, such as previous academic performance and self-perceptions of competence, can also play an important role in shaping the prestige of future occupations (chap. 1, this volume). These child characteristics are also represented in the Eccles-Parsons et al. (1982) model of parent socialization. In sum, Study 2 provides a unique contribution to the literature by demonstrating a significant relationship between parents' occupational prestige expectations and children's occupational choices over a 13-year time span from adolescence to young adulthood.

In Study 3 (Jacobs et al., 2006), parents' expectations for their children's future occupations were examined once again. This time, however, we examined parents' gender-typed occupational expectations and their children's actual gender-typed occupational choices. We found that parents' earlier gender-typed occupational expectations for their children were similar to those held by their adolescent children 2 years later. This could be due to the fact that their children held consistent career goals throughout this time and their parents' expectations merely reflected those goals; however, the finding is consistent with earlier studies suggesting the existence of a relationship between parents' gender stereotypes and children's later achievement choices (Jacobs, 1991; Jacobs & Eccles, 1992).

We found that parents' earlier gender-typed occupational expectations for their children were significantly related to their children's actual gender-typed occupational choices in young adulthood. These relations, however, varied depending on the gender of the parent and of the child, with fathers playing a more powerful role in shaping both their sons' and daughters' career choices than mothers. Previous research examining young adult children's decisions about their careers has supported this finding, suggesting that fathers may play a larger role in influencing their children's career decisions and choices than mothers (Hoffman, Hofacker, & Goldsmith, 1992). In addition, both mothers and fathers played a significant role in shaping their daughters' gender-typed occupational choices. This could be due to daughters being more sensitive to their parents' expectations, or it could be that parents are more aware of their daughters' career aspirations and make their expectations congruent to those of their daughters. In sum, when examining the occupational choices of young adults, it is important not only to examine the gender-typed nature of the occupation (i.e., male typed vs. female typed vs. gender neutral) but also to examine the differential role that both mothers and fathers play in the occupational choices of sons and daughters.

The findings from Study 3 also support the parent socialization model (Eccles (Parsons) et al., 1982) by providing longitudinal evidence of the relation between parents' beliefs and the later motivation of their children to pursue particular fields. Although these data do not explain the ways in which parents' expectations might be communicated or how children's achievement choices are made, the model suggests that parents' roles may shift from sharing perspectives and providing exposure, opportunities, and role modeling at early ages to providing encouragement and guidance for developing interests during adolescence and young adulthood.

Together, the three studies we have presented in this chapter provide important insights into the longitudinal relations between parents' beliefs and expectations and their children's future gender-typed occupational expectations and choices in young adulthood. A major limitation is the homogeneous nature of the sample with regard to ethnicity: The majority of the parents and children examined in our studies were White. It will be important for future research to longitudinally examine the role that parents play in their children's future occupational choices in more ethnically diverse samples.

CONCLUSION AND IMPLICATIONS

Findings from our three studies suggest that adolescents and young adults are making career choices within the context of gender-typed parental expectations and within a gender-typed world of occupational opportunities. Specifically, parents' general beliefs about the world and their child-specific beliefs can have a great bearing on their children's occupational expectations and future occupational choices. There are many nuances to the way in which parents' beliefs and expectations are related to their children's gender-typed occupational choices. For instance, the relation between parents' beliefs and expectations and their children's occupational expectations and choices differed depending on whether the outcome under examination was a male-typed versus female-typed occupation, or a gender-typed versus non-gender-typed occupation. In Study 1, for example, parents' gender role beliefs were more strongly related to their young adult children's decisions to enter female- than male-typed occupations. Another interesting nuance was that both parents' and children's gender impacted the relation between parents' beliefs and expectations and their children's beliefs and occupational choices. In Studies 2 and 3, mothers and fathers had significant impacts on their sons and daughters—but each on certain outcomes and not others. It is therefore important to consider not only the gender of the individual but also the differential roles played by mothers and fathers in shaping the future occupational choices of their sons and daughters.

We know that many factors influence gender-typed occupational choices, including the prestige of the occupation (chap. 1, this volume) and the desire for family-flexible occupations (chap. 7, this volume). Our studies suggest parents are another important factor in shaping children's gender-typed occupational choices. The longitudinal nature of our research has allowed us to identify relationships between parents' earlier beliefs and expectations and children's occupational choices up to 13 years later. Without data spanning the period during which adolescents' early speculations about preferred occupations turn into actual occupational choices in young adulthood, it would not be possible to understand the role that parents play in constructing and supporting the gendered environments in which children fashion their future occupational choices.

If we wish to diminish constraints on children's occupational choices, we need to educate parents, along with teachers, school counselors, principals, and other influential adults, about the important part that gender role attitudes and expectations can play in students' future career choices. By exhibiting more egalitarian gender role attitudes and valuing both gender-traditional and gender-nontraditional careers, we can expand students' future career opportunities. This may be especially important for young women, given the low numbers of women choosing to enter science, technology, engineering, and mathematics (often called "STEM") careers, which are among the most prestigious, most profitable, and most male-dominated careers in the United States. Students who receive encouragement in both traditional and nontraditional occupational domains will be better able to cope with negative socialization pressures from other sources, such as peers and the media, and will be less likely to limit their career interests and pursuits.

REFERENCES

Bleeker, M. M., & Jacobs, J. E. (2004). Achievement in math and science: Do mothers' beliefs matter twelve years later? *Journal of Educational Psychology, 96,* 97–109.

Chhin, C. S., Bleeker, M. M., & Jacobs, J. E. (2006, March). *Gender-typed career choices: The long-term effect of parents' expectations.* Poster presented at the Biennial Meeting of the Society for Research in Adolescence, San Francisco.

Chhin, C. S., Jacobs, J. E., Bleeker, M. M., Vernon, M. K., & Tanner, J. L. (2007). *Great expectations: The relations between parents' early expectations and perceptions of their young adult children's actual achievements.* Manuscript submitted for publication.

Cooper, J., & Weaver, K. D. (2003). *Gender and computers: Understanding the digital divide.* Mahwah, NJ: Erlbaum.

Eccles, J. S., Freedman-Doan, C., Frome, P., Jacobs, J., & Yoon, K. S. (2000). Gender-role socialization in the family: A longitudinal perspective. In T. Eckes & H. M. Trautner (Eds.), *The developmental social psychology of gender* (pp. 333–360). Mahwah, NJ: Erlbaum.

Eccles, J. S. (1993). School and family effects on the ontogeny of children's interests, self-perceptions, and activity choice. In J. Jacobs (Ed.), *Nebraska Symposium on Motivation, 1992: Development perspectives on motivation* (pp. 145–208). Lincoln: University of Nebraska Press.

Eccles, J. S., Wigfield, A., Reuman, D., & Mac Iver, D. (1987, April). *Changes in students' beliefs about four activity domains: The influence of the transition to junior high school.* Paper presented at the Annual Meeting of the American Educational Research Association, Washington, DC.

Eccles (Parsons), J., Adler, T. F., & Kaczala, C. M. (1982). Socialization of achievement attitudes and beliefs: Parental influences. *Child Development, 53,* 322–339.

Hartung, P. J., Porfeli, E. J., & Vondracek, F. W. (2005). Child vocational development: A review and consideration. *Journal of Vocational Behavior, 66,* 385–419.

Helwig, A. A. (1998). Occupational aspirations of a longitudinal sample from second to sixth grade. *Journal of Career Development, 24,* 247–265.

Hoffman, J. J., Hofacker, C., & Goldsmith, E. B. (1992). How closeness affects parental influence on business college students' career choices. *Journal of Career Development, 19,* 65–73.

Jacobs, J. E. (1991). The influence of gender stereotypes on parent and child math attitudes: Differences across grade-levels. *Journal of Educational Psychology, 83,* 518–527.

Jacobs, J. E., Chhin, C. S., & Bleeker, M. M. (2006). Enduring links: Parents' expectations and their young adult children's gender-typed occupational choices. *Educational Research and Evaluation, 12,* 395–401.

Jacobs, J. E., & Eccles, J. S. (1985). Gender differences in math ability: The impact of media reports on parents. *Educational Researcher, 14,* 20–25.

Jacobs, J. E., & Eccles, J. S. (1992). The influence of parent stereotypes on parent and child ability beliefs in three domains. *Journal of Personality and Social Psychology, 63,* 932–944.

Jacobs, J. E., & Eccles, J. S. (2000). Parents, task values, and real-life achievement choices. In C. Sansone & J. M. Harackiewicz (Eds.), *Intrinsic and extrinsic motivation: The search for optimal motivation and performance* (pp. 405–439). San Diego, CA: Academic Press.

Jacobs, J. E., Finken, L. L., Griffin, N. L., & Wright, J. D. (1998). The career plans of science-talented rural adolescent girls. *American Educational Research Journal, 35,* 681–704.

Lips, H. M. (2005). *Sex and gender: An introduction.* New York: McGraw Hill.

Lupart, J. L., Cannon, E., & Telfer, J. (2004). Gender differences in adolescent academic achievement, interests, values and life-role expectations. *High Ability Studies, 15*(1), 25–42.

National Science Foundation. (2002). *National Science Board: Science and engineering indicators—2002* (NSB-02-1). Arlington, VA: Author.

Nakao, K., & Treas, J. (1994). Updating occupational prestige and socioeconomic scores: How the new measures measure up. *Sociological Methodology, 24,* 1–72.

Raty, H., Leinonen, T., & Snellman, L. (2002). Parents' educational expectations and their social–psychological patterning. *Scandinavian Journal of Educational Research, 46,* 129–144.

Schulenberg, J. E., Vondracek, F. W., & Crouter, A. C. (1984). The influence of family on vocational development. *Journal of Marriage and the Family, 46*(1), 129–143.

Trusty, J. (1998). Family influences on educational expectations of late adolescents. *Journal of Educational Research, 91*, 260–270.

Updegraff, K. A., McHale, S. M., & Crouter, A. C. (1996). Gender roles in marriage: What do they mean for girls' and boys' school achievement? *Journal of Youth and Adolescence, 25*(1), 73–88.

U.S. Census Bureau. (2000). *Occupation by sex: 2000.* Retrieved June 22, 2005, from http://factfinder.census.gov/servlet/QTTable?_bm=y&-geo_id=01000US&-qr_name=DEC_2000_SF3_U_QTP27&-ds_name=DEC_2000_SF3_U&-_lang=en&-_caller=geoselect&-state=qt&-format=

Zeldin, A. L., & Pajares, F. (2000). Against the odds: Self-efficacy beliefs of women in mathematical, scientific, and technological careers. *American Educational Research Journal, 37*, 215–246.

9

BIOLOGICAL CONTRIBUTORS TO GENDERED OCCUPATIONAL OUTCOME: PRENATAL ANDROGEN EFFECTS ON PREDICTORS OF OUTCOME

SHERI A. BERENBAUM AND KRISTINA L. KORMAN BRYK

The nature and causes of sex differences in occupational outcomes have generated considerable controversy among the scientific and public communities in the past few years. Of particular concern is the underrepresentation of women in science, math, engineering, and related technical fields, and the salary differential accompanying the sex difference. A corollary not as often discussed is the underrepresentation of men in caring professions such as child care, teaching, and nursing. There is little question that many factors contribute to gendered occupational outcomes. As described in other chapters in this book, some of the factors offered to explain these outcomes include self-perceptions, school experiences, values, and social pressures. These causal influences are generally assumed to originate outside the child (e.g., to be imposed by parents or schools) or to be constructed by the child from observation of the social world. However,

The research reported here was supported by a grant from the National Institutes of Health, HD19644. We thank Matthew DiDonato for his careful reading and thoughtful comments on the chapter. A number of people have contributed to our research, and we particularly thank the pediatric endocrinologists who generously provided access to their patients and answered medical questions; the graduate and undergraduate students who have helped to collect and process data; and Stephen Duck, J. Michael Bailey, Susan Resnick, and Melissa Hines for their collaborations. We are particularly grateful to the families who have participated in our studies.

increasing evidence from other areas of development suggests that the child is not a passive recipient of the social environment.

It is valuable to consider how similar influences might operate for occupational outcomes, that is, how the child's biologically influenced interests and characteristics might influence these outcomes. The child's qualities might affect occupational outcomes directly (e.g., through interests) or indirectly (e.g., through modification of the environment in which the child lives). The goal of this chapter is to describe evidence that gendered interests and characteristics are influenced by biology, particularly the levels of sex hormones present during prenatal development, and to consider how gendered occupational outcomes might arise through joint effects of biology and socialization. Much of the evidence we describe comes from females with congenital adrenal hyperplasia (CAH), who are exposed to moderately elevated androgens during prenatal development. Compared with their unexposed female relatives, females with CAH are more male typical and less female typical in activity interests, some personal and social characteristics, and some cognitive abilities; in contrast, gender identity in females with CAH is female typical. We consider the mechanisms whereby hormones might influence behavior—for example, through alterations in the selection and interpretation of the social environment, particularly those aspects related to sex. We emphasize that biology is not destiny, that social factors also affect psychological sex differences, that sex-differential representation in different occupations reflects social practices as well as individual characteristics, and that findings of hormonal influences on psychological characteristics related to gendered occupational outcomes do not provide justification for unequal treatment of men and women.

SOME BASICS OF HORMONES AND BEHAVIOR

Studies of a variety of nonhuman mammalian species have clearly demonstrated that the development of sex-related physical and behavioral characteristics depends on the levels of sex hormones present during early life.[1] In

---

[1] Androgens and estrogens are the primary sex hormones. Androgens are produced by the testes (the male gonads) as well as by the ovaries (the female gonads) and by the adrenal glands in both males and females. Estrogens are produced directly by the ovaries in females and by the placenta during gestation in both males and females and are produced indirectly by being converted from androgens in both males and females. This means that both males and females produce and respond to both androgens and estrogens, but they do so at different levels at many, but not all, stages of the life span. Males have considerably higher levels of androgens than do females early in development. Androgens are the hormones generally responsible for whether an organism develops physically (and, to some extent, psychologically, as discussed in the chapter) as a male or a female. When high levels of androgens are present, male development takes place; when low or no androgens are present, female development occurs (so the absence of androgens rather than the presence of estrogens causes female development, although estrogens are probably necessary for completely normal female development). Both androgens and estrogens exert physical and behavioral effects at puberty and beyond, and males have higher levels of androgens and lower levels of estrogens than do women at these stages. Androgens and estrogens come in several forms. The forms of androgens that have the most effect on the body and behavior are testosterone, dihydrotestosterone, and androstenedione. The form of estrogen that has the biggest effect is estradiol. Progesterone is also produced in the ovaries, and it plays a large role in reproduction but a smaller role in behavior.

particular, male-typical behaviors arise when the organism is exposed to high levels of androgens during early development (paralleling brain development). This exposure is characteristic of males because androgens are produced in large quantities by the testes, but it can occur in females for a variety of reasons, as discussed below. The importance of androgens for male-typical development has been demonstrated through studies involving experimental manipulation and naturally occurring variations such as gestating close to an animal of the opposite sex (for reviews, see Becker, Breedlove, Crews, & McCarthy, 2002; Breedlove, 1992; M. M. Clark & Galef, 1998; Goy & McEwen, 1980; Ryan & Vandenbergh, 2002). Rodents exposed during the neonatal period to androgen levels that are atypical for their sex also show behavior that is atypical for their sex, including adult sexual behavior, juvenile rough play, adult aggression, and maze performance. Androgens also produce changes in parts of the brain, including the hypothalamus, which is involved in sexual behavior, and the hippocampus, involved in spatial learning (for a review, see Becker et al., 2002).[2]

Primate behavioral development is also affected by early exposure to androgens: Female monkeys treated prenatally are masculinized in several ways, including sexual behavior, rough play, grooming (Goy, Bercovitch, & McBrair, 1988; Wallen, 1996), and some learning abilities (Bachevalier & Hagger, 1991; A. S. Clark & Goldman-Rakic, 1989). Studies in monkeys show that there may be several distinct sensitive periods—even within the prenatal period—for androgen effects on behavior and that it is possible to masculinize the genitalia and behavior independently (Goy et al., 1988). Further, environmental context modifies behavioral effects of hormones (Wallen, 1996). For example, sex differences in rough-and-tumble play occur in all rearing environments, with the size of the difference affected by the environment, whereas differences in aggression and in *presenting* (displaying the female sexual posture) are found only in certain rearing situations, such as rearing with peers and without a mother. Behaviors that show consistent sex differences across social context are most affected by prenatal androgens.

As described in this chapter, human studies of long-term behavioral effects of prenatal androgens have generally confirmed the findings and principles derived from rodent and primate studies. The likely crucial sensitive periods for human behavioral effects of sex hormones occur prenatally, given that human brain structures are formed before birth, and testosterone (the principal masculinizing hormone) is highest in males during prenatal weeks 8 to 24 (Smail, Reyes, Winter, & Faiman, 1981). It is obviously neither feasible nor ethical to manipulate prenatal androgens in human beings, but information

---

[2] Exposure to extreme sex-typical levels of androgens, as in the case of males exposed to above average levels, does not have consistent effects. Studies of nonhuman males show that excess androgen may further masculinize behavior or it may demasculinize behavior (perhaps because exogenous androgen suppresses males' endogenous production), but most often excess androgen has no effects in males (Baum & Schretlen, 1975; Wallen & Baum, 2002).

can be obtained from natural experiments, that is, studies of people with disorders of sexual differentiation whose prenatal androgen exposure is inconsistent with other aspects of biological sex such as sex chromosomes and with rearing (e.g., Money & Ehrhardt, 1972). Such samples are not perfect (particularly with respect to alternative explanations and generalizability, as described below), so it is important to note that recent work in typical populations has provided some convergence of evidence regarding the behavioral importance of prenatal androgens.

The best opportunity to study behavioral effects of prenatal androgens is provided by females with CAH, who have a genetic defect in an enzyme that controls cortisol production, causing them to produce high levels of adrenal androgens beginning very early in gestation. Postnatal treatment with cortisol reduces hormone levels, generally to normal or even below normal levels (Speiser & White, 2003). Genetic females with CAH have external genitalia that are masculinized to varying degrees, but they have ovaries and a uterus and are fertile. They are reared as—and generally identify as—females. They are usually diagnosed at birth and treated with cortisol to reduce androgen excess (or they will experience rapid growth and early puberty) and surgically to feminize their genitalia. If prenatal androgens affect human sex-typed behavior, then females with CAH should be behaviorally more masculine and less feminine than a comparison group of females without CAH—and they are, in many but not all ways, as described below and reviewed in detail elsewhere (Berenbaum, 2001, 2004; Meyer-Bahlburg, 2001).

Nevertheless, girls with CAH are not a perfect experiment, for several reasons. First, their genitalia are masculinized as a result of androgen exposure early in fetal life when the genitalia develop. Most girls receive surgery to normalize their genital appearance, but it is possible that behavioral changes result from social responses to their masculinized genitalia (Quadagno, Briscoe, & Quadagno, 1977) or from their own responses to their genital appearance or surgery.[3] Second, there is variability across patients in the extent to which the disease is controlled, so androgen levels may continue to be elevated throughout life in those with poor disease control. Third, there are other changes associated with CAH that might result in behavioral changes, including abnormalities in other hormones, the treatment itself, and living with a chronic disease. These threats to validity will be considered with the evidence.

---

[3]There are few systematic data describing the postsurgical genital appearance of girls with CAH, and there is considerable controversy about both the anatomic and functional outcome of the surgery in terms of whether the genitalia appear normal to a physician and to the patient herself; how the surgery affects sexual function; and how genital appearance and surgery affect other psychological characteristics, including sexual orientation, gender identity, desire to have children, and overall adjustment. (For a discussion of these issues and some data, see Berenbaum, 2003, 2004, 2006; Berenbaum, Bryk, Duck, & Resnick, 2004; Chase, 1998; Crouch, Minto, Liao, Woodhouse, & Creighton, 2004; Migeon et al., 2002; Minto, Liao, Woodhouse, Ransley, & Creighton, 2003; Warne et al., 2005; Wisniewski et al., 2000; Wisniewski, Migeon, Malouf, & Gearhart, 2004.)

Relevance of Congenital Adrenal Hyperplasia for Understanding Gendered Occupational Outcomes

Females with CAH are of considerable value in understanding the causes of gendered occupational outcomes because they provide an opportunity to separate biological and social origins of the characteristics associated with these outcomes. If, for example, females with CAH differ from typical females on mathematics-related attitudes or coursework or on self-perceived abilities, then it suggests that these characteristics are influenced by prenatal hormones.

What Does It Mean for Hormones to Affect Characteristics Associated With Gendered Outcomes?

The notion that biology might affect gendered occupational outcomes is distasteful to some people. Therefore, it is important to emphasize what it means—and does not mean—for hormones to affect behaviors related to occupation, or, indeed, any outcome. First, hormone effects do not have to be direct. Hormones may, of course, influence specific brain structures that underlie specific behaviors, but it is unlikely that predictors and outcomes related to occupation are simply subserved by a single brain area that is fixed at birth. Hormonal influences on complex behaviors are likely mediated by the social environment. Examples of how this might happen are provided later in the chapter. Second, human behavioral effects of hormones are probably not absolute and fixed. The importance of context has been demonstrated in monkeys, and it seems likely that such effects are even larger for human beings for whom culture is more salient (Wallen, 1996). Third, although some brain structures are established early in development, both structure and function are plastic. There is now good evidence that the brain can change—and does change—in response to environmental events. For example, aberrant emotional experiences associated with maltreatment appear to alter the ways in which the brain processes emotion (Pollak, Klorman, Thatcher, & Cicchetti, 2001). Fourth, hormones have never been found to be the sole cause of any behavior. For all behaviors discussed below, there is evidence to suggest that social factors are also important. It is no longer productive to ask whether a behavior is influenced by nature or by nurture but instead to ask how nature and nurture work together to affect behavior. Fifth, many genetic and biological influences are amenable to environmental modification. Lifestyle changes (e.g., diet, exercise) are widely implemented to reduce disease risk. Cosmetic changes (e.g., contact lenses, hair dye, plastic surgery) are used to improve physical appearance. Educational programs improve the abilities and social behaviors of children with Down syndrome. In general, causes of behaviors may be different from the factors that maintain them or modify them. Sixth, political equality does not depend on biological equality.

All people should be treated the same under the law without regard to the origins of the differences among them. Biological causation does not justify discrimination.

EVIDENCE FOR HORMONAL INFLUENCES ON PREDICTORS OF GENDERED OCCUPATIONAL OUTCOMES

There is no systematic evidence about career choices of women with CAH or any comparable group, but there is good evidence about hormonal influences on behaviors that are related to occupational outcomes, some in a causal way. This includes vocational interests, other interests (e.g., in family), and cognitive abilities. There is also some suggestive evidence regarding other potential influences on occupational outcome, such as personality.

The earliest statements about behavioral effects of androgens came from reports that girls with CAH were tomboys (Money & Ehrhardt, 1972). Those reports were difficult to interpret, however, because of methodological limitations (primarily subjective measures, nonblind interviews, small samples, and inadequate comparisons), and failure to consider alternative explanations (especially the possibility that behavior resulted from parent treatment in response to the appearance of the girls' genitals).

In 1985, we began a project that was initially designed to address these problems. Over the past 20 years, the project has expanded to include study of androgen effects on a variety of behaviors across age. Many of our results are relevant to questions about the development of gendered occupational outcomes. We are not the only ones studying this question, although we are the only ones who have studied participants on multiple occasions across age, and we have a relatively large sample. In the following sections, we describe data from our project as well as relevant data from other labs.

The Study Design

Boys and girls with CAH due to 21-hydroxylase deficiency were recruited through university-affiliated pediatric endocrine clinics in the midwestern United States. Thus, all participants were receiving regular medical treatment for their disease, including cortisol. Letters of invitation were sent to parents, followed by telephone calls to provide additional information and schedule testing sessions (which were done in participants' houses). More than 90% of families contacted participated in the study. Unaffected siblings of similar age to children with CAH were recruited as a comparison group because they provide a control for general genetic and environmental background. On occasion, first cousins were recruited if there was no available sibling. Because not all patients had a same-sex control, relatives of male and female patients were combined to form control groups. Participants represented a range of socioeconomic backgrounds, and the overwhelming majority were Caucasian (partly reflecting the fact that CAH is more common in Whites than in African Americans).

The initial study (Phase I, conducted from 1985 to 1988 in collaboration with Melissa Hines) focused on sex-typed toy preferences and rough-and-tumble play in children aged 3 to 8, including boys and girls with CAH and their unaffected siblings. The next phase of the project (Phase II, conducted from 1988 to 1993) included multiple measures of sex-typed play obtained on two occasions 6 months apart to increase reliability of measurement and examine individual differences in play, following the original children who were then 7 to 12 and adding new children from ages 3 to 12. We also expanded the domains of assessment, to include playmate preference, aspects of personal and social behavior (such as aggression and interest in babies), and cognitive abilities. In the next phase (Phase III, conducted from 1993 to 1999), we followed the children from Phases I and II into later childhood or adolescence and added new children from ages 3 to 18. We added age-appropriate measures, included assessments of gender identity and additional cognitive abilities, and had separate measures for children aged 3 to 8 and 9 to 18. In the last phase (Phase IV, conducted from 1999 to 2006), we again followed participants from earlier phases into adolescence or young adulthood and added new ones aged 9 to 29, again adding age-appropriate measures and having separate measures for participants varying by age (3 to 8, 9 to 15, and 16 and older); we also added measures of sexual orientation and cognitive abilities. At all phases, we also assessed emotional adjustment. Table 9.1 shows an overview of the behavioral domains assessed at each phase. Because participants were added to the study at each phase and only some participated in all phases, this is not a true longitudinal study, but is the only one that has followed participants across age, so we describe it is a "quasi-longitudinal" study.

As would be expected with this design, the number of participants varies across phase, as shown in Table 9.2. Attrition has been low (generally less than 10% from one phase to the next), and 60% of participants have been seen on more than one occasion. Comparisons of participants who drop out versus those who remain in the study have generally revealed no differences on key measures. Some participants missed assessments or have incomplete data (mostly unreturned questionnaires or children too young to understand test instructions). Analyses show little impact of missing data on inferences.

Throughout the project, we have measured multiple aspects of sex-typed behavior with multiple measures obtained from different methods, including observations, tests, self-reports, and parent reports. Measures were chosen to be reliable, age appropriate, sex related (on the basis of other studies), and likely to be sensitive to hormone effects. Hypotheses for all measures were specific and based on evidence regarding hormonal influences on rodent and primate

TABLE 9.1

"Quasi-Longitudinal" Study of Individuals With Congenital Adrenal Hyperplasia (CAH) and Their Relatives: Behavioral Domains Assessed at Each Phase

Behavior	Phase I	Phase II	Phase III	Phase IV
Observed toy play	X	X	X	
Observed rough-and-tumble play	X			
Sex-typed activity interests		X	X	X
Playmate preference	X	X	X	
Aggression		X	X	X
Interest in babies		X	X	X
Gender identity			X	X
Cognitive abilities		X	X	X
Sexuality				X
Emotional adjustment	X	X	X	X

behavior (Becker et al., 2002; Breedlove, 1994) or chosen to assess overall psychological adjustment. The key hypotheses concerned differences between females with CAH and their unaffected sisters—females with CAH were hypothesized to be behaviorally masculinized and defeminized—because animal studies have clearly shown more marked and consistent behavioral effects of excess androgens in females than in males. We did not expect the groups to differ on emotional adjustment.

Males with CAH were studied for several reasons: to study whether behavioral changes in females could be specifically attributed to androgen or might reflect general changes associated with the disease, to provide additional unaffected siblings (some unaffected sisters were actually related to males with CAH), and for comparison with animal studies suggesting few behavioral effects of excess androgen in males. In terms of physical development, males with CAH who are treated with cortisol are generally very similar to males without CAH; untreated males with CAH undergo precocious physical development, including early puberty and ultimately shorter height.

TABLE 9.2

"Quasi-Longitudinal" Study of Individuals With Congenital Adrenal Hyperplasia (CAH) and Their Relatives: Number of Participants at Each Phase

Group	Phase I	Phase II	Phase III	Phase IV
Females with CAH	21	29	46	44
Unaffected female relatives	9	17	25	21
Males with CAH	7	19	31	34
Unaffected male relatives	14	28	44	35
Average age of all participants (years)	5.7	7.8	10.3	15.1

We also studied two separate samples of adolescent and adult females and males with CAH and their unaffected relatives, each assessed on one occasion. The first sample, studied in collaboration with Susan Resnick (see Resnick, 1982), consisted of 58 participants averaging 18.6 years of age (range 11 to 31), including 18 females and 9 males with CAH, 13 unaffected female relatives, and 18 unaffected male relatives. They were assessed on cognition and personality. The second sample was recruited at the same time as the children in Phase I of the quasi-longitudinal study and consisted of 43 participants averaging 19.7 years of age (range 13 to 35), including 11 females and 17 males with CAH, 5 unaffected female relatives, and 10 unaffected male relatives. They were assessed on cognition, aggression and personality, although the sample was too small for meaningful analyses on cognition.

Hormonal Influences on Sex-Typed Activities and Occupational Interests

Our data clearly show that moderate androgen exposure, characteristic of females with CAH, produces large changes on gendered activities and associated interests. In childhood, girls with CAH play much more with boys' toys than do their unaffected sisters, as seen in direct observations of children's play, in girls' self-reports of their activities, and in parents' reports of the girls' activities (Berenbaum & Hines, 1992; Berenbaum & Snyder, 1995). For example, girls with CAH aged 3 to 12 played with boys' toys about 1.5 to 2 times as much as comparison girls. When choosing a toy to keep, 43% of girls with CAH chose a transportation toy at any assessment, whereas 4% of control girls (and 76% of boys) did so. Girls with CAH have scores between those of unaffected girls and boys (with and without CAH, who do not differ from each other).

The effects of androgens on gendered activities extend beyond childhood. Adolescent and adult females with CAH are interested in male-typical activities, as revealed in their own self-reports and in reports from their parents (Berenbaum, 1999, 2005). For example, teenage girls with CAH are more likely than their sisters to report interest in electronics and sports. The effects are very large (ds of approximately 2.0), and, again, girls with CAH are between unaffected girls and boys. Preliminary data from our most recent phase of data collection suggest that adolescent and young adult females with CAH continue to differ from their unaffected sisters in their hobbies, being more interested in male-typical hobbies, such as sports and electronics, and less interested in female-typical hobbies, such as fashion and arts (Berenbaum, 2005). Even on a single self-report measure, the differences are very large, more than 1.5 standard deviations, and women with CAH are again between unaffected women and men (Berenbaum, 2005).

The male-typical interests of females with CAH extend to vocational interests. For example, teenage girls with CAH express interest in male-typical careers, such as engineer, architect, and airline pilot, whereas their unaffected sisters express interest in female-typical careers, such as X-ray technician, ice skater, and hair stylist (Berenbaum, 1999). Again, the differences are large (*d*s of approximately 2.0). Because interests show stability in typical males and females (Low, Yoon, Roberts, & Rounds, 2005; Swanson, 1999), it is likely that adult females with CAH will maintain interest in male-typical occupations, but this awaits empirical test.

The increase in male-typical activity interests in females with CAH is paralleled by a decrease in female-typical interests. Thus, compared with typical females, females with CAH play less in childhood with girls' toys, show less interest in adolescence and adulthood in female-typical activities and hobbies, and are less interested in female-typical careers (Berenbaum, 1999; Berenbaum, Duck, & Bryk, 2000; Berenbaum & Hines, 1992; Berenbaum & Snyder, 1995).

When multiple measures are used, so that reliability is high, there is little overlap in the scores of females with CAH and typical females. Further, there is a "dosage" effect, with sex-atypical interests most pronounced in those with the most exposure to prenatal androgens, as reflected by clinical features (Berenbaum, 1999; Berenbaum et al., 2000).

Our results on activity interests have been confirmed by other investigators with respect to childhood toy play (Meyer-Bahlburg et al., 2004; Nordenström, Servin, Bohlin, Larsson, & Wedell, 2002) and vocational interests in childhood (Servin, Nordenström, Larsson, & Bohlin, 2003). Our findings of a dosage effect have also been confirmed by those examining clinical features (Dittmann et al., 1990; Servin et al., 2003) and extended by those examining behavior in relation to genetic mutation causing CAH, which is a more sensitive indicator of androgen exposure than is clinical phenotype (Nordenström et al., 2002).

Keeping in mind that CAH is not a perfect experiment, it is important to note that alternative explanations for the findings have been tested and generally not supported. This work comes from other labs in addition to ours. First, there is no evidence that behavioral changes result from social responses to the genitalia of females with CAH. Parents report that they treat their daughters with CAH the same as they treat their unaffected daughters (Berenbaum & Hines, 1992), and they wish that their daughters with CAH were less masculine than they are (whereas they wish that their daughters without CAH were more masculine than they are; Servin et al., 2003). Moving behind parent reports to actual observations of parent behavior, the amount of time that girls with CAH spend playing with boys' toys does not increase when parents are present (Nordenström et al., 2002), and parents of girls with CAH were observed to encourage them to play with girls' toys (Pasterski et al., 2005). These results are consistent with those from androgenized female monkeys showing mothers' behaviors to be unrelated to offspring masculine behavior (Goy et al., 1988). Second, behavioral changes in CAH have been found to relate to levels of prenatal—not postnatal—androgen (Berenbaum et al., 2000; Dittmann et al., 1990; Nordenström et al., 2002; Servin et al., 2003). Third, other hormones that are abnormal in females with CAH, such as progesterone and corticosteroids, have smaller and less consistent behavioral effects than androgen, and may actually prevent masculinization (Hull, Franz, Snyder, & Nishita, 1980). Further, behavioral similarities between males with and without CAH suggest that the behavioral changes in females with CAH are unlikely to reflect general disease characteristics or other hormonal abnormalities (for a review, see Berenbaum, 2004).

Data from other labs studying other clinical samples with sex-atypical hormone exposure confirm the findings in females with CAH. One source of evidence comes from individuals with complete androgen insensitivity syndrome (CAIS), who have a male-typical karyotype (XY chromosomal complement), normal testes, and high (male-typical) prenatal androgen levels but who develop as females because they lack the cell receptors to respond to androgens. Individuals with CAIS—who are reared as females—have female-typical activity interests, as measured by reports of their current interests and by retrospective reports of their childhood interests (Hines, Ahmed, & Hughes, 2003; Wisniewski et al., 2000). Another source of evidence about androgen effects on gendered interests comes from individuals with cloacal exstrophy who have a male-typical karyotype, normal testes, and high (male-typical) prenatal androgen exposure but female rearing because of absent or malformed penis. They are reported by themselves and their parents to have male-typical childhood activity interests (Reiner & Gearhart, 2004), although they have not been studied with the objective measures used in children with CAH.

There is also some question about the extent to which findings from CAH females can be generalized to the general population, given that their androgen levels are considerably higher than those of any female without CAH. Thus, it is important to confirm findings in general populations with typical variations in prenatal androgen exposure (for review and discussion of such studies see Cohen-Bendahan, van de Beek, & Berenbaum, 2005). Such evidence comes from two studies that found markers of high testosterone in mother's blood during pregnancy to be associated with masculinized gender-role behavior in daughters later in life. One study examined sex-typed activities in typical girls at age 3½ years in relation to testosterone in their mother's serum during pregnancy (blood samples were collected between weeks 5 and 36 of gestation). Girls who engaged in masculine activities had mothers who had higher testosterone when the girls were in utero than did girls who engaged in feminine activities (Hines, Golombok, Rust, Johnston, & Golding, 2002). Another study examined a broad measure of gender-role behavior in adult females. Behavior was found to be associated with the women's own hormones in adulthood, hormones in mother's blood during pregnancy, and their interaction (Udry, 1994, 2000; Udry, Morris, & Kovenock, 1995). Consistent with suggestions that prenatal weeks 8 to 24 are the key sensitive period, behavior was related to hormones from maternal blood during the second trimester only. It should be noted, however, that there are some questions about the cause of the association between maternal hormones during pregnancy and offspring behavior. Although it is assumed to reflect direct effects of maternal hormones, it is possible that the association reflects genetic effects, especially in light of the fact that the placenta generally protects the fetus from exposure to excess hormones from the mother.

It is important to note that there is some evidence of failure to find androgen effects on interests in typical samples (for review and discussion, see Cohen-Bendahan et al., 2005). First, females with a male co-twin do not appear to differ from females with a female co-twin on childhood play (Elizabeth & Green, 1984; Henderson & Berenbaum, 1997; Rodgers, Fagot, & Winebarger, 1998) or adult interests (Loehlin & Martin, 2000; Rose et al., 2002). Such masculinization would be expected from studies in other species showing that females who gestate between two males are behaviorally masculinized compared with females who gestate between two females (M. M. Clark & Galef, 1998; Ryan & Vandenbergh, 2002). However, the human twin method has not been validated for assessing androgen effects. It is not clear that androgens are transmitted from male to female human fetuses or that androgen exposure is high enough for a human female gestating next to a single male. Second, testosterone in amniotic fluid has not been found to relate, in either boys or girls, to their childhood activities, measured by parent-reported child spatial play experiences (a broader array of gender-related activities was not examined; Grimshaw, Sitarenios, & Finegan, 1995) or sex-typed activities (Knickmeyer et al., 2005). However, both studies had small samples and limited variability, making it difficult to detect what are likely to be moderate effects at best.

Thus, there is now little question that prenatal exposure to moderate levels of androgen masculinizes the interests of females with CAH. Our own studies have been confirmed and extended by others, with findings consistent across countries, methods, and sampling strategies. Further, findings have been confirmed in other clinical samples and in some typical samples. Overall, then, the evidence shows clearly that exposure to elevated androgens during prenatal life is associated with increased interest in male-typical activities and reduced interest in female-typical activities in childhood, adolescence, and adulthood. Effects are large at moderate-to-high levels of androgen (as in females with CAH) but may be somewhat smaller within the range of typical females. Thus, it is highly likely that androgen accounts for a good deal of the difference between the sexes in interests, but it is not clear how much it accounts for variations within each sex. We are currently studying the gendered outcomes that these interests are hypothesized to predict, including occupational interests and occupational choices.

Hormonal Influences on Sex-Typed Personal and Social Correlates of Gendered Outcomes

It is reasonable to ask whether prenatal hormones also influence other characteristics that predict gendered outcomes. There is unfortunately little direct evidence on this point, although it is possible to examine the question empirically. For example, females with CAH might be hypothesized to differ from females without CAH on self-perception, values, and experiences (as discussed in other chapters in this book).

The potential fruitfulness of this approach is demonstrated by evidence showing that females with CAH differ from those without CAH on a number of gendered behaviors that might be important for gendered occupational outcomes, as described below. Androgens appear to affect these characteristics less than activities and interests, but they have not been as well-studied, so it is difficult to make definitive comparisons.

Personal and Social Behaviors

We demonstrated in our project that among children aged 3 to 12 years, girls with CAH are reported by their parents to be less interested in babies than are their unaffected sisters (Leveroni & Berenbaum, 1998). The difference is moderate in size (d of 0.7 compared with a sex difference of 1.0); females with CAH have scores between those of unaffected girls and boys (CAH and unaffected, who do not differ from each other). Although early studies had suggested this (Ehrhardt & Baker, 1974), they had some methodological problems, such as subjective measures. We used a questionnaire developed to differentiate nurturance toward infants versus pets (with the former, but not the latter, showing sex differences; Melson, 1987). Our ideal measure would be observation of children's reactions to babies (e.g., Blakemore, 1981, 1990, 1991), but we have not yet figured out how to do this in children's homes; ethics review boards (to say nothing of parents) probably would not like the idea of our carrying around babies as stimuli in our research! Other studies of adult females with CAH (with instruments of varying quality) have produced results similar to ours: Compared with unaffected females, females with CAH report themselves to be less maternal and less interested in having their own children (Dittmann et al., 1990; Helleday, Edman, Ritzen, & Siwers, 1993; Meyer-Bahlburg, 1999). It is possible that this reflects a psychological response to reduced fertility associated with the disease, but this seems unlikely because women with Turner syndrome (who are completely infertile) do not show reduced interest in babies (Money & Ehrhardt, 1972), nor do the boys with CAH in our study (Leveroni & Berenbaum, 1998).

Females with CAH are also more likely than their unaffected sisters to report that they would use physical aggression in hypothetical conflict situations, especially when they are reporting as adults about their childhood behavior (Berenbaum & Resnick, 1997). These data come from the quasi-longitudinal sample and the two adolescent–adult samples each studied one time. These results confirm an earlier study in females who were prenatally exposed to masculinizing hormones (androgenizing progestins) because their mothers took the hormones as a treatment for miscarriage (Reinisch, 1981): Girls aged 6 to 18 who were exposed to the hormones were more likely than their similar-age unexposed sisters to report that they would use aggression in conflict situations. It is important to note, however, the complexity of androgen effects on aggression in both human and nonhuman animals. For example, in both rodents and primates, aggression in adulthood is affected by treatment with androgens during prenatal, early postnatal, and adult life (e.g., Beatty, 1992; Eaton, Goy, & Phoenix, 1973; Joslyn, 1973; Monaghan & Glickman, 1992); in humans, circulating testosterone is sometimes associated with aggression, with the effects most pronounced in adolescents and when aggression is measured as response to provocation, and there is a bidirectional relation between testosterone and aggression (aggression itself or a related trait, social dominance, may serve to increase androgen levels; e.g., Albert, Walsh, & Jonik, 1993; Bernhardt, Dabbs, Fielden, & Lutter, 1998; Booth, Shelley, Mazur, Tharp, & Kittok, 1989; Monaghan & Glickman, 1992; Olweus, Mattsson, Schalling, & Low, 1980). Androgens may affect aggression by acting directly on the brain and by facilitating the learning of aggression (Joslyn, 1973).

There are many other aspects of personality and social behavior that show sex differences (Ruble, Martin, & Berenbaum, 2006; Wood & Eagly, 2002), but little data to indicate whether they are related to prenatal androgens. There is some suggestion from twin studies that prenatal androgens influence sensation seeking (on which males are usually higher than females): Females with a male co-twin were reported to be masculinized compared with females with a female co-twin on sensation-seeking (Resnick, Gottesman, & McGue, 1993) and rule-breaking (Loehlin & Martin, 2000), although it is possible that the effects reflect a shared postnatal social environment; other studies have failed to find differences on similar traits (Cohen-Bendahan, Buitelaar, van Goozen, Orlebeke, & Cohen-Kettenis, 2004; Rose et al., 2002). It will be interesting to look at these traits in females with CAH as well as to determine whether the latter have lower scores on traits (besides maternal interest) on which females score higher than males, such as emotional expressivity, intimacy in friendships, and depression (Ruble et al., 2006).

Social Relationships

Androgens appear to affect not only individual behavior, but an individual's gendered interactions with others. Because peers are socialization agents who help children to acquire a wide range of behaviors and attitudes (Rubin,

Bukowski, & Parker, 2006), including those related to gender (Fabes, Hanish, & Martin, 2003; Maccoby, 1998; Martin & Fabes, 2001; Ruble et al., 2006), androgen effects on social relationships could produce effects on gendered outcomes.

Data from our project show that girls with CAH are more likely than girls without CAH to report that they play with and prefer boys as playmates (Berenbaum & Snyder, 1995; Hines & Kaufman, 1994), and similar results have been found in Sweden (Servin et al., 2003). The effects are not as large as those for activity interests, which is surprising because the sex difference in peer preferences is very large, larger than that for activity interests (Maccoby, 1998; Ruble et al., 2006). It is important to study peer preferences with observational measures, both to get an accurate estimate of the differences between girls with and without CAH, and to examine the role of sex-typed interests in the development of sex-segregation (Martin & Fabes, 2001).

Evidence from other labs shows that exposure to moderate prenatal levels of androgen also affects sexual orientation, increasing sexual arousal to women. Compared with unaffected sisters, women with CAH are less likely to be sexually attracted to men and more likely to be sexually attracted to women (Hines, Brook, & Conway, 2004; Zucker et al., 1996). The differences are moderate-sized; about one third of women with CAH are bisexual or homosexual, although sampling biases and underreporting may underestimate nonheterosexuality. We are currently studying factors that might differentiate those who are exclusively heterosexual from those who are not, with data from others leading us to hypothesize that these factors are social or cognitive, because amount of androgen exposure has not been found to relate to variation in sexual orientation (Zucker et al., 1996). There is some suggestion that females with CAH are somewhat delayed in "psychosexual milestones" (Meyer-Bahlburg, 2001): They start to date and to engage in heterosexual activities later than females without CAH. It is unclear whether this is directly related to prenatal androgen exposure (in line with the fact that boys mature sexually at a later age than do girls), to heterosexual questioning (in light of data just described), to concerns about their genital appearance (related to their disease or their surgery), or to other factors related to the disease or its treatment.

Hormonal Influences on Cognitive Abilities Correlated With Gendered Outcomes

There is considerable controversy about factors that contribute to the development of cognitive abilities that show sex differences. There are no sex differences in general intelligence, but there are differences in the pattern of intellectual abilities. Males, on average, outperform females on measures of spatial, mechanical, and mathematical abilities, whereas females, on average, outperform males on measures of verbal fluency, verbal memory, emotional perception, and perceptual speed (Halpern, 2000; Ruble et al., 2006). Although some question the existence of some sex differences, the evidence for the cognitive differences listed above is compelling, and even advocates of "gender similarities" (e.g., Hyde, 2005) recognize that some differences exist, although they argue that most are small. It is clear that socialization contributes to some of these sex differences—for example, stereotypes that emphasize women's inferiority in spatial and math abilities (Steele, 1997) and spatial experiences provided to boys but not to girls (Halpern, 2000). There is also good evidence that early androgens affect at least one of these abilities—spatial.

Several studies have found females with CAH to have higher spatial ability than their unaffected female relatives in childhood, adolescence, and adulthood (one study is based on the sample of adolescents and adults we studied with Resnick). The aspects of spatial ability that appear to be enhanced include spatial orientation (rotation) and visualization and targeting (Hampson, Rovet, & Altmann, 1998; Hines, Fane, et al., 2003; Resnick, Berenbaum, Gottesman, & Bouchard, 1986). However, there are some inconsistencies in results (e.g., Helleday, Bartfai, Ritzen, & Forsman, 1994; Hines, Fane, et al., 2003; McArdle & Wilson, 1990), perhaps due in part to statistical power problems or the use of insensitive measures (those that do not show sex differences). The sex differences in spatial ability are smaller than the differences in other psychological traits such as activity interests, so it is challenging to detect differences in androgen-exposed groups, especially with the size of the samples typically studied (for review, see Berenbaum, 2001). Keep in mind that 50 participants per group are needed to detect a difference of 0.5 standard deviations with a one-tailed probability of .05. It would be unlikely that differences between females with and without CAH would be much larger than this, given that sex differences are generally no larger than 0.7 to 1.0 standard deviations.

Consistent with data from females with CAH, males with low early androgen levels due to an endocrine disorder called *idiopathic hypogonadotropic hypogonadism* have lower spatial ability than controls. This likely reflects reduced androgens early in development because in males with this disorder, spatial ability was correlated with testicular volume and did not improve with androgen replacement, and it was not reduced in males with acquired (late-onset) hypogonadism (Hier & Crowley, 1982).

There is also some suggestion from nonclinical samples that typical variations in prenatal androgens are related to variations in spatial ability, although results are not straightforward. In one study, testosterone in amniotic fluid was related to spatial ability in girls at age 7: Girls with higher amniotic (prenatal) testosterone levels had faster (but not necessarily more accurate) performance on a mental rotation task than did girls with lower levels, but effects were found only in a subgroup of girls who used a rotation strategy, and, unexpectedly, girls were faster at rotation than boys (Grimshaw et al., 1995). In a study of female dizygotic twins, those with a male co-twin had higher spatial ability than those with a female co-twin (Cole-Harding, Morstad, & Wilson, 1988). These studies, if replicated, suggest that enhanced spatial ability in females with CAH results directly from effects of androgens on the developing brain and not from social responses to the girls' virilized genitalia or other abnormalities of the disease.

Not much is known about prenatal androgen effects on other cognitive abilities that show sex differences, including those on which males are superior (e.g., mechanical and mathematical abilities) and those on which females are superior (e.g., verbal fluency and memory). It will be interesting to study, for example, whether females with CAH have lower (more male-typical) verbal memory than unaffected females. It may be difficult to get good answers to these questions, however, because sex differences in these abilities are smaller than those in spatial ability, so large samples will be necessary to detect any effects of early androgens.

Hormonal Influences on Gender Identity

Females with CAH are similar to unaffected females in their core gender identity. The overwhelming majority of girls and women with CAH identify as female, albeit with somewhat reduced identification (Berenbaum & Bailey, 2003; Hines et al., 2004; Meyer-Bahlburg et al., 1996, 2004; Zucker et al., 1996). A small minority of females with CAH are unhappy as females (*gender dysphoric*) or live as males, and this number is higher than that in the general population. However, those who are gender dysphoric or male identified are not those with the greatest genital masculinization or the most prenatal androgen excess. Further, gender dysphoria occurs just as often in those (rare cases) in which females with CAH are reared as male (Dessens, Slijper, & Drop, 2005). Data from females with CAH are consistent with data from other individuals with sex-atypical hormone exposure in showing that gender identity is not predicted simply by prenatal androgen exposure, genital appearance, or rearing sex (Cohen-Kettenis, 2005; Mazur, 2005).

The female-typical gender identity of females with CAH has two important implications. First, it means that prenatal androgens do not have large effects on all aspects of sex-related behavior. Second, it means that many aspects of the socialization of females with CAH should be indistinguishable from that of typical females.

Overall Adjustment

It is important to note that psychological masculinization and defeminization in females with CAH occur in the presence of normal emotional adjustment. In all the samples we have studied—the quasi-longitudinal sample as well as the two separate samples of adolescents and adults—adjustment of females and males with CAH was not significantly different than that of unaffected relatives, whether assessed by parent report or self-report, using multiple measures (Berenbaum et al., 2004).

Summary of the Evidence Regarding Hormonal Influences on Predictors of Gendered Occupational Outcomes

It is clear that androgens affect some of the traits that are related to gendered occupational outcomes—especially activities and interests, aspects of spatial ability, and social relationships—and it is reasonable to expect that some of the sex difference in occupational outcome itself is due to a difference in prenatal androgen exposure, although this awaits direct empirical test. It is also highly likely that any hormonal effects on occupational outcome would be mediated by hormonal effects on the traits discussed and perhaps others. This means that studying hormonal effects on occupational outcomes tells us not just about biological contributors to outcomes; more important, it tells us about the developmental pathways by which biology is manifested in behavior.

SPECULATIONS ON THE PATHS FROM HORMONES TO OCCUPATIONAL OUTCOME

It is worth repeating that any hormonal influences on gendered occupational outcomes come about through indirect effects on traits and behaviors that contribute to those outcomes. There is not a part of the brain that directly affects whether someone becomes an engineer or a nurse that is shaped by androgens during prenatal development. The indirect path provides an opportunity for developmentalists to understand the ways in which a child's biological predispositions manifest themselves through the social environment: that is, the ways that a child's preferences lead her down a pathway that causes her to end up in one career versus another. Although we currently have no data to answer this question, we can develop hypotheses and design studies that might eventually produce these data.

Psychological Mechanisms From Hormones to Behavior

A key question concerns the psychological mechanisms that mediate androgen effects on gender development. What causes someone who is exposed to high levels of androgens during prenatal development (typical boys and girls with CAH) to play with toy trucks—or become an engineer, or like the remote control? Consider two possibilities. There are certainly others that could be proposed.

First, it is possible that part of the effect is mediated by basic perceptual or sensory processes. Androgens might bias our perceptual or affective preferences (see also Alexander, 2003). Many characteristics differentiate boys' and girls' toys, such as the use of motion, color, texture, and shape, and these characteristics parallel sex differences found in other domains. When infants look at visual stimuli, boys prefer movement and girls prefer form and color (Serbin, Poulin-Dubois, Colbourne, Sen, & Eichstedt, 2001). In childhood activities, boys use motion more than girls do (Benenson, Liroff, Pascal, & Cioppa, 1997). In drawings, boys tend to draw mechanical and moving objects, use dark and cold colors, and have a bird's-eye perspective. Girls tend to draw human figures, flowers, and butterflies; use light and warm colors; and array items in a row on the ground. Evidence that this reflects biological preferences and not social labels comes from data showing that girls with CAH tend to draw pictures with masculine characteristics (Iijima, Arisaka, Minamoto, & Arai, 2001). In our lab, we have found that when preschool children are given a choice of bears to play with that differ in the characteristics of motion, texture, color, or adornment, boys spend almost all their time with the bear that moves (compared with less than 50% of girls' time) and that among the boys, the time spent playing with the bear correlated with the time playing with a toy truck in a separate free play task (Landy, 2003).

Important evidence for biological-based preferences underlying toy preferences and activity interests comes from two studies of monkeys. Juvenile monkeys are not subjected to the social pressures typical of human children. Nonetheless, they show the same sex-typed toy preferences as human children. In one study, juvenile vervet monkeys allowed to play with six sex-typed human toys played longer with same-sex than opposite-sex toys (Alexander & Hines, 2002). In a second study, juvenile rhesus monkeys given a choice between plush doll-like (girls') toys and wheeled vehicle (boys') toys played with same-sex toys more than opposite-sex toys (Hassett, Siebert, & Wallen, 2004).

Second, androgen effects on behavior might be mediated by basic cognitive processes and the neural substrates that subserve them. Sex differences in spatial ability appear to depend, in part, on sex differences in the use of landmarks versus geometric cues. In one study, men and women were found to differ in brain activation during a navigation task; this may reflect men's use of geometric cues versus women's use of working memory to keep landmark cues active (Grön, Wunderlich, Spitzer, Tomczak, & Riepe, 2000). In rodents, these processes appear to be differentially sensitive to hormones (Williams & Meck, 1991).

Environmental Transactions

Hormones undoubtedly affect behavior by changing the individual's interactions with the environment (physical and social environment). In rodents, hormones affect both the behavior of the organism and others' responses to it, including grooming by the mother and attraction of peers (e.g., M. M. Clark & Galef, 1998). Although this has not been studied in people, it is easy to speculate how this might happen, assuming that prenatal exposure to androgens (in girls with CAH and typical boys) creates some biases that are magnified by the environment. For example, androgens might produce a preference for moving stimuli that is reinforced by the environment through selection by the child and provision by the parents of transportation and action toys. This familiarity and comfort with machines and action might then lead androgen-exposed children (girls with CAH and typical boys) to use computers, which in turn might foster their spatial skills and interest in technical careers. As another example, consider that androgens might reduce interest in infants, which would then cause a child to avoid babysitting and other experiences with babies and therefore not receive benefits from interacting with babies. This lack of reward could lead to further avoidance of babies and reduced opportunity to practice maternal behavior. Of course, these are speculative examples that await empirical assessment.

These are examples of hormone–environment correlations (similar to the genotype–environment correlations discussed by Scarr & McCartney, 1983), in which environments are correlated with an individual's hormone exposure. There may also be hormone–environment interactions, in which the effect of an environment varies for people with different hormone exposure. For example, training in spatial ability may be more beneficial for people whose brains were exposed to moderate levels of androgen during prenatal development. This means that even with the same environment (e.g., a classroom), boys may become increasingly better than girls at processing spatial information. The group differences in spatial ability would become even larger if the relevant environments differed for the groups, for example, playing with spatial toys. Again, this is speculative, but it can also be tested empirically.

Further, all behaviors are shaped by the social environment in which an organism is reared. This is shown clearly in studies of behavioral sex differences in monkeys (Wallen, 1996), as described in the beginning of this chapter, and there appear to be parallels between juvenile monkeys and human children. Primate behaviors that show consistent sex differences across social context are most affected by prenatal androgens, with rough play but not aggression showing consistent sex differences and sensitivity to hormones. Human childhood activities and interests show large sex differences across cultures and are strongly affected by prenatal androgens, whereas aggression shows varying sex differences as a function of context and is not as strongly influenced by hormones.

CONCLUSIONS AND POLICY IMPLICATIONS

The evidence described strongly suggests that some psychological sex differences—including those related to occupational outcomes—are influenced by biological factors, particularly androgen levels present during prenatal development. These effects are complex, however, varying at least in size across different characteristics, and this leaves open the question of factors (both biological and social) that moderate psychological effects of hormones. Further, findings that hormones influence a variety of characteristics suggest that there is no single individual characteristic that affects outcome. This means that it is important to move beyond a single focus on sex differences in cognition to explain sex differences in occupational outcomes.

A long-term longitudinal study of individuals with sex-atypical hormone exposure, such as females with CAH, could provide a unique opportunity to understand how biological predispositions work jointly with socialization to lead to important psychological outcomes. In essence, females with CAH enable empirical study of the transactional processes between the individual and her environment that shape development (a developmentalist's dream). Consider two ways in which this could be valuable. First, a longitudinal study would permit analysis of the relative contribution of prenatal hormones and gendered socialization to changes in predictors of occupational outcome, such as self-perceptions and values (Jacobs, Lanza, Osgood, Eccles, & Wigfield, 2002; Watt, 2004). If females with CAH become more gender typical with age (i.e., differences between females with CAH and unaffected females decrease), this suggests the importance of gender-specific socialization because females with CAH are reared as and identify as girls. However, if females with CAH remain atypical or become more so with age (i.e., differences between females with CAH and unaffected females remain the same or increase), this suggests the importance of self-socialization (e.g., selecting environments consistent with interests) or continuing effects of prenatal androgen.

Second, a longitudinal study in females with CAH would allow a direct examination of the ways in which biological predispositions affect outcome through the social environment. Consider, for example, the hypothetical development of a girl with CAH compared with her unaffected sister. Her interest in toy cars and Legos causes changes in her other behavior—for example, she moves around her environment, values spatial activities, perceives herself to have good spatial abilities, sees herself as someone who can affect her environment, and seeks out school experiences consistent with her interests. These interests also produce social responses from others; for example, parents provide her with toy vehicles, blocks and videogames, and teachers encourage her spatial skills. If she spends more time with boys (as some girls with CAH appear to do), then her boy-typical interests will be reinforced, and she will be influenced by the culture prominent in boys more than that of girls (Maccoby, 1998). Taken together, the child-selected and the adult- and peer-facilitated environment reinforce the girl's interests and abilities related to moving objects and spatial stimuli, facilitating interests and abilities related to science and math. Of course, this is only a hypothetical and sketchy picture, but it is a blueprint to show how studying girls with CAH can substantially enhance our understanding of the processes that produce sex differences in occupational (and other) outcomes.

Given that causes of gendered outcomes have figured prominently in debates about their meaning, it is important to consider the implications for social policy of the evidence that biology affects psychological characteristics related to these outcomes. Biology is not destiny: For all characteristics studied, the differences between females with and without CAH are smaller than the sex differences, which means that hormones do not account for all of the difference between males and females. This is consistent with other evidence showing the importance of social influences on psychological sex differences (e.g., Ruble et al., 2006; Steele, 1997; Wood & Eagly, 2002). Nevertheless, even complete biological determination would not rule out modification by environmental intervention. Evidence from other fields shows that even traits with strong biological contributors can be modified by environmental events. For example, children with phenylketonuria "genetically destined" to have intellectual disability actually have normal IQ when they receive a phenylalanine-free diet throughout early development. Many typical people attempt to modify their genetic risk for disease by exercising and eating well. Further, values about acceptable and desirable behavior are not based on causes of the behavior. For example, antisocial behavior is not acceptable whether it is caused by genes or the rearing environment. It is interesting to consider that most of the controversy about gendered occupational outcomes concerns reasons for women's underrepresentation in technical fields and not men's underrepresentation in caring professions. Some of this undoubtedly reflects the different status, prestige, and financial rewards of technical versus caring professions and the greater power accorded to men than to women. This is why it is not surprising that salaries decline when women enter a profession in considerable numbers. If technical and caring professions were equally valued, it seems likely that the debate about women's underrepresentation in science and math would not be so heated.

Thus, men's and women's differential representation in technical versus caring professions may arise, in part, from sex differences in sex hormones present during early development. It is crucial to remember, however, that biological effects on occupational (and other) outcomes are complex, likely operating through several psychological characteristics and having their effects through the social environment, which may also modify them. It is also important to remember that at least some of the attention given to sex differences in occupational outcomes and their causes relates to the fact that the work of men and women is not accorded equal value in society.

REFERENCES

Albert, D. J., Walsh, M. L., & Jonik, R. H. (1993). Aggression in humans: What is its biological foundation? *Neuroscience and Biobehavioral Reviews, 17*, 405–423.

Alexander, G. M. (2003). An evolutionary perspective of sex-typed toy preferences: Pink, blue, and the brain. *Archives of Sexual Behavior, 32,* 7–14.

Alexander, G. M., & Hines, M. (2002). Sex differences in response to children's toys in nonhuman primates (*Cercopithecus aethiops sabaeus*). *Evolution and Human Behavior, 23,* 467–479.

Bachevalier, J., & Hagger, C. (1991). Sex differences in the development of learning abilities in primates. *Psychoneuroendocrinology, 16,* 177–188.

Baum, M. J., & Schretlen, P. (1975). Neuroendocrine effects of perinatal androgenization in the male ferret. *Progress in Brain Research, 42,* 343–355.

Beatty, W. W. (1992). Gonadal hormones and sex differences in nonreproductive behaviors. In A. A. Gerall, H. Moltz, & I. L. Ward (Eds.), *Handbook of behavioral neurobiology: Vol. 11. Sexual differentiation* (pp. 85–128). New York: Plenum Press.

Becker, J. B., Breedlove, S. M., Crews, D., & McCarthy, M. M. (Eds.). (2002). *Behavioral endocrinology* (2nd ed.). Cambridge, MA: MIT Press.

Benenson, J. F., Liroff, E. R., Pascal, S. J., & Cioppa, G. D. (1997). Propulsion: A behavioural expression of masculinity. *British Journal of Developmental Psychology, 15,* 37–50.

Berenbaum, S. A. (1999). Effects of early androgens on sex-typed activities and interests in adolescents with congenital adrenal hyperplasia. *Hormones and Behavior, 35,* 102–110.

Berenbaum, S. A. (2001). Cognitive function in congenital adrenal hyperplasia. *Endocrinology and Metabolism Clinics of North America, 30,* 173–192.

Berenbaum, S. A. (2003). Management of children with intersex conditions: Psychological and methodological perspectives. *Growth, Genetics & Hormones, 19,* 1–6.

Berenbaum, S. A. (2004). Androgen and behavior: Implications for the treatment of children with disorders of sexual differentiation. In O. H. Pescovitz & E. A. Eugster (Eds.), *Pediatric endocrinology: Mechanisms, manifestations, and management* (pp. 275–284). Philadelphia: Lippincott Williams & Wilkins.

Berenbaum, S. A. (2005, February). Prenatal androgen effects on social and cognitive development. In P. Maki (Chair), *Life span perspective of sex hormones and cognition.* Symposium conducted at the 33rd Annual Meeting of the International Neuropsychological Society, St. Louis, MO.

Berenbaum, S. A. (2006). Psychological outcome in children with disorders of sex development: Implications for treatment and understanding typical development. *Annual Review of Sex Research, 17,* 1–38.

Berenbaum, S. A., & Bailey, J. M. (2003). Effects on gender identity of prenatal androgens and genital appearance: Evidence from girls with congenital adrenal hyperplasia. *Journal of Clinical Endocrinology and Metabolism, 88,* 1102–1106.

Berenbaum, S. A., Bryk, K. K., Duck, S. C., & Resnick, S. M. (2004). Psychological adjustment in children and adults with congenital adrenal hyperplasia. *Journal of Pediatrics, 144,* 741–746.

Berenbaum, S. A., Duck, S. C., & Bryk, K. (2000). Behavioral effects of prenatal versus postnatal androgen excess in children with 21-hydroxylase-deficient congenital adrenal hyperplasia. *Journal of Clinical Endocrinology and Metabolism, 85,* 727–733.

Berenbaum, S. A., & Hines, M. (1992). Early androgens are related to childhood sex-typed toy preferences. *Psychological Science, 3,* 203–206.

Berenbaum, S. A., & Resnick, S. M. (1997). Early androgen effects on aggression in children and adults with congenital adrenal hyperplasia. *Psychoneuroendocrinology, 22,* 505–515.

Berenbaum, S. A., & Snyder, E. (1995). Early hormonal influences on childhood sex-typed activity and playmate preferences: Implications for the development of sexual orientation. *Developmental Psychology, 31,* 31–42.

Bernhardt, P. C., Dabbs, J. M., Fielden, J. A., & Lutter, C. D. (1998). Testosterone changes during vicarious experiences of winning and losing among fans at sporting events. *Physiology & Behavior, 65,* 59–62.

Blakemore, J. E. O. (1981). Age and sex differences in interaction with a human infant. *Child Development, 52,* 386–388.

Blakemore, J. E. O. (1990). Children's nurturant interactions with their infant siblings: An exploration of gender differences and maternal socialization. *Sex Roles, 22,* 43–57.

Blakemore, J. E. O. (1991). The influence of gender and temperament on children's interaction with a baby. *Sex Roles, 24,* 531–537.

Booth, A., Shelley, G., Mazur, A., Tharp, G., & Kittok, R. (1989). Testosterone, and winning and losing in human competition. *Hormones and Behavior, 23,* 556–571.

Breedlove, S. M. (1992). Sexual dimorphism in the vertebrate nervous system. *Journal of Neuroscience, 12,* 4133–4142.

Breedlove, S. M. (1994). Sexual differentiation of the human nervous system. *Annual Review of Psychology, 45,* 389–418.

Chase, C. (1998). Surgical progress is not the answer to intersexuality. *Journal of Clinical Ethics, 9,* 385–392.

Clark, A. S., & Goldman-Rakic, P. S. (1989). Gonadal hormones influence the emergence of cortical function in nonhuman primates. *Behavioral Neuroscience, 103,* 1287–1295.

Clark, M. M., & Galef, B. G. (1998). Effects of intrauterine position on the behavior and genital morphology of litter-bearing rodents. *Developmental Neuropsychology, 14,* 197–211.

Cohen-Bendahan, C. C. C., Buitelaar, J. K., van Goozen, S. H. M., Orlebeke, J. F., & Cohen-Kettenis, P. T. (2004). Is there an effect of prenatal testosterone on aggression and other behavioral traits? A study comparing same-sex and opposite-sex twin girls. *Hormones and Behavior, 47,* 230–237.

Cohen-Bendahan, C. C. C., van de Beek, C., & Berenbaum, S. A. (2005). Prenatal sex hormone effects on child and adult sex-typed behavior: Methods and findings. *Neuroscience and Biobehavioral Reviews, 29,* 353–384.

Cohen-Kettenis, P. T. (2005). Gender change in 46,XY persons with 5-alpha-reductase-2 deficiency and 17-beta-hydroxysteroid dehydrogenase-3 deficiency. *Archives of Sexual Behavior, 34*, 399–410.

Cole-Harding, S., Morstad, A. L., & Wilson, J. R. (1988). Spatial ability in members of opposite-sex twin pairs [Abstract]. *Behavior Genetics, 18*, 710.

Crouch, N. S., Minto, C. L., Liao, L.-M., Woodhouse, C. R. J., & Creighton, S. M. (2004). Genital sensation after feminizing genitoplasty for congenital adrenal hyperplasia: A pilot study. *BJU International, 93*, 135–138.

Dessens, A. B., Slijper, F. M. E., & Drop, S. L. S. (2005). Gender dysphoria and gender change in chromosomal females with congenital adrenal hyperplasia. *Archives of Sexual Behavior, 34*, 389–397.

Dittmann, R. W., Kappes, M. H., Kappes, M. E., Borger, D., Meyer-Bahlburg, H. F. L., Stegner, H., et al. (1990). Congenital adrenal hyperplasia: II. Gender-related behavior and attitudes in female salt-wasting and simple-virilizing patients. *Psychoneuroendocrinology, 15*, 421–434.

Eaton, G. G., Goy, R. W., & Phoenix, C. H. (1973). Effects of testosterone treatment in adulthood on sexual behavior of female pseudohermaphrodite rhesus monkeys. *Nature New Biology, 242*, 119–120.

Ehrhardt, A. A., & Baker, S. W. (1974). Fetal androgens, human central nervous system differentiation and behavior sex differences. In R. C. Friedman, R. M. Richart, & R. L. Vande Wiele (Eds.), *Sex differences in behavior* (pp. 33–51). New York: Wiley.

Elizabeth, P. H., & Green, R. (1984). Childhood sex-role behaviors: Similarities and differences in twins. *Acta Geneticae Medicae et Gemellologiae: Twin Research, 33*, 173–179.

Fabes, R. A., Hanish, L. D., & Martin, C. L. (2003). Children at play: The role of peers in understanding the effects of childcare. *Child Development, 74*, 1039–1043.

Goy, R. W., Bercovitch, F. B., & McBrair, M. C. (1988). Behavioral masculinization is independent of genital masculinization in prenatally androgenized female rhesus macaques. *Hormones and Behavior, 22*, 552–571.

Goy, R. W., & McEwen, B. S. (1980). *Sexual differentiation of the brain.* Cambridge: MIT Press.

Grimshaw, G. M., Sitarenios, G., & Finegan, J. A. (1995). Mental rotation at 7 years: Relations with prenatal testosterone levels and spatial play experience. *Brain and Cognition, 29*, 85–100.

Grön, G., Wunderlich, A. P., Spitzer, M., Tomczak, R., & Riepe, M. W. (2000). Brain activation during human navigation: Gender-different neural networks as substrate of performance. *Nature Neuroscience, 3*, 404–408.

Halpern, D. F. (2000). *Sex differences in cognitive abilities* (3rd ed.). Mahwah, NJ: Erlbaum.

Hampson, E., Rovet, J. F., & Altmann, D. (1998). Spatial reasoning in children with congenital adrenal hyperplasia due to 21-hydroxylase deficiency. *Developmental Neuropsychology, 14*, 299–320.

Hassett, J. M., Siebert, E. R., & Wallen, K. (2004). Sexually differentiated toy preferences in rhesus monkeys [Abstract]. *Hormones and Behavior, 46,* 91.

Helleday, J., Bartfai, A., Ritzen, E. M., & Forsman, M. (1994). General intelligence and cognitive profile in women with congenital adrenal hyperplasia. *Psychoneuroendocrinology, 19,* 343–356.

Helleday, J., Edman, G., Ritzen, E. M., & Siwers, B. (1993). Personality characteristics and platelet MAO activity in women with congenital adrenal hyperplasia (CAH). *Psychoneuroendocrinology, 18,* 343–354.

Henderson, B. A., & Berenbaum, S. A. (1997). Sex-typed play in opposite-sex twins. *Developmental Psychobiology, 31,* 115–123.

Hier, D. B., & Crowley, W. F. (1982). Spatial ability in androgen-deficient men. *New England Journal of Medicine, 302,* 1202–1205.

Hines, M., Ahmed, F., & Hughes, I. A. (2003). Psychological outcomes and gender-related development in complete androgen insensitivity syndrome. *Archives of Sexual Behavior, 32,* 93–101.

Hines, M., Brook, C., & Conway, G. S. (2004). Androgen and psychosexual development: Core gender identity, sexual orientation, and recalled gender role behavior in women and men with congenital adrenal hyperplasia (CAH). *Journal of Sex Research, 41,* 75–81.

Hines, M., Fane, B. A., Pasterski, V. L., Mathews, G. A., Conway, G. S., & Brook, C. (2003). Spatial abilities following prenatal androgen abnormality: targeting and mental rotations performance in individuals with congenital adrenal hyperplasia. *Psychoneuroendocrinology, 28,* 1010–1026.

Hines, M., Golombok, S., Rust, J., Johnston, K. J., & Golding, J. (2002). Testosterone during pregnancy and gender role behavior of preschool children: A longitudinal, population study. *Child Development, 73,* 1678–1687.

Hines, M., & Kaufman, F. (1994). Androgen and the development of human sex-typical behavior: Rough-and-tumble play and sex of preferred playmates in children with congenital adrenal hyperplasia (CAH). *Child Development, 65,* 1042–1053.

Hull, E. M., Franz, J. R., Snyder, A. M., & Nishita, J. K. (1980). Perinatal progesterone and learning, social and reproductive behavior in rats. *Physiology and Behavior, 24,* 251–256.

Hyde, J. S. (2005). The gender similarities hypothesis. *American Psychologist, 60,* 581–592.

Iijima, M., Arisaka, O., Minamoto, F., & Arai, Y. (2001). Sex differences in children's free drawings: A study on girls with congenital adrenal hyperplasia. *Hormones and Behavior, 40,* 99–104.

Jacobs, J. E., Lanza, S., Osgood, D. W., Eccles, J. S., & Wigfield, A. (2002). Changes in children's self-competence and values: Gender and domain differences across grades one through twelve. *Child Development, 73,* 509–527.

Joslyn, W. D. (1973). Androgen-induced social dominance in infant female rhesus monkeys. *Journal of Child Psychology and Psychiatry, 14,* 137–145.

Knickmeyer, R. C., Wheelwright, S., Taylor, K., Raggatt, P., Hackett, G., & Baron-Cohen, S. (2005). Gender-typed play and amniotic testosterone. *Developmental Psychology, 41*, 517–528.

Landy, C. L. (2003). *Characteristics of boys' and girls' toys.* Unpublished undergraduate honors thesis, The Pennsylvania State University, University Park.

Leveroni, C. L., & Berenbaum, S. A. (1998). Early androgen effects on interest in infants: Evidence from children with congenital adrenal hyperplasia. *Developmental Neuropsychology, 14*, 321–340.

Loehlin, J. C., & Martin, N. G. (2000). Dimensions of psychological masculinity–femininity in adult twins from opposite-sex and same-sex pairs. *Behavior Genetics, 30*, 19–28.

Low, K. S. D., Yoon, M., Roberts, B. W., & Rounds, J. (2005). The stability of vocational interests from early adolescence to middle adulthood: A quantitative review of longitudinal studies. *Psychological Bulletin, 131*, 713–737.

Maccoby, E. E. (1998). *The two sexes: Growing up apart, coming together.* Cambridge, MA: Harvard University Press.

Martin, C. L., & Fabes, R. A. (2001). The stability and consequences of young children's same-sex peer interactions. *Developmental Psychology, 37*, 431–446.

Mazur, T. (2005). Gender dysphoria and gender change in androgen insensitivity or micropenis. *Archives of Sexual Behavior, 34*, 411–421.

McArdle, P., & Wilson, B. E. (1990). Hormonal influences on language development in physically advanced children. *Brain and Language, 38*, 410–423.

Melson, G. F. (1987). *The role of pets in the development of children's nurturance.* Paper presented at the Delta Society Conference, Vancouver, British Columbia, Canada.

Meyer-Bahlburg, H. F. L. (1999). What causes low rates of child-bearing in congenital adrenal hyperplasia? *Journal of Clinical Endocrinology and Metabolism, 84*, 1844–1847.

Meyer-Bahlburg, H. F. L. (2001). Gender and sexuality in congenital adrenal hyperplasia. *Endocrinology and Metabolism Clinics of North America, 30*(1), 155–171.

Meyer-Bahlburg, H. F. L., Dolezal, C., Baker, S., Carlson, A. D., Obeid, J. S., & New, M. I. (2004). Prenatal androgenization affects gender-related behavior but not gender identity in 5–12-year-old girls with congenital adrenal hyperplasia. *Archives of Sexual Behavior, 33*, 94–104.

Meyer-Bahlburg, H. F. L., Gruen, R. S., New, M. I., Bell, J. J., Morishima, A., Shimshi, M., et al. (1996). Gender change from female to male in classical congenital adrenal hyperplasia. *Hormones and Behavior, 30*, 319–332.

Migeon, C. J., Wisniewski, A. B., Gearhart, J. P., Meyer-Bahlburg, H. F. L., Rock, J. A., Brown, T. R., et al. (2002). Ambiguous genitalia with perineoscrotal hypospadias in 46,XY individuals: long-term medical, surgical, and psychosexual outcome. *Pediatrics, 110*, e31.

Minto, C. L., Liao, L.-M., Woodhouse, C. R. J., Ransley, P. G., & Creighton, S. M. (2003). The effect of clitoral surgery on sexual outcome in individuals who have intersex conditions with ambiguous genitalia: A cross-sectional study. *Lancet, 361*, 1252–1257.

Monaghan, E. P., & Glickman, S. E. (1992). Hormones and aggressive behavior. In J. B. Becker, S. M. Breedlove, & D. Crews (Eds.), *Behavioral endocrinology* (pp. 261–285). Cambridge, MA: MIT Press.

Money, J., & Ehrhardt, A. A. (1972). *Man and woman, boy and girl*. Baltimore: Johns Hopkins University Press.

Nordenström, A., Servin, A., Bohlin, G., Larsson, A., & Wedell, A. (2002). Sex-typed toy play behavior correlates with the degree of prenatal androgen exposure assessed by CYP21 genotype in girls with congenital adrenal hyperplasia. *Journal of Clinical Endocrinology and Metabolism, 87*, 5119–5124.

Olweus, D., Mattsson, A., Schalling, D., & Low, H. (1980). Testosterone, aggression, physical, and personality dimensions in normal adolescent males. *Psychosomatic Medicine, 42*, 253–269.

Pasterski, V. L., Geffner, M. E., Brain, C., Hindmarsh, P., Brook, C., & Hines, M. (2005). Prenatal hormones and postnatal socialization by parents as determinants of male-typical toy play in girls with congenital adrenal hyperplasia. *Child Development, 76*, 264–278.

Pollak, S. D., Klorman, R., Thatcher, J. E., & Cicchetti, D. (2001). P3b reflects maltreated children's reactions to facial displays of emotion. *Psychophysiology, 38*(2), 267–274.

Quadagno, D. M., Briscoe, R., & Quadagno, J. S. (1977). Effects of perinatal gonadal hormones on selected nonsexual behavior patterns: A critical assessment of the non-human and human literature. *Psychological Bulletin, 84*, 62–80.

Reiner, W. G., & Gearhart, J. P. (2004). Discordant sexual identity in some genetic males with cloacal exstrophy assigned to female sex at birth. *New England Journal of Medicine, 350*, 333–341.

Reinisch, J. M. (1981, March 13). Prenatal exposure to synthetic progestins increases potential for aggression in humans. *Science, 211*, 1171–1173.

Resnick, S. M. (1982). *Psychological functioning in individuals with congenital adrenal hyperplasia: Early hormonal influences on cognition and personality*. Unpublished doctoral dissertation, University of Minnesota, Minneapolis.

Resnick, S. M., Berenbaum, S. A., Gottesman, I. I., & Bouchard, T. J. (1986). Early hormonal influences on cognitive functioning in congenital adrenal hyperplasia. *Developmental Psychology, 22*, 191–198.

Resnick, S. M., Gottesman, I. I., & McGue, M. (1993). Sensation-seeking in opposite-sex twins: An effect of prenatal hormones? *Behavior Genetics, 23*, 323–329.

Rodgers, C. S., Fagot, B. I., & Winebarger, A. (1998). Gender-typed toy play in dizygotic twins: A test of hormone transfer theory. *Sex Roles, 39*, 173–184.

Rose, R. J., Kaprio, J., Winter, T., Dick, D. M., Viken, R. J., Pulkkinen, L., et al. (2002). Femininity and fertility in sisters with twin brothers: Prenatal androgenization? Cross-sex socialization? *Psychological Science, 13*, 263–267.

Rubin, K. H., Bukowski, W., & Parker, J. G. (2006). Peer interactions, relationships, and groups. In W. Damon & R. Lerner (Series Eds.) & N. Eisenberg (Vol. Ed.), *Handbook of child psychology: Vol. 3. Social, emotional, and personality development* (6th ed., pp. 571–645). New York: Wiley.

Ruble, D. N., Martin, C. L., & Berenbaum, S. A. (2006). Gender development. In W. Damon & R. Lerner (Series Eds.) & N. Eisenberg (Vol. Ed.), *Handbook of child psychology: Vol. 3. Social, emotional, and personality development* (6th ed., pp. 858–932). New York: Wiley.

Ryan, B. C., & Vandenbergh, J. G. (2002). Intrauterine position effects. *Neuroscience and Biobehavioral Reviews, 26,* 665–678.

Scarr, S., & McCartney, K. (1983). How people make their own environments: A theory of genotype → environment effects. *Child Development, 54,* 424–435.

Serbin, L. A., Poulin-Dubois, D., Colbourne, K. A., Sen, M. G., & Eichstedt, J. A. (2001). Gender stereotyping in infancy: Visual preferences for and knowledge of gender-stereotyped toys in the second year. *International Journal of Behavioral Development, 25,* 7–15.

Servin, A., Nordenström, A., Larsson, A., & Bohlin, G. (2003). Prenatal androgens and gender-typed behavior: A study of girls with mild and severe forms of congenital adrenal hyperplasia. *Developmental Psychology, 39,* 440–450.

Smail, P. J., Reyes, F. I., Winter, J. S. D., & Faiman, C. (1981). The fetal hormone environment and its effect on the morphogenesis of the genital system. In S. J. Kogan & E. S. E. Hafez (Eds.), *Pediatric andrology* (pp. 9–19). The Hague, the Netherlands: Martinus Nijhoff.

Speiser, P. W., & White, P. C. (2003). Congenital adrenal hyperplasia. *New England Journal of Medicine, 349,* 776–788.

Steele, C. (1997). A threat in the air. How stereotypes shape intellectual identity and performance. *American Psychologist, 52,* 613–629.

Swanson, J. L. (1999). Stability and change in vocational interests. In M. L. Savickas & A. R. Spokane (Eds.), *Vocational interests: Meaning, measurement, and counseling use* (pp. 135–158). Palo Alto, CA: Davies-Black.

Udry, J. R. (1994). The nature of gender. *Demography, 31,* 561–573.

Udry, J. R. (2000). Biological limits of gender construction. *American Sociological Review, 65,* 443–457.

Udry, J. R., Morris, N. M., & Kovenock, J. (1995). Androgen effects on women's gendered behavior. *Journal of Biosocial Science, 27,* 359–368.

Wallen, K. (1996). Nature needs nurture: The interaction of hormonal and social influences on the development of behavioral sex differences in rhesus monkeys. *Hormones and Behavior, 30,* 364–378.

Wallen, K., & Baum, M. J. (2002). Masculinization and defeminization in altricial and precocial mammals: Comparative aspects of steroid hormone action. In D. W. Pfaff, A. P. Arnold, A. M. Etgen, S. E. Fahrbach, & R. T. Rubin (Eds.), *Hormones, brain and behavior* (Vol. 4, pp. 385–423). New York: Academic Press.

Warne, G., Grover, S., Hutson, J., Sinclair, A., Metcalfe, S., Northam, E., et al. (2005). A long-term outcome study of intersex children. *Journal of Pediatric Endocrinology and Metabolism, 18*, 555–567.

Watt, H. M. G. (2004). Development of adolescents' self-perceptions, values, and task perceptions according to gender and domain in 7th- through 11th-grade Australian students. *Child Development, 75*, 1556–1574.

Williams, C. L., & Meck, W. H. (1991). The organizational effects of gonadal steroids on sexually dimorphic spatial ability. *Psychoneuroendocrinology, 16*(1–3), 155–176.

Wisniewski, A. B., Migeon, C. J., Malouf, M. A., & Gearhart, J. P. (2004). Psychosexual outcome in women affected by congenital adrenal hyperplasia due to 21-hydroxylase deficiency. *Journal of Urology, 171*, 2497–2501.

Wisniewski, A. B., Migeon, C. J., Meyer-Bahlburg, H. F. L., Gearhart, J. P., Berkovitz, G. D., Brown, T. R., et al. (2000). Complete androgen insensitivity syndrome: Long-term medical, surgical, and psychosexual outcome. *Journal of Clinical Endocrinology and Metabolism, 85*, 2664–2669.

Wood, W., & Eagly, A. H. (2002). A cross-cultural analysis of the behavior of women and men: Implications for the origins of sex differences. *Psychological Bulletin, 128*, 699–727.

Zucker, K. J., Bradley, S. J., Oliver, G., Blake, J., Fleming, S., & Hood, J. (1996). Psychosexual development of women with congenital adrenal hyperplasia. *Hormones and Behavior, 30*, 300–318.

IV

SOCIAL AND INSTITUTIONAL CONSTRAINTS ON WOMEN'S CAREER DEVELOPMENT

10

GENDERED OCCUPATIONAL OUTCOMES FROM MULTILEVEL PERSPECTIVES: THE CASE OF PROFESSIONAL TRAINING AND WORK IN TURKEY

AHU TATLI, MUSTAFA ÖZBILGIN, AND FATMA KÜSKÜ

Turkey presents a two-track and polarized profile in terms of gender equality in occupational choices and outcomes. Although the proportion of women in higher education, including technical and scientific subjects, and professional work compares well with that in Europe (Healy, Özbilgin, & Aliefendioglu, 2005; Özbilgin & Healy, 2004; Özkale, Küskü, & Sağlamer, 2004), the same pattern of favorable representation is not evident in low-skilled and manual work categories, where Turkey has greater gender segregation (Özbilgin & Woodward, 2003; Woodward & Özbilgin, 1999). The high proportion of women in professional work and training in Turkey is a curious phenomenon for North American and Western European readers, where such egalitarian representation has remained a largely unfulfilled social cause.

OCCUPATIONS AND GENDER IN TURKEY

Any exploration of the current state of women's status and position in the field of employment urges for the understanding of historical legacy of the process of nation-state formation in Turkey. The Proclamation of the Republic

---

The authors made equal contributions to this chapter.

in 1923 was the turning point for the role of women in the Turkish society. Since 1923, sex equality in employment has been deliberately promoted through government policies shaped around the principles of "modernization" and "Westernization." The Turkish experience has been distinct from that in Western European and North American countries, which have promoted equality in employment through legislative sanctions. Gender equality legislation in the field of employment has been rudimentary in Turkey, and the dominant state ideology has been the main force behind the change toward gender equality in the country (Özbilgin, 2000, 2002; Özbilgin & Healy, 2004; Woodward & Özbilgin, 1999).

As has been frequently suggested in the literature, the representation of women plays an important symbolic function during the formation of modern nation-states in developing countries because gender symbols are seen as a "barometer of modernization" against backwardness (Yuval-Davis, 1997, p. 21). Cockburn's (1998) research volume, *The Space Between Us: Negotiating Gender and National Identities in Conflict,* provides examples of the interplay between gender and national identity formation in Cyprus, Ireland, Israel, and Palestine. In search for new national identity, women are made the carriers of both tradition and modernity, with their respective roles in the private sphere as reproducers of national traditions and in the public sphere as symbols of modernity. This results in a kind of primitive feminism of equality that focuses on women's representation in the public space while leaving the subordination in the private space intact and unquestioned (Jayawardena, 1986).

Accordingly, during the formation of the Turkish nation-state, the role and status of women became one of the major areas of intervention for cultural formation based on the principle of republican secularism. The low status of women was equated with underdevelopment, and the modernization movement was mainly marked by the entrance of women into the public space, which was associated with the strengthening of secularism (Arat, 1994; Göle, 1993). Within the framework of the secularist state ideology, the identity of "modern" woman is constructed around the dualities of Islam–West and traditional–modern. Subsequently, the status of women was seen as the determinant of the success of the modernization project.

The presence of women in the public sphere has been supported by the Turkish state with several reforms and services. The first decade of the new Turkish republic witnessed significant legal and societal changes toward the equality of the sexes. In 1926, the new Turkish Civil Code banned polygamy and gave women equal rights to men in matters of divorce and child custody. Political rights were granted to Turkish women through the introduction of the right to vote in local elections in 1930 and the right to vote in elections for and to be elected to the Grand National Assembly in 1934. Other important legislative changes in this era were the prohibition of head and full body covers for women, the introduction of secular education, and lifting the bans on women's employment, all of which militated against the tradition of rigid sex segregation during the Ottoman rule. Tekeli (1982) stated that these rights given to women had two strategic functions: First, they were an important part of dissociating the new secular republic from the ideological and political foundations of the Ottoman Empire, and second, they were the symbol and proof of democratization for the West.

These legal reforms and their implications were further promoted by the strong ideological support of Mustafa Kemal (the founding leader of the Turkish Republic). He encouraged women's entrance into all sectors of employment and created legitimacy for that move through his support of first-generation women professionals of the new republic, who would become role models for subsequent generations of women. However, the beneficiaries of these encouragements and reforms have been a small number of privileged women, whereas the majority of women from lower social classes and rural areas were not reached (Tekeli, 1982). Only the daughters of bureaucracy and the native bourgeoisie were able to reap the benefits of reforms and pursue professional careers. The proximity of middle and upper class women to the central authority as well as the distance of working class and agrarian women from it has allowed for the former's concerns to be supported by the Turkish state, whereas the latter has remained out of the scope of national policymaking.

Nevertheless, these vanguard women have become representations of the "new" woman of the young republic as an emancipated, virtuous, nationalist female hero. Memoirs of and anecdotes from the first generation of professional women in Turkey reveal how they internalized the values and aims of the Kemalist ideology and saw themselves as the pioneers of civilization (Abadan-Unat, 1998; Göle, 1993; Toska, 1998; Urgan, 1999). They felt themselves privileged and emancipated, and being grateful to the republic and Mustafa Kemal, they made incredible efforts to realize the ideal of "new" woman.

Although small in number, the first-generation women of the republic paved the way socially for the existence of women in the public space. However, despite the creation of employment opportunities for women and promotion of women's presence in the public domain, reforms did not attempt to alter either the domestic division of labor or sexual ethics, causing a split between the private and public identities of working women (Kandiyoti, 1997; Tekeli, 1982). As Kandiyoti (1997) argued, "The emancipatory measures directed at women (education, employment, legal reforms) by postcolonial states were never intended to lead to renegotiation of men's existing privileges, but merely to endow women with additional capabilities and responsibilities" (p. 5).

Because the reforms in the Turkish context were made within the framework of the modernization and nationalization projects rather than a framework of women's emancipation, the deeply rooted patriarchal assumptions were left intact, and women continued to be defined primarily in relation to the private sphere with their roles as mothers and wives. As we explain, although this situation has promoted a relatively favorable representation of women in professional training and work in the country, it has also led them to experience gendered outcomes in organizational life.

This chapter situates the gendered outcomes for professional workers in Turkey by reflecting on three interconnected studies, and we identify the intergenerational differences in gendered experiences among young trainees and adult workers. We present the historical legacy, which provides understanding of the current status of gender relations and gendered outcomes, in the context of professional work in Turkey. On the basis of three empirical studies, we present a critical realist account, which illustrates that social reality of gendered occupational outcomes in Turkey can be explained through a layered investigation of micro, meso, and macro situated contexts. The historical and relational approach adopted allows for a reading of gendered outcomes in Turkey as a multilayered issue, having both a path-dependent trajectory suggesting that gendered occupational outcomes should be studied in their historical context and an intergenerational life cycle, namely the interconnected stages of gendered occupational outcomes through training and education to professional work and life. The combined approach adopted here makes it possible to view gendered occupational outcomes as constructed and dynamically negotiated phenomena.

METHOD

The studies that inform this chapter involved both qualitative and quantitative research as well as historical, institutional, and statistical sources. Using a historical and relational approach, we draw on the findings of three distinct field studies, two of which were with employees from the financial services and higher education sectors (Healy et al., 2005; Özbilgin & Healy, 2004; Özbilgin & Woodward, 2003, 2004) and the third with undergraduate engineering students in Turkey (Küskü, Özbilgin, & Özkale, 2007; Özkale et al., 2004; Özkale, Küskü, & Özbilgin, 2005).

At a more philosophical level, the critical realist approach is adopted for the stages of conduct, strategy, and analysis of the three studies. Two basic principles of the critical realist approach are the multilayered nature of reality and the transcending of agency–structure dualism. First, critical realism argues against the flat ontologies of both the positivist tradition that limits scientific inquiry to observable regularities and the interpretivist tradition that focuses on the experiences and interpretations of actors (Keat & Urry, 1975; Layder, 1998). Conversely, a critical realist holds the view that social scientific analysis should investigate the deepest layer of underlying structures and mechanisms that generate the observable phenomena and experiences (Brown, Fleetwood,

& Roberts, 2001). Second, critical realism commits to overcoming the dualism between structure and agency. Within the scope of agency–structure dualism, objectivist accounts ignore any form of human agency, whereas subjectivist approaches reject any objective structure irreducible to individual action or perception (Layder, 1993, 1998). In contrast, critical realism emphasizes the relationality and interdependence between agency and structure and proposes a conception of these two spheres as ontologically different from and irreducible to each other (Robert, 2001).

Another feature of critical realism that informs the discussion in this chapter is the use of multiple research methods to capture the complex, multilayered nature of the interplay between gender and occupational outcomes. Critical realism stands as a relatively open philosophy in the sense of being compatible with different types of research methods and strategies and advocates a multiplicity of methodological strategies and research methods. In that sense, critical realism transcends the artificial boundaries established by both positivism and interpretivism regarding the false dichotomy between qualitative and quantitative research methods (Patomaki & Wight, 2000). As put forward by Brown et al. (2001), "critical realism foregrounds the need to adapt the research methodology to the object and not vice versa. Qualitative and quantitative methods of statistical inference can be assessed in terms of their applicability to the object" (p. 24). Furthermore, the strategy of multiple research methods can be seen as a strategy to reconcile the subjective and objective dimensions of social reality within a single framework. Layder (1998) advocated a multistrategy framework for the investigation of the multilayered nature of social life. To ensure a sound multilevel investigation of the gendered occupational outcomes, the studies analyzed are fed from multiple sources, both qualitative and quantitative.

STUDY 1: THE CASE OF ENGINEERING STUDENTS AND GENDER

Study 1 explored gendered prejudices among engineering students at a state university in Turkey. The study, including the pilot study, was conducted during 2003 and 2005 at Istanbul Technical University (ITU), which is the oldest technical university in Turkey, with a well-established reputation in offering high-quality degrees in engineering. In-depth interviews were conducted with only freshman engineering students, and then a pilot questionnaire survey was administered to all students, including freshman students, with 386 participants (75 female, 311 male). As a result, the final research instrument was formed consisting of three parts that aimed to collect data on students' (a) perceptions of their department's gendered distribution, (b) sets of beliefs on careers and particularly women's careers in engineering, and (c) socioeconomic profiles.

The questionnaire was uploaded to the university Web site and e-mailed to the engineering students. Respondents were 603 students: 133 female and 470 male, equating to a 10% response rate. Although this was a low response rate, the distributive profiles of the respondents in the sample closely mirrored the distribution of male and female students of the school. There is a tendency for researchers to conduct studies on women and engineering exclusively with female participants (Baryeh, Squire, & Mogotsi, 2001; Koushki, Al-Sanad, & Larkin, 1999; Lee, 2002; VanLeuvan, 2004; Zengin-Arslan, 2002). Our study also included male students because they play a major role in sustaining gender order, and therefore the comparison of attitudes and beliefs of male and female students is an important area of investigation (for more detail on this first study, see Küskü et al., 2007; Özkale et al., 2004, 2005).

EUROSTAT (2004) data show that although the proportion of female students now exceeds or closely matches that of male students in higher education in Europe and other industrialized regions of the world, female students are still underrepresented in the field of engineering. Many researchers have studied this phenomenon. For example, Bix (2004) stated that in the United States, women who study engineering encounter several challenges due to the social construction of the field as masculine and male dominated. Similarly, in the Malaysian context, the image of engineering carries the connotations of being a dirty, heavy, manual occupation for strong men and unsuitable for women (Ismail, 2003). This image is further reinforced by the numerical dominance of men in the field, the attitudes of teachers, and the lack of role models and female networks in engineering professional training and work (Hersh, 2000; Siann & Callaghan, 2001; VanLeuvan, 2004). Social learning theory argues that students with less positive attitudes toward mathematics and science will lack the motivation to persist in these fields. Although there has been no evidence to support "gender intensification" hypotheses in longitudinal studies (Jacobs, Lanza, Osgood, Eccles, & Wigfield, 2002; Watt, 2004), several studies have found that during high school, girls' confidence in their mathematics and science abilities remains significantly lower than boys', resulting in girls' underestimation of their mathematics and science competency and feeling less adequate and having lower expectations for success in these technical fields (Guzzetti & Williams, 1996).

The gendering of the engineering profession has historically led to largely male environments structured around male cultural norms and behaviors and very unfriendly environments for women, in which they are often marginalized and discriminated against (Ranson, 2003; Witz, 1992). Consequently, women's success in the field is often contingent on them adopting an explicitly male pattern of career success (Ismail, 2003). Even then, they experience further barriers such as sex discrimination in the workplace. The authors of chapter 7, this volume, argue that lack of flexibility and high work loads in male-dominated professions, combined with women's lower intrinsic values and ability self-concepts for male-typed occupations, constitute significant gender barriers to women's development in such professions. In another study, Zeldin and Pajares (2000) found that male domination in scientific fields has a negative impact on the self-efficacy beliefs of women.

Within this framework, Turkey presents an interesting example for the study of the gendered nature of engineering, where male domination continues to prevail as a cultural construct. Although the proportion of female university students (42.8%) in Turkey is lower than in the developed countries, the proportion of female engineering students is higher than in Europe and other industrialized countries. According to EUROSTAT data, Turkey has one of the highest proportions of female engineering students (34.8%) after Bulgaria and Portugal (35.5% and 35.3%, respectively; for more detail see EUROSTAT, 2004).

Understanding this paradoxical situation calls for a layered investigation of the phenomenon. Turkey's historical trajectory accounts for some of the initial reasons for the relatively favorable representation of women in the engineering study. As explained previously, as part of the modernization project in the country, women were encouraged into professional employment. During this period, the sciences and mathematics were glorified as bastions of modernity, and middle and upper class women dwelling in the cities were encouraged into those areas.

Another structural factor that promoted equality of opportunity in Turkey was the competitive, transparent, and centralized nature of the higher education admission system. Admission to university is based on a nationwide single-stage examination administered by the Öğrenci Seçme ve Yerleştirme Merkezi (Student Selection and Placement Center) every year. Because the exam papers are anonymous and assessed electronically and university placement relies solely on the scores achieved, the process does not allow for gender bias in the form of interview bias or informal relationships. This procedure of university admission provides equality of opportunity for access to privileged fields of study in Turkey, such as engineering and medicine.

However, favorable representation of female engineering students does not mean that the field is free from gender prejudice and discrimination. On the basis of the data from the questionnaire survey, we explored the nature of gendered prejudice leveled at female engineering students as displayed in the beliefs of engineering students.

The questionnaire scale contained 36 items measured by Likert-type scales that ranged from 1 (*strongly disagree*) to 7 (*strongly agree*). Items tapped aspects of beliefs regarding key influences on engineering study and gender. Through principal component exploratory factor analysis with a varimax rotation and extraction of factors having eigenvalues exceeding unity, we identified a 10-dimensional structure, explaining 65% of the total variation, with no cross-loading items. Varimax rotation was chosen to maximize the squared factor loadings in each factor; this simplifies the columns of the factor loading matrix. Factors were sufficiently reliable, excepting Factor 8 (Influence of the Family Context), which displayed marginal internal consistency ($\alpha = .55$). Factor descriptions are contained in Tables 10.1 and 10.2, and correlations among the observed factors in Table 10.3. Gender differences on the factors were analyzed using multivariate analysis of variance in order to understand the nature of gendered prejudices and beliefs. One-way analyses of variance also tested gender differences for individual items to provide understanding of the underlying contribution of each item to significant gender effects for each factor.

Survey participants came from a wide range of engineering disciplines, such as electrical, manufacturing, civil, mechanical, food, chemical, textile, industrial, and physics. General characteristics of the students' backgrounds are presented in Table 10.4.

Female and male respondents displayed similarity across a number of factors. Women, however, scored particularly high on Factor 3, regarding beliefs about women engineers. This was the highest rated factor across the female participants, indicating that female respondents hold highly positive beliefs about women engineers. The highest factor means for male students were for Factors 2 and 5, regarding the positive prospects of engineering and personal aptitude and interest in engineering, respectively. Females' ratings on these two factors were, however, similar to males'. Factors 7, 8, and 9, concerning the influence of family and teachers on the engineering career choices of students, had the lowest reported means by both female and male students, suggesting that Turkish students do not consider these as significant factors in their career choice. Male and female mean ratings are depicted in Figure 10.1, together with factors on which significant gender differences occurred—gender and professional choice, women engineers, women's interest in engineering, and suitability of engineering fields to women (Factors 1, 3, 4, and 6). These findings suggest four main forms of gendered belief and prejudice: Male students displayed higher levels of belief in the impact of gender on professional choice. Female students had a stronger belief than their male counterparts on the success of women engineers. Male students reported stronger beliefs than their female peers that women have lower levels of interest in engineering than their male counterparts, and male students displayed a weaker belief in the suitability of engineering fields to women.

Within the first factor on beliefs on gender and professional choice, there were statistically significant differences with regard to respondent sex on all component items. Male engineering students displayed stronger beliefs on the significance of gender in professional choice than female students, which suggests that male respondents assume stronger gender prejudice than female respondents in the interrelationship between professional choice and gender. There were no significant differences between female and male respondents

TABLE 10.1
Beliefs About Key Influences on Engineering Choice and Gender

Belief	Females (n = 133) M (SD)	Males (n = 470) M (SD)	Total (N = 603) M (SD)
Factor 1: Gender and Professional Choice* (α = .84)			
1. A person's gender is important in choosing a profession as certain professions require certain physical capabilities.*	4.03 (1.99)	4.82 (1.88)	4.64 (1.93)
2. A person's gender is important in choosing a profession because of the working conditions in certain professions.*	4.29 (2.05)	5.12 (1.81)	4.94 (1.89)
3. In my opinion a person's gender is important in choosing a profession.*	3.14 (2.02)	3.98 (2.04)	3.80 (2.06)
4. A person's gender is important in choosing a profession because of socio-cultural expectations.*	3.17 (2.04)	3.66 (1.99)	3.55 (2.01)
5. A person's gender is important in choosing a profession as males and females have different interest areas.*	3.49 (2.06)	4.22 (1.96)	4.06 (2.00)
Total subscale	3.62 (2.03)	4.36 (1.94)	4.29 (1.98)
Factor 2: Engineering Prospects (α = .86)			
6. I believe the quality of living as an engineer is much higher than it is in other professions.	5.06 (1.74)	5.01 (1.52)	5.02 (1.57)
7. I believe the chances of getting promoted are higher in the field of engineering than in any other field.	5.41 (1.66)	5.32 (1.53)	5.34 (1.56)
8. I believe that job opportunities in the field of engineering are more than those in other fields.	5.26 (1.69)	5.16 (1.58)	5.18 (1.60)
9. I believe the salary I get as an engineer will be higher than the salaries people get in other professions.	4.41 (1.68)	4.58 (1.50)	4.54 (1.54)
10. I believe I will acquire much more self-improvement as an engineer than professionals.	5.41 (1.59)	5.48 (1.56)	5.46 (1.56)
Total subscale	5.11 (1.67)	5.11 (1.54)	5.11 (1.57)

(continued)

TABLE 10.1
Beliefs About Key Influences on Engineering Choice and Gender (Continued)

Belief	Females (n = 133) M (SD)	Males (n = 470) M (SD)	Total (N = 603) M (SD)
Factor 3: Women Engineers* (α = .87)			
11. There are many very successful female engineers.*	6.14 (1.49)	4.84 (1.90)	5.13 (1.89)
12. I believe females can generally be very successful in engineering.*	6.14 (1.59)	4.59 (1.83)	4.93 (1.89)
13. There are many very successful female engineers in our country.*	5.77 (1.59)	4.47 (1.87)	4.76 (1.89)
14. I believe engineering is generally a suitable job for females.*	5.78 (1.80)	4.18 (1.83)	4.54 (1.94)
Total subscale	5.96 (1.62)	4.52 (1.88)	4.84 (1.90)
Factor 4: Women's Interest in Engineering* (α = .71)			
15. Female students are not interested in the fields of engineering as they are not guided sufficiently during high school education.	4.07 (1.93)	4.31 (1.79)	4.26 (1.82)
16. Female students are not interested in the fields of engineering as they are not guided sufficiently by their families	4.15 (1.79)	4.47 (1.76)	4.40 (1.77)
17. The lowly proportionate representation of successful female engineers prevents women from choosing engineering as a profession.*	3.28 (2.01)	4.10 (1.93)	3.92 (1.97)
18. Females are generally less interested in engineering.*	4.05 (1.91)	5.11 (1.57)	4.87 (1.71)
19. Female students are not interested in the fields of engineering as these fields do not match with their interests.*	3.89 (1.81)	4.63 (1.61)	4.47 (1.68)
Total subscale	3.89 (1.85)	4.52 (1.73)	4.38 (1.79)
Factor 5: Personal Aptitude and Interest in Engineering (α = .69)			
20. I've been interested in studying engineering since childhood.*	4.62 (2.03)	5.48 (1.70)	5.29 (1.81)
21. I wanted to be an engineer because of my interest in such subjects as maths, physics, and chemistry.	5.75 (1.53)	5.48 (1.73)	5.54 (1.69)
22. I decided to choose this profession because of my abilities and talents.	4.87 (2.00)	4.93 (1.99)	4.92 (1.99)
Total subscale	5.08 (1.85)	5.30 (1.81)	5.25 (1.83)

Factor 6: Suitability of Engineering Fields to Women* (α = .65)			
23. Female students are not interested in the fields of engineering as the job opportunities are limited in this profession.	2.95 (1.90)	2.81 (1.72)	2.85 (1.76)
24. I think that under the working conditions in our country it is difficult to work as a female engineer.*	3.10 (1.93)	3.90 (1.92)	3.72 (1.95)
25. I believe under the working conditions in our country female engineers haven't got enough chance to work as an engineer.*	4.33 (1.96)	3.89 (1.92)	3.99 (1.93)
26. Female students are not interested in the fields of engineering as their physical capabilities do not fit to this profession.*	2.71 (1.80)	3.80 (1.79)	3.56 (1.85)
Total subscale	3.27 (1.90)	3.60 (1.84)	3.53 (1.87)
Factor 7: Influence of Close Family Members (α = .68)			
27. My mother had a great effect on my being an engineer.	2.35 (1.73)	2.43 (1.78)	2.41 (1.77)
28. My father had a great effect on my being an engineer.	2.89 (2.12)	2.84 (2.04)	2.85 (2.06)
29. My brothers and sisters had a great effect on my being an engineer.	2.17 (1.81)	2.09 (1.74)	2.11 (1.75)
Total subscale	2.47 (1.89)	2.45 (1.85)	2.46 (1.86)
Factor 8: Influence of the Family Context (α = .55)			
30. I decided to choose this profession because of the way I was brought up.	2.44 (1.96)	2.48 (2.03)	2.47 (2.02)
31. I decided to choose this profession because of my gender.	1.87 (1.58)	1.61 (1.30)	1.67 (1.37)
32. I decided to choose this profession because of our financial/economic situation.	2.92 (2.10)	3.20 (2.14)	3.14 (2.13)
Total subscale	2.41 (1.86)	2.43 (1.82)	2.43 (1.84)
Factor 9: Influence of Education (α = .76)			
33. My high school teachers had a great effect on my being an engineer.	2.49 (1.91)	2.18 (1.74)	2.25 (1.78)
34. My teachers at the private course had a great effect on my being an engineer.	2.46 (1.82)	2.32 (1.84)	2.35 (1.84)
Total subscale	2.48 (1.87)	2.25 (1.79)	2.30 (1.81)
Factor 10: Influence of the National Context (α = .78)			
35. I believe under the working conditions in our country male engineers get promoted more quickly than the females.	4.20 (2.14)	4.28 (2.00)	4.26 (2.03)
36. I believe under the working conditions in our country male engineers earn more money than the females.	3.62 (2.21)	3.79 (2.05)	3.75 (2.09)
Total subscale	3.91 (2.18)	4.04 (2.0)	4.01 (2.06)

Note. All items were measured by a 1–7 *strongly disagree–strongly agree* Likert scale.
*Denotes significant gender differences.

TABLE 10.2
Factor Descriptions

Factor	No. of items	Reliability coefficient	Eigenvalue	Rotation sum of squared loadings	Variance explained (%)	Cumulative %	M	SD
1	5	.84	5.28	3.49	9.69	9.69	4.20	1.54
2	5	.86	4.25	3.29	9.15	18.84	5.11	1.25
3	4	.87	2.93	3.24	8.99	27.83	4.84	1.62
4	5	.71	2.46	2.38	6.61	34.43	4.38	1.23
5	3	.69	1.87	1.96	5.44	39.87	5.25	1.44
6	4	.65	1.58	1.93	5.36	45.24	3.53	1.31
7	3	.68	1.51	1.89	5.24	50.48	2.46	1.46
8	3	.55	1.28	1.79	4.98	55.46	2.42	1.36
9	2	.76	1.13	1.73	4.80	60.26	2.30	1.62
10	2	.78	1.10	1.69	4.70	64.96	4.01	1.87

Note. Extraction method: principal component analysis; rotation method: varimax with Kaiser normalization. Factor descriptions are contained in Table 10.1.

TABLE 10.3
Pearson Correlations Between Factors

Factor	1	2	3	4	5	6	7	8	9	10
1	1.000									
2	.110**	1.000								
3	-.223**	.183**	1.000							
4	.299**	.185**	-.008	1.000						
5	-.038	.354**	.136**	.097*	1.000					
6	.439**	.034	-.167**	.343**	-.026	1.000				
7	.027	.044	-.042	.023	.037	.037	1.000			
8	.101*	.104*	-.116**	.094*	.070	.129**	.356**	1.000		
9	-.027	.011	-.070	.042	.034	.044	.290**	.318**	1.000	
10	.301**	.147**	-.144**	.237**	.016	.375**	.013	.120**	-.010	1.000

Note. Factor descriptions are contained in Table 10.1.
*p < .05. **p < .01.

TABLE 10.4
General Characteristics of the Students' Parents

Characteristic	Females		Males		Total	
	n	%	n	%	n	%
Mother's education level						
Primary school degree or less	28	21.0	140	29.8	168	27.8
Junior high school degree or middle school degree	9	6.8	30	6.4	39	6.5
High school degree	51	38.3	149	31.7	200	33.2
Undergraduate degree	44	33.1	141	30.0	185	30.7
Graduate degree	1	0.8	10	2.1	11	1.8
Father's education level						
Primary school degree or less	11	8.3	75	16.0	86	14.3
Junior high school degree or middle school degree	8	6.0	26	5.5	34	5.6
High school degree	27	20.3	80	17.0	107	17.8
Undergraduate degree	70	52.6	251	53.4	321	53.2
Graduate degree	17	12.8	38	8.1	55	9.1
Mother's working condition						
Working mother	71	53.4	216	46.0	287	47.6
Housewife	62	46.6	254	54.0	316	52.4

with respect to the second factor on beliefs about engineering, with both female and male students holding positive views on the profession, which conforms with its social image in Turkey. Yet, male students displayed a higher degree of gendered prejudice regarding the questions on women engineers. Significant differences exist between female and male engineering students regarding the third factor related to their beliefs on women in engineering. Female students responded positively to the idea that there are successful women engineers and that engineering is a suitable career for women, whereas male students reported much lower support for these positive statements.

For the fourth factor, on beliefs on women's interest in engineering, both female and male students had similar levels of agreement with the statements relating to females' low interest in the field as being due to absence of proper guidance from their families and during high school. It is interesting that males indicated stronger agreement with the explanation of females not entering engineering because of the lack of successful role models, in contrast to the female students reporting in Factor 3 that there are successful women in engineering. However, despite males endorsing the view that a lack of female role models in engineering explains the lower entrance of women into the profession, these male students reported a higher degree of support than females for the two statements that considered women's lack of interest in engineering as a more innate and essential part of women's nature. This finding demonstrates

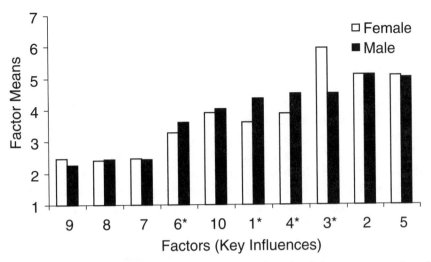

Figure 10.1. Gendered factor means for beliefs about key influences on engineering choice. Asterisks indicate significant factor differences between males and females. Factor descriptions are contained in Table 10.1.

that male students hold gendered prejudices. They believe that women's aptitude and interests are reasons for lower representation of women in the field. Although the facilitative structures in Turkey may partly explain this, it nevertheless tacitly suggests that according to male engineering students, the absence of women in engineering fields is a matter of choice rather than an outcome of structural conditions. Women's aptitude and interest in engineering study alone cannot account for their representation in engineering. Thus, male students' support for these essentialist statements suggests gendered bias.

There was no difference in personal identification of the female and male respondents with engineering as shown in the fifth factor. Both females and males rated their interest in science subjects associated with engineering, as well as their talents and aptitude, to be important in their choice of engineering as a profession. These statements suggest an informed choice through students' experiences and educational achievements. However, male students displayed a stronger belief than their female peers in their affinity from childhood with engineering. For the sixth factor, on beliefs about the suitability of engineering fields to women, female students reported stronger support for the statement that lack of opportunities, rather than innate factors, affected women's suitability for the engineering profession, whereas the latter was considered more strongly by male respondents, who rated women's less suitable physical capabilities as a reason for females' lack of interest in engineering.

For the seventh factor, beliefs on the influence of close family members, and eighth factor, beliefs on the influence of the family context, there were no significant differences between the responses of females and males. However, in general, the students reported very low support for the influence of their parents and siblings. This is an interesting finding for a country where parental influence is comparatively more significant than in other countries on the career choices of individuals, as identified by Özbilgin, Küskü, and Erdoğmus (2005) in their comparative study of Britain, Israel, and Turkey. Similarly, both female and male students gave very low support for the statements that their family background and context had an influence on their choice of engineering. There were no significant gender differences supporting the statements in Factor 9 related to the influence of teachers on career choice. Although there was no statistically significant difference by gender in response to these statements in Factor 10, both male and female students rated at just above the scale midpoint the statement that male engineers enjoy better opportunities for career advancement in the country compared with their female counterparts. There was slightly less support by both groups of students regarding male engineers being paid better than female engineers, with mean ratings just below the scale midpoint.

These findings provide important insights into gendered beliefs regarding engineering study and the engineering profession from a group of Turkish engineering students. The Turkish case presents a challenge to the critical mass hypothesis (Dahlerup, 1988), which suggests that as the proportion of women reaches a critical mass in workplaces, this will engender a further egalitarian change, helping to eradicate gendered prejudice. The Turkish case is unique because the existence of a critical mass of female students in engineering has not altered the taste for gendered prejudice in engineering study. Analysis of our findings unambiguously demonstrates that numerical representation alone does not ensure sufficient protection against gendered prejudice. Nevertheless, numerical representation has a moderating impact on the gendered disadvantage and prejudice that female students may experience. Küskü et al. (2007) explained that female and male students in mixed-sex departments in Turkey reported lower levels of gendered prejudice regarding women in engineering than their counterparts from departments which are male or female dominated. We suggest that gender representation is only one dimension of gendered disadvantage in engineering because complex forms of gendered disadvantage reside at social, cultural, psychological, and economic layers of life. Therefore, reducing gendered disadvantage in engineering should involve multilayered and multidimensional programs that tackle disadvantage in domains as wide as social life, schooling and education, work, and organization. Although the study clearly identified gendered patterns, we must caution against overextrapolation from our results in view of our sample response rate, which did however include participants from across the full range of engineering departments.

STUDY 2: THE CASE OF PROFESSORIAL WORKERS AND GENDER

Study 2 aimed to understand how professorial careers are gendered in the Turkish higher education system. The study was conducted between 2001 and 2004 and based on semistructured interviews with open-ended questions that focused on six themes: careers, progression, inequality, work and life, employment structures, and personal–professional history. The study participants were selected through purposive sampling. We approached 71 professors, of whom 57 (30 men and 27 women) participated in the study. All participants were full professors holding professorial chairs across all cognate disciplines at universities. Their professorships were subject to the progression criteria of Yükseköğretim Kurulu (YÖK; the governing body of the Turkish higher education sector; see http://www.yok.gov.tr). The research took place in six universities in Istanbul and five in Ankara because these two cities are the centers of academic activity in Turkey, accommodating the highest number of universities in the country. The semistructured interviewing method was adopted to allow the narration of issues regarding gender equality and higher education in Turkey as well as personal career experiences seen as appropriate by the participants. The 32-question interview schedule was designed to explore career development in the higher education sector in Turkey and socioeconomic and institutional profiles of the respondents. All interviews were tape recorded, fully transcribed, and translated to English from Turkish (for more detail on this second study, see Healy et al., 2005; Özbilgin & Healy, 2004).

The case of professorial workers in Turkey demonstrates a paradoxical situation similar to the case of the engineering students. Turkey is among the countries having the lowest female labor force participation in Europe, and the percentage of women academics in the country is just above the European Union average of 34.8%. It is interesting that the representation of women academics in the professorial ranks in Turkey displays a limited vertical segregation in the sector compared with its European counterparts. In the European Union, the average representation rate of female professors is only 14%, whereas Turkey has the highest percentage of women professors in Europe of 27% (Özbilgin & Healy, 2004; Woodward & Özbilgin, 1999).

As in the case of engineering students, this favorable outcome is first related to the deliberate ideological state support for women to pursue professional careers as the representatives of the new "modern" republic. In the initial periods of the Turkish Republic in the 1920s, several reforms took place to modernize, Westernize, and secularize the higher education system (Güvenç, 1997). Starting from the 1920s, women were purposely welcome to take academic employment, and until the 1980s the number of women academics gradually increased partly because of that ideological sanctioning (see YÖK Web site: http://www.yok.gov.tr). Moreover, in Turkish society, the academic sector was historically considered a source of "safe," "respectable," and "proper" employment for highly educated women (Kandiyoti, 1997; Zeytinoğlu, 1999). Since the early 1990s, the academic sector has witnessed a rapid expansion (the number of universities went from 29 to 76 between 1990 and 2004, with a 75% increase in the number of full professors), which has led to skill shortages in the sector and increasing career mobility opportunities for women.

Again similar to the impact of the centralized university admission system in the case of engineering students, female academics likewise benefited from the relatively centralized, standardized, and transparent nature of the promotion system in academia. In Turkey, YÖK, a central authority, governs the higher education sector. YÖK legislation defines the performance criteria and mobility requirements that regulate promotions at all academic levels in the sector, including the professorial promotions (Healy et al., 2005). After being qualified by YÖK for the title of professor, candidates need to be appointed to a chair by their local university, which will have its own promotion system. At this stage, Özbilgin and Healy (2004) argued, competition and organizational politics, particularly in the elite universities, may potentially upset the equitable outcomes (p. 8). Still, the considerably gender-neutral, transparent, and standardized system of promotion governed by YÖK regulations has a relatively positive impact on women professors' careers in Turkey and promotes a "greater equality of access to full professorial posts than in many other countries, where such standardization is rare" (Özbilgin & Healy, 2004, p. 8).

Unfortunately, this seemingly transparent and gender-neutral system of promotion and recruitment does not translate into an antidiscriminatory and women-friendly work culture and environment in the higher education sector in Turkey. The qualitative field research conducted with Turkish professors reveals the complex nature of gendered employment relationships in Turkish universities.

When asked whether they think that there are gender inequalities in higher education employment, most of the male and female professors reported the academic domain as free from gender inequality and discrimination, although some accepted that it may not be the case in employment outside of academia. One of the male professors argued, "I do not believe in discrimination in this profession. Women face discrimination in lots of other sectors but not in the university system."[1]

There was a strong belief, particularly among the male professors, in the impossibility of gender discrimination in the highly "prestigious" sphere of academia. The words of a male professor demonstrate this belief: "Gender dis-

---

[1]All of the quotations from participants in this chapter were translated from the Turkish by Mustafa Özbilgin. We obtained permission to use their words and promised to ensure anonymity and confidentiality.

crimination is not a significant issue here and being men or women is beyond question in an academic institution." Still another male professor confidently stated, "There are no barriers to women in Turkey in this area. I've never encountered it even in the most conservative places. Male colleagues also do support [women]."

However, women professors seemed to be more reluctant about displaying their confidence in the ideal of a discrimination-free environment in the academic sector. For instance, one of them argued that the academic sector is no different from other fields of employment, saying, "All the discriminatory factors that exist in social life prevail in academic life as well."

It is ironic that the gendered nature of academic careers becomes apparent when respondents tell about the barriers that they have encountered during their academic employment experience. Male professors report institutional barriers such as promotion procedures, and their female colleagues mention barriers regarding the family life focused around marriage and child care—none of which seemed to be considered constraints for the male professors. Furthermore, in their effort to marry their professional and family lives, all the female professors acknowledged the men's help and support to their career, whereas only 5 of the 30 male professors mentioned the contributions of their immediate families.

Experiences of women professors as they were narrated during the interviews show that female academic careers are developed under the shadow of their domestic responsibilities and realities. As pointed out earlier, despite women having been actively encouraged by the dominant state ideology and policies to pursue professional careers as part of the project of modernizing the country, these policies neither questioned nor undermined the patriarchal culture of the society. Hence, traditional family ideology based on the gendered division of labor, shaped around the idea of women as the homemakers and men as the breadwinners, continues to be a key pillar of Turkish culture (Peker, 1996). Our research findings demonstrate the validity of the gendered division of labor for the case of professorial workers as well. It is ironic that this situation was perceived as "normal" by respondents of both genders and that the gendered career outcomes were neither questioned nor challenged. Although male respondents may be blind to the advantages of the gendered division of labor in regard to their career advancement, women professors were equally oblivious to the negative career outcomes they experienced because of their dual roles.

Although female professors are aware of the difficulties that they face because of their domestic responsibilities, they do not associate this with their career trajectories. One of the female respondents said, "Actually family did not hinder me but when my children were younger I had difficulties in doing research, teaching, working and also taking care of the house." Another tried to consolidate her belief in the existence of sex equality with the difficulties that she had experienced by emphasizing the "difference" between men's and women's experiences:

> I believe that there is equality between the sexes. However, once you enter the academic profession, the difficulties [women and men] face are different. However much men help, responsibilities of caring for the family and children are expected of women.

Accepting their dual role and double burden as "normal" and "natural," Turkish female professors participating in this study failed to challenge either work culture or familial ideology. They tried to adapt themselves to the masculine career paths and values that governed their workplace relationships and culture.

STUDY 3: THE CASE OF BANK WORKERS AND GENDER

Study 3, which sought to reveal the gendered inequalities in the financial services sector in Turkey, was conducted in 1995 in three large retail banks. Two of the case study companies were among the oldest privately owned financial institutions in Turkey, founded in the early 1940s, and the third is one of the largest state-owned commercial financial institutions in Turkey. At the time the research took place, they respectively provided employment to 7,000 workers (41% women); 3,500 workers (41% women); and 11,000 workers (36% women). The representation of women employees in the workforce was above the national average for financial companies (31%) in all of the case study organizations. In all the companies, female staff had higher educational qualifications than the male employees, and female employment was concentrated at the middle ranks of the organizational hierarchy. Women were underrepresented both in the higher echelons of management and in unskilled work, where their representation was very limited because these companies preferred men for such posts.

In this study, data were collected through structured direct questionnaires and semistructured interviews, both of which were devised to investigate gender issues in employment by focusing on the work experiences of participants in relation to sex equality within the scope of their personal lives and professional work. The questionnaires and interviews centered on four key themes: personal histories of participants in their lives, educations, and careers; their perceptions and experiences of equality and discrimination; their patterns of work and employment; and finally, their strategies for accommodation of domestic life and work. The interviews generally lasted about an hour and were tape recorded and fully transcribed. Using a purposive sampling strategy, the study generated 312 (182 female, 130 male) completed questionnaires out of 400 questionnaires sent out and 20 interviews (8 female, 12 male) from 25 potential interviewees who were approached. The average age of respondents was 30, and ages ranged from 18 to 50. Questionnaire respondents came from a spread of socioeconomic and educational backgrounds. Of the interview participants, 4 had completed secondary school, 13 had attended university, and 3 had postgraduate qualifications. Nine were married, and 11 were single. Five of the interviewees were senior managers, 5 middle managers, and 4 junior managers. There were also 6 nonmanagerial grade employees. (For more detail on this third study, see Özbilgin, 1998, 2000; Özbilgin & Woodward, 2003, 2004.)

In the early decades of the 20th century, 27 government-owned national banks were established in Turkey, and they promoted professional careers for Turkish women in conformity with the secularist state ideology. This was followed by the expansion of the banking sector in the 1950s, when more than 30 privately owned banks were established. These privately owned banks also provided women with new employment opportunities in this sector (Özbilgin & Woodward, 2003, 2004).

Since 1955, women's numerical representation has shown a steady decrease (from 43% in 1955 to 35% in the 1990s) in the work force because of the wave of mass migration and urbanization. However, a reverse trend can be witnessed in the banking sector, where women's participation rates increased from 24% to 42% between 1988 and 2001 (Türkiye Bankalar Birliği, 2002). The reason for that positive trend in the sector is twofold. First, mainstream banking and finance organizations in Turkey adopt secular and global policies in their recruitment practices. Second, the increasing number of women with higher technical skills meets the growing levels of demand for skilled workforce in the sector (Özbilgin & Woodward, 2003). Additionally, as in the case of academic employment, women's employment in the banking sector, as pointed out by Seyman (1992), is seen as "socially and morally acceptable" because of the sector's reputation as a provider of secure, prestigious, and safe career opportunities for women. Hence, well-educated young Turkish women are encouraged by significant others to pursue careers in the sector.

However, as indicated earlier, the review of policies, documents, and other in-house publications of the case study companies reveals that women are underrepresented in both the higher and lower levels of the organizations and that they are rather clustered at the middle ranks, whereas male employees enjoy better opportunities in both unskilled and managerial positions. For the case of female employment in the sector, it is only a minority of highly educated women of upper or middle class origin who benefit from career opportunities. Hence, for the female banking sector employees, social class is a stronger antecedent of their status within the sector than it is for their male colleagues (Özbilgin & Woodward, 2004).

The case study research shows that in this sector, sex equality is taken for granted by both human resource managers and employees. Ninety-four percent of survey respondents believed that women enjoy equal opportunities in their companies, and 86% reported that women do not face recruitment barriers. Contrary to that belief of gender-neutral employment, as we discuss through this section, our findings reveal the existence of several demarcation strategies that control women's careers in the field and exclude them from some areas and ranks of the organization. Case studies of these three companies demonstrate the presence of both vertical and horizontal segregation in the financial service sector in Turkey.

Women's employment in the sector is heavily concentrated in areas that involve direct contact with customers, such as marketing, investment, and stock exchange. One of the female respondents commented,

> They specifically prefer women in the personal banking department. . . .
> It must be their appearance. The ones working with us all are pleasant looking. They are also sweet talking. They have the patience to explain everything without losing their patience.

This pattern of women's overrepresentation in customer service jobs suggests the dominance of heterosexist gender ideology in the sector where women's physical appearance or their "feminine" qualities have a determining impact on their occupational and career outcomes. The same gender ideology also results in barriers to women's entrance into male-dominated areas of employment in the organizations. Özbilgin and Woodward (2004) maintained that the current exclusion of women from some occupational areas in the financial service sector is the heritage of the Ottoman tradition, which limited women's free movement in the public domain (p. 678). Words from a male senior manager display this hesitation to let women pursue their career in certain areas: "Ladies also enter the audit department but they, for example, don't go everywhere. But you can send men to branches anywhere in Turkey." This exclusion from male-dominated occupational areas such as auditing is reinforced by the lack of organizational procedures to combat sexual harassment exercised by the customers. One of the female respondents narrated her experience during her employment in the audit department:

> I had a bad experience once. During the branch audit, I always wear mini skirts. When we went to a conservative town, I had a very bad experience. I am not going to do customer visits any longer. The customer did not want to shake my hand. I had a male marketing representative with me. He talked to him and did not even look at me.

In the absence of any organizational support, female financial sector employees develop individual coping strategies such as refraining from these occupational areas that are socially seen as "improper" for women. The experience of the same respondent who thereafter abstained from audit work exemplifies that situation. She reasoned as follows: "Here in this enclosed office, because we are together with our colleagues, we are not affected but I am sure our colleagues in branches are having difficulties."

However, the "enclosed offices" are also not free from sexual harassment, although male respondents deny its existence. Unfortunately, grievance procedures are complicated, and there are no adequate employee training programs to raise awareness regarding the issue. Moreover, victims are required to provide "proof," which can hardly be seen as supportive of the victims because incidents generally take place in private where there will be no witnesses. A female respondent explained the difficulty of "proving" harassment:

> It can be a look or a word. I believe that under every joke there is a sense of truth. They may be implying things with their jokes. What I observe and consider as harassment, if you ask that person, may not be. I say, "Yes, this is harassment," but for them it is not disturbing. Looks, talks, jokes. I don't know what kind of procedure is followed. I mean, I observe things but nothing is really happening. I mean, sometimes the looks are really disturbing. I think if the person who is harassed complains, they would investigate and ask for the reasons. I mean, you may say he looked at me so bad that I felt naked. He will say, "I did not look that way." We cannot prove that. We cannot prove words or looks, You cannot even prove touches. . . . Except for the doctor's report in rape, others are difficult to prove.

Her words also demonstrate that sexually harassing behaviors such as "looks, talks, and jokes" are regarded as "normal" in the work environment and are not associated with women's exclusion and discrimination. This is due to the fact that sexual harassment at work is a taboo topic in Turkey, and organizational culture is constructed around male values. The image of the "ideal worker" in the banking sector is associated with qualities such as being dynamic, hard working, reckless, and quick, all of which traditionally denote masculinity in Turkish society. The implication of this is that female employees are expected to identify with this imagery and to conform to the male norm by isolating work from domestic life.

One of the main features of the male-centered organization of work life in the banking sector in Turkey is the culture of long working hours. The pattern of long working hours and workaholism has been well studied in the U.S. context (Schor, 1991). Working long hours is equated with strong commitment to the organization as well as providing networking opportunities—both of which lead to positive occupational outcomes and career advancement. However, the norm of long work hours functions as an exclusion strategy for women employees, particularly the ones with domestic and child care responsibilities who cannot easily conform. As pointed out earlier, traditional family ideology based on a strong gendered division of labor is prevalent in Turkey. As would be expected, banking sector employees are not immune to that tradition. Our case study research shows that female employees are heavily responsible for domestic work and child care. A female participant pointed to that gendered imbalance:

> Women do not always show it in their work lives but they have difficulties combining home and work. Of course, because most of the domestic responsibility falls on women, such as child care, or routine housework, they are having difficulties there. . . . I think that men's responsibility at home is much less.

Still another female employee argued that because of domestic commitments, work life is being pushed to secondary status for women:

> You cannot always show the same performance as other male colleagues. You are left behind as you have too much responsibility on you. You are lagging behind, naturally. If you have a home and children, as the children become your priority, work becomes a second priority. I don't think that men have any such problem.

These dual responsibilities for women also prevent them from taking advantage of the training, education, and career development opportunities in their organizations, which are organized around male needs and time constraints (see also chap. 7, this volume). It is interesting that some male research participants failed to recognize the existence of these barriers for their female colleagues:

> There are no barriers to the education and training of women. However, I cannot say anything about the ones who experience difficulties due to their own social circumstances. But there is no discrimination in the departments where they work. It may be that her husband does not permit it, or that she doesn't want to leave her child and go to training.

These words display the dominant attitude in the banking profession of perceiving gender imbalances regarding domestic life as natural facts of life, and the difficulties that female employees experience in their work life because of that imbalance as personal problems. Ninety-three percent of respondents believed that barriers to women's career advancement did not exist in their organizations. That attitude covertly implies that gender inequality is perceived as a personal rather than an institutional issue and that it is female employees' failing if they cannot perform as well as their male colleagues in adopting the work life and culture centered on male values, needs, and experiences. In this sector, the ideal worker is expected to separate his or her domestic and work lives. This expectation clearly disadvantages female banking workers who assume primary responsibility for domestic work and child care. It is ironic that male participants confidently claimed that they were better at separating their domestic and work duties then their female colleagues, with a tone that attributed this to their better organizational and professional capabilities rather than to their advantageous position due to holding minor and secondary responsibilities for domestic tasks carried out primarily by their spouses or mothers. The following quote from a male participant illustrates how easily men are able to dissociate themselves from domestic work: "Do men have difficulty in combining home and domestic responsibilities? No, never, domestic life is one thing and occupational work is another."

That insensitivity to gender imbalance in domestic life was also prevalent at the institutional level. The dominant stance taken toward sex equality in the case study companies replicated the state ideology of sex equality that promotes equality between men and women in the field of employment without referring to or dealing with their differences and gendered domestic division of labor. Accordingly, although financial service companies encourage women to take up employment in the sector, they neither attempt to change their male dominated organizational cultures nor take action to accommodate the different needs and priorities of their female employees by providing adequate child care arrangements or family-friendly work–life balance policies.

DISCUSSION

Gendered occupational outcomes can be best understood through a layered and relational investigation of the phenomenon. This chapter operationalizes this proposition by adopting a critical realist perspective. We argue for a methodological approach that will enable critical engagement with data through integration of the socioeconomic forces and institutional dynamics to the analysis of the situational nature of the gendered occupational outcomes in the case of professional work and training in the Turkish case. Our studies reveal that gendered occupational outcomes are sustained and reproduced at three interrelational levels: the macro social and historical level, the meso organizational level, and the micro individual level.

The numerical representation of women in science, engineering, and technology careers is counterintuitively high in Turkey compared with the European and North American countries. Considering that Turkey is a Muslim majority country, this situation presents a curious case. Through three studies in the Turkish context, this chapter presents challenges to the critical mass thesis, explicating that numerical representation is a necessary but insufficient condition for gender equality in careers.

One of the key issues that all three of these studies reveal is the complex nature of gendered occupational outcomes in the Turkish context. The findings of our three case studies suggest that unidimensional explanations for the interplay between gender and professional training and work present an incomplete picture of the reality and understanding of that complex phenomenon and urges for a multilayered and relational treatment of social–structural, organizational, and individual–agentic impacts. In this chapter, we have situated the notion of gendered occupational outcomes in the Turkish case at macro, meso, and micro levels. We explored the impact of familial and state ideology at the macro level and of organizational and institutional context at the meso level. At the micro level, we examined the gendered beliefs and experiences of participants regarding professional study and work.

As we have already maintained, through the cases of engineering students and professorial and bank workers, women are numerically well represented in professional education and employment in Turkey. This favorable representation has both ideological and institutional bases. Institutional transparency plays an important role in reducing the gender bias in the university admission and academic promotion systems. Both systems are characterized by their centralized and standardized processes, providing professors and engineering students with relatively gender-neutral procedural arrangements and thus higher prospects for success compared with their Western European and North American counterparts who do not enjoy the same levels of institutional transparency.

More important, the secularist ideology adopted by the Turkish state since the early 1920s plays a crucial role in the high levels of female representation in professional education and employment. Within the scope of the modernization project in the country, sex equality in the field of employment, particularly in professional occupations, and women's presence in the public space were encouraged as a symbol of the new, modern Turkish state's divorce from its Islamic Ottoman heritage. This ideological support made it possible for upper and middle class Turkish women to pursue professional careers as bank workers, engineers, and academics. Moreover, careers in sectors such as banking and academia were socially constructed as safe, secure, proper, and respectable for women in Turkish society.

However, it is important to note that social class background draws a demarcation line for gendered occupational outcomes in Turkey. The participants in all three studies had both middle class status and family backgrounds. The women who have enjoyed the opportunities opened up by the ideological state support have been well-educated women from big cities and privileged class backgrounds, whereas their sisters from lower social class backgrounds are still facing severe gendered obstacles in entering the labor market. We mentioned earlier that mass migration and urbanization processes starting from the 1960s have led to the deterioration of employment prospects for unskilled, less educated women from rural backgrounds, resulting in high levels of female unemployment in the cities. As Kandiyoti (1997) observed, sex segregation in unskilled jobs is much stronger than in highly skilled occupations in Turkey.

Another weakness of the ideologically driven sex equality agenda in Turkey is the overwhelming indifference to and insensitivity to the impact of the domestic division of labor on women's occupational lives. Although the numerical representation of women in professional occupations has been encouraged by state policies and reforms, traditional family ideology based on the gendered domestic division of labor positioning women as the primary domestic workers has been left unquestioned. Our findings have demonstrated the negative effects of this imbalance on women's careers. Female participants' experiences show that their dual responsibilities in professional and domestic spheres erect barriers that jeopardize their efforts at sustaining a balance of work and life demands. Absence of work–life balance supports at institutional and national levels means that women find themselves observing double shifts because of their disproportionately heavy domestic roles.

This situation is partly due to the paradoxical nature of the sex equality framework in Turkey. Unlike in the developed countries, where legal protectionism to combat gender discrimination in the field of employment is a long-standing tradition, in Turkey the hegemonic understanding of sex equality in employment is shaped by ideological state support within the scope of the modernization project. The Turkish Constitution guarantees that women and men are equal and enjoy equal rights. However, this does not translate into a critical awareness of the persistent gender inequalities in employment and the domestic division of labor. Because sex equality is assumed but not questioned, there is no "equal opportunities" legislation to prevent discriminatory practices and guarantee equal treatment in the workplace. In the absence of necessary legal sanctions, the issue of sex equality depends heavily on the initiative, willingness, and ideological choice of the employer. Not unexpectedly, gendered social order and traditional family ideology also pertain to work organizations. Evidence from our case study organizations shows that male experience is treated as universal, resulting in work culture being constructed around male norms and values. Within this framework, work life is organized around the separation of domestic and work life, and the gendered nature of domestic life and the different needs and priorities that female employees may have are ignored. It is difficult to see how organizations in Turkey may start to take some progressive action to promote sex equality by adopting more family-friendly work–life balance policies without an external push in the form of legal enforcement as in the case of developed countries.

It is not surprising that the family ideology, which is underpinned by traditional gender roles, and discriminatory stereotypes that are embedded in Turkish culture persist not only at the organizational level but also at the individual level. As in the case of engineering students, despite relatively high female representation, strong gendered prejudices are still held, particularly by male students. Similarly, responses of male banking workers and professors in the studies discussed here displayed their belief in gendered stereotypes and the domestic division of labor, which exclude and disadvantage female professionals throughout their careers. It is ironic that women respondents in the case studies, although experiencing negative occupational outcomes, seemed to accept the gendered nature and practice of their profession and the field of employment at large and to question neither imbalance in the domestic division of labor nor its impact on their careers. They, like their male colleagues, had internalized the male-centered values, norms, and rules of the field of professional employment, and unwittingly occupied the gendered "legitimate" space permitted to them.

POLICY IMPLICATIONS

A move forward for sex equality in employment in Turkey calls for action at different levels. As we have demonstrated, numerical representation is only one dimension of the equality agenda because relatively high rates of female presence in professional study and work do not automatically alter the deep-rooted gendered order in the society. Although ideological state support has been an important medium for promoting sex equality in Turkey, it needs to be incorporated within a progressive equal opportunities legislation that will reinforce organizations' adoption of equal treatment and positive action policies for men and women. At the institutional level, organizations need to commit to changing both their cultures and their employment practices around the principles of fairness and inclusion; to acknowledge the different needs and priorities of women; and to tackle discrimination, harassment, and exclusion of women in the workplace. Last but not least, because it is the individual agents who will practice, promote, or obstruct any action taken at the level of organizational and state policy, individuals need to develop a strong personal awareness and critical understanding of the gendered nature of employment.

REFERENCES

Abadan-Unat, N. (1998). *Kum Saatini İzlerken* [Watching the hourglass]. İstanbul, Turkey: İletişim.

Arat, Y. (1994). Toward a democratic society: The women's movement in Turkey in the 1980s. *Women's Studies International Forum, 17,* 241–248.

Baryeh, E. A., Squire, P. J., & Mogotsi, M. (2001). Engineering education for women in Botswana. *International Journal of Electrical Engineering Education, 38*(2), 173–182.

Bix, A. S. (2004). From "engineeresses" to "girl engineers" to "good engineers": A history of women's U.S. engineering education. *NWSA Journal, 16*(1), 27–49.

Brown, A., Fleetwood, S., & Roberts, J. (2001). The marriage of critical realism and Marxism: Happy, unhappy or on the rocks? In A. Brown, S. Fleetwood, & J. Roberts (Eds.), *Critical realism and Marxism* (pp. 1–22). London: Routledge.

Cockburn, C. (1998). *The space between us: Negotiating gender and national identities in conflict*. London: Zed Books.

Dahlerup, D. (1988). From a small to a large minority: Women in Scandinavian politics, *Scandinavian Political Studies, 11*, 275–298.

EUROSTAT. (2004, January 19) *Science and technology: Highest proportion of graduates in science and engineering in Sweden, Ireland and France*. Brussels, Belgium: Author.

Göle, N. (1993). *Modern Mahrem: Medeniyet ve Örtünme* [The forbidden modern: Civilization and veiling]. Istanbul, Turkey: Metis.

Güvenç, B. (1997). *Türk Kimliği: Kültür Tarihinin Kaynakları* [The Turkish identity: Origins of cultural history]. İstanbul, Turkey: Remzi Kitabevi.

Guzzetti, B., & Williams, W. (1996). Gender, text, and discussion: Examining intellectual safety in the science classroom. *Journal of Research in Science Teaching, 33*(1), 5–20.

Healy, G., Özbilgin, M., & Aliefendioglu, H. (2005). Academic employment and gender: A Turkish challenge to vertical sex segregation. *European Journal of Industrial Relations, 11*, 247–264.

Hersh, M. (2000). The changing position of women in engineering worldwide. *IEEE Transactions of Engineering Management, 47*, 345–359.

Ismail, M. (2003). Men and women engineers in a large industrial organization: Interpretation of career progression based on subjective-career experience. *Women in Management Review, 18*(1–2), 60–67.

Jacobs, J. E., Lanza, S., Osgood, D. W., Eccles, J. S., & Wigfield, A. (2002). Changes in children's self-competence and values: Gender and domain differences across grades one through twelve. *Child Development, 73*, 509–527.

Jayawardena, K. (1986). *Feminism and nationalism in the third world*. London: Zed.

Kandiyoti, D. (1997). *Cariyeler, Bacılar, Yurttaşlar: Kimlikler ve Toplumsal Dönüşümler* [Concubines, sisters and citizens: Identities and social transformations]. Istanbul, Turkey: Metis Yayınları.

Keat, R., & Urry, J. (1975). *Social theory as science*. London: Routledge & Kegan Paul.

Koushki, P. A., Al-Sanad, H. A., & Larkin, A. M. (1999). Women engineers in Kuwait: Perception of gender bias. *Journal of Engineering Education, 88*(1), 93–97.

Küskü, F., Özbilgin, M., & Özkale, L. (2007). Against the tide: Gendered prejudice and disadvantage in engineering study from a comparative perspective. *Gender, Work and Organization, 14*(2), 109–129.

Layder, D. (1993). *New strategies in social research*. Cambridge, England: Polity Press.

Layder, D. (1998). *Sociological practice: Linking theory and social research*. London: Sage.

Lee, J. D. (2002). More than ability: Gender and personal relationships influence science and technology involvement. *Sociology of Education, 75*, 349–373.

Özbilgin, M. F. (1998). *A cross-cultural comparative analysis of sex equality in the financial services sector in Turkey and Britain*. Unpublished doctoral thesis, University of Bristol, England.

Özbilgin, M. F. (2000). Is the practice of equal opportunities management keeping pace with theory? Management of sex equality in the financial services sector in Britain and Turkey. *Human Resource Development International, 3*(1), 43–67.

Özbilgin, M. F. (2002). The way forward for equal opportunities by sex in employment in Turkey and Britain. *International Management, Special Issue on Gender Mainstreaming, 7*(1), 55–67.

Özbilgin, M. F., & Healy, G. (2004). The gendered nature of career development of university professors: The case of Turkey. *Journal of Vocational Behavior, 64,* 358–371.

Özbilgin, M., Küskü, F., & Erdoğmuş, N. (2005). Explaining influences on career "choice": the case of MBA students. *International Journal of Human Resource Management, 16*(11), 2002, 2030.

Özbilgin, M. F., & Woodward, D. (2003). *Banking and gender: Sex equality in banking in Britain and Turkey.* London and New York: IB Tauris.

Özbilgin, M., & Woodward, D. (2004). "Belonging" and "otherness": Sex equality in banking in Turkey and Britain. *Gender, Work and Organization, 11*(6), 668–688.

Özkale, L., Küskü, F., & Sağlamer, G. (2004, July). *Women in engineering education in Turkey.* Paper presented at the Annual Conference and Exposition of the American Society for Engineering Education Engineering, Salt Lake City, UT.

Özkale, L., Küskü, F., & Özbilgin, M. (2005, September). *Beliefs on gender and engineering choice: The case of Istanbul Technical University.* Paper presented at the 34th Engineering Education Symposium, Istanbul, Turkey.

Patomaki, H., & Wight, C. (2000). After postmodernism: The promises of critical realism. *International Studies Quarterly, 44,* 213–237.

Peker, M. (1996). Internal migration and the marginal sector. In E. Kahveci, N. Sugur, & T. Nichols (Eds.), *Work and occupation in modern Turkey* (pp. 7–37). London: Mansell.

Ranson, G. (2003). Beyond "gender differences": A Canadian study of women's and men's careers in engineering. *Gender, Work and Organization, 10*(1), 22–41.

Robert, J. M. (2001). Critical realism and the dialectic. *British Journal of Sociology, 52*(4), 667–685.

Schor, J. B. (1991). *The overworked American.* New York: Basic Books.

Seyman, Y. (1992). *Kadin ve Sendika* [Women and trade unions]. Ankara, Turkey: Sosyal Demokrasi Yayinlari.

Siann, G., & Callaghan, M. (2001). Choices and barriers: Factors influencing women's choice of higher education in science, engineering and technology. *Journal of Further and Higher Education, 25*(1), 85–95.

Tekeli, S. (1982). *Kadinlar ve Siyasal Toplumsal Hayat* [Women and sociopolitical life]. Istanbul, Turkey: Birikim Yayinlari.

Toska, Z. (1998). Cumhuriyetin kadın ideali [The republic's ideal of woman]. In A. B. Hacımirzaoğlu (Ed.), *75. Yılda Kadınlar ve Erkekler* (pp. 71–89). Istanbul, Turkey: Tarih Vakfı Yayınları.

Türkiye Bankalar Birliği. (2002). *Turkiye Bankalar Birligi Istatistiksel Veriler* [Statistical data of the Turkish Union of Banks]. Istanbul, Turkey: Author.

Urgan, M. (1999). *Bir Dinazorun Anıları* [Memoirs of a dinosaur]. Istanbul, Turkey: Yapı Kredi Yayınları.

VanLeuvan, P. (2004). Young women's science/mathematics career goals from seventh grade to high school graduation. *Journal of Educational Research, 97,* 248–267.

Watt, H. M. G. (2004). Development of adolescents' self perceptions, values and task perceptions according to gender and domain in 7th through 11th grade Australian students. *Child Development, 75,* 1556–1574.

Witz, A. (1992). *Professions and patriarchy.* London and New York: Routledge.

Woodward, D., & Özbilgin, M. F. (1999). Sex equality in the financial services sector in Turkey and the UK. *Women in Management Review, 14,* 325–332.

Yuval-Davis, N. (1997). *Gender and nation.* London: Sage.

Zeldin, A. L., & Pajares, F. (2000). Against the odds: Self-efficacy beliefs of women in mathematical, scientific, and technological careers. *American Educational Research Journal, 37,* 215–246.

Zengin-Arslan, B. (2002). Women in engineering education in Turkey: Understanding the gendered distribution. *International Journal of Engineering Education, 18,* 400–408.

Zeytinoğlu, I. U. (1999). Constructed images as employment restrictions: Determinants of female labour in Turkey. In Z. F. Arat (Ed.), *Deconstructing images of "the Turkish woman"* (pp. 183–197). New York: Palgrave.

11

ADVANCING WOMEN FACULTY IN SCIENCE AND ENGINEERING: AN EFFORT IN INSTITUTIONAL TRANSFORMATION

ABIGAIL STEWART AND DANIELLE LAVAQUE-MANTY

The "leaky pipeline" image often used in the literature on gender and careers in science and engineering implies a damaged route to a final destination: If only we can keep girls and young women from slipping through the cracks on their way through the pipeline, science can "retain" them. But where and when does the pipeline end? When has an "occupational outcome" been definitively achieved? Being hired into a tenure track job in academic science or engineering seems like one possibility, but women remain less likely to receive tenure in those positions than men (Valian, 1999). Acquiring tenure should surely count as a safe stopping place, except that even tenured women faculty in science and engineering are promoted more slowly, earn less on average, and are more likely to exit academe than their male counterparts (Etzkowitz, Kemelgor, & Uzzi, 2000; Long, 2001; Valian, 1999). There is no doubt that a pipeline problem exists for women in science and engineering. However, slow progress toward gender equity among faculty in science and engineering over the past 20 years, particularly at the highest ranks, in spite of an increased proportion of science and engineering doctorates earned by women, has led researchers to investigate ways in which the climate of academic science might contribute both to women "leaking" from the academic pipeline and to their low status within the academy (Bronstein & Farnsworth,

1998; Etzkowitz et al., 2000; Sears, 2003; Sonnert & Holton, 1996; Valian, 1999). It is a fair assumption that the relative absence of women at the end of the pipeline, their low status, and their low morale might all be important factors in the choices being made by girls and younger women. Thus, conditions at the endpoint may be contributing to the difficulty in changing those very conditions.

In addition to helping girls and women stay in the pipeline, then, we also need to change the gendered nature of the system as a whole. In one sense, this is an impossible task because the gendered aspects of science are not separable from our larger, gendered society. However, there is also a more positive way to look at the situation: Change in any part of the system requires adjustment in other parts, thereby creating other changes. Thus, fostering the careers of women who already hold faculty positions in science and engineering— changing the environment in which they operate—may increase the likelihood that girls and young women will stay in the pipeline, partly because they will have more role models to look up to but also for deeper reasons that we will make clear later in this chapter.

Women science and engineering faculty must work not only within the broader gendered systems of their disciplines but also within the smaller systems of their own particular departments and universities. Supported by a 5-year grant from the National Science Foundation's ADVANCE initiative to improve recruitment and retention of female science and engineering faculty members at research universities, the ADVANCE project at the University of Michigan (UM; this project was directed by Abigail Stewart and employed Danielle LaVaque-Manty) conducted a study of its academic climate for science and engineering faculty in 2001 with the goal of observing how men and women faculty in these fields experienced their work environments.[1] The study was initiated under the assumption that aggregate data about difficulties faced by women in science and engineering at UM would help ADVANCE target intervention efforts to improve recruitment, retention, and promotion of tenured and tenure-track women faculty in those fields as well as to increase the visibility and authority of women scientists and engineers in leadership posi-

---

[1]The other 31 institutions were funded in three rounds. The first included UM as well as the University of Wisconsin—Madison; the University of Washington; Hunter College; New Mexico State University; Virginia Polytechnic Institute and State University; Utah State University; the University of Texas at El Paso; the University of Puerto Rico—Humacao. The second round included the University of Rhode Island; the University of Montana; the University of Maryland Baltimore County; the University of Colorado at Boulder; the University of California, Irvine; the University of Alabama at Birmingham; Kansas State University; Georgia Institute of Technology; Earth Institute at Columbia University; and Case Western Reserve University. The third round included Cornell University; Rensselaer Polytechnic Institute; California State Polytechnic University, Pomona; the University of Maryland, Eastern Shore; the New Jersey Institute of Technology; Marshall University; Duke University; the University of North Carolina at Charlotte; Iowa State University; William Marsh Rice University; the University of Illinois at Chicago; the University of Arizona; Brown University.

tions. The interventions undertaken thus far will be discussed below, following a presentation of the baseline climate data.

DATA

Before conducting the survey, ADVANCE already had basic demographic data indicating that women were underrepresented on the faculties in science and engineering departments at UM relative to the pool of women completing doctorates in the relevant fields. This underrepresentation was consistent with national trends. Nationwide, faculty positions held by women in the natural sciences increased from 22% to 31% between 1991 and 2001, and in engineering, the increase in the same period began from a lower level (4%) and doubled (to 8%). Graduate student rates also increased during this period but (as can be seen in Figure 11.1) at all times were substantially higher than faculty rates.

Further, nationally as at UM, the higher the level of pay and prestige an academic position carries, the less likely it is that a woman will hold it. Thus, there are more women at community colleges and liberal arts institutions than at top research universities, more women "off track" in part-time and/or

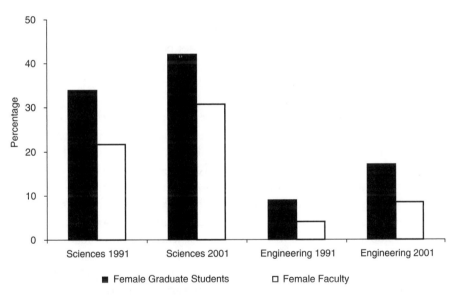

Figure 11.1. National percentages of female graduate students and faculty, 1991 and 2001. Source for graduate student data: National Science Foundation, Division of Science Resource Statistics (2004). Source for faculty data: National Science Foundation, Division of Science Resource Statistics (1991, 2003).

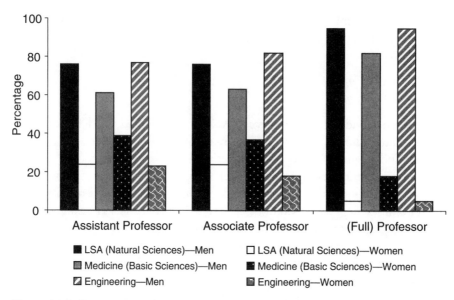

Figure 11.2. Percentages of male and female faculty by rank in literature, science, and the arts (natural sciences); medicine (basic sciences); and engineering at the University of Michigan, 2000–2001. Data from University of Michigan M-Pathways Human Resources Management System (2000–2001). LSA = literature, science, and the arts.

temporary positions than in full-time tenured or tenure track slots, and more women in assistant professor than full professor positions. This latter pattern held both nationally and at UM when the ADVANCE program began (data for faculty in science and engineering by gender and rank at UM in 2000–2001 are presented in Figure 11.2).

The UM ADVANCE climate study compared women scientists and engineers with two other groups: men scientists and engineers and women social scientists (for details, see Stewart, Stubbs, & Malley, 2002). The sample included all female tenure track science and engineering faculty at or above the rank of assistant professor ($n = 259$); a random subsample of male tenure track science and engineering faculty at or above the rank of assistant professor, stratified by race and rank ($n = 339$); and all female tenure track social science faculty at or above the rank of assistant professor who were in colleges that also have science faculty ($n = 156$). The overall response rate was 38%. Women of both academic groups responded at a higher rate than men: 50% female scientists and engineers and 47% female social scientists versus 26% male scientists and engineers. On the one hand, this was a matter of some concern because the goal was to assess gender differences. Given this difference in response rate, it was possible that the sample of male respondents was less representative of all male scientists and engineers than was that of female respondents. To assess that possibility, male and female respondents were compared with the overall sample pools of men and women separately in terms of a few variables available for all faculty (track [tenure, research, clinical], race–ethnicity, school or college of appointment, and rank). For both men and women, respondents did not differ from the pool as a whole on those variables; thus, the male and female respondents appear to be equally representative.

The research design allowed ADVANCE to assess whether differences in perception and satisfaction were attributable to gender (e.g., if the experiences of women scientists and engineers resembled those of women social scientists but not men scientists), to factors more generally relevant to the science and engineering context (e.g., if experiences were similar for men and women scientists and engineers and different for women social scientists), or to factors affecting women in science and engineering only (e.g., if experiences were unique to women scientists and engineers compared with both of the other groups). The study revealed that women scientists and engineers were least satisfied with their positions at UM and that many aspects of academic life that could be negative for all women faculty were even worse for women in science and engineering.

The survey revealed important differences in male and female scientists' household structures, contract renegotiation packages, service, and mentoring. Female scientists and engineers were more likely than male scientists to be single and less likely to have both a partner and children; female scientists and engineers who did have partners were more likely to have considered leaving UM for the sake of their partners' careers. If partnered, female scientists and engineers were more likely than male scientists and engineers to have a partner who worked full time, and that person was more likely to be a full-time UM faculty member. Thus, women scientists and engineers, because they are more likely to either not be partnered (and therefore have no one at home to provide assistance, even if they have no dependents) or have a partner who works full time (and therefore operate in a two-career household), are probably more burdened by household responsibilities than their male counterparts, more than half of whom have a partner who has no paid employment or only part-time paid employment.

Women scientists also received fewer items in contract renegotiation packages than their male counterparts, although their initial hiring packages were comparable. This outcome is consistent with a pattern of greater attention to equity for new hires than for faculty already in the system and with a pattern of accumulating disadvantage, which will be discussed in more detail below (see Valian, 1999).

Women served on more committees than men but were not more likely to chair them—a situation in which greater amounts of service were not rewarded with commensurate opportunities for leadership.

Although male scientists and engineers reported an average of nearly five male mentors in their departments, female scientists and engineers reported an average of just over two male mentors in their departments, a significantly lower number, and of particular importance in units where few or no senior women were present and where most or all mentoring would therefore have to be offered by men. In addition, women scientists and engineers at the assistant professor level reported an average of more than three areas in which they were receiving no mentoring compared with less than one for men scientists and engineers and between one and two for women social scientists at the same rank. Looked at another way, fewer than half of the women scientists and engineers who were assistant professors reported mentoring of any kind in five of the eight mentoring areas: networking, department politics, obtaining resources, advocating for them, and balancing work and family. (The other three areas were serving as a role model, advising about career advancement, and advising about publication.) These findings are disturbing in light of research connecting effective mentoring and positive career outcomes in science and engineering (Etzkowitz et al., 2000; Sonnert & Holton, 1996).

The survey also showed that women scientists and engineers were less satisfied than either their male counterparts or the women social scientists with their positions at UM. Further, 40% of the women faculty in science and engineering reported experiencing gender discrimination within the past 5 years, and 20% reported experiences of unwanted sexual attention. These indicators suggest that women scientists and engineers were at higher risk of attrition as a function of dissatisfaction and unpleasant working conditions than were men scientists and engineers or women social scientists on the faculty.

In assessing the departmental climate in more detail, ADVANCE researchers created scales of items. This data reduction strategy minimized the likelihood of findings resulting from chance and maximized measurement reliability (for a general account of the measurement approach used here, see Cronbach, 1990). Nine scales were used to assess departmental climate. Of the scales constructed to assess features of department climate (Positive Climate, Tolerant Climate, Egalitarian Atmosphere, Scholarly Isolation, Felt Surveillance, Race/Gender Tokenism, Chair as Fair, Chair as Able to Create Positive Environment, Chair as Committed to Racial/Ethnic Diversity), there were significant group differences in all but one (Scholarly Isolation). On an aggregate measure combining all of the scales, and on each of the eight indicators listed above, women scientists and engineers reported the most negative climate. Women scientists and engineers were significantly less likely than their male counterparts to rate their departmental climate as supportive and significantly less likely than either men scientists and engineers or women social scientists to rate their departmental climate as tolerant of diversity or their department gender atmosphere as egalitarian. Women scientists and engineers were significantly more likely than men scientists and engineers or women social scientists to report having felt race or gender tokenism in their department—being expected to represent the "point of view" of their race or gender. They were also significantly more likely than men scientists and engineers to report having felt surveillance in their department; this scale included items such as, "I feel under constant scrutiny by my colleagues," and "I have to work harder than my colleagues to be perceived as a legitimate scholar." Overall, then, there was clear evidence that the climate for women in science and engineering departments felt more negative than the climate in those same departments felt to men or than the social science departments felt to women.

INTERVENTIONS

The findings from the study demonstrated a need to improve the academic climate for women scientists and engineers at UM. For example, the fact that women scientists and engineers were more likely than their male counterparts to be partnered with other academics pointed to the need to help place those partners if UM was to successfully recruit more women. The burden of a "double shift" that falls disproportionately on women scientists and engineers suggested a need for other family-friendly policies that might lighten or at least recognize that burden. Mentoring disparities revealed a need to educate senior faculty about the importance of providing career advice to junior faculty and to institute more equitable approaches rather than allowing junior women to continue to fall through the cracks. The importance of department chairs' roles in fostering or failing to foster positive, gender-equitable climates was made abundantly clear, and ADVANCE encouraged a variety of new and expanded approaches to training for new department chairs, including adoption of a "best practices" document that stressed three key features of good leadership: transparency, uniformity or equity, and helpfulness (Waltman & Hollenshead, 2005).

Viewing the university as a system allowed ADVANCE to approach the climate problems from multiple points of entry, intervening at several levels. Specific interventions, which will be discussed in more detail, included the following: Individual faculty members were invited to compete for Elizabeth Crosby grants to help bolster individual women's careers; departments were invited to apply for grants that would allow them to design their own new approaches to recruiting, retaining, and promoting women faculty; and university-wide policy changes addressing family-friendly policies, recruitment, and the tenure clock were initiated.

ADVANCE draws on systems theory as well as social movement theory—particularly with respect to the problems of "degrouping" and fostering positive collective identity, which will be discussed later in the chapter—and other conceptual tools from the social sciences to make gender visible to scientists and engineers. Because these groups prize objectivity and empiricism so highly, they often imagine that their disciplines and departments do not suffer from gender bias. However, scientists and engineers find data and experimental results very persuasive. Thus, discussion of the existence of "gender schemas," as demonstrated in many studies in experimental psychology summarized by Virginia Valian (1999), can play a key role in persuading scientists that gender bias exists. Valian has stressed that gender schemas are hypotheses, not consciously held, about what men and women are like. They are beliefs that have a basis in statistical realities—more women are stay-at-home parents than men, for example, and more men are engineers than women—and that shape expectations of other people. Both men and women use gender schemas, and to similar degrees.

Gender schemas disadvantage women working in fields that primarily employ men. Both men and women undervalue the performance of women and overvalue the performance of men in "masculine" jobs, even when they intend to be fair and objective in their evaluations. For example, in a study conducted by Steinpreis, Anders, and Ritzke (1999), both male and female psychology faculty were significantly more likely to recommend hiring "Brian Miller" than "Karen Miller" for faculty positions in psychology, although "Brian" and "Karen" had identical curricula vitae, with the sole difference being the candidate's name at the top of the page. In addition to undervaluing the performance of other women, women internalize gender schemas and undervalue their own work as well, beginning at an early age. As noted in chapter 7, this volume, girls tend to underestimate their abilities in math and believe themselves to be better at traditionally "feminine" tasks, "whether or not these fields reflect their true ability profiles" (p. 198).

Reliance on gender schemas (and therefore evaluation bias) is particularly likely in situations in which women are tokens or minorities (see Yoder, 2002). When one woman or very few women work in a typically masculine environment, they register constantly as gender outliers on their colleagues' radars, even when those colleagues are not consciously aware that this is the case. As more women enter the environment, the salience of gender and reliance on gender schemas decreases. When women constitute approximately 30% of the workplace, "critical mass" has been reached. At this point, the salience of gender is minimized (although not absent; see chap. 10, this volume), and the presence and proportion of women in the pool is likely to remain stable. Recruitment and retention remain a constant battle in the absence of critical mass, with women continuing to "leak" from the workplace more rapidly than men.

Evaluation bias and the relevance of critical mass are empirically verifiable, and another of Valian's concepts—"accumulation of disadvantage"— is easily modeled and is consistent with the salary and other career patterns of women in academic science and engineering. Earlier in this chapter, we noted that the university typically offers equitable start-up packages to male and female faculty. Unless scrupulous attention continues to be paid to gender equity when it comes time to offer salary raises, evaluation bias is likely to occur, often at such small levels that women who complain are accused of raising a fuss about nothing, or "making a mountain out of a molehill" as Valian put it in one of her recorded lectures (Valian, 2001; see also Valian's Web tutorials on this topic: http://www.hunter.cuny.edu/gendertutorial/tutorials.htm). However, as Valian also noted, "mountains *are* molehills, piled one on top of the other." For example, a computer simulation of a promotion process within an eight-tiered hierarchy in which the first level is staffed by equal numbers of men and women and in which a mere 1% of the variability in selections for promotion at each level is accounted for by a bias in favor of men produces a top tier that is 65% male (Martell, Lane, & Emrich, 1996). Similarly, inequities as small as 1%, recurring and accumulating over a period of 20 or more years, can result in substantial salary disparities among senior faculty. Disadvantages can accumulate in other realms as well, such as publishing and occupying leadership roles. Those without leadership experience lack the credentials to move up an administrative ladder; however, leadership roles are typically assigned rather than chosen, and given gender schemas, are more likely to be assigned to men than women.

Here, then, is where improving the climate for women faculty in science and engineering can have an effect on girls and young women in the pipeline that extends beyond that of ensuring the presence of role models in their classrooms. Establishing a critical mass of women in these fields has the potential to reduce the salience of gender schemas, decrease evaluation bias, and slow the accumulation of disadvantage, not only for women faculty but also for female students. In the next sections we review the strategies the ADVANCE project used to attempt to accomplish these goals.

Faculty Recruitment

One of the most successful and surprising interventions ADVANCE has generated at UM is a faculty committee whose purpose is to help department chairs and hiring committees develop successful strategies for recruiting and hiring women faculty (see Stewart, LaVaque-Manty, & Malley, 2004). This committee, called Strategies and Tactics for Recruiting to Improve Diversity and Excellence (STRIDE), has nine members—six men and three women—all of whom are highly regarded tenured faculty in science and engineering fields and none of whom knew anything about gender schemas, evaluation bias, or critical mass prior to their involvement with ADVANCE. Their status as scientists and engineers is crucial to their role in educating others, granting them the legitimacy that is not immediately available to social scientists when presenting social science theory and research to scientists and engineers. Further, in order to be able to address recruitment issues for others, STRIDE members undertook a self-education process (studying social science literature on gender) that amounted to consciousness raising, which made them particularly well equipped to speak to colleagues whom one might think of as standing on the other side of an epistemological divide that STRIDE members themselves had only recently crossed.

During the 1st year of its existence (2002–2003), STRIDE developed a presentation designed to clarify the demographic situations in various fields, to alert department chairs and committees to university policies and tools (like the dual-career placement office and university funds available to aid in placing spouses and partners of new hires) that could help with recruiting, and to explain the nature of gender schemas and evaluation bias. On the most obvious and pragmatic level, teaching those responsible for recruiting and hiring about gender schemas and evaluation bias can help them avoid overlooking candidates whom they might otherwise dismiss, thereby improving the immediate hiring process. However, STRIDE also hopes that the effects of this knowledge will radiate beyond the hiring process and into the everyday practices of evaluation that can affect retention and climate as well. The pragmatic need that departments face—hiring more women, whether to satisfy the administration or, in many cases, because they want to provide more role models for their own graduate students—opens the door to what might be called a kind of "stealth activism" that has the potential to generate epistemological shifts in individuals, spark new conversations among the faculty, and create change in the system as a whole. Figure 11.3 is an illustration that STRIDE uses in its presentations. Getting others to understand (and believe in the existence of) the feedback loop depicted here should in itself interrupt the dynamic depicted, at least in a small way. Note also, though, the role of "lack of critical mass" in stimulating reliance on gender schemas in the lower right corner of the figure. If recruitment could be improved to a degree that would establish critical mass, even without changing anyone's understanding of gender schemas and evaluation bias (a perhaps unlikely scenario), the loop—the system—would also be disrupted.

We believe that STRIDE has been effective in both of these ways. First, STRIDE now offers several 2-hour workshops every fall to those heading and serving on search committees. In addition to the presentation itself, all participants are provided with their own copies of key articles presenting relevant research as well as other resource materials. They are also given practice in problem-solving dilemmas that arise in search committees in small groups. Beyond whatever effects these workshops have on the thinking of those who attend them, STRIDE has gone out of its way to recruit allies who commit to learning more about gender and science and to serving as liaisons between STRIDE and their own departments. These allies are part of a larger group called Friends and Allies of STRIDE Toward Equity in Recruiting (acronym: FASTER), and they attend two-part sessions in which they, like STRIDE,

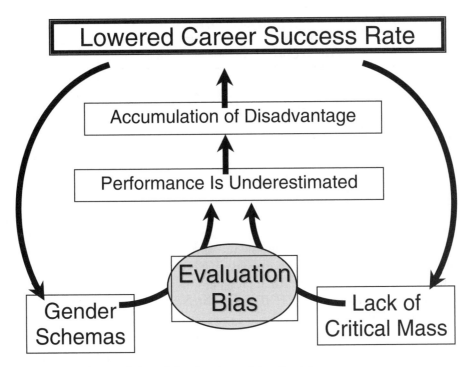

Figure 11.3. Accumulation of disadvantage: A feedback loop.

study social science literature on gender and science in some detail. Thus, the number of faculty members in science and engineering (and beyond—STRIDE has begun to address faculty in other fields as well) who have a solid understanding of the ways in which women scientists and engineers are disadvantaged grows slowly larger.

Second, there has been a clear increase in the number of women faculty hired since STRIDE began its activities. Table 11.1 shows the proportions of men and women hired from 2001 to 2006 in each of the three colleges that employ the largest number of scientists and engineers at UM. Note the marked, and statistically significant, increase in the proportion of women hired comparing the 2 "pre-STRIDE" years (academic years 2001 and 2002) with the 4 "post-STRIDE" years (2003–2006), $\chi^2(1, N = 241) = 10.38, p = .001$. In raw number terms, 10 women scientists and engineers were hired in the three largest colleges during the first 2 years, indicating an average of 5 women scientists and engineers per year in the pre-STRIDE years; in the 4 post-STRIDE years, this rate nearly tripled: 57 women scientists and engineers were hired, or an average of 14.3 women scientists and engineers per year.

Although many factors no doubt contributed to departments' motivation and willingness to hire more women, STRIDE directly provided departments

TABLE 11.1
Men and Women Hired in Natural Science and Engineering Departments
in Three University of Michigan Colleges

College	Academic years 2001–2002		Academic years 2003–2006	
	Men	Women	Men	Women
Medical School (basic sciences)	2	2	21	11
College of Engineering	33	3	50	23
College of Literature, Science, and the Arts (natural sciences)	28	5	40	23
Total % of women		14		34

with tools and ideas to aid in recruitment. Moreover, of 16 women hired in the first year, 12 were hired into departments that had STRIDE presentations (and all chairs were exposed to STRIDE presentations and could have made use of the recruitment handbooks STRIDE also distributes). It is reasonable to conclude that STRIDE, having addressed so many audiences and drawn specific attention to useful policies and resources, contributed to the increase in the number of women hired. For example, many search committees and department members STRIDE met with were unaware that the university has resources to aid in placing spouses and partners of new faculty, and some were unaware of university policies regarding maternity and the tenure clock. Further, anecdotal evidence suggests that at least one department successfully recruited a highly regarded female candidate away from strong competitors partly because of specific advice from STRIDE.

Interactive Theater

Another intervention designed to educate faculty and administrators at UM about gender (in science and engineering specifically, but also in academia in general) relies on a theater troupe called Center for Research on Learning and Teaching (CRLT) Players. The troupe was founded in 2000 to advance multicultural teaching and learning through interactive theater. In collaboration with the ADVANCE program, this theater program developed brief sketches depicting gendered interaction dynamics and gender stereotypes that can influence faculty meeting discussions of candidates, mentoring of women junior faculty by senior faculty (particularly men), and discussions of candidates by tenure committees. In postsketch interactions with the audience, actors remain "in role" and explore with faculty audiences the motivations and reactions of the various characters. In depicting their characters, the actors draw not only on social science literature but also on the results of the climate study we described earlier.

The sketches have the potential to be explosive if used within a single department, where audience members may map the identities of "difficult" characters directly onto their colleagues. Further, having a conversation with actors pretending to be faculty members may sound childish and unappealing to many faculty at first (though evidence is that faculty generally find them very illuminating; see LaVaque-Manty, Steiger, & Stewart, in press). Sketches are available to science and engineering units on request, with performances paid for by ADVANCE, but in order to promote serious engagement with the sketches, they are most often performed for groups drawn from many departments and at dinners hosted by college deans.

Many faculty have reported that they notice connections between what they see in the sketches and what they see in their departments and that they also pay attention to new things after the performances. Research findings about how "tokens" are perceived and are constrained as well as findings about how power differentials (by gender and by rank) operate to create awkward and unprofitable social interactions are reflected in the sketches. CRLT Players attempt to encourage faculty audiences not only to develop new insights into what may sometimes happen in their departments but also to develop new strategies for interacting with their colleagues. For example, following the presentation of a sketch depicting a problematic discussion of a tenure case, senior faculty are invited to step into the discussion at a key point to "replay" and redirect it. The actors and audience then talk about how and why that faculty member's choices either did or did not improve the situation. This sketch is shown early in the tenure season to both department-level and college-level participants in the tenure evaluation process to get them thinking ahead about ways of preventing and responding to varieties of evaluation bias they may encounter during upcoming tenure reviews.

Network of Women Scientists and Engineers

According to Erika Apfelbaum (1979), relations of domination and subordination entail a process in which a subordinate group is first "marked" in some way that sets it apart from the dominant group—thereby rendering it ineligible for the rights and privileges to which the dominant members are entitled—and is then "degrouped" so that its members, separated from one another, have no basis for organizing. To maintain the illusion that subordinated groups—and, therefore, subordination—do not exist, a mythical standard of "universality" is created that "everyone" is imagined to be capable of meeting, although members of the subordinated group in fact lack access to resources they would need to meet that standard, such as education or hiring credentials. Illusions of true universality and social mobility are maintained by integrating tokens into the dominant group. Questioning the apparently "universal" values of the dominant group is understood as troublemaking, deviance, or a request for special privileges. To challenge the "universal" system that guarantees their continuing subordination, those who have been degrouped have to be able to regroup, or articulate a positive collective identity for themselves (Apfelbaum, 1979; Stewart & Zucker, 1999).

Women in academic science and engineering often find themselves token members of their departments. In the absence of specific institutional support, they have little incentive to identify as "women" in ways that would challenge the idea that academic science "universally" and neutrally accepts all qualified scientists. For them, to point out bias in the system is to invite stigmatization— to render their gender explicitly salient. Many women scientists and engineers at UM were initially wary of the ADVANCE project and reluctant to participate in the networking opportunities it provided because they perceived such networking as an opportunity to invite stigma. For many of them, making their way through the pipeline had required embracing the belief that the system really was neutral and universal. Identifying with women colleagues looked like a way of taking a step backwards through proclaiming their own weakness.

Like their male counterparts, women scientists are most easily persuaded by data. They were the first group to whom the results of the ADVANCE climate survey were presented, and their input—their interpretations of the findings—was solicited. Being provided with the evidence first gave them the opportunity to have their own private experience validated as not so unique and not so different from other women's. Moreover, in giving them the news first, the project tried to ensure that they would not be surprised or blindsided by their colleagues' reactions to the data. Finally, the fact that the research team consulted the women themselves throughout the process of collecting and interpreting the data created greater confidence in the data and a sense that there was a serious effort being made to minimize the likelihood of the data being "used against them."

The UM ADVANCE grant included funding for a "Network of Women Scientists and Engineers," but because no such group actually existed at the beginning of ADVANCE's interventions, there was no clarity about how to create it or whether it would be valued. ADVANCE asked women faculty who attended early presentations of the climate data what their concerns were, what they would like ADVANCE to do for them, and what kinds of events they would like to attend. In other words, ADVANCE asked them to begin defining a group identity by collectively defining both their own concerns and their own proposed solutions to those concerns.

The earliest presentation of the climate survey data was given during a dinner to which all tenured and tenure track women faculty in science and engineering were invited. Many of the 65 women who attended were surprised to meet so many other women scientists there, having grown accustomed to being the only woman, or one of very few, in their own departments. They decided to hold more social events—lunches and dinners that served as pressure-free networking opportunities. They also requested leadership training and access to better mentoring.

As noted above, the climate survey showed that women faculty tend to serve on more committees than men but are not rewarded by having more opportunities to lead those committees. In addition, ADVANCE found through the Network conversations that women faculty are frustrated by their lack of access to leadership positions in general. In response to the request for leadership training, ADVANCE organized and funded several extremely popular leadership training and negotiation workshops. Following this, some members of the Network created a highly successful leadership retreat of their own. They decided where and when to hold it, what kinds of panels to have, and whom to invite to serve as panelists. ADVANCE supplied labor (support staff) and part of the funding for the retreat.

The women faculty's emphasis on the importance of leadership roles for women was justified by the actual situation. When the ADVANCE project began at UM in 2002, there were no women department chairs in the School of Medicine and there never had been any. Now there are three. One of the eight science departments in the College of Literature, Science, and the Arts was led by a woman interim chair in 2002. When the man who had been hired to succeed her resigned his position after only 1 year, she agreed to take up the role on a permanent basis, having thought quite a bit about the relationship between gender and leadership and about her own skills during that period. Another woman in this college, who was also a member of STRIDE, became chair of her department during this period. Another female STRIDE member, who was associate chair of her department, when invited to serve on the dean search committee in the College of Engineering, made a choice that would not have occurred to her prior to her participation in ADVANCE activities: She agreed to serve on that committee only if she could chair it. In short, women science and engineering faculty members have been viewed as resources for leadership roles in the post-ADVANCE period, and they have viewed their own capacities differently too. Following the same logic underlying the creation of the original Network, ADVANCE also initiated a monthly networking lunch for women department chairs in science and engineering.

Providing leadership training and opportunities for women faculty through the Network is one way ADVANCE attempts to address the problem of accumulation of disadvantage. Those women who are serving on more committees than men without getting to chair them are accumulating disadvantage; their male counterparts, chairing slightly more committees while serving on slightly fewer, are accumulating advantage, experience, and better looking curricula vitae than the women. When it comes to administrative and other leadership appointments, the men will look like "better" candidates than the women, according to the "universal" and "impartial" meritocratic norms of the academy. These patterns need to be changed. Although it is helpful for individuals to see ways in which they have begun to accumulate disadvantages so that they can attempt to intervene in these processes themselves, it is also crucial that those above them—those in a position to nominate or appoint others to leadership roles—become aware of these patterns as well.

Gender schemas and evaluation bias contribute to women's lowered chances of being appointed to leadership roles at all levels. In one of the experiments Virginia Valian described in her lectures (Porter & Geis, 1981), both men and women, when shown a photograph of five people seated at a table, are likelier to guess that one of the men in the photograph is the "leader" of the group, even when the person sitting at the head of the table—the seat typically associated with leadership—is a woman. Women not only have a harder time gaining leadership roles in the first place but also a harder time in gaining the respect or deference that is automatically granted to men when men hold those roles.

As noted above, the climate survey revealed that women science and engineering faculty at UM receive less mentoring than their male counterparts. This lack of mentoring also contributes to women's accumulation of disadvantage. Women have less access to information, advice, sponsorship, and opportunities for collaboration than men do. Noting this lack, the Network of Women Scientists and Engineers decided to create their own cross-departmental mentoring program. ADVANCE created a Web page on which would-be mentors offer self-descriptions and contact information for would-be mentees in search of advice. ADVANCE also holds mentoring events to help mentors and mentees connect with one another. In addition, ADVANCE has contributed to institutionalizing better mentoring policies through its work with a university-wide committee, Gender in Science and Engineering, which is discussed below, and the development of a career advising handbook that is widely distributed to both senior and junior faculty.

Grants to Individuals and Departments

As another method of redressing accumulated disadvantage, ADVANCE offers Elizabeth Crosby awards (grants of up to $20,000) to individual faculty for work that will further the careers of women scientists and engineers. Men and women are both eligible to apply, provided that the funds will be used to foster the careers of women. To date, 47 Crosby grants have been awarded and have been used to pay for research assistance, conference travel, research seed funding, and speakers series and workshops within and across disciplines, among other things. These grants play at least a small part in helping to retain women faculty by helping them develop stronger portfolios for tenure and promotion on the one hand and increasing their satisfaction with and connection to UM on the other.

ADVANCE also provides Departmental Transformation Grants of up to $100,000, to be used for periods of up to 3 years, to individual departments or groups of departments to support activities that will lead to significant transformation in the environment for women faculty. Twelve Departmental Transformation Grants have been awarded thus far and have been used to provide teaching releases to women faculty, create interdepartmental mentoring fora, and invite potential job candidates to give talks early in their careers and outside the usual hiring season to cultivate early connections that might improve the recruitment of women faculty.

Departmental Transformation Women Grants offer departments incentives to assess their own environments and generate ideas that might not only improve their own microclimates but also might be adopted by other departments or colleges or university-wide. Participation in the application process, even when a department ultimately does not receive an award, requires that faculty within the department (and sometimes across departments) engage in conversation about issues like evaluation bias and accumulation of disadvantage. Like STRIDE and CRLT Players, these grants help make gender visible to scientists and engineers, and they bring the intelligence and creativity of a large number of people to bear on the pragmatic questions of what can be done about these problems—not in the abstract, but in the near future, and with a relatively small amount of money.

The goal of ADVANCE is to transform the system at UM substantially during the 5-year grant period. As we have noted, women are affected most directly and most consistently by the microclimates in their own departments. In addition to inviting departments to apply for Departmental Transformation Grants and to make use of STRIDE during their recruitment processes, ADVANCE has helped create a training program for new chairs, who can have an enormous effect on recruitment, retention, and departmental climate (Bensimon, Ward, & Sanders, 2000). Cultivating an awareness of gender schemas, evaluation bias, and accumulation of disadvantage in new chairs can help them create better departmental recruitment and evaluation practices along with a better climate in general. For similar reasons, ADVANCE also offers workshops to newly promoted full professors, whose new authority can also influence departmental dynamics, especially if they are assisted in learning some intervention strategies. At the first workshop of this kind, many new male full professors sought advice about what they could do to curb the impact of powerful and unpleasant individual department members creating a hostile climate for women. Their active pursuit of advice on this point was encouraging evidence of their capacity to make a difference in those climates in the future.

University-Wide Policy Change

In January 2001, UM president Lee Bollinger convened a Gender in Science and Engineering (GSE) Committee to plan and initiate interventions to improve the climate for women scientists and engineers at UM. In April 2003, President Mary Sue Coleman and Provost Paul Courant charged three subcommittees with a combined membership of 21 senior faculty (12 men and 9 women), drawn from six colleges and 13 departments, to

- examine and evaluate institutional policies and practices that might differentially impact the progress of women faculty in science and engineering fields. These will likely include policies dealing with appointment, promotion, and tenure; practices that result in disproportionately higher percentages of women in nontenured ranks; the under-representation of women in leadership positions in these fields; an evaluation of the success of current family-sensitive policies in the pre-tenure probationary period (e.g., stopping the tenure clock, modified duties);
- recommend and set goals for improved institutional policies and practices;
- recommend instruments to measure outcomes and ensure accountability of the leadership at multiple institutional levels. (Coleman & Courant, 2003)

The three committees—Recruitment, Retention and Leadership; Family Friendly Policies and Faculty Tracks; and Faculty Evaluation and Development—operated independently, and as a result, in some cases policies were examined and discussed in more than one committee. On March 29, 2004, they reported to the GSE Committee on their findings and detailed recommendations for possible policy changes.[2] Taken together, the three committees made more than 50 recommendations. However, a few issues arose in all three committees and as a result took on special weight; these included mentoring, dual-career family-related partner policies, child care and parental care policies, and the rigid tenure clock. A wide range of policies and practices were discussed, debated, and evaluated both within the committees and on campus more generally. A number of institutional policy or practices were altered immediately.

Mentoring

At least two of the committees (Recruitment, Retention and Leadership and Faculty Evaluation and Development) made efforts to provide definitions of and rationales for mentoring generally and for different kinds of mentoring.

---

[2]For the three reports of the subcommittees, see University of Michigan (2004a, 2004b, 2004c).

Although there was no effort to legislate mentoring practices or policies at the university level, particular colleges—including the liberal arts college housing eight natural science disciplines and the engineering college—undertook the task of encouraging better mentoring in a formal manner. Efforts were made to make good use of ADVANCE-sponsored programs, such as the CRLT Players' sketch about faculty career advising and the career advising handbook. In one college, departments were provided with a template outlining the elements of a mentoring policy that should be considered and were required to develop and implement their own policy within broad guidelines. In short, a practice that had long been defended as best left to be worked out between individuals in private was publicly defined as a resource for professional development to which all faculty had a right. Under that definition, administrators recognized their responsibility to ensure equitable access to that resource. Implementation is certainly uneven, but the terms of discussion of faculty career advising have shifted.

Dual-Career Family-Related Partner Policies

Recognition of the particular need to address the careers of faculty members' partners led to formalization and enhancement of existing partner placement policies. The Provost's Office invested considerable effort into organizing an improved Web site for faculty and their partners to use in interpreting university policy (http://www.provost.umich.edu/faculty/family/dual-career/index.html) and publicly committed substantial staff resources to providing partner services and budgeting for incentive funding for some kinds of positions. Efforts were redoubled to articulate as explicitly as possible the university's commitment to supporting the needs of dual-career households of faculty recruited to Ann Arbor. For example, the brochure aimed at couples begins as follows:

> To maintain and strengthen its excellence the University must recruit and retain an outstanding faculty. Many faculty members who are being recruited by the University of Michigan—Ann Arbor have partners who are accomplished professionals in their own right. Therefore, the ability of a dual career partner to find a suitable career opportunity is often a key factor in the recruitment process and ultimately in the couple's decision. The Dual Career Program was created in response to this need. (UM, n.d.-a, p. 1)

In addition, the three largest colleges collaborated in creating a full-time staff position to provide further support to partners and to facilitate negotiation of partner placements across colleges. During the academic year 2004–2005, the provost's office dual-career staff met with 160 partners of potential faculty and helped identify positions for 62 of them; some sort of incentive funding was provided for 38 of those. Although these programs were mostly in place before the GSE Committee recommendations, they were integrated, formalized, and advertised in a new way—all of which enhanced their visibility and therefore their efficacy.

Child Care and Parental Care Policies

As a direct result of the GSE Committee recommendations, the provost's office committed to create additional child care spaces in university-subsidized child care centers, with a particular focus on full-time infant care, which was identified in the GSE reports as a particularly scarce commodity. In her announcement to the campus community regarding the university's new child care commitments, President Coleman said,

> Reliable access to child care services can significantly enhance the ability of faculty, staff and students to pursue their academic and professional goals and to contribute fully to the University. This is an increasingly important dynamic in our efforts to recruit and retain the very best talent. (Greene, 2005, p. 1)

In addition, the university broadened and deepened its policies on "modified duties" (usually involving release from teaching, among other things) for new parents (to cover, e.g., adoption) and on extension of the tenure clock for female faculty who became new parents. Some colleges went further, extending these policies to cover male faculty who became new parents and asserted that they were providing at least 50% of the care to the child. In addition, some colleges articulated explicitly that these policies applied to other family care demands, such as elder and partner care. The authors of chapter 7, this volume, note that girls in their study who aspired to male-dominated occupations in the 12th grade and who also planned to have children were most likely to "leak" from the math and science pipeline in the coming years once they became aware of the difficulty of combining work and family in traditionally masculine fields. Like other climate improvements addressed in our chapter, better child care policies may contribute not only to retention of current faculty but also, in the long term, to fewer leaks in the science and engineering pipeline.

Flexible Tenure

Perhaps the most radical recommendation that emerged from the GSE Committees related to tenure—the most sacred of all academic cows. Here the committees noted that the rigidity of the tenure clock did not suit women faculty's lives and careers well and advised that efforts be made to create some greater flexibility to accommodate women's lives. In response to this analysis, the provost appointed a faculty committee to review the possibilities and make recommendations. That committee recommended that the university

> adopt policies that create more flexibility in the tenure probationary period. Our central recommendation is that each school and college identify a presumptive time of tenure review and then create fair and consistent policies that may accelerate or postpone the tenure review for faculty members depending on their situations. To permit such policies to develop in the schools and colleges, two crucial changes need to be made in University policy: 1) revising Regents' Bylaw 5.09 to extend the maximum probationary period from the current eight years to ten years, so that schools and colleges have the freedom to provide longer tenure probationary periods when that is justified by their policies; 2) oversight of school and college policies by the Provost or Chancellor to ensure that school and college policies define fair and clear criteria for decisions about accelerating or postponing the timing of the tenure review. We also recommend a new policy to make it possible for faculty members to work part time and remain on the tenure track, accruing years of service on a prorated basis. These recommendations are intended to adapt the institution of tenure to the realities of contemporary scholarship and faculty life. (UM, n.d.-b, ¶3)

At the time of this writing, the campus is debating this policy change. Whether the changes are adopted, the fact that the current policy and practice is being recognized as one that was adopted at a particular point in history to accomplish particular goals for a particular constituency is something new and significant. This changes the climate, with or without the policy change.

Changing policies is important, in part because policies enable some practices and prevent others. Changing policies is also important because policies both reflect and shape the way we think—about careers, about "merit," about what counts as success. Open discussion of the disparate impact of these policies on women and men is often uncomfortable because it always reopens the possibility that difference will—again—be identified as deficit. However, it also opens up other possibilities—for differences to be recognized and accommodated in new ways. When that happens, the climate actually improves.

CONCLUSION

After only 5 years, at the time of this writing, it is too early to tell what the combined effects of ADVANCE's interventions have been or will be. Further, with so many interventions being carried out simultaneously, presumably catalyzing and building on one another, we are unlikely ever to be able to tease apart the effects of individual efforts. Nevertheless, a number of efforts have been made and continue to attempt to assess the effects of particular programs (see Stewart, Malley, & LaVaque-Manty, in press). To what extent have departments been motivated to apply for Departmental Transformation Grants by what they have learned from STRIDE presentations? How many women have been tenured who might otherwise not have been, not only because they received Crosby Awards that boosted their careers, but also because key senior faculty in their departments began to think a bit differently after engaging with a performance from the CRLT Players? Would the GSE Committee ever have been created in the first place, much less have produced so much policy change, in the absence of ADVANCE?

These questions will never be sorted out because there are no baseline data in many instances and certainly no untreated comparison groups on the UM campus. However, if the efforts we have been making at UM (and at the other institutions also currently engaging in ADVANCE projects) succeed, we should continue to see improvement in the climate for women faculty in science and engineering, which was assessed at baseline and again in Fall 2006. The data are currently being analyzed. We should, sooner rather than later, see women reach critical mass in some fields. If that happens, we should also soon see more young women entering and staying in the pipeline and, happily, confronting fewer barriers over the course of their careers. That is the most optimistic scenario, and one worth realizing. It requires that institutions remain committed to this project over a long period of time—a period that permits meaningful change in the demographic makeup of departments in the context of academic tenure guaranteeing long and secure careers to faculty as well as little growth in the overall size of the professoriate. Continuing to monitor and foster this transformation will take more than a 5-year National Science Foundation grant; it will require significant commitment for 10 to 20 years. We hope that price will be acceptable, given that we know already the cost of failing to make that commitment—continued underrepresentation of women in science and engineering.

REFERENCES

Apfelbaum, E. (1979). Relations of domination and movements for liberation: An analysis of power between groups. In W. G. Austin & S. Worchel (Eds.), *The social psychology of intergroup relations* (pp. 188–204). Belmont, CA: Wadsworth.

Bensimon, E. M., Ward, K., & Sanders, K. (2000). *Department chair's role in developing new faculty into teachers and scholars*. Bolton, MA: Anker.

Bronstein, P., & Farnsworth, L. (1998). Gender differences in faculty experiences of interpersonal climate and processes for advancement. *Research in Higher Education, 39*, 557–585.

Coleman, M. S., & Courant, P. (2003, April). *Charge to the committee* [Memo]. Unpublished document.

Cronbach, L. (1990). *Essentials of psychological testing*. New York: Harper & Row.

Etzkowitz, H., Kemelgor, C., & Uzzi, B. (2000). *Athena unbound: The advancement of women in science and technology*. New York: Cambridge University Press.

Greene, D. M. (2005). University to expand child care programs. *The University Record Online*. Retrieved July 26, 2007, from http://www.umich.edu/~urecord/0405/Apr25_05/02.shtml

LaVaque-Manty, D., Steiger, J., & Stewart, A. J. (in press). Interactive theater: Raising issues about the climate with science faculty. In A. J. Stewart, J. E. Malley, & D. LaVaque-Manty (Eds.), *Transforming science and engineering: Advancing academic women*. Ann Arbor: University of Michigan Press.

Long, J. S. (Ed.). (2001). *From scarcity to visibility: Gender differences in the careers of doctoral scientists and engineers*. Washington, DC: National Academy Press.

Martell, R. F., Lane, D. M., & Emrich, C. (1996). Male–female differences: A computer simulation. *American Psychologist, 51*, 157–58.

National Science Foundation, Division of Science Resource Statistics. (1991). *Characteristics of doctoral scientists and engineers in the United States: 1991*. Arlington, VA: Author.

National Science Foundation, Division of Science Resource Statistics. (2003). *Characteristics of doctoral scientists and engineers in the United States: 2001* (NSF 03-310). Arlington, VA: Author.

National Science Foundation, Division of Science Resource Statistics. (2004). *Science and engineering degrees: 1966–2001* (NSF 04-311). Arlington, VA: Author.

Porter, N., & Geis, F. L. (1981). Women and nonverbal leadership cues: When seeing is not believing. In C. Mayo & N. Henley (Eds.), *Gender and nonverbal behavior* (pp. 39–61). New York: Springer Verlag.

Sears, A. W. (2003). Image problems deplete the number of women in academic applicant pools. *Journal of Women and Minorities in Science and Engineering, 9*, 169–181.

Sonnert, G., & Holton, G. (1996). Career patterns of women and men in the sciences. *American Scientist, 84*, 63–71.

Steinpreis, R. E., Anders, K. A., & Ritzke, D. (1999). The impact of gender on the review of the curricula vitae of job applicants and tenure candidates: A national empirical study. *Sex Roles, 41*, 509–528.

Stewart, A. J., LaVaque-Manty, D., & Malley, J. E. (2004). Recruiting female faculty members in science and engineering: Preliminary evaluation of one recruitment model. *Journal of Women and Minorities in Science and Engineering, 10*, 361–375.

Stewart, A. J., Malley, J. E., & LaVaque-Manty, D. (Eds.). (in press). *Transforming science and engineering: Advancing academic women*. Ann Arbor: University of Michigan Press.

Stewart, A., Stubbs, J., & Malley, J. (2002). *Assessing the academic work environment for women scientists and engineers*. Ann Arbor: University of Michigan, Institute for Research on Women and Gender.

Stewart, A. J., & Zucker, A. (1999). Regrouping social identities. *Feminism & Psychology, 9*, 261–265.

University of Michigan. (2004a, March). *Gender in science and engineering: Report of the Subcommittee on Faculty Evaluation and Development*. Retrieved July 27, 2007, from http://www.umich.edu/~advproj/GSE-_Faculty_%20Evaluation_%20 Development.pdf

University of Michigan. (2004b, March). *Gender in science and engineering: Report of the Subcommittee on Faculty Recruitment, Retention and Leadership*. Retrieved July 27, 2007, from http://www.umich.edu/~advproj/GSE-_Family_Friendly_Policies.pdf

University of Michigan. (2004c, March). *Gender in science and engineering: Report of the Subcommittee on Family Friendly Policies and Faculty Tracks*. Retrieved July 27, 2007, from http://www.umich.edu/~advproj/GSE-_Family_Friendly_Policies.pdf

University of Michigan. (n.d.-a). *Dual Career Program at the University of Michigan—Ann Arbor: A guide for prospective or new faculty members and their partners*. Retrieved August 3, 2007, from http://www.provost.umich.edu/programs/dual_career/ DualCareerBrochure9201.pdf

University of Michigan. (n.d.-b). *Report of the committee to consider a more flexible tenure probationary period*. Retrieved August 3, 2007, from http://www.provost.umich. edu/reports/flexible_tenure/work_of_the_committee.html

University of Michigan M-Pathways Human Resources Management System. (2000–2001). [Faculty data]. Unpublished data.

Valian, V. (1999). *Why so slow? The advancement of women*. Cambridge, MA: MIT Press.

Valian, V. (2001). *The advancement of women in science and engineering: Why so slow?* Webcast retrieved from http://webcast.rice.edu/speeches/20010329valian.html

Waltman, J., & Hollenshead, C. (2005). *Creating a positive departmental climate: Principles for best practices*. Retrieved July 26, 2007, from http://www.umich.edu/~advproj/ principles.pdf

Yoder, J. (2002). 2001 Division 35 Presidential Address: Context matters: Understanding tokenism processes and their impact on women's work. *Psychology of Women Quarterly, 26*, 1–8.

12

THE CONTINUING TECHNOLOGICAL REVOLUTION: A COMPARISON OF THREE REGIONS' STRATEGIES FOR CREATING WOMEN-INCLUSIVE WORKPLACES

CHRISTINA M. VOGT

Historically, women have not always been welcomed into the scientific community, yet they have often been coopted into the science and engineering professions to provide lower cost labor necessary to combat temporary workforce shortages (Oldenziel, 2000). Economic restructures have entailed the feminization of many job structures in which women earn lower wages than their male counterparts and have less opportunity for advancement. For example, women in all branches of science, including the more recent information communication technology (ICT) sector, not only receive less compensation but are more often relegated into employment with stifled upward mobility (International Labour Organization [ILO], 2002a, 2004a; Natsuko, 2002). These points raise the question of how the differences in payment-to-education ratios for men and women will continue to devaluate women's "learning–earning" link. In this chapter, women's employment and educational statistics from the United States, the European Union 15 (EU15; the 15 member countries of the European Union prior to 2004: Austria, Belgium, Denmark, Finland, France, Germany, Greece, Ireland, Italy, Luxembourg, the Netherlands, Portugal, Spain, Sweden, and the United Kingdom), and Japan are mined and then compared to gather an equality profile. These countries are the focus because the majority of all new technologies are patented in these three regions (U.S.

Patent Office, 2003). From this, I trace the participation of women in science, technology, engineering, and math (often abbreviated as "STEM") careers before and after the endorsement of globalization, where there has been a shift in ideology from a human capital to a "knowledge economy." Because most efforts to remedy gendered participation in these fields have been through targeting female educational preparation (the "knowledge-based" approach), I empirically test whether equivalent educational preparation translates into equitable occupational outcomes for males and females across these three geographic regions. I then analyze differences between the levels of gender equity measures across the three regions by comprehensive review of international and national policy and legal initiatives and their corresponding effects on labor force demographics.

Finally, I cast this current problem of underutilization of women as a historic one, originating from lingering discriminatory patterns. Despite recent social developments in gender equality, in scientifically advanced nations women lag behind men economically. Although today's woman has many more opportunities than in the past, patriarchal traditions inhibit her full participation in the current technological advancement. My intent is to underscore that the same discriminatory patterns are still pervasive.

HISTORICAL BASIS FOR THE UNDERUTILIZATION OF WOMEN IN SCIENCE AND TECHNOLOGY

Nussbaum (1999) stated that political and economic thought must view gender oppression as a problem of justice. She based this argument on the fact that women in many societies are not treated as ends in their own right but instead as means for the ends of others. Historically, unequal social, economic, and political circumstances have left women with unequal access to opportunities and liberties. As a major segment of the disenfranchised, women had been struggling for access into U.S. and European universities and the labor force since the mid 19th century (Oldenziel, 2000; Solomon, 1985). Japan did not allow women access into colleges of science until 1913 (Tsugawa & Konami, 2005). Unfortunately, admission was only half the battle: In the United States (Sloan, 1975) and Europe (Canal, Oldenziel, & Zachmann, 2000), women in universities experienced difficulties because higher education institutions did not provide contexts conducive to their staying. Those who did enter often could not study science and, especially, engineering because women were deemed unsuitable for scientific curricula (Sloan, 1975). Women's biology was thought to cast female students predominantly as future wives and mothers.

As a result of industrialization (the "machine age"), mechanical engineering and science professions flourished during the late 19th and early 20th centuries. Throughout the first half of the 20th century, however, fewer than 1% of engineering students in the United States (Sloan, 1975), Japan (Ministry of Health, Labour and Welfare, 2002), and Western Europe (Canal et al., 2000) were women. Professional engineering organizations denied women membership, so they had virtually no avenue for professional networking. Therefore, organizations were formed to rally for the betterment of women, such as the Swedish Association for Female Engineering Students in 1901 (Berner, 2000); the Women's Engineering Society in the United Kingdom in 1919; and the Society of Women Engineers in the United States in 1950, following an unsuccessful attempt to establish it in 1943. In 1958, the Society of Japanese Women Scientists was established; however, it was not until 1992 that the Society of Japanese Women Engineers formed.

Women devised strategies to gain entry to the science and engineering professions during the 20th century (Canal et al., 2000). One predominant strategy throughout the United States and Europe involved women's attainment of multiple science or mathematics degrees. A second strategy involved concentration in specializations, which although opening the doors to certain jobs for women may also have served to create the gendered divide in scientific careers—that is, "pink" jobs.

Although women had to overcome barriers to employment, at times they were coopted into the science and engineering professions because of depleted labor pools (see Canal et al., 2000). The infamous World War II "Rosie the Riveter" campaigns were a call to women to fill male-vacated positions in U.S. and European factories and laboratories. Typically, women were assigned to lower paying and less prestigious positions than men. In fact, many women with college degrees were given jobs as laboratory assistants or engineering aides (Oldenziel, 2000). These overqualified women frequently worked in sex-segregated departments doing jobs that men with lesser education had previously performed before their call to war.

Post–World War II, several transitions occurred throughout the world's labor forces. In the United States, many women returned to their former roles as homemakers (Oldenziel, 2000) but in the early 1960s began to reemerge in the workforce with the dawning of the electronic and aerospace industries. Women continued developing a presence in engineering because of the 1960s women's movement (McIlwee & Robinson, 1992; Sloan, 1975). Title IX of the 1972 Education Amendments to the Higher Education Act broadened education options for many women by prohibiting sexual discrimination by any educational institution receiving federal funds. Despite this, throughout the 1970s women still made up only approximately 5% of engineering graduates (National Science Foundation [NSF], 2000). Western Europe had a wide variation on statistics in women's representation across the professions. Some countries, such as Greece (1950–1960 statistics), had representation as high as 44% for women in architecture and 10% in chemical engineering (Chatzis &

Nicolaid, 2000), although most other countries reported fewer than 2% in engineering and related professions (ILO LABORSTA, 2005). In Japan, women engineers were fewer than 0.5% (ILO LABORSTA, 2005). By contrast, in Eastern Europe and the Soviet states, women still held a large percentage of midlevel science and engineering posts because they were coopted into establishing emergent socialist governments post–World War II (Gouzevitch & Gouzevitch, 2000; Lopez-Claros & Zahidi, 2005). However, women were rarely in the top positions in the Soviet bloc.

Endeavors to overcome obstacles facing women who studied engineering in the United States, Japan, and the EU15 made some progress: By 1980, women made up approximately 10% of the engineering graduates in the United States, with a higher number in science and math (NSF, 2000). There were fewer women in these programs in Western Europe (ILO LABORSTA, 2005) and even fewer—less than 1%—in Japan (ILO LABORSTA, 2005). In the United States, affirmative action programs throughout the 1970s and 1980s probably enhanced the number of women willing to study engineering because this improved their chances for securing jobs on graduation. As presented later in this chapter, positive discrimination (i.e., affirmative action) laws were not enacted in the EU15 until as late as the 1980s (ILO, 2004a) and in Japan in the 1990s (Ministry of Health, Labour and Welfare, 2002).

WOMEN'S PROGRESS IN SCIENTIFIC EDUCATION

In developed nations such as the United States, member states of the EU15, and Japan, women's attainment of higher education was the result of previous economic expansion and development rather than more recent global education initiatives (Stromquist, 2007). However, after several decades of educating women to boost their participation in engineering and computing classes, the higher education profiles for these regions are remarkably similar, with women very underrepresented (see Table 12.1). Although the higher education system is somewhat different in the United States, the European Union, and Japan, women still tend to be overrepresented in fields such as education, the social sciences, and humanities and underrepresented in computing, mathematics, the physical sciences, and engineering (United Nations Educational, Scientific and Cultural Organization [UNESCO], 2003). This explains a major source of income differential when women and men join the labor force (Burk, 2005; ILO, 2002a; Stromquist, 2007).

The United States

Growth rates of female university students and faculty in sciences and engineering in the United States have been somewhat flat for the past decade.

TABLE 12.1
Women's Share of Positions in Related Fields to Gender Equality

Country	ICT/engineering, computer professional (% F)	Tertiary students (% F/% M)[a]	Tertiary engineering students (% F)[b]	Tertiary STEM students (% F)[c]	Full professors, all/engineering and technical (% F)[b]
Austria	14	53/44	7.5	20.7	9.5/3.8
Belgium	15	65/55	6.2	42.0	9.0/4.4
Denmark	16	73/52	16.5	21.0	10.9/1.3
Finland	17	95/77	20.6	15.7	21.2/6.7
France	17	60/47	5.6	44.2	16.1/6.9
Germany	17	40/42	3.1	30.0	9.2/3.9
Greece	N/A	72/65	N/A	N/A	11.3/NA
Iceland	N/A	70/39	4.0	18.1	13/3.8
Ireland	14	56/44	5.6	49.2	NA/NA
Italy	N/A	61/46	13.5	19.1	16.4/6.5
Japan	17	45/53	17.0	18.0	6.8/2.8*
Netherlands	15	59/55	6.8	16.9	9.4/3.2
Norway	16	90/58	4.2	17.2	15.7/5.1
Portugal	N/A	62/45	13.0	21.6	20.9/5.2
Spain	14	64/54	4.6	29.7	17.6/3.6
Sweden	20	93/60	16.6	18.6	16.1/7.6
Switzerland	10	39/49	N/A	19.1	16.5/11.1
United Kingdom	15	70/57	7.4	36.2	15.9/5.2
United States	20	94/70	19.0	50.0	20.9/5.8

Note. Data refer to the most recent year available during the period 1992–2001. Data vary by country in the European Union 15. Data for Austria, Belgium, France, Ireland, Norway, and the United Kingdom are from the European Commission (2004). Data for Germany, Iceland, Finland, the Netherlands, and Spain are from the central statistics offices in each country. Data for Japan are from Ministry of Education, Science and Technology, Sports and Culture (2004). U.S. data were obtained from personal communications with Bureau of Labor Statistics personnel. The U.S. data are for the number of women in computing careers, though not necessarily ICT related. Although somewhat inconsistent in classification, they provide a baseline to illustrate the concerns of women's underrepresentation by region. All values are rounded. ICT = information communication technology; F = female; M = male; STEM = science, technology, engineering, and math; N/A = no reliable data exist for women in these fields.
[a]Data are from United Nations Economic Commission for Europe (2003). U.S. data are from National Science Foundation (2004).
[b]Female professional and technical workers (% of total). Women's share of positions is defined according to the International Standard Classification of Occupations (ISCO-88) to include physical, mathematical, and engineering science professionals; life science and health professionals; teaching professionals (and associate professionals); and other professionals and associate professionals. European data were extracted from European Commission (2004). Japan's data are from Ministry of Education, Science and Technology, Sports and Culture (2004) and include science and engineering professors. U.S. data are from National Science Foundation (2004) and Gibbons (2004).
[c]Extracted from European Commission (2003). U.S. data are from National Science Foundation (2004).

Women currently secure approximately 25% of the degrees in computer science—having dropped from approximately 33% in the 1980s. In physics and engineering, U.S. female college students obtain approximately 20% of the awarded degrees (Huang, Taddese, & Walter, 2000). Despite efforts to increase women's presence in engineering doctoral programs, women today receive only 19% of those doctoral degrees (NSF, Division of Science Resources Statistics, 2004). Although women are receiving nearly half of all awarded doctoral degrees, this has not translated into better jobs for women, who secure the majority of nontenured professorial positions. At the full-professorial rank, women make up only 27% of the total at 4-year institutions (American Association of University Women, 2004). In the sciences, the Commission on the Advancement of Women and Minorities in Science, Engineering and Technology Development (2000) reported that of women science faculty, only 29% held tenured positions compared with 58% of the men. The representation of female full professors drops to 14% in engineering and science combined (NSF, 2000), and narrowing the segment to only engineering, women make up approximately 10% of the total professors, where the majority of these are either ranked as associate or assistant level (NSF, 2004). The remaining are likely lecturers or adjuncts.

Japan

Post–World War II, the Americans reconfigured the Japanese education system according to the U.S. model. Influenced by U.S. postwar policies, in 1947, the Japanese allowed women greater access to postsecondary education (Tsugawa & Konami, 2005). Today, more than 90% of Japanese students graduate from high school and more than 40% from university or junior college. Unlike the United States or most EU15 countries, at 4-year universities, male students outnumber females (see Table 12.1). The opposite is true of junior colleges, where Japanese women make up 90% of the graduates. In Japan, the total number of graduate students is relatively small, having to do with tradition, because Japan has been primarily a manufacturing country where "company men" have been the mainstay of the nation's economy. Consequently, most research and development projects have been conceived in corporate laboratories, negating the need for abundant university graduate programs.

However, modernization cannot be avoided: According to Tsugawa and Konami (2005), 18% of Japanese female undergraduates major in mathematics and physics, 31% in chemistry, and 43% in biology. According to the ministry, the number of women entering graduate school has increased as well. At the master's level, females make up 19% of science candidates: 12% in mathematics and physics, 20% in chemistry, and 31% in biology. At the doctoral level, the female representation in science is 13%, and of that 13%, 8% are majoring in mathematics and physics, 12% in chemistry, and 23% in biology. At the faculty level, women are only 12% of total faculty members. In the natural sciences, women are approximately 4% of the full professors, 7% of the associate professors, 12% of the lecturers, and 19% of the research associates (Tsugawa & Konami, 2005).

In industry, government, and academia combined, Japan's gender statistics report that male researchers have increased by a multiple of 1.6 from 1985 to 1999, whereas for females, the rate of increase has nearly tripled. The rate of increase for women scientists was 3.2, and for women engineers, 7.2. This suggests that although the absolute number of women researchers remains low, the number of women scientists and engineers is multiplying faster than the number of men in these fields (Tsugawa & Konami, 2005). One of the reasons for the rapid growth of women majoring in engineering seems to be that unlike science, engineering qualifications allow entry into a diverse range of professions inside Japan's massive manufacturing conglomerates. Similar to the United States and the EU15, representation of Japanese women in life sciences is the highest. However, what is most impressive is that for a country that had few female scientists and fewer than 1% in engineering through the 1990s (ILO LABORSTA, 2005), Japanese women have made great advances throughout the past decade.

European Union

Across the European Union, statistics vary by country, but definite progress is occurring. As described earlier, women in science and engineering were quite common in the EU25 countries (the EU15 plus an additional 10), which include Eastern Europe, but until recently, in the EU15, women's representation was much lower. In research universities, women are lagging in science, math, and computing. In engineering, manufacturing, and construction, overall in the EU15, women constitute 20.6% of employees in these fields (on par with the United States). In Portugal, Italy, Sweden, Denmark, and France, women's representation exceeds that within the United States (see Table 12.1). EU15 faculty employment ratios display similar trends to the United States and Japan: The higher the professorial rank, the fewer the women. In the EU15, fully tenured faculty (i.e., equivalent to full professor) in engineering and technology range from 1.3% in Denmark to 11.1% in Switzerland (see Table 12.1). Women in research positions outside academia present a different picture. In government, women's engineering and technology researcher statistics for reporting EU15 countries are as follows: Germany (16.6%), Norway (17.2%), Denmark (22.7%), Austria (26%), Portugal (36.9%), Spain (38.8%), and Iceland (40.8%; Bell, Chopin, & Palmer, 2006). Like women elsewhere, they usually hover at the bottom rungs of seniority (Bell et al., 2006; European Commission, 2003; ILO, 2002a, 2004a; Lopez-Claros & Zahidi, 2005).

Summary

These statistics show that despite intensive efforts to involve more women in engineering and related fields, women today are visibly underrepresented. Because technological advancement has become associated with quality of life in the global economy, new challenges for gender equity issues will be fundamentally associated not only with women's education and training but potentially with their sustained employment in science and technology fields.

ANTIDISCRIMINATION POLICIES, TREATIES, AND MULTILATERAL AGENCIES

The emergence of telecommunications and ICT has spawned a global society and the ideal of a "model global citizenship." To monitor this phenomenon, the United Nation's international governmental organizations and nongovernmental organizations (NGOs) have become the fora for countries to collectively cooperate in forging this new world order. Fortunately, at the United Nations level, gender equality remains a primary goal. To implement equality, several treaties, endorsements, project documents, and policies have emerged. Perhaps the first were the ILO's conventions on equal remuneration (ILO, 1951) and discrimination (ILO, 1958). After the establishment of International Women's Year in 1975, proclamation of the United Nations Decade for Women from 1976 to 1985, and the adoption of the Beijing Declaration and Platform for Action in the Fourth World Conference on Women in 1995 (see http://www.un.org/womenwatch/daw/beijing/platform/), women's status has been monitored more closely worldwide.

A later United Nations treaty, the Convention for the Elimination of All Forms of Discrimination Against Women (CEDAW; see United Nations, Division for the Advancement of Women, Department of Economic and Social Affairs, n.d.) is not legally binding, yet it obligates signatory governments to eliminate laws and practices conflicting with its goals. According to the United Nations Division for the Advancement of Women (2002), acceptance of the convention commits states to undertaking measures to end discrimination against women, and periodically each signatory government must report its progress to the United Nations. However, what each country must do de facto in order to implement antidiscriminatory laws and policies remains vague. To address this shortcoming, "gender mainstreaming" has emerged, requiring governments to pass new gender laws and implement detailed policies with corresponding programs that are incorporated into a nation-state's governments and public or private institutions. Analysis of United Nations scientific project documents can provide material for speculation about the promotion of gender equality in scientific communities. Historically, access strategies (i.e., a "raise the numbers" approach) have not addressed core issues of patriarchal struc-tures in science and technology careers, whether in academia, government, or commercial firms. In Min-Woptika's (2000) longitudinal analysis of United Nations documents, the majority of documents by UNESCO; UNIFEM, the United Nations Development Fund for Women; and the World Bank addressing the issues of women in science and engineering have been pub-lished since 1994. Although liberal wording (i.e., *access strategy*) occurs in the majority of the documents before the Beijing conference in 1995, post-1995 there is mention of both access and transformation strategies—of the work-force and education.

It is alarming that the issue of gender in science was not addressed by UNESCO until as late as 1999, as noted in a 2005 declaration (UNESCO, 1999, 2005). Since that time, expressions mentioning both men and women have appeared in its declarations. The 2005 declaration calls for not only an access strategy but also inclusion that will evolve scientific development by bas-ing scientific progress on "meeting the needs of all humankind." Creating more female-friendly spaces certainly increases women's attraction to and sur-vival in these fields. A radical approach challenges understanding of science, approaches to science, and applications of scientific knowledge. That may require women's increased involvement in setting the scientific agenda through greater participation on scientific boards—a priority in the European Union because of serious adherence to United Nations gender mainstreaming policies. It is laudable that by 2004, women in Norway, Finland, and Sweden made up slightly less than 50% of the scientific board members (Bell et al., 2006). Because adherence to policy and international conventions is essential for many European Union countries, laws include provisions to advance gender-neutral family leave policies, with continuing advancement opportunities, and pay equality that continues after childcare. This continues to open the doors to these professions for women; otherwise, women may be simply asked to sacri-fice more for less (see chap. 10, this volume). Accordingly, in 2000, the United Nations noted that women provide approximately 65% of the world's labor in formal (i.e., such as employment by a publicly or privately registered firm) and informal (i.e., such as home-based employment) settings (United Nations Department of Economic and Social Affairs, 2000).

Country-Specific Legislation to Enforce Gender Equality

True and Mintrom (2001) argued that CEDAW has not had a significant effect on women's equality. Although that may be correct, what have resulted are enhanced discrimination laws and gender mainstreaming policies that have raised women's status on several key indicators (ILO, 2004a). Moreover, although it is difficult to directly link, since the implementation of CEDAW the number of women in scientific professions has increased in Japan and the

European Union, as demonstrated by statistics from the ILO LABORSTA (2005) database.

The United States

The United States has not ratified CEDAW or its optional protocol (United Nations Division for the Advancement of Women, 2000), yet it had antidiscrimination laws earlier than either the European Union or Japan. The United States strengthened its antidiscrimination employment laws in the 1960s. The Equal Pay Act of 1963, which is part of the Fair Labor Standards Act of 1938, is administered and enforced by the Equal Employment Opportunity Commission. The Equal Employment Act prohibits sex-based wage discrimination between those working in the same establishment and performing under similar working conditions. The Civil Rights Act (CRA) of 1964 prohibits discrimination in the provision of public accommodations, governmental services, and public or private education. In particular, Title VII of the CRA applies to private employers, labor unions, and employment agencies. After this act was passed, the CRA of 1991 was created to amend the CRA of 1964 by strengthening laws that banned discrimination in employment.

In the United States, the legal system has been the primary method for enforcing gender equality. During the past decade, women's lawsuits have increased sharply, perhaps because affirmative action measures have weakened. It is interesting to note that discrimination cases have not been filed under the Equal Pay Act but rather as direct merit suits, where the second largest category occurs under Title VII, indicating that a range of discriminatory practices pervades the workforce (Equal Employment Opportunity Commission, 2005). Problems with U.S. labor laws are momentous because the onus for proving job similarity and maintaining workplace compliance remains with the employee, not the employer or government (Burk, 2005). Although Bell (2005) has proven that U.S. women executives in women-led firms earn between 15% and 20% more in total compensation than women in male-led firms, the United States is unlikely to reintroduce its once-aggressive affirmative action programs.

In education, Title IX, also now referred to as the Patsy T. Mink Equal Opportunity in Education Act, demanded that gender equality be implemented in federally funded school programs. Several landmark cases have been filed in the past few years to curtail its power. Additionally, the recent 2006 revisions to Title IX regulations allow K–12 nonvocational single-sex schools, classes, and extracurricular activities in elementary and secondary schools for a variety of vague purposes such as the achievement of governmental or educational objectives deemed important (Klein, 2007). In short, gender equality measures in the United States are being challenged as unnecessary in the current political and business sphere.

The European Union

Although antidiscrimination laws have been enacted in all EU15 countries, in the European Union, member nations vary in their implementation of gender policy and equality. The influential European Women's Lobby (EWL) is the largest coordinating body of national and European nongovernmental women's organizations in the European Union and has wielded a great deal of power in the implementation of gender mainstreaming. Coordinating high-level interventions, such as linking political decision makers and women's organizations, grants the EWL its powerful stance in the political arena. In fact, the EWL has stalled countries from entering the European Union until archaic laws have been superseded with newer gender-sensitive legislation. Turkey offers the latest case in point (see chap. 10, this volume).

Gender equality has clearly been given priority in the Northern European countries: Finland, Norway, Sweden, Denmark, and Iceland occupy the top positions of the United Nations' human development indicators (HDI), gender development indicators (GDI), gender empowerment measures (GEM), and World Economic Forum rankings (see Table 12.2). However, this has not necessarily translated into more women participating in the workforce. At the latest Lisbon review meeting, women's employment had not reached its interim target of approximately 60%. At the Beijing +10 meeting in 2005, many goals had still not been actualized (EWL, 2005). Recommendations included improving child care facilities throughout the union, boosting women's participation in scientific professions, accounting for gender equality in all union activities and encouraging national governments to allocate European Union funds for ongoing minimization of gender inequalities. The 2006 European Commission sponsored report entitled *Developing Anti-Discrimination in Europe: The 25 EU Member States Compared* (Bell et al., 2006) noted that a high proportion of European Union citizens did not understand their rights in employment discrimination. Consequently, the courts have had few discrimination cases filed because of the burdens placed on plaintiffs. Finally, using the legal system in European Union member nations to compare national with European Union discrimination laws is a relatively recent phenomenon.

Japan

Post–World War II, the Constitution of Japan (1946) was rewritten. Because of the efforts of Beate Sirota Gordon, Article 14 designates equality for Japanese men and women. Japan's Article 24 decrees equal rights in marriage. However, because of the patriarchal Japanese society, these did little for women's emancipation as indicated by the current status of women in Japan more than 60 years later (Natsuko, 2002).

Like the European Union, using the courts to hear discrimination cases is a relatively new phenomenon. In 1989, the first sexual discrimination lawsuit

TABLE 12.2
HDI, GEM, GDI, WEF, and CEDAW Ratification

Country	HDI	GEM	GDI	Gini Index[a]	WEF[b]	CEDAW (date ratified)[c]
Norway	1	2	1	25.1	2	1981
Iceland	2	1	2	N/A	3	1985
Sweden	3	3	3	25.0	1	1980
Australia	4	11	4	32.0	10	1983
Netherlands	5	6	7	32.6	14	1991
Belgium	6	15	8	25.0	20	1985
United States	7	10	5	40.8	17	N/A
Canada	8	9	6	31.5	7	1981
Japan	9	44	13	24.9	38	1985
Switzerland	10	13	12	33.1	34	1987
Denmark	11	4	9	24.7	4	1983
Ireland	12	16	16	35.9	16	1985
United Kingdom	13	17	11	36.0	8	1986
Finland	14	5	10	25.6	5	1986
Luxembourg	15	N/A	18	30.8	26	1989
Austria	16	7	14	N/A	28	1980
France	17	N/A	17	32.7	13	1983
Germany	18	8	15	35.2	9	1985
Spain	19	14	20	32.5	27	1984
New Zealand	20	12	19	N/A	6	1985
Italy	21	32	21	36.0	45	1985
Israel	22	23	22	35.5	37	1991
Portugal	23	21	23	38.5	23	1980
Greece	24	40	24	38.4	50	1983
Cyprus	25	34	25	N/A	N/A	1985

Note. Data are from the United Nations Development Program (2003). The Human Development Index (HDI) measures a country's overall standard of living, education, income, infant mortality and average lifespan. The Gender Development Index (GDI) factors in gender differences for HDI measures. The Gender Empowerment Measure (GEM) measures women's advancement in a society's economic and political spheres, measured by such criteria as wages and women in parliament, administrative and management positions, technical professions, and corporate professions. A Gini Index is a calculation used by economists where a value of 0 represents perfect economic equality, and a value of 100 absolute inequality. The World Economic Forum's (WEF) measures for gender equality examine both basic provisions as in the GDI but also empowerment measures like the GEM. Japan has a much higher (i.e., higher = worse) GEM ranking because of greater gender inequality than other nations ranking in the 10 top positions of HDI and GDI measures. Japan has a high HDI because it is a developed nation offering a high quality of life overall. In contrast, the United States has a smaller GEM indicator than Japan because U.S. women do have more economic opportunities than Japanese women. However, the United States has the largest Gini Index, indicating incisive inequality because the gaps between the upper and lower echelons of society are the greatest. In the United States, this inequality may be most often related to socioeconomic status, with single mothers remaining one of the most seriously disadvantaged groups (Peterson, 2002). Although single mothers in Japan are also struggling, the inequality index is lower because differences in pay have never been as large. Overall, Japanese maintain good living standards because of better distribution of wealth and resources, more adequate health care, and a high level of education for its citizens. Like the European Union, Japan is more egalitarian in terms of wage equality. As expected, the Northern European nations are at the top of the GEM and WEF rankings with lower Gini Indices than most countries. Data are from the United Nations Development Program (2003). CEDAW = Convention for the Elimination of all Forms of Discrimination Against Women.
[a]Data from World Bank (2003).
[b]For the World Economic Forum (WEF) ranking categories, see the headings in Table 12.3. The WEF has adopted its own measure, which is most similar to the GEM.
[c]Data from United Nations Division for the Advancement of Women (2002).

was filed, and the Japanese word for *sexual harassment* (i.e., *sekuhara*) originated (Yoneda, 2002). In 1985, Japan ratified CEDAW. Like many countries without gender discrimination laws, since CEDAW's ratification Japan has passed substantial legislation in support of working women. The Equal Employment Opportunity Law (EEOL) was enacted in 1986, and the Child-Care and Family-Care Leave Law was enacted in 1992 (see ILO, 2002b, 2004b). In 1994, the Ministry of Health, Labour and Welfare subsidized family support centers by providing operational expenses for child care, which were instituted to attract more women into the workforce. In 1999, the Japanese government began enforcing the revised EEOL, which called for more equal treatment of men and women in the workplace. More recently, the Basic Law for a Gender-Equal Society (ILO, n.d.) mandated that every citizen fully participate in society regardless of gender (Natsuko, 2002). This decree specified that yearly reports on the implementation of gender-specific policies be compiled and published. One example stated that the Japanese government would increase the number of female members of the government advisory council to 30% by the year 2005—a requirement for gender-equal participation in planning and decision making (Natsuko, 2002). To date, this goal remains unmet, but the government must measure and report progress yearly.

Since the EEOL was enacted, the number of female workers in Japan has climbed to almost 25 million. Nearly half of all eligible women now account for 48% of the entire workforce (ILO, 2002a). Japanese law has provided government support for companies that implement affirmative action programs. Unfortunately, shortly after the enactment, unofficial job offers to men were 60% in the technical sector and 30% in the administrative sector (Natsuko, 2002).

Summary

Japan has made progress, but this may be because it had to make large-scale improvements to comply with CEDAW. In the EU15, despite setbacks, faith in the gender mainstreaming process has continued the implementation of necessary laws, policies, and procedures. For U.S. women, the situation appears to be worsening because companies seem intent on overlooking gender discrimination, and women face enormous economic and professional penalties when filing antidiscrimination lawsuits (Burk, 2005).

DO LABOR LAWS CREATE WORKFORCE EQUITY?

Despite higher education levels for women, they are not well established in the labor force. As shown in Table 12.3, the United States (with 46%) had the highest share of women administrative and managerial workers compared

TABLE 12.3
Women's Empowerment in Several Spheres

Country	Health and well-being[a]	Corporate boards (% F)[b]	Management administration (% F)[c]	Women in parliament (%)[d]	Economic participation[a]	Economic opportunity[a]
Norway	9	21.1	30	36	13	3
Iceland	6	4.8	29	30	17	7
Sweden	1	16.9	30	45	5	12
Netherlands	8	7.3	26	37	32	16
Belgium	16	3.0	31	35	35	37
United States	42	12.8	46	14	19	46
Japan	3	0.4	10	7	33	62
Switzerland	7	7.7	28	25	43	42
Denmark	2	12.8	26	38	8	1
Ireland	12	4.1	29	13	37	51
United Kingdom	28	7.4	33	18	21	41
Finland	4	10.5	28	38	12	17
Austria	13	5.2	27	34	42	22
France	17	6.5	N/A	32	31	9
Germany	10	6.7	36	32	20	28
Spain	5	3.8	30	36	45	34
Italy	11	2.6	21	12	51	49
Portugal	20	0.8	32	19	27	18
Greece	22	6.5	26	14	44	48

Note. Countries are ranked by their human development indicators.

[a]Data from the 2005 World Economic Forum rankings (Lopez-Claros & Zahidi, 2005). Health and well-being represents rankings of women's access to nutrition, health care, reproductive facilities, and issues of fundamental safety and integrity of person. Economic participation and economic opportunity concern the quality of women's economic involvement beyond their mere presence as workers.

[b]Ethical Investment Research Service research (Maier, 2005) provides a global picture of the level of female representation on corporate boards across Europe, North America and Asia Pacific. The research looked at all board members, both executive and nonexecutive. The study included nonexecutive board members because the distinction between full-time and part-time members has become blurred. Women directors are more likely to be part-time nonexecutive directors than full-time executive directors. In general, if full-time directors only were counted, the percentage of women would be lower. Data are from March 2004.

[c]Some countries showed a decline in the number of management and administrative positions for women since the 1996–1999 period. These include Ireland, Spain, Denmark, and Portugal. Data are from International Labour Organization (2002a) and are rounded.

[d]Parliament is equivalent to the U.S. Congress.

with Japan's at approximately 10%. The European Union averaged approximately 30%, with Italy the exception at 21%. The ILO (2004a) underscored that women continue to be most underrepresented in senior posts.

In Japan, this is mainly caused by differences in men's and women's career advancement to management positions (ILO, 2002a). Since the EEOL was enacted, the ratio of female managers has nearly doubled. Still, women only account for 2% of department directors, 3% of division managers, and 8% of section heads. More detailed figures on women's participation in senior posts and government and corporate boards are listed in Table 12.1. According to a survey in Japan (ILO, 2004a), women tend to be in nonmanagement tracks for the following reasons: There are not enough capable women to promote (54.1%), women leave before acquiring the skills to become managers (33.9%), too few women are capable of management (28.4%), women do not go on business trips or travel for business (21%), and managers with families are unsuitable (4.5%).

Likewise, a survey of 75 senior U.S. ICT executives showed that companies were not promoting women to management positions (ILO, 2004a). According to Doty (2002), a survey of 2,067 ICT professionals showed that executives' primary reasons for gender bias in promotion included their fear that women managers would need family leave to bear children and doubts as to whether women could manage a predominantly male production team. However, the survey also found women rated on par with men in key managerial attributes: loyalty, reliability, and skills. Although 68% of respondents also said women were better organized than their male counterparts, 76% concluded that men had better chances for being mentored into management.

According to the European Commission (2004), "The same level of education as men and comparable qualifications are not enough to guarantee a woman's career in informatics" (p. 31). Occupying less than 30% of the private sector jobs across the European Union, women are significantly underrepresented, with Belgium and Austria having below average participation rates.

A study of U.K. employees (Davis, Neathey, Regan, & Willison, 2005) also determined that pregnancy was a primary concern for continued employment, especially for posts offering promotion. Not wanting to hire temporary workers, companies asked the remaining workers to compensate for the employee absent on family leave—perhaps creating further disharmony.

The world over, history continues to repeat itself: Women's biological capacity to produce offspring often creates career incompatibility for women scientists and engineers (see chaps. 7 and 10, this volume). According to Thom (2001),

> Sue V. Rosser, dean of Ivan Allen College at the Georgia Institute of Technology, surveyed academic women scientists and engineers who received

NSF Professional Opportunities for Women in Research and Education (POWRE) awards in 1997, 1998, and 1999, asking them, among other questions, about the most significant challenges they face as they plan their careers. Balancing work and family responsibilities, a great concern among 62% of the respondents in 1997, was cited by an even greater 77% of the women in 1999. (pp. 77–78)

Workplace discrimination claims much of the responsibility for these problems, with penalties for childbearing and a dearth of policies to support working mothers as perhaps the largest obstacles (European Commission, 2004; ILO, 2004a; Lopez-Claros & Zahidi, 2005). In fact, one third of *Fortune* magazine's worldwide list of "most powerful women" had stay-at-home husbands; however, some also quit their jobs to prioritize family (Morris, 2002). Forty-nine percent of women who remain in their careers full time have no children compared with 19% of men (Lopez-Claros & Zahidi, 2005). Statistics across the United States, the European Union, and Japan demonstrate that to varying degrees, laws alone do not remedy the gender gap or the "mommy trap" in employment.

ANALYSIS OF GENDER INEQUALITY IN PAY SCALES

Given the employment data discussed thus far in this chapter, the current education-boosting or knowledge-based economic paradigm cannot justify at least three social questions related to education and gender equity. First, there exists the gap of educational credentials and pay scales between males and females (Livingstone, 1998; Persson & Jonung, 1998; Tinker, 1990; Wong, 1981). Second, shifts of economic structures do not necessarily bring about more decent jobs, upgraded occupational skills, or higher incomes because usually only individuals who have access to education and/or high-level job retraining can benefit from the changes in liberalized economic economies (Farrell, 1995; Livingstone, 1998). Third, economic restructuring entails the feminization of many jobs where women then earn less than their male counterparts (ILO, 2004a).

Two methods to measure returns from educational investment have been documented: One correlates years of schooling with the growth of gross domestic product; the second correlates years of schooling with individual life earnings. Liu and Armer (1993) duplicated Psacharopoulos's (1987) analysis of the returns from different educational attainment levels, finding that the societal rate of return (e.g., better health and literacy resulting in higher HDI and GDI indicators) was high for elementary education, low for secondary education, and least for tertiary education. Conversely, the personal rate of return (i.e., as noted in GEM indicators) was greatest for tertiary education.

Because I am discussing an educated populace (i.e., people trained in advanced scientific fields), the question emerges: How do males and females differ in their rates of return from higher education? Consequently, I mined the data available (1994–2003) from the longitudinal ILO LABORSTA database (ILO LABORSTA, 2005) to extract the annual incomes for all EU15 countries, the United States, and Japan. For each country, the averages in the manufacturing sector data were used; however, there is no guarantee of job equivalence by country.

Average fertility rates (Office of Economic and Cultural Development [OECD], 2003) were multiplied by 6% for one child and 13% for two children and subtracted from women's cumulative salary to factor in the childbearing penalty for developed nations (ILO, 2004a). Only full-time workers were considered, and no calculation was made for change of status into senior positions or management because it is difficult to ascertain who will be promoted and who will not. However, in all three regions, women are not likely to remain in the workforce full time for the same number of years as men (ILO, 2002a, 2004a), nor are they as likely to move into higher level positions (see Table 12.3). The formulae applied for men (Equation 1) and women (Equation 2) are as follows:

$$\text{Men} = \sum [\text{base salary} \, (y1 \ldots y10)] * \text{annual increase} \, (y1 \ldots y10)$$
$$* \text{currency conversion rate} \tag{1}$$

$$\text{Women} = \sum (1 - \text{average gender wage gap}) * [\text{base salary} \, (y1 \ldots y10)]$$
$$* \text{annual increase} \, (y1 \ldots y10) * [1 - \text{absolute value} \, (\text{fertility rate})$$
$$* \text{penalty}] * \text{currency conversion rate} \tag{2}$$

Results in Table 12.4 indicate that women are greatly undercompensated in the workforce—maybe more so than these results indicate, because this calculation is a conservative estimate. Although enacted legislation to combat pay inequality exists, obvious wage gaps remain, especially when the fertility rate is factored into women's pay. However, with continued pressure from the ILO in Europe, women's wages have recently further closed in on men's. Ironically, the higher the post, the wider the pay gap—women with higher levels of education may not close the gap but instead widen it. In the United States during 2001, women earned 76% of men's pay overall: 71% in managerial and professional jobs and 67% in executive administrative posts. Fewer women with doctorates are tenured in university settings. In the EU15, women with higher levels of scientific education are more often in administrative and government jobs earning less than men in the private sector (European Commission, 2003). In Japan, dramatic opportunity and workplace inequalities occur between well-educated male and female employees in all sectors.

TABLE 12.4
Estimated Longitudinal Wages of Professionals from 1994 to 2003

Country	Males	Females	Female wages as percentage of male wages
Austria	244,770	175,755	72
Belgium	261,640	181,720	70
Denmark	502,250	370,725	74
Finland	235,120	163,735	70
France	187,800	127,115	68
Germany	211,040	155,090	73
Greece	N/A	N/A	N/A
Iceland	224,685	167,130	74
Ireland	230,650	146,700	64
Italy	N/A	N/A	N/A
Japan	260,160	156,510	60
Netherlands	319,905	214,715	67
Norway	409,915	295,250	72
Portugal	N/A	N/A	N/A
Spain	N/A	N/A	N/A
Sweden	259,790	205,280	79
Switzerland	472,560	324,865	69
United Kingdom	292,880	202,725	60
USA	235,000	163,561	70

Note. Wages are in Euros. Countries for which reliable gender-disaggregated data are unavailable (those marked N/A) have had large gender pay gaps. All EU15 countries have made progress recently in implementing more gender-equal pay scales (International Labour Organization [ILO], 2004a). Accuracy is subject to the data provided by the ILO LABORSTA (2005). All data are approximated and rounded.

Table 12.4 shows that the earning gap is higher than the Northern European countries often report. This is a consequence of higher fertility rates than much of Southern Europe and Japan. Also, according to the ILO LABORSTA (2005) database, most of Northern Europe did not have real pay equality until the mid to late 1990s. Recently, all EU15 countries have made progress in implementing more gender equal pay scales (ILO, 2004a).

EMERGENT GLOBAL TRENDS: THE GOOD AND BAD NEWS

It is distressing that the literature concurrently cites the great gains for women in science, computing, and engineering fields alongside the pending labor shortages in technology workers—a point I have noted with concern after reading numerous news articles. Very recently, the OECD (2005) advised Japan that women's labor was needed to expand its long-sagging economy. Demographic changes no doubt forecast impending labor shortages: Birth rates are declining while populations are growing older. In 2003, the United Nations Economic Commission for Europe (UNECE) forecast that by 2050, every third person in Europe and North America will be aged over 60, and the proportion of those below age 20 will decline to approximately 20%. In Japan, the labor shortage is in technical employment and continues to rise (Ohmi, 2005). One has to seriously question whether the clamor for women to enter the workforce sincerely addresses gender equality as a human right or whether this persists as the historical call to bolster a depleted technological labor force.

Natsuko (2002) argued that although more Japanese women are obtaining higher education, only 1 in 6 female employees are being hired for professional and technical positions. Even worse, when the EEOL was passed, the number of permanent female employees was 70%, but by 2002 this dropped to 53%. By contrast, the percentage of nonpermanent employees has reached nearly 47%, of whom approximately 80% are part-time workers (ILO, 2004a; Natsuko, 2002). Although the number of women working alongside men has increased, it is impossible to ignore the fact that women are being used for convenient, low-cost labor (Japan NGO Network for CEDAW, 2003; Natsuko, 2002).

In the United States, the employment situation is equally disturbing. Through 2006, new jobs in the economy exceeded the number of workers by approximately 4 million, and this shortage was at the professional level involving knowledge workers (Ellis, 2002). To fill this need, the number of contract or contingent employees is expected to rise dramatically within the next few years. Some studies have predicted that up to 30% of the American workforce may then be other than full-time permanent employees, such as contractors and consultants (Ellis, 2002), of which women tend to be the temporaries and men are generally the contractors and consultants—implying that under this employment scheme, men would tend to be better compensated (ILO, 2004a).

In Europe, the number of nonpermanent employees has also been steadily rising. At the same time, intense union discussions to organize part-time workers have been central in the European Union debates (European Trade Union Confederation, 2005). In the United States, full-time workers are more than twice as likely as part-time workers to be union members: 15.3% and 7.2%, respectively (Bureau of Labor Statistics, 2005). Although Walton (2000) of the World Bank Group has noted that trade and labor unions have benefited women and minorities, over the past several decades, movement in the United States has been away from union or government interventions. The same trend has been the case in Japan, but to a lesser degree, because Japan's unions have been and still are stronger than those in the United States; however, in the midst of mobilization efforts, women in the part-time or nonpermanent workforce face similar challenges to those in the United States.

The technological labor market may also become more uncertain. Use of part-time and nonpermanent employees has grown concurrently with the ICT economy. Companies have profited from work options such as flexible scheduling, telecommuting, and offshore job displacement. From a free-market perspective, it is in companies' economic interest to reduce their number of permanent employees as much as possible and to turn to the lower personnel costs afforded by nonpermanent employees. Many companies want to have nonpermanent employees perform work comparable to that of their permanent employees. This trend indicates that the quality of nonpermanent employees is rising, but the wage and benefit differentials between permanent and non-permanent employees clamors for intervention (ILO, 2004a). Otherwise, many of the nonpermanent, predominantly U.S. women workers may retire in poverty (Lee & Shaw, 2002). To a lesser extent, Japanese women also have the same concerns (Higuchi, 1998) as do women in the EU15—in particular, the United Kingdom (Equal Employment Opportunity Commission, 2005), where women's ratio of pay is the lowest in the EU15.

Although reproductive rights have unshackled women from the home, cultural pressures still curtail many talented women from pursuing top-level high-technology careers. It seems that most women still cannot have the best of both worlds because corporate or social policies on parenting and parental leave, the availability and cost of day care, and corporate or family attitudes cumulatively affect women's long-term advancement and earnings. Because of rapid innovation and shortened product life cycles, women cannot simply drop out of the technological workforce and reenter easily. Supportive governmental policies do not necessarily predict success. For example, according to a study by the OECD (2002), the negative impact of childbirth on a woman's career is particularly high in Germany, where new mothers can request 3 years' leave with limited pay. Many women simply do not, or cannot, reenter the workforce after this prolonged break. Alternatively, countries such as Sweden and Denmark offer 1 year of paid maternity leave, after which most women return to the workforce. In the Netherlands, if either parent requests a part-time schedule, the employer must grant it, and part-time work has become widely accepted. In the European Union, consensus is growing that fathers are entitled to take paternity leave, as evidenced by gestures such as Tony Blair's conciliatory leave on the birth of his child.

In Japan, there is a child care leave system that allows either parent to take time off work for child care purposes until the child is 1 year old, but only about half of the women who are eligible take leave. Often this is because working mothers do not have the support of their workplaces (Natsuko, 2002). Even worse, they find themselves unemployed after announcing their pregnancy (Japan NGO Network for CEDAW, 2003). The United States has the least friendly child care leave policy (see Table 12.5). U.S. mothers do not get paid for leave and subsequently cannot take extended leave unless they can endure serious financial penalties. Thus, no matter how many policies are implemented, they remain impotent if women cannot take advantage of them.

TABLE 12.5
Overall Employment Statistics

Country	Women in labor force (% F)	Unemployed (% F/% M)	Part-time employment (% F/% M)	Service/manufacturing (% F/% F)	Maternity leave and pay (weeks/% pay)
Austria	51	4.2/4.3	24.4/2.6	N/A	16/100
Belgium	40	8.9/7.7	N/A	88.2/10.7	15/[a]
Denmark	73	6.2/5.0	22.9/10.3	85.9/12.2	18/90
Finland	64	8.9/9.2	14.7/7.5	81.9/14.1	13.5/70
France	49	10.9/8.7	24.1/5.1	86.6/12.4	16/100
Germany	49	9.5/10.4	35.2/5.5	82.4/15.6	14/100
Greece	38	14.6/6.2	10/2.9	65.7/12.9	17/100
Iceland	79	2.9/3.6	31.2/10.2	N/A	12/80
Ireland	49	3.9/4.8	33.2/7.1	82.5/15.6	18/70
Italy	37	11.6/6.7	23.4/4.8	76.8/19.2	20/80
Japan	48	4.9/5.5	40.2/13.7	N/A	14/60
Netherlands	56	4.4/4.2	59.9/15	89.0/8.6	16/[a]
Norway	69	4.0/4.9	33.0/9.2	N/A	16/80–100
Portugal	55	7.2/5.5	N/A	67.8/12.9	18/100
Spain	43	15.9/8.2	16.3/2.4	81.3/13.9	16/100
Sweden	76	4.4/5.3	20.3/7.3	87.5/11.1	14/100
Switzerland	59	4.5/3.8	45.3/7.7	N/A	14/80
United Kingdom	55	4.1/5.5	39.7/8.8	87.3/11.9	18/[a]
United States	60	5.7/6.3	17.1/6.9	80.0/64.0	12/0

Note. Service/manufacturing industry data from the *United Nations Statistical Yearbook 2000* (2004). Labor force, unemployment, part-time employment data from United Nations Statistics 2000–2003. Data are rounded. Note that women are overrepresented in both part-time and service professions, indicating a lower wage base. F = female; M = male; N/A = no data available.

[a] The rates vary in these countries, where the initial amount is higher than the amount for remaining leave. Moreover, in some countries such as the United Kingdom and Sweden, the leave may be longer, but there is less pay for longer leave periods (see http://www.childpolicyintl.org).

In reviewing the three regions, each has its strengths and weaknesses. Although the United States has a slight overall lead in the numbers of women in tertiary engineering and computing sciences slated to enter the technical workforce, the EU15 and Japan are gaining. Also, although U.S. women are at higher levels in the commercial workplace, fewer are in top government posts, which may explain why family leave policies are so grim. In contrast, the European Union has a larger number of women in government, which may explain why social policies are so female friendly. Concurrently, enormous pressure is being applied to entice more European Union women into science and technology professions, as evident from their gender mainstreaming approaches. Japan has made enormous strides, given that they began this endeavor much later. It would not be surprising if the European Union and Japan further close in on or surpass the United States because they are more aggressive in their gender mainstreaming strategies and their technological labor forces are facing more serious shortages. Outside the scope of this chapter, the more drastic outsourcing of U.S. jobs to foreign companies could further undermine U.S. women's progress in the labor market.

POLICY IMPLICATIONS AND NEEDED REFORM MEASURES

Ideally, the adoption of more stringent positive discrimination or affirmative action systems might ensure that more women reach the top of their fields. Also, strengthening unions would benefit women. In all three regions, men should be encouraged to participate more in the home because women perform the bulk of unpaid work such as housework, childcare, and care for the elderly. However, what is needed may not be probable; therefore, I summarize here by region some more realistic short-term measures to further gender equality.

The United States needs better enforcement of Title IX. The trend toward single-sex schooling is troubling, and opponents need to fight to reverse this bias. To combat wage inequalities, the Paycheck Fairness Act of 2007 should be passed to strengthen the inadequate U.S. employment laws. The U.S. Congress introduced a bill, the Paid Family and Medical Leave Act of 2005. This bill has not yet been passed, but it would extend the Family and Medical Leave Act of 1993. If voted in, it would provide up to 12 weeks of paid leave regardless of gender. This gender-equal leave is preferable because it would not put women at a disadvantage in the eyes of employers whereas a maternity leave policy might. Finally, the United States should ratify the already signed United Nations treaty, CEDAW, because this would give women a platform from which to rally for greater equality. This treaty was slated for reintroduction in the Senate in late 2007.

In the case of Japan, CEDAW has accelerated the implementation of gender equality policies. However, strong backlash is still common because of the long-standing male-dominated culture. In academia, the male hierarchical structure of the *koza* system, in which professors hold near-absolute power over their subordinates, has been extremely problematic for women. Sadly, there is little remedy in the Japanese court system, which can take an unrealistic amount of time to hear a discrimination case. Moreover, restitution is often paltry. Because these court cases were nonexistent until recently, they are inadequate to legislate gender discrimination cases. In the home, Japanese men contribute very little time (i.e., usually about 30 minutes daily; Tsuya, 2004), and this leaves nearly all the household chores and child-rearing to women—who may also work long hours and endure several hours of commuting to and from work. Married working women may have to endure great hardships to succeed—especially in demanding academic and research positions. Overall, there is a dire need to raise the consciousness of both males and females to accommodate more working women, especially scientists and engineers, because women in these professions are not held in high esteem, especially by their male colleagues.

Each EU15 country has its own court system to implement its national laws on gender discrimination. Issues surrounding implementation of CEDAW and the compliance with European Union protocols are not homogenous with some countries having much less work to do, as indicated in the GDIs in Table 12.2. The 2006 report entitled *Developing Anti-Discrimination in Europe: The 25 EU Member States Compared* (Bell et al., 2006) has mentioned a massive education campaign informing European Union workers of their rights, strengthening existing laws, and streamlining procedures to file discrimination lawsuits. The European Commission plans to monitor the progress of these programs over the next few years. From the same European Commission report, public survey respondents in the EU25 felt that schools and universities had the greatest role in combating discrimination (42%); parents had the next most important role (40%), followed by the media (34%) and the government (31%). A close look at the respondents' answers makes it evident that education to change culture and the next generation may be perceived as more important than changes in the government or companies.

Although statistic laden, I hope that this chapter is also enlightening. My goal was to illustrate several key points: First, women worldwide tend to perceive that higher levels of education help them to compete in the labor market (Stromquist, 2007), but ironically, higher levels of education may create greater pay inequality. Second, in the scientific world—whether in academia, government, or private sectors—the higher the post, the fewer the women. Third, hiring more women into the technical labor force may result from an impetus to reverse the technical labor shortages rather than a genuine concern with gender equity. Finally, women are penalized because of their combined roles as worker and primary caretaker. These historical factors continue to deal women a losing hand in the labor market, especially as they age.

REFERENCES

American Association of University Women. (2004). *Tenure denied: Cases of sex discrimination in academia*. Retrieved March 20, 2005, from http://www.aauw.org/newsroom

Bell, L. (2005). *Haverford College economics professor Linda Bell explores gender pay gap; finds women executives make 15–20% more in women-led firms* [Press release]. Retrieved July 14, 2006, from http://www.socialfunds.com/news/release.cgi/4167.html

Bell, M., Chopin, I., & Palmer, F. (2006). *Developing anti-discrimination in Europe: The 25 EU Member States compared* (European Commission Rep., ISBN 2-930399-33-3). Utrecht, the Netherlands: Human European Consultancy.

Berner, B. (2000). Educating men: Women and the Swedish Royal Institute of Technology, 1880–1930. In A. Canal, R. Oldenziel, & K. Zachmann (Eds.), *Crossing boundaries, building bridges: Comparing the history of women engineers 1870s–1990s* (pp. 75–102). Amsterdam, the Netherlands: Overseas Publishers Association.

Bureau of Labor Statistics. (2005). *Table 1. Union affiliation of employed wage and salary workers by selected characteristics*. Retrieved March 28, 2005, from http://www.bls.gov/news.release/union2.t01.htm

Burk, M. (2005). *Cult of Power: Sex discrimination in corporate America and what can be done about it*. New York: Scribner.

Canal, A., Oldenziel, R., & Zachmann, K. (2000). *Crossing boundaries, building bridges: Comparing the history of women engineers 1870s–1990s*. Amsterdam, the Netherlands: Overseas Publishers Association.

Chatzis, K., & Nicolaid, E. (2000). A pyrrhic victory: Greek women's conquest of a profession in crisis. In A. Canal, R. Oldenziel, & K. Zachmann (Eds.), *Crossing boundaries, building bridges: Comparing the history of women engineers 1870s–1990s* (pp. 253–278). Amsterdam, the Netherlands: Overseas Publishers Association.

Civil Rights Act of 1964, Pub. L. 88-352. Title VII of the Civil Rights Act of 1964, Vol. 42, USC, 2000e (1964).

Civil Rights Act of 1991 (Pub. L. 102-166), enacted on November 21, 1991102d CONGRESS 1ST SESSION H.R.1 (1991).

Commission on the Advancement of Women and Minorities in Science, Engineering and Technology Development. (2000). *Land of plenty: Diversity as America's competitive edge in science, engineering and technology*. Retrieved August 2, 2007, from http://www.nsf.gov/pubs/2000/cawmset0409/cawmset_0409.pdf

The Constitution of Japan. (1946). Retrieved July 26, 2007 from http://www.constitution.org/cons/japan.txt

Davis, S., Neathey, F., Regan, J., & Willison, R. (2005). *Pregnancy discrimination at work: A qualitative study* (Working Paper No. 23). Retrieved May 23, 2006, from http://www.eoc.org.uk/cseng/research/wp23_qualitative_study.pdf

Doty, N. (2002, September 20). Does IT favor men? *Enterprise Systems, 17*(9), 56. Retrieved July 12, 2005 from http://www.acm.org/technews/articles/2002-4/0920f.html#item18

Ellis, C. M. (2002, September 30). The future of base pay. *Perspectives: A Sibson Consulting Publication, 10*(3). Retrieved August 2, 2007, from http://www.sibson.com/publications/perspectives/Volume_10_Issue_3/e_article000095890.cfm

Equal Employment Opportunity Commission. (2005). *EEOC litigation statistics, FY 1992 through FY 2004*. Retrieved March 12, 2005, from http://www.eeoc.gov/stats/litigation.html

Equal Pay Act of 1963, Pub. L. No. 88-38, (EPA), 29 USC, Section 206(d).

European Commission. (2003). *Women and science statistics and indicators: She-figures 2003*. Retrieved August 2, 2007, from http://www.ec.europa.eu/research/science-society/pdf/she_figures_2003.pdf

European Commission. (2004). *Widening women's work in information and communication technology*. Retrieved May 21, 2005, from http://www.ftu.namur.org/222-ict/

European Commission. (2006). *Eurostats. She-figures*. Retrieved February 1, 2007, from http://ec.europa.eu/research/science-society/pdf/she_figures_2006_en.pdf

European Trade Union Confederation. (2005). *TUC conference: EU constitution*. Retrieved July 31, 2005, from http://www.etuc.org/a/1043.

European Women's Lobby. (2005). *Beijing +10. 1995–2005: Review of the implementation of the Beijing Platform for Action by the European Union*. Retrieved March 21, 2005, from http://www.womenlobby.org/pdf/beijing-en.pdf.

Fair Labor Standards Act of 1938, Pub. No. 1318, 29 U.S.C. 29 U.S.C. ch. 8, 676, 52 Stat. 1060 (1938).

The Family and Medical Leave Act of 1993, Pub. L. No. 103-3 (1993) (enacted).

Farrell, J. (1995). Educational cooperation in the Americas: A review. In J. Puryear & J. Brunner (Eds.), *Education, equity, and economic competitiveness in the Americas: An inter-American dialogue project* (pp. 67–102). Washington, DC: Organization of American States.

Gibbons, M. (2004). *The year in numbers*. Washington, DC: American Society of Engineering Education.

Gouzevitch, D., & Gouzevitch, I. (2000). A woman's challenge: The Petersburg Polytechnic Institute for Women, 1905–1918. In A. Canal, R. Oldenziel, & K. Zachmann (Eds.), *Crossing boundaries, building bridges: Comparing the history of women engineers 1870s–1990s* (pp. 103–126). Amsterdam, the Netherlands: Overseas Publishers Association.

Higuchi, K. (1998). *Women in an aging society*. Retrieved July 21, 2005, from http://www.un.org/Depts/escap/pop/apss141/chap6.htm

Huang, G., Taddese, N., & Walter, E. (2000). *Entry and persistence of women and minorities in college science and engineering education* (NCES 2000-601). Washington, DC: National Center for Educational Statistics.

International Labour Organization. (1951). *Convention 100 Equal Remuneration Convention, 1951.* Geneva, Switzerland: Author.

International Labour Organization. (1958). *Convention 111 Discrimination (Employment and Occupation) Convention, 1958.* Geneva, Switzerland: Author.

International Labour Organization. (2002a). *Breaking through the glass ceiling: Women in management.* Retrieved March 10, 2005, from http://www.ilo.org/public/english/support/publ/xtextww.htm

International Labour Organization. (2002b). *Child-Care and Family-Care Leave Law—Japan.* Retrieved July 24, 2007, from http://www.ilo.org/public/english/employment/gems/eeo/law/japan/care.htm

International Labour Organization. (2004a). *Breaking through the glass ceiling: Women in management. An update.* Retrieved March 15, 2005, from http://www.ilo.org/public/english/bureau/inf/pr/2004/9.htm

International Labour Organization. (2004b). *Law on Securing Equal Employment Opportunity and Treatment between Men and Women in Employment (EEOL)—Japan.* Retrieved August 2, 2007, from http://www.ilo.org/public/english/employment/gems/eeo/law/japan/eeol.htm

International Labour Organization LABORSTA. (2005). [data file]. Retrieved April 2, 2005, from http://laborsta.ilo.org/

International Labour Organization. (n.d.). *The basic law for a gender-equal society—Japan.* Retrieved July 19, 2006, from http://www.ilo.org/public/english/employmeny/gems/eeo/law/japan/gender.htm

Japan NGO Network for CEDAW. (2003). *CEDAW: Summary report 2003.* Retrieved May 21, 2005, from http://www.jaiwr.org/jnnc/20030701jnncsummary report(en).pdf

Klein, S. (2007). *Education equality.* Retrieved February 2, 2007, from http://www.feminist.org/education

Lee, S., & Shaw, L. (2002). *Gender and economic security in retirement.* Retrieved June 12, 2005, from http://www.iwpr.org/pdf/D456.pdf

Liu, C., & Armer, J. M. (1993). Education's effect on economic growth in Taiwan. *Comparative Education Review, 37*(3), 304–321.

Livingstone, D. W. (1998). *The education–jobs gap: Underemployment or economic democracy.* Boulder, CO: Westview Press.

Lopez-Claros, A., & Zahidi, S. (2005). *Women's empowerment: Measuring the global gender gap.* Geneva, Switzerland: World Economic Forum.

Maier, S. (2005 August). *How global is good corporate governance?* (EIRIS Research Briefing). Retrieved October 1, 2007, from http://www.eiris.org/files/research%20publications/howglobalisgoodcorpgov05.pdf

McIlwee, J. S., & Robinson, J. G. (1992). *Women in engineering: Gender, power and workplace culture*. Albany: SUNY Press.

Ministry of Education, Science and Technology, Sports and Culture. (2004). *School basic survey*. Retrieved June 23, 2005, from http://www.mext.go.jp/english/news/2004/05/04052401/002.pdf

Ministry of Health, Labour and Welfare. (2002). *Labour statistics*. Retrieved March 10, 2005, from http://www.mhlw.go.jp/english/database/db-l/index.html

Min-Woptika, S. (2000, March). *A longitudinal analysis of multilateral organizations' approach to women in science*. Paper presented at a meeting of the Comparative and International Education Society, Washington, DC.

Morris, B. (2002, October 14). Trophy husbands arm candy? Are you kidding? While their fast-track wives go to work, stay-at-home husbands mind the kids. They deserve a trophy for trading places. *Fortune*. Retrieved August 2, 2007, from http://money.cnn.com/magazines/fortune/fortune_archive/2002/10/14/330033/index.htm

National Science Foundation. (2000). *Women, minorities, and persons with disabilities in science and engineering: 2000* (NSF 00-327). Arlington, VA: Author.

National Science Foundation, Division of Science Resources Statistics. (2004). *Women, minorities and persons with disabilities in science and engineering: 2004* (NSF 04-317). Arlington, VA: Author.

Natsuko, I. (2002, January–February). Women's social progress in Japan and future issues. *Journal of Japanese Trade & Industry, 21*(3), 12–32.

Nussbaum, M. C. (1999). *Sex and social justice*. New York: Oxford University Press.

Office of Economic and Cultural Development. (2002). *Labour market and social policy*. Retrieved April 30, 2005, from http://www.oecd.org/dataoecd/35/25/34687379.pdf

Office of Economic and Cultural Development. (2003). *Annual report*. Retrieved April 13, 2005, from http://www.oecd.org/

Office of Economic and Cultural Development. (2005). *Economic survey of Japan 2005*. Retrieved August 13, 2005, from http://www.oecd.org/document/61/0,2340,en_33873108_33873539_34274621_1_1_1_1,00

Ohmi, N. (2005). Problems of foreign worker policy in Japan—From the labor union viewpoint. *Japan Labor Review, 2*(4), 107–124.

Oldenziel, R. (2000). Multiple entry visas: Gender and engineering in the U.S., 1870–1945. In A. Canal, R. Oldenziel, & K. Zachmann (Eds.), *Crossing boundaries, building bridges: Comparing the history of women engineers 1870s–1990s* (pp. 11–49). Amsterdam, the Netherlands: Overseas Publishers Association.

Paid Family and Medical Leave Act of 2005, H.R. 3192, 109th Congress (2005).

Paycheck Fairness Act, S.R. S.77/H.R. 781, 110 Congress (2007).

Persson, I., & Jonung, C. (Eds.). (1998). *Research in gender and society: 2. Women's work and wages*. New York and London: Routledge.

Peterson, J. (2002). *Feminist perspectives on TANF reauthorization: An introduction to key issues for the future of welfare reform*. Retrieved May 2, 2005 from http://www.iwpr.org/pdf/e511.html

Psacharopoulos, G. (Ed.). (1987). *Economics and education: Research and studies*. New York: Pergamon Press.

Sloan, M. E. (1975). Women engineers in the United States. *Educational Horizons 53*, 102–105.

Solomon, B. M. (1985). *In the company of educated women: A history of women and higher education in America*. New Haven, CT: Yale University Press.

Stromquist, N. (2007). Global education. In S. Klein (Ed.), *Gender equity handbook* (pp. 33–44). Mahwah, NJ: Erlbaum.

Thom, M. (2001). *Balancing the equation: Where are women and girls in science, engineering and technology?* New York: National Council for Research on Women.

Tinker, I. (1990). *Persistent inequalities: Women and world development*. New York: Oxford University Press.

Title IX, Education Amendments of 1972, Pub. L. No. 92-318, Sec. 901, 86 Stat. 373 (1972).

True, J., & Mintrom, M. (2001). Transnational networks and policy diffusion: The case of gender mainstreaming. *International Studies Quarterly, 45*, 1–47.

Tsugawa, A., & Konami, Y. (2005). *Women scientists in Japan—History and today*. Retrieved April 23, 2005, from http://homepage3.nifty.com/jwef/jp_html/tugawapaper.html

Tsuya, N. O. (2004, April). *Gender, employment and housework in Japan*. Paper presented at the Annual Meeting of the Population Association of America, Boston.

United Nations Department of Economic and Social Affairs. (2000). *The world's women 2000: Trends and statistics*. New York: Author.

United Nations Development Program. (2003). *Gender empowerment measures*. Retrieved March 23, 2005, from http://www.undp.org/hdr2003/indicator/pdf/hdr03_table_23.pdf

United Nations Division for the Advancement of Women. (2000). *Optional Protocol to the Convention on the Elimination of All Forms of Discrimination against Women*. Retrieved June 12, 2006, from http://www.un.org/womenwatch/daw/cedaw/protocol/

United Nations Division for the Advancement of Women. (2002). *CEDAW*. Retrieved March 12, 2005, from http://www.un.org/daw

United Nations Division for the Advancement of Women, Department of Economic and Social Affairs. (n.d.). *Convention on the Elimination of all Forms of Discrimination against Women*. Retrieved August 2, 2007, from http://www.un.org/womenwatch/daw/cedaw/

United Nations Economic Commission for Europe. (2003). *Economic survey of Europe, 2003 No. 1*. Retrieved March 21, 2005, from http://www.unece.org/ead/pub/surv_031.htm

United Nations Educational, Scientific and Cultural Organization. (1999). *Declaration on science and the use of scientific knowledge*. Budapest, Hungary: Author.

United Nations Educational, Scientific and Cultural Organization. (2003). [Data file]. Retrieved March 12, 2005, from http://www.uis.unesco.org/ev.php?URL_ID= 5187&URL_DO=DO_TOPIC&URL_SECTION=201

United Nations Educational, Scientific and Cultural Organization. (2005). *Declaration of agreement in support of girls and women in information and communication technology*. Tunis, Tunisia: Author.

United Nations Statistical Yearbook 2000. (2004). Geneva: United Nations Publications.

U.S. Patent Office. (2003). *Trilateral patent statistics*. Retrieved April 10, 2005, from http://www.uspto.gov/

Walton, M. (2000). Unions in a global labor market. Retrieved April 2, 2005, from http://www.worldbank.org/wbi/mdf/mdf1/unions.htm

Wong, A. K. (1981). Planned development, social stratification, and the sexual division of labor in Singapore. *Journal of Women in Culture and Society, 7*(21), 434–452.

World Bank. (2003). *World development indicators: GenderStats Database*. Retrieved April 10, 2005, from http://www.worldbank.org

Yoneda, M. (2002). *International standards of gender equality and Japan—The impact on Japan*. Retrieved July 11, 2007, from http://www.dawncenter.or.jp/english/ publication/edawn/0212/inter.html

AUTHOR INDEX

Numbers in italics refer to listings in the references.

Abadan-Unat, N., 269, *294*

Acker, S., 49, *51*

Adair, R., 176, *191*

Adler, T. F., 15, *22*, 80, 93, 107, *111*, 140, 148, *169*, 197, 198, *211*, 212, 216, 233

Ahmed, F., 245, *260*

Albert, D. J., 248, *256*

Alexander, C. M., 47, *53*

Alexander, G. M., 253, *257*

Alfeld, C., 121, *142*

Alfeld-Liro, C., 175, *189*

Aliefendioglu, H., 267, 270, 283, *295*

Allison, P. D., 127, *139*

Alpert, A., 155, *169*

Alsaker, F. D., 32, *51*

Al-Sanad, H. A., 272, *295*

Altmann, D., 250, *259*

American Association of University Women, 3, *21*, 33, 47, 50, *51*, 196, *210*, 328, *346*

Anders, K. A., 306, *321*

Anderson, M. Z., 47, *52*, 176, *190*, 197, *212*

Apfelbaum, E., 311, 312, *320*

Arai, Y., 253, *260*

Arat, Y., 268, *294*

Arisaka, O., 253, *260*

Armer, J. M., 338, *348*

Armour, M., *51*

Armstrong, P. I., 29–31, 48, *51*

Arnold, K. D., 207, *214*

Astin, H. S., 30, *51*

Australian Bureau of Statistics, 94, *110*

Australian Council for Educational Research, 95, *110*

Bachevalier, J., 237, *257*

Bahr, M., 88, *112*

Bailey, J. M., 251, *257*

Baker, R. W., 182, *189*

Baker, S., 247, *261*

Baker, S. W., *259*

Bancroft-Andrews, C., *191*

Bandura, A., 47, *51*, 56, 77, 78, 80, *172*, 178, 188, *189*, 197, *211*

Barbaranelli, C., 47, *51*, 77, 80

Barber, B. L., 57, 82, 89, *113*, 122, *140*, 148, *169*, 175, *191*, 197, 198, *211*, *213*, *214*

Barnes, H., 182, *189*

Barnett, R. C., 208, *211*

Baron-Cohen, S., *261*

Bartfai, A., 250, 260

Baruch, G. K., 208, *211*

Baryeh, E. A., 272, *294*

Bates, J. E., *52*

Baum, M. J., 237n2, *257*, *263*

Baumert, J., 57, 82, 118, 119, 121, 123, 124, 128, *140–142*, 168, *169*, 197, *213*

Beatty, W. W., 248, *257*

Becker, J. B., 237, 242, *257*

Bell, J. J., *261*

Bell, L., 332, *346*

Bell, M., 329, 331, 333, 345, *346*

Benbow, C. P., 5, 6, *21*, *23*, 28, *54*, 137, *141*, 208, *213*

Benenson, J. F., 253, *257*

Bensimon, E. M., 315, *320*

Bentler, P. M., 150, 155–156, *168*

Bercovitch, F. B., 237, *259*

Berenbaum, S. A., 238, 243–252, *257*, *258*, 260–263

Berner, B., 325, *346*

Bernhardt, P. C., 248, *258*

Best, J. W., 59, 80

Betz, M. E., 56, 73, 80

Betz, N. E., 47, *52*, 197, 198, *211*

Bikos, L. H., 28–31, *53*

Bishop, J., 55, 80

Bix, A. S., 272, *294*

Blais, M. R., 182, *191*, *192*

Blake, J., *264*

Blakemore, J. E. O., 247, *258*

Bleeker, M. M., 28, *52*, 174, *190*, 196, *212*, 218, 219, 221, 224, 225, *232*, *233*

Board of Studies, 91, *110*

Boggs, K. R., 47, *52*

Bohlin, G., 244, *262*, *263*

Bollen, K. A., 155, *168*

Bong, M., 5, *21*, 93, *110*

Boomsma, A., 146, *168*

Booth, A., 248, *258*

Borger, D., *259*

Bornholt, L. J., 93, *110*

Bouchard, T. J., 250, *262*

Boyle, M. H., 38, *51*

Bradley, S. J., *264*

Brain, C., *262*

Braverman, M. T., *81*

Breedlove, S. M., 237, 242, *257*, *258*

Bridgeman, B., 4, *21*, 88, *110*

Brière, N. M., 182, *192*

Briscoe, R., 238, *262*

Bronstein, P., 299, *320*

Brook, C., 249, *260*, *262*

Brosnahan, A., *81*

Brown, A., 270, 271, *294*

Brown, S. D., 47, *53*, 56, *81*

Brown, T. R., *261*

Browne, M. W., 156, *168*

Bryk, A. S., 33, 38, *51*, *53*, 126, *140*, 168, *168*

Bryk, K. K., 244, 252, *257*

Buchmann, C., 28, 31, 50, *51*

Buitelaar, J. K., 248, *258*

Bukowski, W., 249, *263*

Bureau of Labor Statistics, 195, 196, 199, *211*, 341, *346*

Burk, M., 326, 332, 335, *346*

Byars-Winston, A. M., 29, *52*

Byrne, B. M., 147, 149–151, 153, 155, *168*

Callaghan, M., 5, *24*, 272, *296*

Campbell, J., *52*

Canal, A., 324, 325, *346*

Cannon, E., 216, *233*

Caprara, G. V., 47, *51*, 77, 80

Carlson, A. D., *261*

Carnegie Commission on Higher Education, 30, *51*

Carr, D., 196, 200, 209, *211*

Carrington, B., 5, *22*

Casserly, P., 196, *211*
Castellino, D. R., *52*
Catsambis, S., 49, *51*
Chase, C., 238n3, *258*
Chatzis, K., 325, *346*
Cheong, Y. F., 38, *53*
Chhin, C., 28, *52*
Chhin, C. S., 196, *212*, 221, 224, 225, 229, *232*, *233*
Chipman, S. F., 57n1, *80*
Chopin, I., 329, *346*
Cicchetti, D., 239, *262*
Ciccocioppo, A., 28, *51*
Cioppa, G. D., 253, *257*
Civil Rights Act of 1964, *346*
Civil Rights Act of 1991, *346*
Clark, A. S., 237, *258*
Clark, M. M., 237, 246, 254, *258*
Cliff, N., 97, *110*, *111*
Cockburn, C., 268, *295*
Cohen, J., 66, *80*, 179, *189*
Cohen, P., 66, *80*
Cohen-Bendahan, C. C. C., 245, 246, 248, *258*
Cohen-Kettenis, P. T., 248, 251, *258*, *259*
Coladarci, T., 57, *81*
Colbourne, K. A., 253, *263*
Cole-Harding, S., 251, *259*
Coleman, M. S., 316, *320*
Collins, L. M., 38, *51*
Commission on the Advancement of Women and Minorities in Science, Engineering and Technology Development, 328, *346*
Congdon, R. T., 38, *53*
Connell, J. P., 172, 178, *189*
Conseil de la science et de la technologie, 171, *190*
The Constitution of Japan, 333, *346*
Conway, G. S., 249, *260*
Cooney, G. H., 93, *110*
Cooper, J., 215, *232*
Cortina, K. S., 138, *141*
Courant, P., 316, *320*
Crandall, V. C., 75, 77, 78, *80*, 197, *211*

Crawford, K. M., 32, *53*, 208, *213*
Creighton, S. M., 238n3, *259*, *261*
Crews, D., 237, *257*
Crombie, G., 29–31, 48, *51*, 147, 149–151, *168*
Cronbach, L., 304, *321*
Crouch, N. S., 238n3, *259*
Crouter, A. C., 218, 224, *233*, *234*
Crowley, W. F., 250, *260*
Cudeck, R., 156, *168*
Curran, P. J., 125, *140*

Dabbs, J. M., 248, *258*
Dahlerup, D., 282, *295*
Dalton, B., 28, 31, 50, *51*
Daniels, J. A., 29, *53*
Davis, S., 337, *347*
Davis-Kean, P. E., 93, *113*, 174, 175, *190*, *191*
Deci, E. L., 172, 178, *190*
De Lisi, R., 57n1, *80*
Dessens, A. B., 251, *259*
Dick, D. M., *262*
Dittmann, R. W., 244, 245, 247, *259*
Dodge, K. A., *52*
Dolezal, C., *261*
Domene, J. F., 109, *112*, 208, *214*
Donohue, S., *81*
Doolittle, A. E., 58, *80*
Doty, N., 337, *347*
Dow, K. L., 4, *22*
Drop, S. L. S., 251, *259*
Duck, S. C., 244, 252, *257*
Dumka, L. E., 28, *52*
Duncan, S. C., 147, 155, *169*
Duncan, T. E., 147, 155, 156, *169*
Durik, A., 174, 178, *190*
Durik, A. M., 89, *113*
Du Toit, M., 132n1, *141*
Du Toit, S., 132n1, *141*

Eagly, A. H., 248, 256, *264*
Eaton, G. G., 248, *259*
Eccles, J. S., 4, 5, *22–24*, 31, 33, 47, *51*, 56, 57, 76–78, *80*, 82, 87, 89, 92, 93, 95, 106, 107, *111–113*, 116, 118–123, 125, 135, 138, 139,

140–143, 147, 148, 167, 169, 174, 175, 189–191, 196–200, 203, 207, 211–214, 216–219, 221, 229, 230, 232, 233, 255, 260, 272, 295

Eccles (Parsons), J. S., 5, 12, 15, 22, 87, 89, 92, 93, 106, 107, 111, 112,197, 212, 213, 216–218, 225, 228–230, 233

Edler, E., 29, 54

Edman, G., 247, 260

Ehrhardt, A. A., 238, 240, 247, 259, 262

Eichstedt, J. A., 253, 263

Eisenhart, M. A., 207, 212

Elizabeth, P. H., 246, 259

Elliott, R., 176, 191

Ellis, C. M., 341, 347

Emrich, C., 307, 321

Epperson, D. L., 176, 191

Equal Employment Opportunity Commission, 332, 342, 347

Equal Pay Act of 1963, 347

Erdoğmuş, N., 282, 296

Ernest, P., 78, 80

Ethington, C. A., 5, 22, 107, 111

Etzkowitz, H., 299, 300, 304, 321

European Commission, 327n, 329, 337–339, 343n, 347

European Trade Union Confederation, 341, 347

European Women's Lobby, 333, 347

EUROSTAT, 272, 273, 295

Fabes, R. A., 249, 259, 261

Fagot, B. I., 246, 262

Faiman, C., 237, 263

Fair Labor Standards Act of 1938, 347

Family and Medical Leave Act of 1993, 347

Fane, B. A., 250, 260

Farmer, H. S., 28, 29, 31, 32, 47, 52, 176, 190, 197, 199, 212

Farnsworth, L., 299, 320

Farrell, J., 338, 347

Feather, N. T., 122, 140, 198, 207, 212

Feingold, A., 6, 22

Feldhusen, J. F., 29, 52

Fennema, E., 6, 22, 24, 174, 190

Fielden, J. A., 248, 258

Finch, J. F., 125, 140

Finegan, J. A., 246, 259

Finken, L. L., 217, 233

Finn, J. D., 55, 80

Fitzgerald, L. F., 92, 112

Flanagan, C. A., 51, 212

Fleetwood, S., 270, 294

Fleming, S., 264

Forgasz, H. J., 88, 89, 90, 111, 112

Forsman, M., 250, 260

Fortier, M. S., 176, 178, 187, 188, 190

Fouad, N. A., 29, 52

Francis, B., 29, 30, 52

Franz, J. R., 245, 260

Fraser, B. J., 182, 190

Fredricks, J., 175, 190

Freedman-Doan, C., 217, 232

Friedman, L., 6, 22, 58, 68, 81

Frome, P. M., 175, 189. 197, 212, 217, 232

Frost, L. A., 6, 22, 174, 190

Frost-Olsen, S., 191

Fuligni, A. J., 148, 169

Fuller, C., 198, 214

Futterman, R., 22, 80, 93, 111, 112, 140, 197, 198, 211, 213

Galef, B. G., 237, 246, 254, 258

Garrett, J., 57, 82, 123, 138, 141, 142, 197, 213

Gassin, E. A., 29, 31, 52

Gearhart, J. P., 238n3, 245, 261, 262, 264

Geffner, M. E., 262

Geis, F. L., 314, 321

Gerber, S. B., 55, 80

Gibbons, M., 327, 347

Gilbert, L. A., 208, 212

Glickman, S. E., 248, 262

Goff, S. B., 22, 80, 93, 111, 112, 140, 197, 198, 211, 213

Golding, J., 245, 260

Goldman-Rakic, P. S., 237, *258*
Goldsmith, E. B., 230, *233*
Göle, N., 268, 269, *295*
Golombok, S., 245, *260*
Goodnow, J. J., 93, *110*
Gottesman, I. I., 248, 250, *262*
Gottfredson, L. S., 28, *52*, 207, *212*
Gouzevitch, D., 326, *347*
Gouzevitch, I., 326, *347*
Goy, R. W., 237, 244, 248, *259*
Green, D. R., 93, *111*
Green, R., 246, *259*
Greene, D. M., 318, *321*
Griffin, N. L., 217, *233*
Grimshaw, G. M., 246, 250, *259*
Grön, G., 253, *259*
Grover, S., *264*
Gruehn, S., 75, *82*, 115, 121, 124, 137, 139, *140, 142*
Gruen, R. S., *261*
Guay, F., 183, *191*, 198, *213*
Güvenç, B., 283, *295*
Guzzetti, B., 272, *295*

Hackett, G., 47, *52, 53,* 56, 73, *80, 81,* 197, 198, *211, 261*
Hagger, C., 237, *257*
Hall, R. M., 188, *190,* 196, *212*
Hallett, M. B., 208, *212*
Halpern, D. F., 250, *259*
Hampson, E., 250, *259*
Hanish, L. D., 249, *259*
Harold, R., 5, *22*
Harold, R. D., 77, 78, *80*
Hartung, P. J., 50, *53,* 229, *233*
Harvey, M., 198, *213*
Hassett, J. M., 253, *260*
Hau, K.-T., 117, *141*
Hayes, A., 198, *212*
Healy, G., 267, 268, 270, 283, 284, *295, 296*
Hedin, B. A., 188, *190*
Helleday, J., 247, 250, *260*
Heller, K. A., 4, *22,* 87, *111*
Helwig, A. A., 218, *233*
Henderson, B. A., 246, *260*

Hernandez, D., 198, *214*
Hersh, M., 272, *295*
Hewitt, N. M., 175, 188, *191*
Heyn, S., 124, *140*
Hier, D. B., 250, *260*
Higuchi, K., 342, *347*
Hill, N. E., 28, 31, *52*
Hill, O. W., 188, *190*
Hill, P., 95, *112*
Hindmarsh, P., *262*
Hines, M., 243–245, 249–251, *257, 258, 260, 262*
Hochschild, A. R., 208, *212*
Hofacker, C., 230, *233*
Hoffer, T. B., 9, *23,* 58, *81*
Hoffman, J. J., 230, *233*
Holland, D. C., 207, *212*
Hollenshead, C., 305, *322*
Hollinger, C. L., 198, *212*
Holton, G., 300, 304, *321*
Hood, J., *264*
Hoogland, J. J., 146, *168*
Hoogstra, L., 57, *82*
Hoogstra, L. A., 57, *81*
Hopp, C., 6, *22,* 174, *190*
Hosenfeld, I., 128, *141*
House of Representatives Standing Committee on Education and Training, 88, *111*
Huang, G., 328, *348*
Hubbard, M., 35, *52*
Hughes, I. A., 245, *260*
Hull, E. M., 245, *260*
Hunt, J. B., 55, *81*
Hutson, J., *264*
Hyde, J. S., 6, *22,* 174, 178, 188, *190,* 250, *260*

Iijima, M., 253, *260*
International Labour Organization, 323, 326, 329–331, 335, 336n, 337–342, *348*
International Labour Organization LABORSTA, 326, 329, 332, 339, 340, *348*
Ismail, M., 272, *295*

Jacobs, J. E., 4, 5, *22*, *23*, 28, *52*, 118, 120, *141*, 147, 148, 167, 168, *169*, 174, *190*, 196–198, *212*, *213*, 216–219, 221, 224, 225, 229, 230, 232, *233*, 255, 260, 272, *295*

Japan NGO Network for CEDAW, 341, 342, *348*

Jayawardena, K., 268, *295*

Jensen, J. A., 57, *81*

Jodl, K. M., 5, *23*

Johnston, K. J., 245, *260*

Jonik, R. H., 248, *256*

Jonung, C., 338, *349*

Jöreskog, K. G., 132n1, *141*, 156, *169*

Joslyn, W. D., 248, *260*

Jozefowicz, D. M., 197, 198, 199, 203, *211*, *213*

Kaczala, C. M., 5, 15, *22*, 80, 93, *111*, *112*, *140*, 148, *169*, 197, 198, *211*, 213, 216, 233

Kahle, J., 5, *23*

Kahn, J. V., 59, *80*

Kandiyoti, D., 269, 284, 292, *295*

Kappes, M. E., *259*

Kappes, M. H., *259*

Kaprio, J., *262*

Kaufman, F., 249, *260*

Kaufman, P., 57, *81*

Keat, R., 270, *295*

Keating, D. P., 34, 37, *54*, 109, *112*, 208, *214*

Keiley, M. K., 160, 162, *169*

Kelly, K. R., 29, *52*

Kemelgor, C., 299, *321*

Kilpatrick, J. R., 57, 75, *81*

Kimball, M. M., 6, *23*

Kimmel, L., 9, *23*, 58, *81*

Kittok, R., 248, *258*

Klein, S., 332, *348*

Klorman, R., 239, *262*

Knickmeyer, R. C., 246, *261*

Köller, O., 57, *82*, 116–119, 121, 123, 124, 128, 138, *140–142*, 197, *213*

Konami, Y., 324, 328, 329, *350*

Koushki, P. A., 272, *295*

Kovenock, J., 245, *263*

Krapp, A., 118, *141*

Küskü, F., 267, 270, 272, 282, *295*, *296*

Lamon, S. J., 6, *22*

Landy, C. L., 253, *261*

Lane, D. M., 307, *321*

Langford, J. E., *52*

Lanza, S., 118, *141*, 167, *169*, 197, *213*, 255, 260, 272, *295*

Lapan, R. T., 47, *52*

Larkin, A. M., 272, *295*

Larose, S., 174, 183, 187, *190*, *191*, 198, *213*

Larson, L. M., 29, *53*

Larsson, A., 244, *262*, *263*

LaVaque-Manty, D., 307, 311, 320, *321*

Layder, D., 270, 271, *295*

Leder, G. C., 88, 89, 90, *111*, *112*

Lee, J. D., 5, *23*, 272, *295*

Lee, S., 342, *348*

Lee, V. E., 57, *81*, 198, 199, *214*

Leinonen, T., 218, *233*

Lent, R. W., 47, *53*, 56, *81*

Leong, F. T. L., 50, *53*

Leveroni, C. L., 247, *261*

Levy, F., 55, *81*

Lewis, P., *52*

Li, F., 155, *169*

Liao, L.-M., 238n3, *259*, *261*

Lightbody, P., 174, *190*

Lingard, B., 88, *112*

Linn, M. C., 6, *23*

Linver, M. R., 175, *191*

Lips, H. M., 4, *23*, 88, *112*, 198, *213*, 229, *233*

Liroff, E. R., 253, *257*

Little, T. D., 168, *169*

Liu, C., 338, *348*

Livingstone, D. W., 338, *348*

Loehlin, J. C., 246, 248, *261*

Long, J. S., 299, *321*

Lopez-Claros, A., 326, 329, 336n, 338, *348*

Lord, S. E., 123, *140*

Losier, G. F., 182, *191*
Low, H., 248, *262*
Low, K. S. D., 244, *261*
Lubinski, D., 6, *23*, 28, *54*, 137, *141*, 208, *213*
Lüdtke, O., 119, 125, *141*, *142*
Lupart, J. L., 216, *233*
Lutter, C. D., 248, *258*
Lutz, M. M., 209, *213*

Ma, X., 56, 57, 76–79, *81*, 176, 187, *191*
Maaz, K., 137, *143*
MacCann, R., 90, *112*
Maccoby, E. E., 249, 255, *261*
Mac Iver, D., *51*, 219, *232*
Madill, H. M., *51*
Madsen, E. R., 57, *81*
Maier, S., 336, *348*
Malanchuk, O., 5, *23*, 174, *190*
Malley, J., 302, *321*
Malley, J. E., 307, 320, *321*
Malouf, M. A., 238n3, *264*
Mandleco, B. L., *191*
Marchant, G. J., 182, *191*
Marini, M. M., 198, *213*
Marion, S. F., 57, *81*
Marjoribanks, K., 28, 29, 31, 32, 48, *53*
Marsh, H. W., 12, *23*, 116–120, 125, 135, *141*
Martell, R. F., 307, *321*
Martin, A. J., 88, *112*
Martin, C. L., 248, 249, 259, *261*, *263*
Martin, N. G., 246, 248, *261*
Martino, W., 88, *112*
Masters, G., 95, *112*
Mathews, G. A., *260*
Matier, M., 176, *191*
Mattsson, A., 248, *262*
Mau, W. C., 28–32, *53*, 196, *213*
Mazur, A., 248, *258*
Mazur, T., 251, *261*
McAllister, T., *81*
McArdle, P., 250, *261*
McBrair, M. C., 237, *259*
McBride, B. A., 209, *213*
McCarthy, M. M., 237, *257*

McCartney, K., 254, *263*
McCloy, R., *52*
McEwen, B. S., 237, *259*
McGillicuddy-De Lisi, A., 57n1, *80*
McGue, M., 248, *262*
McHale, S. M., 218, *234*
McIlwee, J. S., 325, *349*
McNeilly, M. K., *191*
McWhirter, E. H., 29, 47, *53*
Meck, W. H., 253, *264*
Meece, J. L., 4, 5, 22–23, *80*, 87, 93, 107, *111*, *112*, 140, 148, 169, 197, 198, *211–213*
Meinster, M. O., 208, *213*
Melson, G. F., 247, *261*
Mendez, L. M. R., 32, *53*, 208, *213*
Meredith, W., 126, *141*
Metcalfe, S., *264*
Meyer-Bahlburg, H. F. L., 238, 244, 247, 249, 251, 259, *261*, *264*
Michael, A., 5, *23*
Midgley, C., *51*, *80*, 107, *111*, 140, 211
Migeon, C. J., 238n3, *261*, *264*
Miller, C., *212*
Miller, J. D., 9, *23*, 58, 60, 64, *81*
Miller Buchanan, C., *51*
Mills, M., 88, *112*
Minamoto, F., 253, *260*
Ministère de l'Éducation, du Loisir et des Sports du Québec, 171, 188, *191*
Ministry of Education, Science and Technology, Sports and Culture, 329, *349*
Ministry of Health, Labour and Welfare, 325, 326, 335, *349*
Minto, C. L., 238n3, 259, *261*
Mintrom, M., 331, *350*
Min-Woptika, S., 331, *349*
Mogotsi, M., 272, *294*
Möller, J., 116, 117, 138, *141*, *142*
Monaghan, E. P., 248, *262*
Money, J., 238, 240, 247, *262*
Montgomerie, T. C., *51*
Morishima, A., *261*
Morrill, W. H., 47, *52*

Morris, B., 338, *349*
Morris, N. M., 245, *263*
Morstad, A. L., 251, *259*
Mossenson, L., 95, *112*
Murnane, R., 55, *81*
Muthén, B. O., 127, *142*
Muthén, L. K., 127, *142*

Nagy, G., 57, *82*, 123, *142*, 197, 198, *213*
Nakao, K., 224, *233*
Nakeo, K., 202, *213*
Nash, S. C., 198, *213*
Nasir, N. S., 20, *24*
National Center for Education Statistics, 3, *23*, 195–198, *213, 214*
National Committee for the Mathematical Sciences of the Australian Academy of Science, 4, *23*
National Council of Teachers of Mathematics, 56, 77, *82*
National Education Longitudinal Study of 1988, 32, *53*
National Science Board, Committee on Education and Human Resources, Task Force on National Workforce Policies for Science and Engineering, 4, *23*
National Science Foundation, 3, 4, *24*, 196, *214*, 215, *233*, 325, 326, 328, *349*
National Science Foundation, Division of Science Resources and Statistics, 115, *142*
National Science Foundation, Division of Science Resources Statistics, 301, *321*, 328, *349*
Natsuko, I., 323, 335, 341, 342, *349*
Nauta, M. M., 176, *191*
Neathey, F., 337, *347*
Nelson, C., 9, *23*, 58, *81*
Nelson, L., *191*
New, M. I., *261*
Nguyen, D., 28, *53*
Nicolaid, E., 326, *346*
Nishita, J. K., 245, *260*

Nordenström, A., 244, 245, *262, 263*
Northam, E., *264*
Nottingham, J., *52*
Novack, D. R., 198, 207, *214*
Novack, L. L., 198, 207, *214*
Nowlin, P., *52*
Nussbaum, M. C., 324, *349*

Oakes, J., 196, 200, *214*
Oatley, K., 49, *51*
Obeid, J. S., *261*
O'Brien, K. M., 57, *82*, 89, *113*, 175, *191*, 197, *214*
O'Doherty, S., 88, *112*
Office of Economic and Cultural Development, 339, 340, 342, *349*
Office of Michigan Merit Award Program, 124, *142*
Ohmi, N., 341, *349*
Oldenziel, R., 323–325, *346, 349*
Oliver, G., *264*
Olson, D. H., 182, *189*
Olweus, D., 248, *262*
O'Neill, R., 119, *141*
O*NET OnLine, 35, *53*
Orlebeke, J. F., 248, *258*
Osgood, D. W., 118, *141*, 197, *213*, 255, *260*, 272, *295*
Osgood, W., 167, *169*
Osipow, S. H., 92, *112*
Özbilgin, M. F., 267, 268, 270, 282–284, 287, 288, *295–297*
Özkale, L., 267, 270, 272, *295, 296*

Packard, B. W., 28, *53*
Paid Family and Medical Leave Act of 2005, *349*
Pajares, F., 173, 174, *191*, 229, *234*, 273, *297*
Palmer, F., 329, *346*
Parker, J. G., 249, *263*
Parsons, J. E., 4, *22*, 87, *111*, 148, *169*
Parsons, S., 28, 29, *54*
Pascal, S. J., 253, *257*
Pasterski, V. L., 244, *260, 262*
Pastorelli, C., 47, *51*, 77, *80*

Patomaki, H., 271, *296*
Paulson, S. E., 182, *191*
Paycheck Fairness Act, *349*
Peck, S. C., 20, *24*
Peker, M., 285, *296*
Pelletier, L. G., 182, *192*
Perrone, K. M., 47, *53*
Persson, I., 338, *349*
Petersen, A. C., 6, *23*
Peterson, J., 334n, *349*
Pettus, W. C., 188, *190*
Phoenix, C. H., 248, *259*
Pintrich, P. R., 118, *143*
Pohlmann, B., 138, *142*
Pollak, S. D., 239, *262*
Porfeli, E. J., 229, *233*
Porter, N., 314, *321*
Poulin-Dubois, D., 253, *263*
Psacharopoulos, G., 338, *350*
Pulkkinen, L., *262*

Quadagno, D. M., 238, *262*
Quadagno, J. S., 238, *262*
Quatman, T., 29, *54*

Raggatt, P., *261*
Ramirez, C. A., 28, *52*
Ransley, P. G., 238n3, *261*
Ranson, G., 272, *296*
Ratelle, C. F., 183, *191*, 198, *213*
Raty, H., 218, *233*
Raudenbush, S. W., 33, 38, *51*, *53*, 126, *140*, 168, *168*
Reese, C., 207, 208, *214*
Regan, J., 337, *347*
Reiner, W. G., 245, *262*
Reinisch, J. M., 248, *262*
Resnick, S. M., 243, 248, 250, 252, 257, 258, *262*
Reuman, D., *51*, 219, *232*
Reuman, D. A., *212*
Reyes, F. I., 237, *263*
Richardson, P. W., 5, *24*
Riepe, M. W., 253, *259*
Rimmele, R., *140*
Risinger, R., 47, *52*, 176, *190*, 197, *212*

Ritzen, E. M., 247, 250, *260*
Ritzke, D., 306, *321*
Rivkin, D., *52*
Robert, J. M., 271, *296*
Roberts, B. W., 244, *261*
Roberts, J., 271, *294*
Robinson, C. C., *191*
Robinson, J. G., 325, *348*
Rock, J. A., *261*
Rodgers, C. S., 246, *262*
Roeder, P. M., *140*
Roeser, R. W., 7, 20, *24*, 123, *140*, 175, *190*
Rogosa, D., 33, *53*
Rojewski, J. W., 29, 31, 32, *53*
Rose, K. C., 208, *213*
Rose, R. J., 246, 248, *262*
Rosenthal, R., 6, *24*
Rotella, S. C., 28, *52*
Rothlisberg, B. A., 182, *191*
Rounds, J., 244, *261*
Rovet, J. F., 250, *259*
Roy, R., 174, 187, *190*
Rubin, D. B., 6, *24*, 127, *142*
Rubin, K. H., 248, *263*
Ruble, D. N., 248–250, 256, *263*
Rust, J., 245, *260*
Ryan, B. C., 237, 246, *263*
Ryan, M., 6, *22*, 174, *190*
Ryan, R. M., 172, 178, *190*

Sağlamer, G., 267, *296*
Saldana, D., 57, 73, *82*
Sameroff, A., 5, *23*
Sanders, C. E., 6, *23*
Sanders, K., 315, *320*
Sandler, B. R., *190*, 196, *212*
Saner, H., 33, *53*
Satorra, A., 127, *142*
Sayer, A. G., 146, 148, 157, *169*
Scantlebury, K., 5, *23*
Scarr, S., 254, *263*
Schaefers, K. G., 176, 177, 187, *191*
Schafer, J. L., 95, *112*, 127, *142*
Schalling, D., 248, *262*
Schiefele, U., 118, *140*, 196, *212*

Schnabel, K. U., 75, *82*, 115, 118, 121, 124, 136, 137, 139, *140–142*, 168, *169*

Schoon, I., 28, 29, *54*, 177, *191*

Schor, J. B., 289, *296*

Schretlen, P., 237n2, *257*

Schulenberg, J. E., 224, *233*

Schwanzer, A., 125, *142*

Scott, J., 176, *191*

Sears, A. W., 300, *321*

Sedlacek, W. E., 47, *53*

Sells, L. W., 4, 9, *24*, 30, *54*, 55, *82*, 87, *112*, 115, 139, *142*, 197, *214*

Sen, M. G., 253, *263*

Senécal, C., 183, *191*, 198, *213*

Serbin, L. A., 253, *263*

Servin, A., 244, 245, 249, *262, 263*

Seyman, Y., 287, *296*

Seymour, E., 175, 188, *191*, 196, *214*

Shapka, J. D., 34, 35, 37, *54*, 109, *112*, 208, *214*

Shaw, L., 342, *348*

Shelley, G., 248, *258*

Sherman, J. A., 30, *54*

Shernoff, D. J., 57, *82*

Shimshi, M., *261*

Siann, G., 5, *24*, 174, *190*, 272, *296*

Siebert, E. R., 253, *260*

Signer, B., 57, 73, *82*

Simpkins, S. D., 93, *113*

Sinclair, A., *264*

Singer, J. D., 33, 38, *54*

Siryk, B., 182, *189*

Sitarenios, G., 246, *259*

Siwers, B., 247, *260*

Slijper, F. M. E., 251, *259*

Sloan, M. E., 324, 325, *350*

Smail, P. J., 237, *263*

Smoller, J., 174, *192*

Snellman, L., 218, *233*

Snyder, A. M., 245, *260*

Snyder, E., 243, 244, 249, *258*

Solar, C., 89, *112*

Solomon, B. M., 324, *350*

Sonnert, G., 300, 304, *321*

Sörbom, D., 132n1, *141*, 156, *169*

Spade, J., 207, 208, *214*

Speiser, P. W., 238, *263*

Spitzer, M., 253, 259

Squire, P. J., 272, *294*

Stanley, J. C., 5, *21*

Statistisches Bundesamt, 115, *142*

Steele, C., 250, 256, *263*

Stegner, H., *259*

Steiger, J., 311, *321*

Steinpreis, R. E., 306, *321*

Stewart, A. J., 302, *321*, 307, 311, 312, 320, *321*

Stewin, L. L., *51*

Stinson, D. W., 55, *82*

Stocks, R., 174, *190*

Streblow, L., 138, *142*

Strenta, C. A., 176, 188, *191*

Stromquist, N., 326, 345, *350*

Stryker, L. A., 155, *169*

Stubbs, J., 302, *321*

Subotnik, R. F., 207, *214*

Sullins, E. S., 198, 207, *214*

Swanson, J. L., 244, *263*

Sydow, H., 125, *142*

Taddese, N., 328, *347*

Tanner, J. L., 224, *232*

Tartre, L. A., 6, *24*

Tashiro, J. S., 198, *214*

Taylor, K., *261*

Tekeli, S., 269, *296*

Telfer, J., 216, *233*

Tharp, G., 248, *258*

Thatcher, J. E., 239, *262*

Thom, Mary, 337, *350*

Tinker, I., 338, *350*

Tinto, V., 174, *191*

Title IX, Education Amendments of 1972, *350*

Tomczak, R., 253, *259*

Tomlinson-Keasey, C., 207, *214*

Toska, Z., 269, *296*

Tovell, D. R., *51*

Trautwein, U., 57, *82*, 119, 120, 123, 125, *141–142*, 197, *213*

Treas, J., 202, *213*, 224, *233*

True, J., 331, *350*

Trusty, J., 224, *234*

Tsugawa, A., 324, 328, 329, *350*
Tsuya, N. O., 345, *350*
Türkiye Bankalar Birliği, 287, *297*

Udry, J. R., 245, *263*
United Nations Department of
  Economic and Social Affairs,
  331, *350*
United Nations Development Program,
  334n, *350*
United Nations Division for the
  Advancement of Women, 330,
  332, 334n, *350*
United Nations Division for the
  Advancement of Women,
  Department of Economic and
  Social Affairs, 330, *350*
United Nations Economic Commission
  for Europe, 327n, 340, *350*
United Nations Educational, Scientific
  and Cultural Organization, 326,
  331, *351*
United Nations Statistical Yearbook
  2000, 343, *351*
University of Michigan, 316n2, 317,
  319, *322*
University of Michigan M-Pathways
  Human Resources Management
  System, 302, *322*
Updegraff, K. A., 57, 77, *82*, 89, 93,
  113, 197, 198, 207, *214*, 218, *234*
Updegraff, K. J., 175, *191*
Urgan, M., 269, *297*
Urry, J., 270, *295*
U.S. Census Bureau, 64, *82*, 215, 226,
  234
U.S. Department of Education, 56, *82*
U.S. Department of Labor, Women's
  Bureau, 196, *214*
U.S. Department of Labor Employment
  and Training Administration, 91,
  96, *113*
U.S. Patent Office, 323–324, *351*
Uzzi, B., 299, *321*

Valdez, I., *81*
Valian, V., 299, 300, 303, 306, 307, *322*

Vallerand, R. J., 174, 182, 187, *191, 192*
van de Beek, C., 245, *258*
Vandenbergh, J. G., 237, 246, *263*
van Goozen, S. H. M., 248, *258*
VanLeuvan, P., 29, 30, 54, 272, *297*
Vernon, M. K., 224, *232*
Vida, M., 77, 78, 82, 122, 138, *140*,
  175, *190*
Viken, R. J., *262*
Vondracek, F. W., 224, 229, *233*

Walberg, H., 56, *82*
Wallen, K., 237, 239, 253, 254, 260,
  263
Walsh, D., 174, *190*
Walsh, M. L., 248, *256*
Walter, E., 328, *347*
Waltman, J., 305, *322*
Walton, M., 341, *351*
Wang, J., 56, *81*
Wang, M. C., 55, *80*
Ward, K., 315, *320*
Wardrop, J. L., 28, 47, *52*, 176, *190*,
  197, *212*
Ware, N. C., 57, *81*, 198, 199, *214*
Warne, G., 238n3, *264*
Watermann, R., 137, *143*
Watson, C. M., 29–31, 48, 50, *54*
Watt, H. M. G., 5, 24, 56, 57, 75, 77,
  78, 83, 89, 91, 93, 95, 97, 107,
  109, 113, 118, 120, *143*, 167,
  168, *169*, 175, 176, *192*,
  196–198, 207, *212, 214*, 255,
  264, 272, *297*
Weaver, K. D., 215, *232*
Webb, R. M., 28, *54*
Wedell, A., 244, *262*
Wellborn, J. G., 172, 178, *189*
Wendler, C., 4, *21*, 88, *110*
West, S. G., 125, *140*
Wheelwright, S., *261*
White, P. C., 238, *263*
Wigfield, A., 4, 5, *23*, 24, *51*, 87, 92,
  93, 95, 106, *111–113*, 118, 119,
  140, 141, 143, 167, *169*, 175,
  190, 196, 197, *212, 213*, 219,
  232, 255, 260, 272, *295*

Wight, C., 271, *296*
Wilkins, J., 76, *81*
Willett, J. B., 38, *54*, 146, 148, 157, 160, 162, *169*
Williams, C. L., 253, *264*
Williams, W., 272, *295*
Willis, S., 5, 6, *24*
Willison, R., 337, *347*
Willms, J. D., 38, *51*
Wilson, B. E., 250, *261*
Wilson, J. R., 28, 29, 32, *54*, 251, *259*
Wilson, J. W., 55, *83*
Wilson, P. A., 28, 29, 32, *54*
Wilson-Relyea, B. J., 56, *83*
Winebarger, A., 246, *262*
Winter, J. S. D., 237, *263*
Winter, T., *262*
Wisniewski, A. B., 238n3, 245, *261*, *264*
Witz, A., 272, *297*
Wong, A. K., 338, *351*
Wood, W., 248, 256, *264*
Woodhouse, C. R. J., 238n3, *259*, *261*

Woodward, D., 267, 268, 270, 283, 287, 288, *296*, *297*
World Bank, 334n, *351*
Wright, J. D., 217, *233*
Wunderlich, A. P., 253, *259*

Yee, D., *212*
Yeung, A. S., 117, 118, *141*
Yoder, J., 306, *322*
Yoneda, M., 335, *351*
Yoon, K. S., 217, *232*
Yoon, M., 244, *261*
Youniss, J., 174, *192*
Yuval-Davis, N., 268, *297*

Zachmann, K., 324, *346*
Zahidi, S., 326, 329, 336n, 338, *348*
Zeldin, A. L., 229, *234*, 273, *297*
Zengin-Arslan, B., 272, *297*
Zeytinoğlu, I. U., 284, *297*
Zucker, A., 312, *321*
Zucker, K. J., 249, 251, *264*

SUBJECT INDEX

Ability beliefs, 92–93
Abstract thinking, 9
Academic domain, 17, 18
    in Turkey, 283–286
    women faculty in. *See* Women
        faculty advancement (study)
Academic self-concepts, 116
Access strategies, 331
Accumulation of disadvantage, 303,
    306–307, 309, 313–314
Activism, stealth, 308
Adolescents, aggression in, 248
Adrenal androgens, 238
Adrenal glands, 236n1
Advanced course enrollment,
    128–129, 131–135, 137–138,
    175–176
ADVANCE program (at University of
    Michigan), 17–18, 300–307,
    310–315, 317, 319–320

Affirmative action programs, 344
    and female engineering students, 326
    in Japan, 335
    in United States, 332
Aggression, 237, 247–248, 254
Algebra II, 9, 69, 74, 77, 79
Androgen effects. *See* Prenatal androgen
    effects (study)
Androgenizing progestins, 248
Androgens, 16, 236n1
    dosage effect of, 244
    exposure to extreme sex-typical
        levels of, 237n2
    moderate exposure to, 243
    prenatal exposure to, 246
Androstenedione, 236n1
Antidiscrimination laws, in United
    States, 332
Application-oriented mathematics, 78
Article 14 (Japanese Constitution), 333

Article 24 (Japanese Constitution), 333
Arts, underrepresentation of men in
    the, 5
Asian countries, 4
Asian females, 68
Attachment, institutional, 186, 187
Attainment value, 118
Attitudes
    parental gender-role, 221–224, 229
    toward mathematics, 76–78,
        197–198
    toward science, 197–198
Australia. *See also* New South Wales,
    Australia
    advanced science/math education,
        participation levels in, 4
    government policy regarding girls'
        math education in, 88
    HDI/GEM/GDI/WEF/CEDAW
        ratification in, 334
    math courses in, 11
    sex-stereotyped career motivations
        in. *See* Sex-stereotyped career
        motivations (study)
Australian National University, 32
Austria, 327, 329, 334, 337, 340, 343
Autonomy support, 173, 176–178,
    183–185, 187

Babies, interest in, 247, 254
Bachelor's degrees in math or computer
    science, 115
Banking companies, 17
Bank workers, in Turkey, 286–291
"Barometer of modernization," 268
Barriers
    to academic employment, 285
    to bank jobs, 288, 290–291
    to professional plans, 208
Barriers to promotion, 17
Base model, 67
Basic Law for a Gender-Equal Society
    (Japan), 335
Behavior, hormones and, 239
Beijing Declaration and Platform for
    Action, 330

Belgium, 327, 334, 337, 340, 343
Belonging, feelings of, 174
Best practices document, 305
Between-person change model,
    154–159
BIJU. *See* "Learning Processes, Educa-
    tional Careers, and Psychosocial
    Development in Adolescence
    and Young Adulthood"
Biological predispositions, 15–16
Birth rates, 340
Black females, 68
Blair, Tony, 342
Block method, multiple-regression, 66
Bollinger, Lee, 316
Brain development, 237, 239
Bulgaria, 273
Bureau of Labor Statistics, 35

CAH. *See* Congenital adrenal
    hyperplasia
CAIS (complete androgen insensitivity
    syndrome), 245
Calculus, 9–10
    as critical filter on college major, 55,
        72, 75
    encouraging students to take, 76–77
    importance of taking, 57
Canada, 34
    HDI/GEM/GDI/WEF/CEDAW
        ratification in, 334
    high schools in, 33
    occupational-prestige index, lack of,
        48
Career, combining family with, 198–199
Career advising handbook, 314, 317
Career choices
    and mathematics coursework, 67–69
    measures of, 64–65
    statistical procedures for predicting,
        66–67
Career planning, 207–208
Career self-efficacy, 56, 73
CEDAW. *See* Convention for the
    Elimination of All Forms of
    Discrimination Against Women

Center for Research on Learning and
Teaching (CRLT) Players,
310–311, 317
CFI. *See* Comparative fit index
Chairing committees, 303, 315
Chairs, department, 305
Change group, 203–204
Childbearing penalties, 338, 339, 342
Child care, 209, 290, 318
Child-Care and Family-Care Leave Law
(Japan), 335
Child care leave, 342
Childrearing, 345
Child-specific beliefs, of parents,
218–219
Civil Rights Act of 1964, 332
Civil Rights Act of 1991, 332
Cloacal exstrophy, 245
Clustering effect, 126–127
Cognitive abilities, 249–251
Coleman, Mary Sue, 316, 318
College admission
and high school coursework, 12
in Turkey, 273
College enrollment
history of women's, 324–326
in science and engineering, 9–10
College majors
calculus as critical factor for female
choice of, 75
math achievement effect for male
choice of, 75–76
mathematics and choice of, 57
and mathematics coursework, 69–73
measures of, 64–65
statistical procedures for predicting,
67
Colleges and universities, anti-
discrimination role of, 345
Commission on the Advancement of
Women and Minorities in
Science, Engineering and
Technology Development, 328
Committees
leadership of, 313
service on, 303

Comparative fit index (CFI), 156–158
Competence, feelings of, 177, 178, 184,
186, 188
Complete androgen insensitivity syndrome (CAIS), 245
Computer science, 328
Confounding variables, 59
Congenital adrenal hyperplasia (CAH),
16, 238–256
characteristics of, 236
design of study, 240–243
environmental interactions of girls
with, 253–254
future research on, 255–256
and gendered occupational outcomes, 239
and hormonal influences on characteristics associated with gendered outcomes, 239–240
and hormonal influences on cognitive abilities, 249–251
and hormonal influences on gender
identity, 251
and hormonal influences on
personal/social behaviors,
247–248
and hormonal influences on sex-
typed activities/occupational
interests, 243–246
and hormonal influences on social
relationships, 248–249
males with, 242
overall adjustment of girls with,
251–252
psychological mechanisms associated
with, 252–253
and surgery, 238n3
Consciousness raising, 308
Contingent employees, 341
Contract employees, 341
Contract negotiations, 303
Convention for the Elimination of All
Forms of Discrimination Against
Women (CEDAW), 19,
330–332, 334, 335, 344, 345
Cooperative learning environments, 5

Corporate boards, 336
Corticosteroids, 245
Cortisols, 238
Cost, task-value, 118
Courant, Paul, 316
CRA. *See* Civil Rights Act of 1964;
    Civil Rights Act of 1991
Critical filter, math as, 8–10, 30, 33, 115
    and calculus, 72, 73
    in career choices, 87
    and longitudinal study, 45–46, 50
    Sells' identification of, 4
    for social stratification, 55–56
Critical mass, 282, 306–308
Critical realism, 270–271
CRLT Players. *See* Center for Research
    on Learning and Teaching Players
Cross-cultural studies, 21, 31
Curricular effects on career choices
    (study), 55–79
    calculus and female choice of college
        major, 75
    lack of mathematics coursework
        effects for females, 74–75
    math achievement and male choice
        of college major, 75–76
    method, 60–67
    negative mathematics coursework
        effect for males, 74
    policy implications of, 77–79
    results, 67–73
    retaining students in advanced
        mathematics courses, 76–77
Cyprus, 334

Decade for Women, 330
Demandingness, job. *See* Job demand-
    ingness
Denmark, 327, 329, 333, 334, 340, 342,
    343
Departmental climate, 304–305
Departmental Transformation Grants,
    315
Depression, 209
Developing Anti-Discrimination in Europe
    (Bell et al.), 333, 345
Dihydrotestosterone, 236n1

Doctoral degrees, 301, 328
Dominance analysis, 97
Domination and subordination,
    relations of, 311–312
"Double shifts," 17, 305
Drawings, 253
Dual-career couples, 208, 303, 317–318
d value, 97

Eastern Europe, 326, 329
Economic disadvantage, 19
Economic opportunity, 336
Economic participation, 336
Economics (major), 70, 72
Economic spheres, 336
Education. *See also* Title IX of 1972
    Education Amendments to the
    Higher Education Act
    of boys, 88
    as college major, 72, 73
    level of required, 203, 207
    parental levels of, 37
    progress in scientific, 326–330
Educational aspirations, 27
    and gender, 32, 46
    and gender/math achievement,
        43–45
    and mathematics, 56
    over time, 29, 36, 44–46
    of parents for children, 218–219
    and prestige level of occupation,
        28–30
    and real occupations, 28
    trajectories for, 41–45
Educational choices, gendered, 88–91
Educational productivity, model of, 56
Educational systems
    and mathematics coursework, 58
    in the United States and Germany,
        120–123, 136–137
EEOL (Equal Employment Opportunity
    Law) (Japan), 335
Elizabeth Crosby grants, 305, 314–315
Emergent global trends, for workplaces,
    340–344
Emotional adjustment, 251–252
Employment statistics, 343

Empowerment
    in economic spheres, 336
    in mathematics education, 78–79
Engineering
    faculty, 328
    historical basis for underutilization of
        women in, 324–326
    as male environment, 272
    male/female faculty percentages in,
        302
    math coursework in, and college-
        major selection of, 69, 72, 73
    persistence in, 177
Engineering students, 16–17
    female, 273, 324, 325, 328
    tertiary, 327, 328
    in Turkey, 271–282
Engineering students' beliefs (in Turkey)
    on gender and professional choice,
        274, 275
    on influence of close family mem-
        bers, 277, 282
    on influence of education, 277, 282
    on influence of family context, 277,
        282
    on influence of national context,
        277, 282
    on personal aptitude/interest in
        engineering, 276, 281
    on prospects in engineering, 274,
        275, 280
    on suitability of engineering fields to
        women, 277, 281
    on women engineers, 276, 280
    on women's interest in engineering,
        276, 280, 281
English achievement
    gendered perceptions of, 100–101
    in the United States vs. Germany,
        123–125
English courses/coursework
    contemporary English, 90, 91, 94,
        99, 100
    differences in U.S. and German, 138
    gender differences in selection of, 99,
        104–109
    in New South Wales, Australia, 90,
        91

3-unit English, 90, 91, 94, 99, 100
2-unit general English, 90, 91, 94,
    99, 100
    U.S. vs. German levels of, 125
English-related educational and career
    choices, 10–13, 92, 104–106,
    108–109
Environment, hormones and, 239,
    253–254
EQS program, 150, 157
Equal Employment Opportunity
    Commission, 332
Equal Employment Opportunity Law
    (EEOL) (Japan), 335
Equality in employment, 268
Equality profile, 18–19
Equal Pay Act of 1963, 332
Equal remuneration, 330
Equity, 305
Estradiol, 236n1
Estrogens, 236n1
Ethnicity–race, 66
    and occupational aspirations, 29, 57
    and persistence in S&T, 176
EU15. See European Union 15
EU25 (European Union 25), 329
European Commission, 337, 345
European Union, 283
    and antidiscrimination
        policies/treaties/multilateral
        agencies, 332, 333
    emergent global trends in, 341–344
    and historical basis for underutiliza-
        tion of women, 324–326
    pay-scale inequality in, 339, 340
    women's empowerment in, 336–338
    women's progress in scientific educa-
        tion in, 327, 329
    workplace policy implications/reform
        measures needed for, 345
European Union 15 (EU15), 323,
    326–329, 333, 335, 339, 342,
    344, 345
European Union 25 (EU25), 329
European Women's Lobby (EWL),
    333
EUROSTAT data, 272, 273
Evaluation bias, 307, 309, 314

EV theory. *See* Expectancy-value theory
EWL (European Women's Lobby), 333
Executives, female, 332
Expectancies
    of success, 118
    values vs., 93, 118, 197
Expectancy-value model, 11, 197
    of academic choice, 56
    for gendered educational/
        occupational choices, 92–93
    of gendered math participation, 87
Expectancy-value theory (EV theory),
    116, 118–120, 139

Faculty. *See also* Women faculty
        advancement (study)
    female, 328–329
    recruitment of, 307–310
    in Turkey, 283–286
Fair Labor Standards Act of 1938, 332
Family, combining career and, 198–199
Family and Medical Leave Act of 1993,
    344
Family-flexible jobs, 204, 206, 207, 210
Family-friendly policies, 305
Family leave, 344
Family-related influences, 14–16
Family-related partner policies, 317–318
Family support centers, 335
FASTER. *See* Friends and Allies of
        STRIDE Toward Equity in
        Recruiting
Fathers
    and child care, 318
    gender-typed occupational expecta-
        tions of, 226–228, 230
    and household duties, 209
Federally-funded school programs, 332
Feedback, 308
Female development, 236n1
Female-dominated occupations
    examples of, 201
    females changing to, 202
    flexibility of, 199
    self-concepts of ability in, 197–198
    underrepresentation of men in, 235

Females. *See also* Women
    with CAH. *See* Congenital adrenal
        hyperplasia
    learning environments for, 5
Feminization of jobs, 338
Fertility, 247
Fertility rates, 339, 340
Finland, 327, 331, 333, 334, 340, 343
Flexible scheduling, 209, 341–342
Flexible tenure, 318
Fortune magazine, 338
4-unit (4U), 90
France, 327, 329, 334, 340, 343
Friends and Allies of STRIDE Toward
        Equity in Recruiting (FASTER),
        308, 309
Full professorship
    women's share of positions of,
        327–329
    workshops for the newly promoted
        to, 315
Future Business Leaders of America, 209

GDI. *See* Gender development indicator
GEM. *See* Gender empowerment
        measure
Gender
    and earning potential, 4
    economic disadvantage of, 19
    and educational aspirations/math
        achievement, 43–45
    and longitudinal study, 46–47
    and math achievement, 6, 30–34
    and occupational prestige/math
        achievement, 40–41
    and parental influence on occupa-
        tional expectations, 15
    and persistence in S&T, 176, 177
    and self-perception of ability, 160–162
Gender bias, 306
Gender development indicator (GDI),
    333, 334
Gender discrimination, 304
Gender dysphoric, 251
Gendered occupational outcomes in
        Turkey (study), 267–294

bank workers (study 3), 286–291
   discussion, 291–294
   engineering students (study 1),
      271–282
   method, 270–271
   policy implications of, 294
   professional workers (study 2),
      283–286
   and women in Turkey, 267–270
Gender empowerment measure (GEM),
   333, 334
Gender identity, 251
Gender in Science and Engineering
   (GSE) Committee, 314, 316
Gender mainstreaming, 330, 333, 344
Gender outliers, 306
Gender role attitudes, 221–224, 229
Gender schemas, 306, 309, 314
Gender-specific socialization, 255
Gender stereotypes, 217–218
Gender symbols, 268
Gender tokenism, 305
Gender-typed occupational expectations,
   225–228
Gender visibility, 305–306, 315
Genitalia
   masculinized, 237, 238
   surgery on, 238n3
Germany
   bachelor's degrees in math/computer
      science in, 115
   course choices in, 116
   educational system in, 120–123
   employment statistics in, 343
   HDI/GEM/GDI/WEF/CEDAW
      ratification in, 334
   maternity leave in, 342
   professional wages in, 340
   school tracking in, 12
   women in government research in,
      329
   women's empowerment in, 336
   women's share of positions in, 327
Gifted students, 29, 32
Gini index, 334
Global perspective, 7

Goodness-of-fit statistics, 156–157. *See
   also* RMSEA
Gordon, Beate Sirota, 333
Government, women in, 336, 344
Government advisory councils, 335
Government policy, 48
GPA. *See* Grade point average
Grade 9
   math achievement in, 33, 40–41
   overall GPA in, 37
Grade 12
   enjoyment of science in, 198
   math coursework in, and college-
      major selection, 69–73
Grade 13, 34
Grade point average (GPA)
   Grade 9 overall, 37
   Grade 12 science, 176
   in science, 184
   and self-perception of ability, 163–167
Graduate students, 301, 328
Grants, 314–315
Greece, 325, 327, 334, 340, 343
Grooming, 253
Growth-curve modeling (hierarchical
   linear modeling), 13, 30, 32–33
GSE Committee. *See* Gender in Science
   and Engineering Committee
Gymnasium (German school), 12,
   121–123, 128, 137

Harassment, 289
Hauptschule (German school), 121
HDI. *See* Human development indicator
Health care, women's empowerment in,
   336
Helpfulness, 305
Helping professions, underrepresentation
   of men in the, 5
Hierarchical linear modeling, 38, 168
Higher education
   rate of return from, 339
   in Turkey, 283–286
   women's progress in scientific,
      326–330
Higher School Certificate (HSC), 90–91

High school course selection (study),
115–139
  course enrollment, 131–135
  gender/achievement/self-concept/
    intrinsic value in, 129–131
  gender differences in, 127–129
  and gendered occupational choices,
    137–138
  in Germany vs. the United States,
    116, 120–121
  I/E model/EV model/gender effects,
    116–120
  impact of educational systems on,
    136–137
  limitations/outlook, 138–139
  method, 123–127
  purpose of study, 122–123
  results, 127–135
High School Transcript Study, 55
Hippocampus, 237
Hiring packages, initial, 303
Hormonal influences, 236–256
  on behavior, 236–240
  CAH's importance in understanding,
    239
  on characteristics associated with
    gendered outcomes, 239–240
  on cognitive abilities, 249–251
  design of study, 240–243
  and environmental interactions,
    253–254
  future research on, 255–256
  on gender identity, 251
  on overall adjustment, 251–252
  on personal/social behaviors,
    247–248
  psychological mechanisms associated
    with, 252–253
  on sex-typed activities/occupational
    interests, 243–246
  on social relationships, 248–249
Hormones, 16, 236–237
Household chores, 209, 290, 344, 345
Household structures, 303
HSC. *See* Higher School Certificate

Human development indicator (HDI),
333, 334
Humanities, underrepresentation of
  men in the, 5
Hypothalamus, 237

Iceland, 327, 329, 333, 334, 340, 343
ICT. *See* Information communication
  technology
Idiopathic hypogonadotropic hypogo-
  nadism, 250
I/E model. *See* Internal/external frame of
  reference model
ILO. *See* International Labor Organi-
  zation
ILO LABORSTA database, 332, 339
Individualized learning environments, 5
Information communication technology
  (ICT), 323, 327, 337, 341–342
Inquiry Into the Education of Boys, 88
Interactive theater, 310–311
Internal/external frame of reference
  model (I/E model), 116–120
International Labor Organization
  (ILO), 330, 337
International Standard Classification of
  Occupations (ISCO-88), 327
International Women's Year, 330
Interventions to increase women's
  participation in STEM careers,
  6–7, 17–18
Intrinsic value
  and attitudes toward math/science,
    197, 198
  defined, 93, 118
  and English participation, 108
  gender differences in, 128
  and male-dominated occupational
    aspirations, 204, 206–207
  and math participation, 107
  measurement of, 210
  and self-concept, 119, 125–126
Involvement
  academic, 183, 185–187
  in academic work, 174, 177

emotional, 183
parental, 184, 185, 189
Ireland, 327, 334, 340, 343
ISCO-88 (International Standard Classification of Occupations), 327
Israel, 334
Istanbul Technical University (ITU), 271–282
Italy, 327, 329, 334, 340, 343
ITU. *See* Istanbul Technical University

Japan
and antidiscrimination policies/treaties/multilateral agencies, 331, 333–335
emergent global trends in, 340–344
and historical basis for underutilization of women, 324–326
pay-scale inequality in, 339, 340
women's empowerment in, 336, 337
women's progress in scientific education in, 327–329
workplace policy implications/reform measures needed for, 345
Job content, 199, 203
Job demandingness, 203, 207
Job flexibility (study), 195–210
analyses/results of, 203–207
and attitudes toward math/science, 197–198, 207
and career planning, 207–208
and combining career/family, 198–199, 207
and dual-career couples, 208
hypotheses for, 196–199
method, 200–203
and occupational characteristics, 199
policy implications for, 209
rationale for study, 199–200
Job satisfaction, 304
Junior colleges, 328

Kandiyoti, D., 269
Kemal, Mustafa, 269
Knowledge economy, 324

Knowledge workers, 341
Koza system, 345

Labor force, 325, 343
Labor laws. *See* Legislation, gender-equality
Labor shortages, 340–341
Lagrange Multiplier Test, 157
Language arts, self-perceived ability in, 157–161, 163–167
Latent growth curve (LGC) modeling, 13, 145–168
hierarchical linear modeling approach to, 168
measuring change over time with, 146–148
scarce applications of, 167
testing for academic grades as time-varying predictor of change, 162–167
testing for gender as time-invariant predictor of change, 159–162
testing for validity of multiple-domain, 148–159
within-person (Level 1) model, 148–154
Latinos, 57
Laval University, 172
Law (major), 70, 72
Lawsuits, 332, 333, 335, 345
Leadership roles, 307, 314
Leadership training, 313
"Leaky pipeline," 196, 299
Learning–earning link, 323
Learning environments, 5
"Learning Processes, Educational Careers, and Psychosocial Development in Adolescence and Young Adulthood" (BIJU), 123–133, 138
Legislation, gender-equality, 331–338
country-specific, 331–335
effectiveness of, 335–338
Level 1 (within-person) factors, 38, 148–154

Level 2 (between-person) factors, 38, 148, 154–159
LGC modeling. *See* Latent growth curve modeling
Liberal arts
    female faculty advancement in, 317
    math coursework in, and college-major selection of, 71–73
Life satisfaction, 4
Life sciences, 329
Lifestyle, personal, 17
Logistic regression, 204
Longitudinal studies, 7, 21, 32, 34–35
Longitudinal Study of American Youth (LSAY), 9, 58–60
Luxembourg, 334

Malaysia, 272
Male development, 236n1
Male-dominated occupations, 199, 201, 209
    concentration of males in, 88
    and females with CAH, 243–244
    and mothers' gender role attitudes, 222–224, 229
    underrepresentation of females in, 88
Males
    with CAH, 242
    educational needs of, 88
    in English-related careers, 108–109
    expected success in mathematics by, 56
    and household chores, 344
Male-typical activities, 243
Male-typical karyotype, 245
Management administration, 335–337
Manufacturing, women in, 329, 343
Mardia's normalized estimate, 156
Marriage, equal rights in, 333
Maternity leave, 342, 343
Maternity policies, 310
Math achievement, 8–10, 27–50
    and career choice, 59n2, 67–69
    and college majors, 73, 75–76
    early, 47
    in early high school, 30, 33

and educational aspirations/gender, 43–45
and gender, 6, 30–34
gendered perceptions of, 99–101
measures of, 64
and occupational achievement/gender, 40–41
scoring of, 36
in the United States vs. Germany, 123–125
and verbal achievement, 116
Math achievement longitudinal study, 34–50
    and critical filter model, 44–46
    and early math achievement, 47
    and gender effects, 46–47
    limitations/future directions of, 49–50
    method for, 34–37
    policy implications of, 47–49
    results of, 38–45
Math competence
    parents' beliefs regarding child's, 217–218
    perceived, 37
Math courses/coursework
    and career choices, 67–69
    and college majors, 69–73
    expectancy of success in learning, 56
    female self-selection out of, 57–58
    gender differences in selection of, 99, 101–103, 106–107
    lack-of-coursework effects for females, 74–75
    mathematics achievement vs., 59n2
    Maths in Practice (MIP), 90
    Maths in Society (MIS), 90
    4-unit (4U), 90
    3-unit (3U), 90
    measures of, 60–64
    negative effect for males, 74
    in New South Wales, Australia, 90, 91
    number of classes taken in, 57n1
    retaining students in advanced, 76–77
    U.S. vs. German levels of, 125

Mathematics
    as critical filter. *See* Critical filter,
        math as
    intrinsic value of, 210
    self-perceived ability in, 157–161,
        163–167
    student understanding of role of,
        78–79
Math-related educational and career
    choices, 103–104, 106–107
Math self-efficacy, 56
Maths in Practice (MIP), 90
Maths in Society (MIS), 90
Measurement model, 153
Media, 345
Medicine
    male/female faculty percentages in,
        302
    math coursework in, and college-
        major selection of, 71–73,
        76n4
    persistence in, 177
Men. *See* Males
Mentors/mentoring
    of female faculty, 304, 305, 316–317
    in ICT, 337
    lack of, 314
Michigan Study of Adolescent Life
    Transitions (MSALT), 123–134,
    138, 175, 200, 219–221
Ministry of Health, Labour and Welfare
    (Japan), 335
Ministry of Human Resources and
    Social Development (Canada),
    48
MIP (Maths in Practice), 90
MIS (Maths in Society), 90
Miscarriage, treatment for, 248
Missing data problem, 127
"Model global citizenship," 330
Modernization, 268
"Modified duties" policy, 318
"Mommy trap," 338
Monkeys, 237, 253, 254
"Most powerful women" (named by
    Fortune), 338

Mothers
    and child's educational aspirations,
        218–219
    education level of, 175
    gender-typed occupational expecta-
        tions of, 226–227, 230
    and male-dominated occupations,
        222–224, 229
    and self-efficacy, 221–223, 229
Motion, 253, 254
Motivation. *See* Scientific motivation;
    Sex-stereotyped career motiva-
    tions (study)
Motivational dispositions, 188–189
MSALT. *See* Michigan Study of Adoles-
    cent Life Transitions
Multiple-domain latent growth curve
    model, 148–159
    between-person, 154–159
    within-person, 148–154
Multiple imputation, 94, 95
Multiple regression techniques, 66

National Child Development Study,
    177
National Education Longitudinal Study
    of 1988 database, 32, 57
National identity formation, 268
National Opinion Research Council
    coding system, 224
National Science Foundation, 18, 75,
    300, 338
Natural sciences, 302, 329
Navigation task, 253
Negative coursework effect, for males,
    74
Netherlands, 327, 334, 340, 342, 343
Networking, 311–314
Network of Women Scientists and
    Engineers, 312
Neutral occupations, 199, 201, 202
New South Wales (NSW), Australia,
    11, 88–91
New Zealand, 334
Nonpermanent employment, 341, 342
Nontenured professorial positions, 328

Norway, 327, 329, 331, 333, 334, 340,
    343
NSW. *See* New South Wales, Australia

Occupational aspirations. *See also*
    Career choices
    and gender, 46–47
    gendered, 104–106
    and math achievement, 27
    measurement of, 201–202
    over time, 29–30, 196
    parental influence on, 15
    parental role in, 78
    of parents for children, 225–230
    and real occupations, 28
    and socioeconomic status, 57
Occupational choices, gendered, 90–92
Occupational classification system(s)
    Australian National University's, 32
    lack of Canadian, 48
    National Opinion Research Council's,
        224
    O*NET 98 content model, 91, 92
    Standard (U.S.), 35
Occupations
    characteristics of, 199, 203
    prestige level of. *See* Prestige level of
        occupation(s)
Odds ratios (ORs), 128–129
OECD (Office of Economic and
    Cultural Development), 340
Office of Economic and Cultural Devel-
    opment (OECD), 340
Offshore job displacement, 342
Öğrenci Seçme ve Yerleşturne Merkezi,
    273
O*NET 98 database, 35, 91, 92, 96
Ontario, 34
ORs. *See* Odds ratios
Ottoman Empire, 269
Ovaries, 236n1
Overall GPA, 37

Paid Family and Medical Leave Act of
    2005, 344
Parental care, 318

Parental communication, of expecta-
    tions, 15
Parental education, 37
Parental expectations, 174, 175
Parental support, 182–185, 187, 282
Parents
    antidiscrimination role of, 345
    career-aspirations encouragement
        role of, 78
    professional background of, 177
Parents' beliefs and expectations
    (study), 215–232
    child-specific role of, 218–219
    data set used in, 219–220
    gender role attitudes of parents
        (study 1), 221–224, 229
    gender-typed occupational expecta-
        tions of (study 3), 225–228,
        230–231
    general occupational expectations of
        (study 2), 224–225, 229–230
    policy implications of, 231–232
    questions presented by, 219
    role of general beliefs/behaviors,
        217–218
    theoretical perspective on, 216–217
Parent socialization model, 15,
    216–217, 225, 229–231
Partners' careers, 303, 310, 317–318
Part-time employment
    in academia, 319
    in Netherlands, 342
    women in, 341, 343
Paternity leave, 342
Patsy T. Mink Equal Opportunity in
    Education Act. *See* Title IX of
    1972 Education Amendments to
    the Higher Education Act
Paycheck Fairness Act of 2007, 344
Payment-to-education ratios, 323
Pay-scale inequality, 338–340
Peer preferences, 249
Penis, 245
Perceived Math Ability subscale,
    147–148
Perceived math competence, 37

Performance, undervaluing female, 306, 309

Permanent employment, 341, 342

Persistence in science and technology, 171–189
longitudinal studies of, 174–178
policy implications of, 189
and Québec Scientific Career Project, 178–186
sociomotivational model of, 172–174

Personal behaviors, hormonal influences on, 247–248

Personality factors, 177

Personal lifestyle, 17

Personal rate of return, 338

Phenylketonuria, 256

Physical science, 210

Physics, 328

"Pink" jobs, 325

Placenta, 236n1, 246

Playmates, 249

Policy implications
for Australian education, 88
for educational/occupational aspirations, 47–49
for female faculty advancement, 316–319
for job flexibility, 209
for math coursework, 58, 77–79
for parental expectations, 232
for persistence in science and technology, 189
for prenatal androgen, 254–256
for school curriculum, 77–79
for sex-stereotyped career motivations, 109–110
for Turkish employment, 294
for workplaces, 344–346

Portugal, 273, 327, 329, 334, 340, 343

Positive discrimination, 326. *See also* Affirmative action programs

Postsecondary education
degrees in, 195
and gender, 46–47
promotion of, 48–49

POWRE (Professional Opportunities for Women in Research and Education) awards, 338

Pregnancy, 245–246, 337, 342

Prenatal androgen effects (study), 235–256
on cognitive abilities, 249–251
environmental transactions, 253–254
on gender identity, 251
and hormones/behavior, 236–240
and overall adjustment, 251–252
on personal/social behaviors, 247–248
policy implications of, 254–256
psychological mechanisms, 252–253
on sex-typed activities/occupational interests, 243–246
on social relationships, 248–249
study design, 240–243

Presenting behavior, 237

Prestige level of occupation(s)
in academic domain, 301–302
aspirations over time for, 29, 36
and educational aspirations, 28–30
and gender, 40–41, 47
and math achievement, 40–41
and mathematics, 56
measures of, 64–65
and mother's job status, 175
and parental expectations, 224–225, 229–230
scoring of, 35
trajectories for, 38–41

Primates, 237, 254

Probationary period, 319

Proclamation of the Republic (of Turkey), 267–268

Professional careers, 16–17

Professional engineering organizations, 325

Professional Opportunities for Women in Research and Education (POWRE) awards, 338

Professional women, in Turkey, 269, 283–286

Progesterone, 236n1, 245
Provincial policy, 48
Psychological mechanisms, hormonal
    influences on, 252–253
Psychological well-being, 4
Psychosexual milestones, 249
Puberty, 236n1, 242
"Purpose in life," 209

QSCP. *See* Québec Scientific Career
    Project
Quasi-longitudinal study, 241
Québec, 171
Québec Scientific Career Project
    (QSCP), 172, 175, 178–187, 189
    implications of, 189
    individual differences in trajectories,
        180–181
    motivational/familial/pedagogical
        factors, 181–184
    overview of, 178–180
    sociomotivational factors, 184–186

Race. See Ethnicity–race
Race tokenism, 305
Realschule (German school), 121
Reasoning, 9
Recruitment, faculty, 307–310
Relations of domination and subordi-
    nation, 311–312
Reproductive rights, 342
Republican secularism, 268
Researchers, women as, 329
RMSEA. *See* Root-mean-square error of
    approximation
Rodents, 253
Role models, 209
    in engineering, 280, 281
    female faculty as, 300, 308
    and math curriculum, 78
    mother with high job status as, 175
    in Turkey, 269
Root-mean-square error of approximation
    (RMSEA), 156–158. *See also*
    Goodness-of-fit statistics
"Rosie the Riveter" campaign, 325

Rosser, Sue V., 337
Rotation task, 250
Rough-and-tumble play, 237, 241, 254
Rule-breaking behavior, 248

Salary raises, 307
School board policy, 48
Schooling, years of, 338
School programs, 332
Schools, anti-discrimination role of, 345
School tracking. *See* Tracking systems
Science
    enjoyment of, 198
    faculty, 328
    intrinsic value of, 210
    self-perceived ability in, 157–159,
        161–167
    women in, 329
Science, technology, engineering, and
    math fields. *See* STEM fields
Science and technology (S&T),
    171–178, 180
Science majors, 65n3
Science teacher, support from, 176, 178,
    187
Scientific boards, 331
Scientific education
    strategies for women in, 325
    women's access to, 324
    women's progress in, 326–330
Scientific motivation, 172–173,
    181–183, 185, 187–189
Search committees, faculty, 308
Secondary schools, in Germany, 120–123
"Second shift," 208
Secularism, 268
Sekuhara, 335
Self-concept, 118, 119, 125–126, 128,
    131–136, 197–198
    of math ability, 202–204, 206, 210
    of science ability, 210
Self-Description Questionnaire, 119
Self-determination, 172–174, 176, 183,
    184, 186, 187
Self-efficacy, 188, 198
    career, 56, 73

and gender role attitudes, 221–223, 229

and persistence, 172, 173

Self-perceived ability, 145–168

    academic grades as time-varying predictor of change, testing for, 162–167

    data used in, 147–148

    gender as time-invariant predictor of change, testing for, 159–162

    hypothesized models of, 151, 152

    in math, 37

    measuring change over time in, 146–148

    multiple-domain latent growth curve model, testing validity of, 148–159

Self-socialization, 255

Sells, Lucy, 4, 55, 87, 115

SEM. *See* Structural equation modeling

Sensation seeking, 248

Service industries, 343

SES. *See* Socioeconomic status

Sex hormones, 16, 236–237

Sex-stereotyped career motivations (study), 87–110

    educational choices, 88–91

    English participation, gendered, 107–109

    gender differences in participation, 98–99

    gender/motivation/achievement, 99–101

    influences on participation choices, 101–106

    math participation, gendered, 106–107

    method, 94–97

    occupational choices, 90–92

    policy implications for, 109–110

    rationale for study of, 88

    results, 98–109

    theories of, 92–93

Sexual harassment, 17, 289, 335

Sexual orientation, 249

Single mothers, 334

Single-sex schooling, 332, 344

Social behaviors, hormonal influences on, 247–248

Social classes, 269, 287, 292

Social environment, hormones and, 239

Social events, 313

Social learning theory, 272

Social relationships, hormonal influences on, 248–249

Social sciences, female faculty in, 302, 304

Social stratification, 55

Societal rate of return, 338

Society of Japanese Women Engineers, 325

Society of Japanese Women Scientists, 325

Society of Women Engineers, 325

Socioeconomic status (SES), 57, 66, 123

Sociomotivational factors, 184–186

Sociomotivational model, 13–14, 172–174

Soviet states, 326

The Space Between Us (C. Cockburn), 268

Spain, 327, 329, 334, 340, 343

Spatial skills, 6, 250, 251, 253, 254

S&T. *See* Science and technology

Stable group, 203, 204

Standard Occupational Classification System, 35

Statistics Canada, 48

Stealth activism, 308

STEM fields (in science, technology, engineering, and math)

    attracting more high school graduates into, 75

    and calculus, 78

    costs of underrepresentation of women in, 18, 65n.3

    data's importance in, 305–306

    female graduate students in, 301

    gender-related statistics for, 215

    historical basis for underutilization of women in, 324–326

STEM fields, *continued*
  hypotheses for low female participation in, 196–197
  interventions to increase women's participation in, 6–7
  shortage of people entering, 3–4
  tertiary students in, 327
  underrepresentation of women in, 195–196
  women faculty in. *See* Women faculty advancement (study)
Strategies and Tactics for Recruiting to Improve Diversity and Excellence (STRIDE), 307–310, 313, 315
STRIDE. *See* Strategies and Tactics for Recruiting to Improve Diversity and Excellence
Structural equation modeling (SEM), 145–146, 149, 150, 153, 154, 157, 162, 167–168
Structure–agency dualism, 271
Structured opportunities, 173, 177, 183, 185, 187
Student Attitude Questionnaire, 147–148
Student characteristics, measures of, 65, 66
Subordination, relations of domination and, 311–312
Success expectancies, 92, 93
Support
  autonomy, 173, 176–178, 183–185, 187
  parental, 182–185, 187, 282
  teacher, 176, 178, 182–185, 187
Sweden, 327, 329, 331, 333, 334, 340, 342, 343
Swedish Association for Female Engineering Students, 325
Switzerland, 327, 334, 340

Talent perceptions, 93
Task value, 118
Teacher support, 176, 178, 182–185, 187
Technology patents, 19
Telecommuting, 342
Temporary employees, 341

Tenure, 299, 302, 310, 318–319
Tertiary students
  rate of return for, 339
  women's share of, 327
Testes, 236n1, 237
Testosterone, 236n1
  and aggression, 248
  in amniotic fluid, 246
  in mother's blood, 245
  in prenatal males, 237
Theory-oriented mathematics, 78
Thom, Mary, 337–338
3-unit (3U), 90
Title IX of 1972 Education Amendments to the Higher Education Act, 325, 332, 344
Tokenism, 305
Tokens, perception of, 311
Tomboys, 240
Toy preferences, 241, 243, 244, 253
Tracking systems, 12
  in German schools, 121
  in U.S. schools, 60, 121
Training programs, 315
Transformation strategies, 331
Transparency, 305
Turkey, 16, 17
  class differences in, 269
  and European Union, 333
  rights of women in modern, 268–269
  women's role in modern, 267–268
Turkish Civil Code, 268
Turkish Constitution, 293
Turner syndrome, 247
21-hydroxylase deficiency, 240
Twins, 246, 248, 251
2-unit (2U), 90

UM. *See* University of Michigan
UNECE (United Nations Economic Commission for Europe), 340
Unemployed women, 343
UNESCO, 331
Uniformity, 305
Unions, 341, 344
United Kingdom, 325, 327, 334, 337, 340, 342, 343

United Nations, 330–331
United Nations Economic Commission
    for Europe (UNECE), 340
United States
    advanced science/math education
        participation levels in, 3–4
    and antidiscrimination
        policies/treaties/multilateral
        agencies, 332
    bachelor's degrees in math/computer
        science in, 115
    course choices in, 116
    educational system in, 120–123
    emergent global trends in, 341–344
    employment statistics in, 343
    HDI/GEM/GDI/WEF/CEDAW
        ratification in, 334
    and historical basis for underutiliza-
        tion of women, 324–326
    pay-scale inequality in, 339, 340
    school tracking in, 12
    secondary math coursework in, 89
    secondary students in, 9
    women's empowerment in,
        335–337
    women's progress in scientific
        education in, 326–328
    workplace policy implications/
        reform measures needed for,
        344
Universality, 311–312
Universities. See Colleges and
    universities
University of Michigan (UM), 17–18.
    See also Women faculty advance-
    ment (study)
University preparation year, 34
Unwanted sexual attention, 304
U.S. Congress, 344
U.S. Department of Education, 56
U.S. Department of Labor, 35
Utility value, 93, 97n1, 106–108, 118

Valian, Virginia, 306, 307
Values, expectancies vs., 93, 118, 197
Varimax rotation, 273–274
Verbal achievement, 116

Victoria, Australia, 90
Voting rights, 268

Wage gap. See Pay-scale inequality
Wages, professional, 340
WEF rankings. See World Economic
    Forum rankings
Westernization, 268
Whites, CAH more common in, 241
Within-person change model, 148–154
Women. See also Females
    gender symbols of, 268
    historical basis for workplace under-
        utilization of, 324–326
    interventions to increase, in male-
        dominated professions, 6–7
    math achievement and career choice
        by, 67–69
    as role models, 78
    self-selection out of math courses by,
        57–58
    as single heads of households, 4
Women faculty advancement (study),
    299–320
    data regarding, 301–305
    grants for, 314–315
    interactive theater for, 310–311
    interventions for, 305–319
    networking for, 311–314
    recruitment for, 307–310
    university-wide policy change for,
        316–319
Women-inclusive workplaces, 323–346
    and anti-discrimination
        policies/treaties/multilateral
        agencies, 330–335
    emergent global trends regarding,
        340–344
    and historical basis for underutiliza-
        tion of women, 324–326
    and labor laws, 335–338
    and pay-scale inequality, 338–340
    policy implications/reform measures
        needed for, 344–346
    and progress in scientific education,
        326–330
Women-led firms, 332

Women's Engineering Society, 325
Women's movement, 325
Working hours, 17, 289
Work–life balance, 17, 293, 338
Work options, 341–342
Workplaces
    gender wage gap in, 340
    overall employment statistics, 343
    women-inclusive. *See* Women-inclusive workplaces

women's empowerment in segments
    of, 336
women's share of positions in, 327
Workshops, 315
World Economic Forum (WEF) rankings,
    333, 334
World War II, 325

Yükseköğretim Kurulu (YÖK),
    283, 284

ABOUT THE EDITORS

Helen M. G. Watt, PhD, is a faculty member at Monash University, Melbourne, Australia, and has previously served on the faculties of the University of Michigan, Ann Arbor; University of Western Sydney, Sydney, Australia; University of Sydney, Sydney, Australia; and Macquarie University, Sydney, Australia. She has received national and international early career awards since obtaining her PhD in educational psychology and measurement from the University of Sydney in 2002. Her interests include motivation, mathematics education, gendered educational and occupational choices, motivations for teaching, and teacher self-efficacy.

Jacquelynne S. Eccles, PhD, serves as the McKeachie Collegiate Professor of Psychology, University of Michigan, Ann Arbor. She received her PhD from the University of California, Los Angeles, in 1974 and has served on the faculties at Smith College, Northville, Massachusetts; the University of Colorado, Boulder; and the University of Michigan, Ann Arbor. In 1998–1999, she was the interim chair of psychology at the University of Michigan, Ann Arbor. She also chaired the MacArthur Foundation Network on Successful Pathways Through Middle Childhood and was a member of the MacArthur Research Network on Successful Pathways Through Adolescence. She was

Society for Research on Adolescence (SRA) program chair in 1996, has served on the SRA Council, and is now past president of the SRA. She served as program chair and president for the American Psychological Association (APA) Division 35 (Society for the Psychology of Women) and chair of the National Academy of Sciences Committee on After School Programs for Youth. Her awards include the Spencer Foundation Fellowship for Outstanding Young Scholar in Educational Research, the American Psychological Society's Cattell Fellows Award for Outstanding Applied Work in Psychology, Society for the Psychological Study of Social Issues' Kurt Lewin Award for outstanding research, the Thorndike Life Time Achievement Award from Division 15 of APA, the Hill Award for Life Time Achievement from the Society of Research on Adolescence, the Mentor Award from Division 7 of APA, The Wei Lun Lectureship Award from the Chinese University of Hong Kong, and an Honorary Doctorate from the Catholic University of Leuvan, Belgium. She is a fellow of the APA, the American Psychological Society, the Society for the Psychological Study of Social Issues, and the National Academy of Education. She has conducted research on topics ranging from gender-role socialization and classroom influences on motivation to social development in the family, school, peer, and wider cultural contexts. Much of this work focuses on the socialization of self-beliefs and the impact of self-beliefs on many other aspects of social development. Her most recent work focuses on (a) ethnicity as a part of the self and as a social category influencing experiences and (b) the relation of self-beliefs and identity to the transition from mid to late adolescence and then into adulthood.